Thomas Hardy's 'Facts' Notebook

A Critical Edition

Edited by
WILLIAM GREENSLADE

ASHGATE

© William Greenslade, 2004

Published by

Ashgate Publishing Limited	Ashgate Publishing Company
Gower House	Suite 420
Croft Road	101 Cherry Street
Aldershot	Burlington
Hants GU11 3HR	VT 05401-4405
England	USA

Ashgate website: http://www.ashgate.com

British Library Cataloguing in Publication Data
Hardy, Thomas, 1840-1928
   Thomas Hardy's "Facts" notebook : a critical edition. -
(The nineteenth century series)
1.Hardy, Thomas, 1840-1928 - Notebooks, sketchbooks, etc.
2.Hardy, Thomas, 1840-1928 - Criticism and interpretation
I.Title II.Greenslade, William
828.8'03

Library of Congress Cataloging-in-Publication Data
Hardy, Thomas, 1840-1928.
   Thomas Hardy's "Facts" notebook / William Greenslade.--Critical ed.
      p. cm. -- (The nineteenth century series)
   Includes bibliographical references and index.
   ISBN 1-84014-235-9 (alk. paper)
     1. Hardy, Thomas, 1840-1928--Notebooks, sketchbooks, etc. I. Title: "Facts"
notebook. II. Greenslade, William. III. Title. IV. Nineteenth century (Aldershot, England)

PR4750.F25 2003
823'.8--dc21

2002042681

ISBN 1 84014 235 9

Typeset by Bournemouth Colour Press, Parkstone, Poole.
Printed and bound in Great Britain by TJ International Ltd, Padstow, Cornwall.

Contents

The Nineteenth Century Series
General Editors' Preface

The aim of the series is to reflect, develop and extend the great burgeoning of interest in the nineteenth century that has been an inevitable feature of recent years, as that former epoch has come more sharply into focus as a locus for our understanding not only of the past but of the contours of our modernity. It centres primarily upon major authors and subjects within Romantic and Victorian literature. It also includes studies of other British writers and issues, where these are matters of current debate: for example, biography and autobiography, journalism, periodical literature, travel writing, book production, gender, non-canonical writing. We are dedicated principally to publishing original monographs and symposia; our policy is to embrace a broad scope in chronology, approach and range of concern, and both to recognize and cut innovatively across such parameters as those suggested by the designations 'Romantic' and 'Victorian'. We welcome new ideas and theories, while valuing traditional scholarship. It is hoped that the world which predates yet so forcibly predicts and engages our own will emerge in parts, in the wider sweep, and in the lively streams of disputation and change that are so manifest an aspect of its intellectual, artistic and social landscape.

Vincent Newey
Joanne Shattock

University of Leicester

Acknowledgements

In preparing this edition I have been fortunate in the support I have received from Hardy scholars, curators and librarians. First, I acknowledge my indebtedness to Professor Michael Millgate. More than 30 years ago he revealed the intrinsic and potential significance of the notebook for Hardy studies in his book *Thomas Hardy: His Career as a Novelist* (1971), which is not to forget the innovative work of Christine Winfield at about the same time. In the course of my own work on 'Facts', Michael Millgate has given me much encouragement, advice and searching criticism, in meticulous comments on successive drafts. Dr James Gibson has been generous in putting his profound knowledge of Hardy's works at my disposal and Dr Phillip Mallett has been a much-valued source of support and advice. It need hardly be said that whatever shortcomings there may be in this edition, they are entirely my responsibility.

Like so many other students of Hardy I have benefited enormously from the enthusiastic support of Richard de Peyer, formerly Curator of the Dorset County Museum, Kate Hebditch, formerly Deputy Curator, and Judy Lindsay, the Director. I am also very grateful to Lilian Swindall who has generously given me the benefit of her expert knowledge of the Thomas Hardy Memorial Collection in response to my many enquiries, and to the Museum staff, generally, for their friendly assistance at all times. Dorset's other fine resource for the study of Hardy is the Dorset County Reference Library, Dorchester, with its incomparable collection of primary and secondary Hardy material, together with works on Dorset history and topography. In my use of these collections, which include some very scarce items, Nick Lawrence and his colleagues have been unstinting in their assistance over many years, and I owe them a huge debt of gratitude. I should also like to thank the librarians and archivists of the following institutions: the British Library and the British Library Newspaper Library (Colindale); the London Library; the County Record Offices of Dorset, Somerset and Worcester; also the libraries of the universities of Birmingham, Bristol, Cambridge, London (Senate House Library) and the West of England, Bristol (St Matthias and Bolland libraries).

I am glad to acknowledge the permission granted to me by the Trustees of the Will of Eva Anne Dugdale, proprietors of the Hardy copyrights, to publish the 'Facts' Notebook in its entirety. I am also grateful to Macmillan Press (now Palgrave) for allowing me to draw on some of the material contained in my essay 'Rediscovering Thomas Hardy's "Facts" Notebook', in *The Achievement of Thomas Hardy*, edited by Phillip Mallett (Macmillan, 2000), pp. 171–86.

I am grateful to the British Academy and the Faculty of Humanities of the University of the West of England, for making awards which enabled me, through periods of research leave, to devote time to the editing of the notebook.

I would like to thank the following people who in various ways have generously assisted me in bringing this edition to completion: Dr Rosemarie Bailey, Jo Draper, U.A. Fanthorpe, Dr Chris Fletcher (Department of Manuscripts, British Library), Helen Gibson, Isabel Greenslade, Stella Greenslade, Chris Hatcher, C.M. Houlston-Jackson (Oxford Brookes University), Stephen Lester (British Library Newspaper Library, Colindale), Dr Robin Jarvis (University of the West of England), Karen Jones, Sarah

Leigh, John Lucas (Emeritus Professor of English, Loughborough University and Nottingham Trent University), Keith Maiden, Keith McClelland (Middlesex University), Eleanor McGrath, Professor Vincent Newey (University of Leicester), David Parker, Ruth Peters, Dr Steve Poole (University of the West of England), Jill Pope, Dr Fred Reid, Dr Terence Rogers (Bath Spa University College), Professor Joanne Shattock (University of Leicester), Judith Stinton, Professor John Stokes (Kings College, London), Furse Swann, Colin Thomas, Hugh Torrens (Emeritus Professor of Geology, University of Keele), Eddie Wainwright, Shirley Wickham (formerly of the Dorset County Reference Library) and Chris Woods (Dorset Record Office, Dorchester).

I am grateful to my editors at Ashgate, Ann Donahue, Erika Gaffney and Liz Greasby, for their care in seeing the manuscript through to publication. I would also like to thank Carol Lucas for her meticulous copy-editing and Carol Marks for so efficiently typing the index. I am particularly grateful to Basil Greenslade for all his scholarly advice and unflagging support. Finally, I owe a huge debt to my daughters, Hannah and Emily, in exercising so much patience over the years I have been involved in the preparation of the notebook.

List of Abbreviations

Bailey: J.O. Bailey, *The Poetry of Thomas Hardy: A Handbook and Commentary* (Chapel Hill: University of North Carolina Press, 1970)

Boswell-Stone: L.C. Boswell-Stone, *Memories and Traditions Recorded by L.C. Boswell-Stone* (London: Richard Clay, 1895)

Brady: Kristin Brady, *The Short Stories of Thomas Hardy: Tales of Past and Present* (Basingstoke: Macmillan, 1982)

CL: *The Collected Letters of Thomas Hardy*, ed. Richard Little Purdy and Michael Millgate, 7 vols (Oxford: Clarendon Press, 1978–88)

CMT: *A Changed Man and Other Tales*

CP: *Thomas Hardy: The Complete Poems*, ed. James Gibson (London: Macmillan, 1976)

CPW: *The Complete Poetical Works of Thomas Hardy*, ed. Samuel Hynes, 5 vols (Oxford: Clarendon Press, 1982–95)

CS: *Thomas Hardy: The Complete Stories*, ed. Norman Page (London: J.M. Dent, 1996)

Cullen Brown: Joanna Cullen Brown, *Hardy's People* (London: Allison & Busby, 1991)

DCC: *Dorset County Chronicle, Somersetshire Gazette, And General Advertiser For the South and South-West of England*

DCM: *Dorset County Museum*

DN: *Daily News*

DNHAS: Dorset Natural History and Archaeological Society

ELH: Emma Lavinia Hardy

FED: Florence Emily Dugdale

Frampton: *The Journal of Mary Frampton From the Year 1779 Until the Year 1846*, ed. Harriet Georgiana Mundy (London: Sampson Low, Marston, Searle & Rivington, 1885)

GND: *A Group of Noble Dames*

Hutchins: John Hutchins, *The History and Antiquities of the County of Dorset* (1774), eds W. Shipp & J.W. Hodson, 4 vols (3rd edn, Westminster: J.B. Nichols & Sons, 1861–73; rpt East Ardsley, Wakefield: E.P. Publishing, 1973).

Life and Work: *The Life and Work of Thomas Hardy*, ed. Michael Millgate (Basingstoke: Macmillan, 1984)

LLE: *Late Lyrics and Earlier*

LLI: *Life's Little Ironies*

LLI, 1996: *Life's Little Ironies*, ed. Alan Manford (Oxford: Oxford University Press, 1996)

LN: *The Literary Notebooks of Thomas Hardy*, ed. Lennart A. Björk, 2 vols (Basingstoke: Macmillan, 1985)

Mayor, 1987: *The Mayor of Casterbridge*, ed. Dale Kramer (Oxford: Oxford University Press, 1987)

Millgate, 1971: Michael Millgate, *Thomas Hardy: His Career as A Novelist* (1971; London: Macmillan, 1994)

Millgate, 1982: Michael Millgate, *Thomas Hardy: A Biography* (1982; Oxford: Oxford University Press, 1985)

MV: *Moments of Vision*

OED: *Oxford English Dictionary*

PDNHAS: *Proceedings of the Dorset Natural History and Archaeological Society*

Pinion: F.B. Pinion, *A Hardy Companion* (1968; London: Macmillan, 1976)

PN: *The Personal Notebooks of Thomas Hardy*, ed. Richard H. Taylor (London: Macmillan, 1979)

PPP: *Poems of Past and Present*

Public Voice: *Thomas Hardy's Public Voice: The Essays, Speeches and Miscellaneous Prose*, ed. Michael Millgate (Oxford: Clarendon Press, 2001)

PW: *Thomas Hardy's Personal Writings*, ed. Harold Orel (London: Macmillan, 1967)

Ray: Martin Ray, *Thomas Hardy: A Textual Study of the Short Stories* (Aldershot: Ashgate, 1997)

Telegram: *Weymouth, Portland and Dorchester Telegram*

Tess, 1988: *Tess of the d'Urbervilles*, eds Juliet Grindle and Simon Gatrell (Oxford: Oxford University Press, 1988)

TH: Thomas Hardy

THFH: *Thomas Hardy: Family History*, ed. Norman Page, 5 vols (London: Routledge / Thoemmes Press, 1998)

THJ: *Thomas Hardy Journal*

TL: *Time's Laughingstocks*

TLS: *Times Literary Supplement*

Trumpet-Major, 1991: *The Trumpet-Major*, ed. Richard Nemesvari (Oxford: Oxford University Press, 1991)

Walpole, Letters: Horace Walpole, *The Letters of H. Walpole, Earl of Orford*, ed. Peter Cunningham, 9 vols (London: Richard Bentley, 1857–59)

Winfield: Christine Winfield, 'Factual Sources of Two Episodes in *The Mayor of Casterbridge*', *Nineteenth-Century Fiction* 25 (2) (September 1970): 224–31

Woodlanders, 1985: *The Woodlanders*, ed. Dale Kramer (Oxford: Oxford University Press, 1985).

WP: *Wessex Poems*

WT: *Wessex Tales*

WT, 1991: *Wessex Tales*, ed. Kathryn R. King (Oxford: Oxford University Press, 1991)

Critical Introduction

I

Thomas Hardy and his wife Emma completed their move from Wimborne Minster to Dorchester in the last week of June 1883. Among their effects, they brought with them an accumulation of notebooks, the product of Hardy's habitual note-taking of many years: the 'Architectural Notebook', the 'Schools of Painting' notebook, the 'Trumpet-Major Notebook', one book of 'Literary Notes', the '1867' notebook, and the 'Studies, Specimens &c' notebook. Many others, probably pocket-books dating from the 1870s, would not survive the later Max Gate bonfires. Altogether, 12 MS notebooks of this kind have been preserved, and these include the notebook which Hardy began soon after he was settled in Dorchester, the subject of this edition – 'Facts From Newspapers, Histories, Biographies, & other chronicles – (mainly Local).'[1]

After the death of Hardy's second wife, Florence, in 1937, the co-executor of her will, Irene Cooper Willis, had custody of these so-called 'Commonplace Books', and by 1962 'Facts' (as I shall abbreviate it) had been deposited in the Thomas Hardy Memorial Collection in the Dorset County Museum, Dorchester, listed as 'Literary Notes III'. Along with seven other notebooks, it was put on microfilm in 1975.[2]

In compiling and composing his own 'ghosted biography', *The Life and Work of Thomas Hardy* (published posthumously as *The Early Life* and *The Later Years*),[3] Hardy made no secret of his dependence on what he variously referred to as his 'notebooks', 'pocket-books', 'diaries' and 'memoranda'. The real extent of his private note-taking can now only be guessed at, following the destruction of much of it by Hardy himself, and later by Florence and by his literary executor Sydney Cockerell, who in corresponding about the notebooks of another poet, A.E. Housman, wrote that he had 'spent a whole morning burning (by his instructions) similar notebooks by Thomas Hardy.'[4] But whatever this private archive had amounted to by 1913 (the date of the source for the final entry in 'Facts'), in the light of what is known of the voluminous holograph literary remains of Victorian contemporaries such as Meredith and Hopkins, the volume of Hardy's note-taking is not likely to have been exceptional.[5]

Towards the end of July 1883, within a month of his settling in Dorchester, Hardy began his new notebook, 'Facts', a substantial, stoutly bound volume, suggestive of a deliberate enterprise, and into which he would enter 690 items. And like almost all of Hardy's other surviving notebooks, it carried at his death the injunction 'to be destroyed uncopied'. However, in spite of Cockerell's determination to carry out Hardy's injunctions to the letter, Florence Hardy managed to preserve 'Facts', together with other notebooks necessary for the task of completing the *Life*.[6]

In its earliest phase the composition and make-up of 'Facts' was far from straightforward, partly because of the erratic sequencing of entries over the first 11 pages of the notebook. After the first entry (from a review of a work by the economic historian Thorold Rogers) Hardy evidently involved Emma in copying a backlog of items which had been accumulating, from at least 1876, as cuttings and notebook entries, all of which they had brought with them from Wimborne.[7] Emma wrote up extracts from J.F. Pennie's

Tale of a Modern Genius (1827) and entered items from newspapers and magazines – the *Daily News*, *The Times*, the *Saturday Review*, the *Pall Mall Gazette* and *Harper's Bazar* from 1882 to early 1883, with some entries from current papers to October 1883. Hardy took over the note-taking in late November (11c) and thereafter established a reasonably consistent forward momentum.

But in mid-March 1884, with his first entry from early issues of the *Dorset County Chronicle* (27c), Hardy began a new phase in 'Facts', one with which the notebook has been particularly associated. Even when interrupted by the appearance of other fascinating sources – a volume of memoirs, an autobiography, or contemporary newspaper reports too intriguing to ignore – Hardy hardly deviated from what appears to have been a preconceived plan of recording as much as he could, in as short a time as he could, from issues of the *Dorset County Chronicle* ('old DCC' as he called it) of each of the five years 1826–30. Starting at the beginning of each calendar year the procedure was to work through the files to, more or less, the end of the year, before moving on to the next. Four of these years were covered over a period of eight weeks. There is evidence that he borrowed batches of the old files from the office of the *Chronicle* nearby in High West Street, Dorchester, for private use at his home in Shire-Hall Place.[8] It was his good luck to have had access to so obliging a proprietor. Hardy did not have to expose his copying (or Emma's) to public view in the Dorset County Museum.

In the 1820s and 1830s, the *Dorset County Chronicle, Somersetshire Gazette, And General Advertiser for the South and South-West of England* was a weekly newspaper, published on Thursdays, price 7 pence.[9] It consisted of four pages (each 55 x 38.5 cm), a page-size similar to that of a modern English broadsheet. Each page held five columns of closely-set small type with little typographical variety, except for page 1 which was largely given over to advertisements and announcements. The paper was routinely, but not consistently, divided into standard sections which included: 'Original Notices' (reviews), 'London Mails' and foreign news, 'Provincial intelligence', that is, news from Western counties, especially Dorset, 'Accidents & Offences', court cases from all quarters, market news and an editorial. In taking his material from any part of the paper, Hardy did not restrict himself merely to Dorset news, important as this would be to him, but ranged more widely over English and foreign reports. The combination of the disciplined reading of the weekly issues of 'old DCC', over a period of two months, with the impact on him of the mass of this material itself, from the Dorset and England of the post-Waterloo world of his parents' youth, must have been an experience that stayed with him for the rest of his life.

The sequence running through 1826 was the most sustained of all, consisting of 146 items from January to November (items 27c–60b). The file for 1827 yielded 65 items in a rather complex series, which included the first of the lengthy court case entries, mainly handled by Emma. By the beginning of May 1884, with the papers of 1828 and 1829 read through, Hardy had accumulated 350 entries, including a return to a formidable report of an action for damages (November 1826), which in the notebook ran to 11 pages, mostly entered by Emma. So by May 1884 the bulk of the immediate task had been completed, although the newspapers of 1830 were still to be tackled. Important source material had been identified for *The Mayor of Casterbridge* which Hardy had been actively planning since early in 1884, and to the writing of which he now turned in earnest.

The 113 items which were to be taken from 1830 papers fell into a much protracted and intermittent later phase of the note-taking, lasting from the summer of 1884 until 1890, as the enterprise gave way to the demands of writing *The Mayor*, *The Woodlanders*, a range of short fiction and, subsequently, *Tess*. There is consequently a marked slowing-down of the rate of entry of the 1830 *DCC* items: 16 entries between May and July 1884, only 17 between August and November 1884, a further six items through to late December. By the beginning of 1885 Hardy had worked through to May 1830. He then entered a further 23 items to take the coverage up to July (153a) but this was carried out over 14 months (January 1885–March 1886). A further batch of 40 entries was taken from the July–October 1830 issues, in late 1886 or 1887. Eight final *DCC* entries from November and December 1830 (192a–192h, [193]c) follow sometime between March 1888 and September 1890. And at this point Hardy entered the final 'old DCC' item ([193]c), from the issue of 9 December 1830.

The predominance of the *Dorset County Chronicle* as a source in 'Facts' has tended to obscure the importance to him of the 'Histories, Biographies and other chronicles' of Hardy's title. Entries early in the notebook, from Pennie's *Tale of a Modern Genius*, J.F. Molloy's *Court Life Below Stairs*, Hutchins's *History and Antiquities of the County of Dorset*[10] and Horace Walpole's *Letters* and *Reminiscences*[11] are followed, in the late 1880s and onwards, by extracts from Molloy's *Peg Woffington*, Marie Liechtenstein's *Holland House* and memoirs by R.H. Gronow, Mary Frampton, and the artist W.P. Frith. Lucia Boswell-Stone's charming *Memories and Traditions*, recapturing pre-Victorian Dorchester, came to hand in 1895. From some of this material, especially that from Frampton and Liechtenstein, Hardy took references to families in the immediate neighbourhood of his own birthplace who were household names – Pitt, Fox (Fox-Strangways), Walpole and Wellesley. These striking 'accidents of locality'[12] he could not ignore (see Appendix Two).

The final phase of the notebook (items 194a–[221]a), with entries made very sporadically over more than 20 years (1890–1913), combines the characteristics of both common-place book and scrapbook. A new feature is the pasting-in of cuttings from journals and newspapers. During these years he appears to have left the notebook unused for long periods. Page-numbering, which had been consistently entered on alternate pages, was now given up. Yet 'Facts' was still the natural repository for documents prompted by new interests, notably Hardy's assembly of material for the poem 'Panthera',[13] his extract from the *Memoir* of Bishop Walsham How (1898), probably entered when he was considering the 'Postcript' to *Jude the Obscure* for the Wessex edition of 1912, and a clutch of pasted-in cuttings from 1902 and 1912 on the subject of Dorchester's old theatres.

II

The genesis and development of 'Facts' are inseparable from the decisive change in the direction of Hardy's writing life in the early 1880s, when, with his return to the Dorset district of his childhood and youth, he committed himself to what Michael Millgate has rightly described as an 'orderly falling back upon his oldest, deepest, and surest creative resources'.[14] It follows from this commitment that Hardy would refamiliarize himself with the environment of his childhood in pre-railway Dorset, and with the exceptionally rich oral testimony about the immediate past – the Dorset of the Napoleonic and post-Napoleonic years – already communicated to him by his parents, his paternal grandmother, and many elderly people he knew and talked to. One of them, an old employee of his father's, was a former smuggler. The recording by Hardy in *Life and Work* of his father's own memories (quoted from earlier memoranda) is particularly notable.[15] So when in March 1884 he came to the reading of the old *Dorset County Chronicle*, the record which emerged in 'Facts' was less an innocent text than one which authenticated and enlarged on, from public sources, what he had long ago heard from the private testimony of his family. The talk of family and neighbourhood (which included not only Bockhampton but Puddletown) was confirmed and capped repeatedly by the old papers' reporting. Here, for example, he found reports of the quarrelsome rivalry between the Bockhampton band and the Fordington mummers on Christmas Eve 1827, which reached the Borough Quarter Sessions and the Assizes of January 1828 – his uncle, John Hardy, and the Keates family of Bockhampton being involved as plaintiffs. The report must have made compelling reading, confirming (or contradicting), striking facts, no doubt first encountered through the talk of his extended family.

But the man who absorbed himself in family anecdote is also an 'educated observer', in Raymond Williams's phrase.[16] The notebook equipped Hardy with the documentary authority he needed to address an educated metropolitan readership, of which he was inescapably a part, a readership largely ignorant of the 'unrecorded culture' which Hardy was uniquely equipped to embody in his art.[17] His sense of its significance, is in Simon Gatrell's words, 'a substantial part of what lies behind the growth of Wessex, as is the role he cast for himself as a mediator between it and the educated middle classes ... who were quite ignorant of the substance and the richness of such remote and rural life'.[18] 'Facts' had a special function for one who saw 'tradition in both ways'.[19]

The immediate practical function of 'Facts' was to provide 'material which might prove useable in the writing of stories and poems'.[20] This is the aspect of the notebook which has prompted most comment, even though only a small proportion of what Hardy recorded was of this type. Of the 690 items in the notebook, only a relatively small number comprise, directly or indirectly, source material for his poetry and fiction, and there is considerable variation in the possibilities these entries offer. At least 50 items can be identified as providing incidents, plotlines, details of characterization, and factual information of various kinds which figure in his poems, short stories and fiction. A dozen of these serve as direct or indirect source information for *The Mayor of Casterbridge*, the composition of which lay immediately before him that spring. Within the first 30 items which he copied from the 1826 papers, he identified a report of a bankruptcy hearing in Launceston (30a) and of a wife sale in Brighton (32g), both of them key sources for this novel.[21] Certain items, sometimes in pairs or triads, provide events, actions or episodes whose completeness Hardy has seized on and reproduced in their major outlines: the wife sale in *The Mayor*, the avenging mantrap in *The Woodlanders*, the death of Durbeyfield's horse, Prince, in *Tess* – each is the composite of two or three separate but cognate entries.[22] There are other items whose status as source material is more problematic in that they provide not so much literal relationships as correspondences: a bodysnatcher is paid £12 per head (literally) by anatomists (61a), a girl leaves her illegitimate baby under a hayrick (148a) – suggestive material for episodes in *The Woodlanders* (ch.16) and *Tess of the d'Urbervilles* (ch.14).

The common factor in much of what Hardy selects is the anecdotal, the germ of a story. This emerges clearly where Hardy is at work assigning material from the same source to two different notebooks, 'Literary Notes' and 'Facts', which for 30 years he maintained simultaneously. From a *Cornhill Magazine* article of October 1881 on the Hungarian romantic poet, Nikolaus Lenau, Hardy assigned to 'Literary Notes' comments of conventional critical appreciation: Lenau 'deserves to be more widely recognised'. However the 'Facts' entries from the same source, also noted at the same date for entry in 'Literary Notes', comprise serviceable material for narrative treatment. We learn of the melancholy surroundings of Lenau's family home, set 'in a dismal graveyard', but also a story of the poet's fit of madness on his wedding day: 'Bride & mother, halting at an inn on the way to him hear that … [he] has been put into a straight waistcoat' (24f, 24g). While 'Literary Notes' is for philosophical and aesthetic reflection – that which is quotable – 'Facts' generally comprises material which is narratable, here a familiar 'satire of circumstance'.[23]

In *The Mayor*, Lucetta Farfrae, in her bedroom, thinks she hears someone, in the room below, reading out a report of 'some extraordinary crime' from 'the *Casterbridge Chronicle*'.[24] In the real *Chronicle*, as 'Facts' records, crime, extraordinary and petty, is insistently present – murder, highway robbery, theft and fraud of all kinds, horse-stealing, bodysnatching, and particularly in issues of 1830, machine-breaking and incendiarism. The newspaper carries lengthy reports of the law in action, both locally and nationally, and verdicts of transportation or death. Convicts in chains are on the move in coaches from prison to hulks, and from hulks to ship.[25] Petty offenders are whipped in front of thousands of spectators. Suicides, for love, or loss of money, or for shame, figure prominently.[26] Indeed one item is a portmanteau of two suicides and a murder (173a). But violence, too, characterizes the frequent reports of accidents, farcical or sad, especially coach and waggon disasters; all of this in addition to reports of elopements and abduction, and the routine of race meetings, country sports, balls, dinners and the Dorset theatre. Hardy's keen sense of the ludicrous which threads through the notebook is not absent from his treatment of petty crime. The ingenious Howarths, 'burglars of Frome', hold prayer meetings at their house, but rob the church; the wife had 'a silk dress made out of clergyman's gown & passed him wearing it' (69a). One predicament, recorded repeatedly in 'Facts', evidently held a peculiar fascination for Hardy – the necessity of sharing a room, at an inn, with a stranger, with the risk of the theft of clothes, or of money, and the ultimate threat of murder,[27] but again such incidents may carry a farcical potential. Some items are chosen because they provide technically necessary information, such as a detailed description of a wrestling bout (106d). Hardy's pursuit of factual authentication can on occasion lead to a certain cold-blooded suppression of the full context from which it derives. An item which he heads 'Dress of the Period' (45g) is based on a report of an inquest on a drowned man, 'supposed to have been in the water eight or nine days'. Precise details of the clothes worn by commercial travellers in 1829 (96e) are taken from a case of two con-men on the run, the description in *DCC* simply intended to aid their arrest.[28]

A reader familiar with Hardy can hardly miss the recognizable pattern of many of the entries, a baldly ironic reversal, often producing sensational outcomes, marked by the grotesque or the macabre: a woman superstitiously floats a candle on water in order to discover the whereabouts of a drowned child but only succeeds in setting fire to her house which burns to ashes (57b); a young man taps on his fiancée's window at night and is killed by the girl's father who takes him for a burglar (32d); a man who is drunk attempts suicide and is discovered to have been a temperance lecturer (6c); a nurse employed at a workhouse and discharged for being drunk on the doorstep, returns as an inmate, when it is revealed that she is the daughter of a naval commander (23i). A special mode of reversal emerges in a number of episodes of temporal dislocation or 'foreshortening', involving sudden, unpremeditated decisions to marry, or to escape from marriage:[29] 'Young man in Church renovating monument – comes down ladder & marries young woman' (120a); 'Young man put up at pub. h. at Barnsley for a night – the servant took his fancy – licence obtained – married next morning' (132c); or the three examples of wife sales from *DCC* (items 32g, 74b, 116c). *Jude the Obscure* with its marryings, separations and remarryings, is not far off.

Hardy is also clearly intrigued by episodes involving the opposite dynamic: inaction, the extreme prolongation of an action, or postponement of desire, in episodes which also range widely in their tone. For want of an event to report, an editor fills his paper with items from the Bible; 'so great was the dearth of news' that he 'began with 1st Gen. & got to 10th Ex. before anything happened' (55d). Two members of the gentry meet on horseback in a narrow lane, each refusing to give way; one enquires of the other, after some hours, whether he might borrow his newspaper from him 'when you have done' (37f). But in 'Long engagement', the story of a couple who wait for 30 years for the opportunity to be married (82f), pathos tempers the absurd, prompting a comment from *DCC* with which Hardy clearly identified himself – 'W^d it not have been better to wait till death'.

In combing through his sources, it is likely that Hardy wrote out only a fraction of what he must have read, so as a record of his reading, as opposed to his note-taking, the notebook is far from complete. Hardy could not have failed to register, in issues of newspapers and magazines which we know he read through, a large number of items which were significant to him, but which he did not choose to note. Having made a number of entries from *DCC* about a sensational case of the abduction of a Miss Turner by Edward Wakefield, in 1826–27 (29a, 48d, 49b, 63c), he did not copy but could not have missed reading a further *DCC* report of 21 September 1826 (p.1, col.3) which spelled out Miss Turner's plight as vulnerable heiress.[30]

Of course, it is impossible to know why certain items were included and others not. For instance, in his reading in 'Biographies and other chronicles', of the notebook's title, Hardy consulted Captain Gronow's *Reminiscences* of 1862, where from p.210 he noted a comment on Byron (155c). But it is inconceivable that Hardy did not pause over pp.212–14, where Gronow recorded his memories of his school-friend Shelley whom he last saw on the seashore at Genoa, shortly before the poet's death. Yet these poignant recollections of Hardy's much-loved Shelley go unentered. Similarly, Gronow's memorable 20-page account of the battles of Quatre Bras and Waterloo, is not included. 'Facts' provides, tantalizingly, a severely abbreviated version of the full script of Hardy's reading in all these sources.

III

A striking feature of the notebook is the active presence in it of Hardy himself as editor and commentator as well as mere summarizer. There are numerous occasions on which Hardy evaluates the importance of entries, in some cases even as they are being entered. He is also drawn to embroider items which connect with the world of his childhood. Whether through a transcription of a whole report, or through an apparently insignificant textual intervention, Hardy's connection with the lives and stories of people (predominantly of his parents' generation) is attractively reaffirmed. An extract taken from *The Tale of a Modern Genius* by J.F. Pennie, an obscure Dorset writer of the 1820s, records a sad story involving a smuggler, his sweetheart and 'jilt', and 'her favoured beau', an excise officer, named James Wallis (3a). Hardy cannot resist adding in pencil 'was this the Wallis, who lived at Lower House, & whom g.f^r knew?' 'Ancestors of the present Habgoods, I suppose', he responds, when coming across a Wimborne Habgood in Hutchins (19d). 'Tom Garth?', he queries of an item on the son of General Garth, of Puddletown, the equerry to George III (45c), as he confirms and sometimes corrects the public record. There are other items which prompt Hardy to get ahead of the facts contained in a report, to supply personal details which the newspaper would not dare to print but which were familiar to him, and usually more enlightening. Of James Balston, the tenant of Admiston Hall (Athelhampton) near Puddletown, he faithfully notes the official news – '100 persons from neighb^g villages sitting round his hospitable board ... country dancing kept up' – then inserts the unofficial data: 'kept mistress (Dibbin by name) & children at New Mill cottage. Mrs Beasant was one' (82a). While *DCC* muffles its reports of the establishment in the language of deference, Hardy points up what was probably common knowledge. His pithy interjections give these figures life and individuality; a story seems on the tip of his pen.

'Facts' reveals that both Hardy and Emma were diligent in their pursuit of certain court cases, concerning damages for adultery and indictments for abduction, smuggling and murder. On occasion they would follow a case through a number of issues, over a period of weeks, but since other items came to their attention as they read through the files, it became necessary to maintain firm control over the case in hand; this was achieved through cross-referencing forward or back. The 'Bligh vs Wellesley', crim.con. case of 1826, assured of extensive reporting by the fact that the defendant was Wellington's nephew, William Long-Wellesley, is referenced on pages 59 and 93, and on 120 which marks the inception of an 11-page extract, the longest in the notebook (120e).

As the notebook grew in scale and range of subject matter Hardy increasingly became his own editor. An item from February 1826 concerning the impact on the Yeovil glove trade of imported French gloves (27f) is updated with further economic news 'later on in the year'. He returns to a murder case a year after it had been first entered by Emma (14e), and annotates it with supplementary information concerning the suicide of the sweetheart of the victim, a labourer of 22: 'his death seemed to have preyed on her mind – took to drink – drowned herself (after kissing his likeness) in harbour'. Here the impetus was not merely to tidy up the report, but to bring out the distressing effects of the labourer's death on his 'sweetheart ... Jane Dare, prostitute'. Hardy thus both witnesses and elaborates a narrative of despair that ends in suicide.

An unobtrusive detail can show the narrative imagination at work where the convention of reliable transcription becomes a secondary matter. An item, 'Lady escapes detectives', reads as follows: 'Bow St. officers ... come down to country village where she has taken cottage – she sees them from w^w answers door (slipping on cap) saying that the lady is not home – steps out at back, leaving them in parlour' (81a). The phrase 'slipping on cap' is a piece of metonymic amplification which Hardy stitched seamlessly to the narrative in front of him. He heads another item 'Tender Thief': 'Last week Mrs Oxford, late Mrs Allen, of the Carriage Inn Coombe Down, received a ring wh. was stolen from her 12 years since, inclosed in a note from the person /man/ who stole the ring. [Handsome woman probably]' (117d). 'Tender Thief', 'man' and 'handsome woman probably' are Hardy's inventions; a narrative line is here being sketched out – perhaps a romantic connection between the thief and his victim. To a note of a report of 'Illicit cider shops' which sell 'cider without licence – & £10 fine' (90e), Hardy adds 'in out of the way villages', a detail compressing a precise socio-geographical context for a transgressive activity beyond the reach of publicity and reflecting his own knowledge of remotest Dorset (the echoes of 'Weydon-Priors', in the first chapter of The Mayor, are not hard to find). Sometimes Hardy notes down his almost spoken queries: 'What had she done?' he asks of the Dean of Worcester who threatened to revoke his 'permission granted for use of Worcester Cathedral for approaching Musical Festival if Miss P. be allowed to sing' (161c). 'What does the man want?' he asks of a drearily misogynistic correspondent to the Daily News in 1899 (196a). These precise interrogatives suggests something of the force of Hardy's instinctual response to evidence of moral and social censoriousness.

IV

The central phase of the notebook, with its concentrated record of entries from DCC for the years 1826–29, leaves a powerful impression of a region in the grip of sustained economic depression and social privation. The 'once flourishing' town of Frome, with 8000 of its 13 000 inhabitants dependent upon a depressed wool trade, has not 'recovered from the depression like the towns in the north' (53b). The glove trade of Yeovil is at risk from French imports which threaten 'ruin to honest tradesmen', and deprives 'thousands of poor' of the 'means of subsistence' (27f). Hardy was also aware of the effect of these hard times on the middle class – the core readership of DCC. In 'Fall of Townsman' respectable 'business-clothiers' are reduced to 'breaking stones on the road' to earn their allowance from the parish (50b). The general distress, and the crime it gives rise to, comes through in Hardy's terse summaries: 'Great distress and poverty in the country at this period (1826) – Suicides: horse-stealing: highway robbery frequent. Talk of grant of pub. money necessary' (50a).

Following the Napoleonic Wars the situation of the workfolk, in Dorset, as elsewhere in Britain, was perilous. Dorset had itself 'become a by-word for the low wages, poor housing and bad conditions of farm-workers'.[31] A series of poor harvests had led to escalating food prices and plummeting living standards. E.P. Thompson has detailed the pressures which 'served, directly or indirectly, to tighten the screw upon the labourer ... High rents or falling profits: war debt and currency crises: taxes on malt, on windows, on horses: Game Laws, with their paraphernalia of gamekeepers, spring-guns, mantraps and (after 1816) sentences of transportation'.[32] Hardy's entries on the rural unrest in Dorset and the southern counties which reached a climax in 1830, reflect the increasing tension of that year, with the mobilization of troops and special constables and the formation of a 'corps of Yeomanry' in Dorchester in late November 1830.[33] For a while the threat of widespread revolt had produced real fear among the propertied classes. In November there were riots in the Blackmoor Vale and, for early December 1830 (his final entry from an 'old DCC'), Hardy noted this item:

> The disturbances – assemblages in neighb[d]. of Shaftesb[y]...destroyed some machines: thence to the residence of the clergyman from whom they demanded, with threats, a considerable reduction of tithes: 5 of the ring leaders captured by party of armed yeomen: brought to county gaol...a mob collected, & openly burnt a threshing machine...Barn burnt at Bere...Many labourers out of employ – distress great. (193c)[34]

Hardy's reading of class conflict in the period is suggested by a fascinating juxtaposition of two items taken from the same issue of the DCC. A report of conspicuous consumption from which he enters in great detail the extraordinary quantity of food and drink laid on by a newly elected Somerset MP (170c) is set against a chilling account of the execution of three incendiaries at Kenn (171a), also in Somerset, at which 5000 spectators are present and the full panoply of the power of the State is on display (troops of yeoman cavalry, 150 special constables). Hardy's interest in the ritualized, intensely theatrical character of public justice can also be seen from several entries which record public whipping as the punishment for petty misdemeanours (41b, 94c, 144d and 158a).

Indeed, Hardy reveals himself as particularly acute about forms of custom which had survived from the eighteenth century and earlier. 'Facts' opens up a rich seam of the near-obsolete and – to Victorian eyes – the scandalous, which finds its fullest imaginative realization in The Mayor but is also a presence in The Woodlanders. He records practices, once prevalent as custom, but now fallen into disrepute or outlawed by Act of Parliament, such as the burying of the bodies of suicides at crossroads with a stake driven through the heart (4b), discontinued about 1830, and the trade in corpses for the use of anatomists which was ended in 1832. In his youth he saw the effect of efforts by the landed interest, and the Church, to remoralize the people's culture. Clergy encouraged friendly societies and village clubs with decorous habits such as 'club walks' round villages, with banners, wands and ribbons; the consumption of intoxicating drink and tobacco on such occasions was banned.[35] 'Facts' offers evidence of a lively fair-culture in the late 1820s, but by the 1840s these neighbourhood fairs (long the subject of erratic attempts at regulation or abolition) and certain calendar holidays came under increasing surveillance as vestiges of a barbarous old order.[36]

The Hardy who read 'old DCC' was looking back 60 years from the 1880s to the strangeness of the world before his birth. He was a Victorian of the so-called 'age of equipoise', with positivist leanings who, with part of himself at least, took for granted the existence of a watershed which divided the years of his coming to maturity, as a man and a writer, from the years before the first Reform Act, the new Poor Law, the arrival of the railways and the abolition of the Corn Laws. On the far side of this watershed was a culture that was rough, 'primitive', unregulated in character and marked by the persistence of customary traditions and practices. The contrast between the old culture and Victorian modernity is embodied brilliantly in the conflict between the improvisatory, volatile Henchard and the rational, modernizing Farfrae.

V

If 'Facts' had gone the way of other papers in one of Hardy's or Cockerell's bonfires, Hardy's devotion to its compilation and Emma's contribution to it would have remained quite unknown. For no explicit allusion to the notebook has yet been found anywhere in Hardy's published writings.[37] In Hardy's lifetime its existence was known exclusively to him and his two wives. But if this was the case, why did Hardy go to such lengths to obscure some of his sources, by erasing or excising items? For one of the difficulties the manuscript poses is the evidence of the erasure or crossing-out of particular items, or the excision of half-pages of the notebook. Hardy made erasures by heavy scrawling through by pen, or scraping out with a sharp blade. In an item about a fraudulent cattle dealer erasing entries from his books by acid (9b), he gives a further clue as to how he might have achieved obliteration on the page. Some items are scrawled through sufficiently lightly to make them 'recoverable', while other items cannot be deciphered since the superimposed scrawl coheres as an alternative script.

Of the eight erased items only four (52c, 56d, 111d, 117f) can be identified with any certainty from lines which can be read or from words not fully erased. Two of these are sources for *The Mayor*. The first (52c), concerns a soldier who could not get out of bed in the morning and was forced to parade in his night clothes (leading to his suicide); this was the source for the humiliation of Abel Whittle by his employer Henchard (*Mayor*, ch. 15). The second (56d), is a humorous ditty, in praise of smoking, of no apparent significance. The third (111d), is a source for Henchard's oath to forswear drink (*Mayor*, ch. 2). A further erasure, 'Waggoner asleep in his waggon – night Bridport R^d – meets coach – shaft of waggon enters breast of leader' (117f), has been heavily scrawled through in ink: this is something of a puzzle since another item, 'Dark night' (162g), which has as good a claim to be a source for the death of Prince in *Tess*, is not erased.[38] Hardy also made three excisions of, presumably, sensitive material. Of these items, a checking of surrounding passages suggests that at least one further incident, the miscarriage and death of a woman, brought on by seeing an effigy of herself (f.34r&v) offers an almost certain source for the death of Lucetta Farfrae (*Mayor*, chs 39–40). Two further reports relating to bankruptcy proceedings (f.28r&v) may also constitute source material.

It is not possible to be certain about when these erasures and excisions were made, nor about whether Hardy had any consistent plan of self-censorship. If he had such a plan he evidently failed to carry it through; perhaps it did not seem to be worth the time and trouble. His scrawlings-through may have been intended to prevent him from reusing material. The excisions might have been made to allow Hardy to refer to material when he did not have the notebook beside him. Almost all the recoverable erasures are of material which he was to use in his fiction, and so it might be concluded that he felt the need to cover his tracks by obliterating his sources. But what had Hardy to be defensive about since only he and his wives had access to the notebook? Having prefaced the notebook with the injunction 'to be destroyed uncopied', he may have made precautionary erasures as an insurance against not being heeded by his literary executors – yet half-heartedly, in an impulse of revision of a notebook which, like his 'Literary Notes', he could never bring himself to abandon. The working notebooks which he had kept up from the 1860s had been destroyed, although they had provided the unworked material not only for fiction but for poems and *Life and Work*. But the surviving notebooks had their own *raison d'être* as irreplaceable resources and, in the case of 'Facts', as a record of recovery of the past, an intensely personal *aide-mémoire*.[39]

Hardy was sensitive to being thought a mere rural Naturalist, one who was dependent on the 'trifles of useful knowledge ... the accidents and appendages of narrative' when 'the exhibition of human nature' and its 'elementary passions' was a prime duty of a novelist.[40] But Virginia Woolf appears to have believed that Hardy had nothing to fear in this respect, when in 1926 she recorded in her diary a conversation with him. He was, she wrote, 'immensely interested in facts; incidents; & somehow, one could imagine, naturally swept off into imagining & creating without a thought of its being difficult or remarkable; becoming obsessed; & living in imagination.'[41] She saw Hardy's singular absorption in the local and the oddly contingent as presenting not so much a problem as a creative opportunity. Facts and the transforming pressure of his imagination were in dynamic continuum, not in awkward tension.

Woolf was, of course, quite unaware of the existence of 'Facts', yet her diary note wonderfully evokes Hardy's transformation of incident, happenings, found by chance or searched for, into imagined human experience, answering to the test proposed in a passage in *Life and Work* that 'the uncommonness must be in the events, not in the characters'.[42] But his 'living in imagination' was promoted, too, by memory and an acute sense of the past. If some items in 'Facts' can be recognized, in varying degrees, as 'sources', or providing the germ of a narrative, many others appear to trigger his exceptional powers of recall. As Hardy explained in 1912, his 'inquiries' (surely a veiled reference, in part at least, to 'Facts') could 'correct tricks of memory',[43] just as his memory could correct the record. And no other surviving notebook of Hardy's comes as close to that intense interplay between memory and invention which so characterizes his poetry and prose. Whether or not the process of recovery crystallized in poem or story, its aim was, as he put it, 'to preserve for my own satisfaction a fairly true record of a vanishing life'.[44] Yet exposed, randomly, on the pages of the notebook, that 'vanishing life' offers itself, fugitively, as precarious, violent, oppressive and lawless. Such raw data would not have been found acceptable, or even credible, by many late Victorian readers. There were indeed good reasons for Hardy wishing to keep this 'rough music' in its place.

Notes

1. The 'Architectural Notebook' is edited by C.J.P. Beatty as *The Architectural Notebook of Thomas Hardy* (Dorchester: *DNHAS*, 1966). The 'Schools of Painting' notebook, the two 'Memoranda' notebooks and the 'Trumpet-Major Notebook' are gathered in *The Personal Notebooks of Thomas Hardy*, ed. Richard H. Taylor (London: Macmillan, 1979). The three volumes of 'Literary Notes', together with the '1867' notebook, are edited by Lennart A. Björk as *The Literary Notebooks of Thomas Hardy*, 2 vols (London: Macmillan, 1985). *Thomas Hardy's 'Studies, Specimens &c Notebook'* is edited by Pamela Dalziel and Michael Millgate

(Oxford: Clarendon Press, 1994). 'Poetical Matter' is available only on microfilm at the Beinecke Rare Book and Manuscript Library, Yale University, the original having been lost or destroyed.

2. *The Original Manuscripts and Papers of Thomas Hardy* (18 reels): (East Ardsley, Wakefield: E.P. Microform, 1975), reel 9. The earliest published mention of 'Facts' is by R.L. Purdy, *Thomas Hardy: A Bibliographical Study* (Oxford: Oxford University Press, 1954), p. 195, p. 219. Critical attention to the notebook begins with Christine Winfield's 'Factual Sources of Two Episodes in *The Mayor of Casterbridge*', *Nineteenth-Century Fiction* 25 (2) (September 1970): 224–31; and, above all, with Michael Millgate's *Thomas Hardy: His Career as A Novelist* (1971; London: Macmillan, 1994), pp.237–41, 396–7, 400–401). Thereafter 'Facts' has been variously treated by a number of other critics including: Norman Page, *Thomas Hardy* (London: Routledge, 1977); Kristin Brady, *The Short Stories of Thomas Hardy* (Basingstoke: Macmillan, 1982); Samuel Hynes (ed.), *The Complete Poetical Works of Thomas Hardy* 5 vols (Oxford: Clarendon Press, 1982–95); Frank B. Giordano, *'I'd Have My Life Unbe': Thomas Hardy's Self-Destructive Characters* (Montgomery, AL: University of Alabama Press, 1984); Simon Gatrell, 'The Early Stages of Hardy's Fiction' in Norman Page (ed.), *Thomas Hardy Annual* no.2 (London: Macmillan, 1984), pp.3–29; Charlotte Lindgren, 'Thomas Hardy: Grim Facts and Local Lore', *Thomas Hardy Journal* 1 (3) (October 1985): 18–27; Joanna Cullen Brown, *Hardy's People* (London: Allison and Busby, 1991); Pamela Dalziel (ed.), *Thomas Hardy: The Excluded and Collaborative Stories* (Oxford: Clarendon Press, 1992); Martin Ray, *Thomas Hardy: A Textual Study of the Short Stories* (Aldershot: Ashgate, 1997). The fullest description of all the surviving notebooks is to be found in Barbara Rosenbaum, *Index of English Literary Manuscripts Vol. IV (1800–1900), Part Two (Hardy–Lamb)* (London and New York: Mansell, 1990).

3. F.E. Hardy, *The Early Life of Thomas Hardy 1840–1891* (London: Macmillan, 1928); *The Later Years of Thomas Hardy 1892–1928* (London: Macmillan, 1930).

4. John Carter, 'A Further Note on A.E. Housman', *TLS* (14 March 1968), p.278.

5. Virginia Woolf, who like Hardy, read 'with a pen and notebook', left 67 volumes of notes, including one with the title 'Hardy' (Brenda R. Silver, *Virginia Woolf's Reading Notebooks* (Princeton, NJ: Princeton University Press, 1983), xi, 202).

6. Michael Millgate, *Testamentary Acts* (Oxford: Clarendon Press, 1992), p.161.

7. There was a precedent for such division of labour early on in the composition of a notebook. Lennart Björk remarks that in 'Literary Notes' Hardy 'wrote the first entry of the notebook proper … only to show how he wanted the material copied' (*LN*, i, xxxv). Emma had made a significant contribution to the note-taking for 'Literary Notes' from spring 1876. She had made a fair copy of the manuscript of *Desperate Remedies*, and had written some leaves of *The Return of the Native* manuscript. Emma and Hardy's co-operation continued well into the 1880s. It is clear that her assistance was valuable to Hardy, in her transcribing the lengthier and more tedious items (such as 97c or 120e). Of the 690 items which make up the notebook, it is a reasonable estimate that Emma entered 45.

8. *CL*, v, 210; vii, 62.

9. Founded in 1821, *The Dorset County Chronicle, Somersetshire Gazette, And General Advertiser For the South and South-West of England* was described in 1832 as being 'conducted on conservative principles, and in unison with those of the Church of England, and in the present conflicting state of public opinion, advocates those principles worthy of its patronage' (James Savage, *Dorchester and Its Environs* (Dorchester, 1832). It was relaunched in August 1854 as a 20-page paper (four columns) (C.H. Mayo, *Bibliotheca Dorsetiensis* (London: C. Whittingham and Co., 1885), p.79)). Entries from the *Dorset County Chronicle* appear sporadically in other notebooks before the inception of 'Facts': 'A Shorthorn Cow – the highest price ever given was for "The Duchess of Geneva" – 7000 guineas', from *DCC* (13 September 1877, p.14) appeared in *Literary Notes* (i, 116). Another *Literary Notes* item is a report of a speech on India by a Captain Digby (*DCC*, 8 November 1877, 4–5), (*LN*, i, 116, 354n). The 'Trumpet-Major Notebook' contains a reference from an 1829 *DCC* to 'Trial of Kennedy for shooting at Rev. H. Willoughby' (*PN*, 168), an episode later followed up extensively in 'Facts' (97c). Later, in 1888, after the bulk of the work for 'Facts' had been

completed, Hardy spotted a *DCC* report of the suicide of an Army Officer in 1888 (*DCC*, 2 August 1888, p.12) which furnished him with details of the sensational murder of Alec d'Urberville by Tess, and which he pasted into a copy of *Tess* presented to Florence Dugdale in 1911 (*Millgate, 1971*, 265, 401(fn)).

10. Hardy enters notes from Hutchins both in 'Literary Notes 1' in 1876 (*LN*, i, 60–62, 308–10n (items 584, 586–601)) and in 'Facts' (19a–19f, 20h) – again from pasted-in material from another notebook, probably of 1881. There are additional items (188a–189f) from Hutchins in 'Facts', from 1888.

11. Hardy had known about Walpole's letters as early as the 1860s (*Millgate, 1982*, 112). A note from this source was copied into 'Literary Notes 1' sometime between July 1878 and May 1879 (*LN*, i, 118 (item 1097)). Notes from Walpole were first entered into what must be described as an 'ur-notebook', of at least 80 pages, probably in 1881; they were then pasted into 'Facts' (items 20i–23h, 23j–24e) with additional items entered in 1885 or 1886 (151a) and, again, much later, in, or about, 1910 ([211]a–212a).

12. The phrase comes from his Preface to *The Dynasts* and refers to, for example, the presence of George III and his ministers in Dorset during the war with Napoleon, and the 'memories and traditions' of preparations for French invasion, on the Dorset coast. See the Preface to the Wessex Edition of *The Dynasts* (1913), reprinted in *PW*, 39. (See William Greenslade, 'Rediscovering Thomas Hardy's "Facts" Notebook', in Phillip Mallett (ed.), *The Achievement of Thomas Hardy* (Basingstoke: Macmillan, 2000), pp.171–86, p.173; reproduced with permission of Palgrave Macmillan.)

13. These passages (almost certainly entered at the British Museum by Florence Dugdale, at Hardy's request) were taken from Basnage's *History of the Jews* (London: J. Beaver & B. Lintot, 1708) ([205]a:ii), and *The Sepher Toldoth Jeshu: The Jewish Life of Christ*, ed. G.W. Foote and J.M. Wheeler (London: Progressive Company, 1885) ([205]a:i, [205]a:iii), a narrative (with some of its sensitive passages retained in Latin) which tells the story of an alternative lineage for Christ – his descent from a Greek soldier, Jacob Panthera and Miriam. Taken together with Hardy's entries from Ernest Crawley's *The Tree of Life: A Story of Religion* (London: Hutchinson, 1905) ([205]a:iv), a translation of *Origen contra Celsum* ([205]b–[205]d), and an interesting editorial aside ('Vide also Haeckel, Strauss etc.'), these sources point to a particular interest of Hardy's, in the Edwardian years, in revisionary studies of Christ's origins and significance.

14. *Millgate, 1982*, 247.

15. *Life and Work*, 128–9, 222–3.

16. Raymond Williams, *The Country and the City* (1973; London: Hogarth Press, 1985), p.206.

17. Simon Gatrell, 'Wessex' in Dale Kramer (ed.), *The Cambridge Companion to Thomas Hardy* (Cambridge: Cambridge University Press, 1999), pp.19–37 (pp.24–5) and *Millgate, 1971*, 236.

18. Gatrell, 'Wessex', p.24

19. Williams, *The Country and the City*, p.206.

20. *Millgate, 1982*, 248.

21. Sources for *The Mayor of Casterbridge* already established, are three reports of wife sales (32g, 74d and 116c); a report of the decline of Weyhill fair (117g), a Dorchester Tradesman's Dinner (94d), a bankruptcy hearing (30a), a humiliation of a soldier (52c) and the swearing of oath to abstain from liquor (111d). To these can be added a further undoubted source – a report of a wrestling bout (106d) whose terminology Hardy carefully reproduces in his description of the physical struggle between Henchard and Farfrae in the hay loft (*Mayor, 1987*, 271–4) and three indirect sources: a further report of a decline of a fair (at Hindon), 'Gone down' (54g), a report of a feud between the rival bands of Fordington and Bockhampton mummers (81b), and a pasted-in cutting recording a bull rushing at a woman at a cattle fair (143c).

22. Items 32g, 74b and 116c contribute to the wife sale in *The Mayor*, items 31a and 32c to the mantrap episode in *The Woodlanders*, and items 117f and 162g to the accident involving Prince in *Tess*.

23. Hardy's treatment of *Recollections of My Youth* (London: Chapman & Hall, 1883) by the French historian Ernest Renan, found passages of a philosophical character going to 'Literary

Notes' (*LN*, i, 175–6 (1387–94)), while into 'Facts' went an episode, together with amplifying realist touches, which recounts the rejection of Renan's grandmother by a priest whom she had sheltered, at the risk of her life, during the Revolution (160c). A further example of simultaneous noting is Hardy's copying extracts from Marie Liechtenstein's *Holland House* (1874) into 'Facts' (items 180a–183a) while others were entered in 'Literary Notes 1' in 1887 (*LN*, i, 187, 396n (item 1454)).

24. *The Mayor, 1987*, 247.
25. As Hardy had heard too from his father (*Life and Work*, 222–3).
26. See Giordano, '*I'd Have My Life Unbe*', p.12.
27. See items 77c, 84a, 91f, 97a, 142d and 187b.
28. See *DCC*, 5 March 1829, p.3, col.4 (note to 'Facts' item 96e).
29. Kristin Brady writes of the 'farcical foreshortening of the process of courtship' played out in stories such as 'Tony Kytes The Arch Deceiver' or the 'History of the Hardcombes' from 'A Few Crusted Characters' (*LLI*) (*Brady*, 143).
30. *DCC* reported that Mr Leigh of Lyme Park 'who possesses immense estates in Cheshire, which lie contiguous to those of Mr Turner of Shrigley Park, was on the point of paying his addresses to Miss Turner, when she was carried off by Mr Wakefield' which 'put a stop to the preliminaries of so advantageous an alliance as regards property, and upon the result of the trial of Mr Wakefield depends whether Mr Leigh's hand and estates shall be joined with the hand and estates of Miss Turner' (*DCC*, 21 September 1826, p.1, col.3).
31. J.H. Bettey, *Man and the Land: 150 Years of Dorset Farming 1846–1996* (Dorchester: *DNHAS*, 1996), p.9.
32. E.P. Thompson, *The Making of the English Working Class* (1963; Harmondsworth: Penguin Books, 1968), p.245. See also, E.J. Hobsbawm and George Rudé, *Captain Swing* (London: Lawrence and Wishart, 1969), ch.2; Barbara Kerr, *Bound to the Soil: A Social History of Dorset* (1968; East Ardsley, Wakefield: E.P. Publishing, 1975), p.106; Bettey, *Man and the Land*, p.9; Eric Evans, *The Forging of the Modern State: Early Industrial Britain 1783–1870* (1983; 2nd edn, London: Longman, 1996), pp.147–51.
33. This was hastily formed at the King's Arms, Dorchester in early December. So quickly were events unfolding in the county by this time that, exceptionally, *DCC* brought out a second emergency edition with 'latest intelligence' (*DCC*, 2 December 1830, p.4. col.3).
34. Hardy's preoccupation with the 1830–31 disturbances may be reflected in a significant change he made to his story 'The Three Strangers' before its inclusion in *Wessex Tales* for Macmillan in 1888. In the 1883 serial version the sheep-stealer, and his brother 'with no work to do' live at Anglebury (Wareham); in the 1888 version this became 'Shottsford-Forum', that is, Blandford, the change reflecting 'Hardy's efforts to associate Summers with the unrest in the Vale of Blackmoor' – although in fact Wareham was not altogether immune from rioting (Kathryn King, in *WT*, 1991, 228n; Bettey, *Man and the Land*, p.11).
35. See Fred Reid, 'Art and Ideology in *Far From the Madding Crowd*', *Thomas Hardy Annual* no.4 (Basingstoke: Macmillan, 1986): 91–126 (p.100). The effect of evangelical religion and a powerful Anglican revival had been felt as early as the first decade of the century through such organizations as the Society for the Suppression of Vice (Thompson, *The Making*, 442–3). The revival also led to new liturgical disciplines which made old church bands, such as the one in which Hardy's father and grandfather played, unacceptable: the Stinsford quire was disbanded in 1841 under the new authority of the Revd Arthur Shirley (see C.M. Jackson-Houlston, *Ballads, Songs and Snatches* (Aldershot: Ashgate, 1999), pp.148–9).
36. For references to fairs in the notebook see, among others, 46a, 62c, 67b, 67c, 87c & 89a. See David Jones, 'Rural Crime and Protest', in G.E. Mingay (ed.), *The Victorian Countryside* 2 vols (London: Routledge, 1981), ii, 566–79 (p.571), Alun Howkins, 'The Taming of Whitsun: The Changing Face of the Rural Holiday', in E. Yeo and S. Yeo (eds), *Popular Culture and Class Conflict 1590–1914* (Brighton: Harvester Press, 1981), pp.187–208; Hugh Cunningham, 'The Metropolitan Fairs: A Case Study in the Social Control of Leisure', in A.P. Donajgrodzki (ed.), *Social Control in Nineteenth Century Britain* (London: Croom Helm, 1977), pp.163–84; David Kerr Cameron, *The English Fair* (Stroud: Sutton Publishing, 1998).

37. A near allusion is contained in a note added by Hardy to his poem 'The Beauty' (*LLE, CP,* 616–17), the wording of which is virtually identical with an entry in 'Facts' (90a), from *DCC*, itself taken from a London newspaper (the only source Hardy gives). He also refers to his 'papers', which must have been 'Facts', when corresponding, in 1911, about allusions to smuggling in 'The Distracted Preacher' (see *Ray*, 56–7). His most striking (though still guarded) allusion to material in 'Facts' occurs in a letter to Frederic Harrison (20 June 1918; *CL*, v. 270), where he cites three 'Facts' entries, with their *DCC* sources, but does not mention the notebook.

38. See Appendix One: Erasures and Excisions, erasure 7 (item 117f) and the note to item 162g.

39. One of Hardy's comments on the future of his 'memoranda' may be noted: 'his having being asked when old if he would object to their being printed, as there was no harm in them, and his saying passively that he did not mind' (*Life and Work*, 210).

40. 'The Profitable Reading of Fiction', *Forum* (New York) (March 1888): 57–70 (*PW*, 112–13).

41. See *The Diary of Virginia Woolf*, ed. A.O. Bell, 4 vols [vol. III: 1925–1930] (London, Hogarth Press, 1980), iii, 96.

42. *Life and Work*, 154.

43. General Preface to the Novels and Poems [Wessex Edition] (1912) (*PW*, 44–50 (p.46)).

44. General Preface to the Novels and Poems in *PW*, 46.

Textual Introduction

Bibliographical Description

The notebook, measuring 23.8 x 19.5 cm (including spine), is a library-style stationery binding with 16 ruled-paper sections sewn onto two tapes and with a hollow and no head bands. The covering is half leather with black watered cloth siding. The leather is maroon morocco and has blind tooling along the edges on the face. The spine is decorated with simple double-fillet gold lines. Inside the covers there are cloth-reinforced endpapers with non-pareil marbling. On the top left-hand corner of the first endpaper is a Booklabel (5.0 x 3.7 cm) 'FROM THE LIBRARY // OF // THOMAS HARDY, O.M. // MAX GATE'.

Pagination and Gatherings

All pages are ruled; the reinforced endpapers are unruled. The notebook is paginated, in pencil, on alternate pages, that is, on the recto of the leaf, in the top right corner, to f.96r (p.191). Thereafter, to f.111r (p.[221]), pagination has been erased, with the exception of f.101r (p.201). The last two leaves of gathering 10, and the leaves of gatherings 11–16, are all blank (equivalent to 140 pages).

    Gathering 1. 9 leaves. *Prelims* i, v: reinforced endpaper on which is written in TH's hand (pencil), '<u>Facts</u>. To be destroyed uncopied', ('To be destroyed uncopied' is partially erased); ii, r&v: loose leaf; ii, r: 'p.162' in TH's hand (pencil); ii, v blank; iii, r&v blank; 1–7r&v: *Gathering 2*. 11 leaves. 8r&v: loose leaf; 9r&v: both blank; 10: stub on which leaf pasted, r&v [orig. page 77]; 11: stub on which leaf pasted, r&v [orig. page 79], excision in lower half: (9.8 x 16.8 cm); 12: stub on which leaf pasted, r&v [orig. page 81]; 13–18r&v. *Gathering 3*. 10 leaves. 19–28; 28r&v: excision at base (2.0 x 18.0 cm). *Gathering 4*. 10 leaves. 29–30r&v; 31r&v: Excision at base (7.0 x 17.8 cm); 32–33r&v; 34r&v: excision at base (7.0 x 17.5 cm); 35–38r&v. *Gathering 5*. 12 leaves. 39–50r&v. *Gathering 6*. 12 leaves. 51–62r&v. *Gathering 7*. 12 leaves. 63–74r&v; 72r: pasted-in cutting (2.0 x 6.7 cm). *Gathering 8*. 13 leaves. 75–87r&v. *Gathering 9*. 11 leaves. 88r&v: excision in upper half (2.0 x 17.0 cm); 89–92r&v; 92v–93r: 1 loose cutting (10.8 x 6.8 cm); 93r: pasted on inner edge in two cols at 90°, on verso hotel bill, receipted (20.0 x 17.9 cm) 94–96r&v: 97v: pasted-in cutting (3.0 x 7.0 cm); pasted-in leaf (5.6 x 16.8 cm) 98r: pasted-in cutting (19.5 x 6.9 cm); part of a leaf, pasted-in (13.2 x 9.5 cm); 98v: pasted-in cutting, col.1 (12.9 x 20.7 cm); col.2 (12.9 x 20.7 cm). *Gathering 10*. 14 leaves. 99–101r&v; 102r: pasted-in cutting (18.7 x 17.3 cm); 102v: pasted-in cutting, (i) col.1 (21.4 x 8.7 cm); col.2 (13.4 x 8.7 cm) (ii) col.2 (6.5 x 8.6 cm); 103r: pasted-in, leaves (10) (17.8 x 10.0 cm); 103v: blank; 104r; 104v: blank; 105r; 105v: blank; 106–108r&v; 109r: pasted-in cutting (21.6 x 6.9 cm); col.2 (21.6 x 6.9 cm); 109v: pasted-in cutting: (i) col.1 (3.2 x 6.9 cm) (ii) col.1 (17.5 x 6.9 cm) col.2 (5.0 x 7.2 cm); 110r: pasted-in cutting col.1 (21.2 x 6.2 cm); col.2 (8.0 x 6.2 cm) 110v: pasted-in cutting, col.1 (21.4 x 7.0 cm); col.2 (21.5 x 7.0 cm); col.3, (i) (2.6 x 7.0 cm), (ii) (2.3 x 7.0 cm), both at 90°; 111r: pasted-in cutting (11.0 x 12.2 cm); 111v: blank; 112r&v: blank. *Gatherings 11–15*. 66 leaves. 113–174 r&v: blank. *Gathering 16*. 10 leaves. 175–181r&v: blank; 182–184r&v: stubs.

Editorial Procedures

A 'Typographical Facsimile'

The aim of this edition is to produce, as closely as is practicable, a typographical representation of the (largely) handwritten manuscript of the notebook. A decision has been taken to adhere, as far as possible, to the length of the line of the transcriptions by Thomas Hardy, and by his wife Emma, of the almost exclusively prose material culled from the 'newspapers, histories, biographies, & other chronicles' that Hardy referred to on the title page of the notebook. In extending this procedure, normally reserved for poetical matter, to a notebook of prose extracts, I have endeavoured to preserve for the reader a clear visual sense of Hardy's editorial activity, as, with Emma's help, he transcribed, considered and from time to time returned to items which he had chosen for transcription. Authorial matter, such as additions, cross-references and emendations, has been reproduced.

It follows from the retention of the line-length of the notebook's handwritten entries, that words and phrases which have been interlineated by Hardy in the manuscript should be interlineated in this edition, rather than placed on the line in editorial parentheses. With the generous co-operation of the publisher, this has been achieved by the extension of line-spacing to double, for all handwritten matter. Where Hardy's interlineations have been written small, an appropriately small font size has been used to represent it. This procedure has not been adopted in the case of a pasted-in 10-page insertion ([205]a:i–iv) in the hand of Florence Emily Dugdale; here the line has been regularized, although the double spacing, appropriate for a handwritten source, has been maintained. All pasted-in printed matter from newspapers and periodicals has been reproduced in single spacing, with the line-length regularized.

Excisions and Erasures

As Michael Millgate puts it with reference to one particular erased notebook item ('Sobriety and its beneficial consequences' (111d)), 'an effort has been made, presumably by Hardy himself, to render the notebook entry illegible'. Millgate adds that 'other notes have been effectively scored through or scraped away, and some have been removed altogether'. He goes on to suggest that it is impossible 'to make a positive identification of material excised in this way, but in some instances it is at least possible to determine the source of the item, and in the case of the *Dorset County Chronicle* the particular issue and page from which the note must originally have been taken' (*Millgate, 1971*, 240). With regard to the erasures, the results of an examination of ink pigmentation (undertaken at the Conservation Department of the British Library, 2001) have been incorporated in the descriptions detailed in Appendix One. Examples of erased or partially erased items are itemized and gathered together, with textual notes, source notes and annotation in Appendix One. Examples of passages from the notebook which have been excised by cutting out are also brought together along with information about the possible source of the excision; examples of excisions are referred to by the number of the folio in which they occur.

Annotation Principles

There are four types of note deployed. Where the hand in which the item is inscribed is not that of Hardy, this is mentioned (otherwise the hand used is assumed to be Hardy's). In addition a textual note and annotation of the item are included, if appropriate. Where entries are the result of both Hardy and Emma's work, their respective contributions are specified. The source is cited in each case. The small number of items for which no source is traceable are noted as 'unidentified'. Standard sources are abbreviated in accordance with the list of abbreviations. The purpose of the textual note is to comment on the appearance of the script (such as when pencil is deployed in contrast to the usual inked script) and to draw attention to other miscellaneous features of an item, including the anomalous position of an item on the page. The annotation of items includes the glossing of obscure terms, the location of places mentioned and brief biographical details of individuals cited. Persons, subjects and topics are cross-referenced across the notebook, as required. Standard abbreviations, italicized in the annotation, are used for Hardy texts, and for certain secondary sources.

Editorial Conventions

Punctuation

Where there is an ambiguity between comma, dash and stop then the sense of the passage determines the reading, and where stops and small dashes are indistinguishable they are regularized to stops.

Irregularly placed apostrophes, for example lordships' for lordship's, are retained and noted.

The omission or incomplete transcription of accents is noted.

All marks of punctuation are placed inside closing quotation marks, even if the original varies.

Missing full stops are supplied.

Random, irregular markings, usually at the end of items serving no grammatical purpose, are normally not recorded.

Markings which separate elements within an item are retained.

Inconsistent use of quotation marks and parentheses is not regularized.

Dashes under slash marks, indicating paragraph or line breaks, are omitted, as are tails to slash marks.

Dotted brackets are treated as ordinary brackets.

Abbreviations

Common abbreviations, that is, 'wh' for 'which', are retained.

All cases of raised letters as in '15.ᵗʰ' with a period or a dash beneath the raised letter, are regularized by omitting the period or short dash; raised letters are retained.

In the case of 'Mr', 'Mrs', 'Dr', the position of the 'r', if not already raised, is regularized by raising it in all cases.

The characteristic half-circle round the abbreviation 'cut' (for cutting) is rendered as a bracket.

The inconsistent use of the stop after 'ibid.' is regularized, but underlinings are omitted.

The dotted asterisk is regularized to a normal asterisk.

The characteristic sign for 'and etcetera' is regularized to '&c'.

Spacing

Handwritten items are transcribed with double spacing between the lines.

Transcriptions of newspaper and periodical cuttings are single-spaced.

Indentation in entries is consistently represented by four spacebar hits.

Variations in lengths of dashes are regularized.

Ellipses are regularized to three spaced periods.

The position of 'ibid' is regularized at the end of the line.

Alterations and Erasures

Obvious slips of the pen (including anticipatory slips) or unintentional smudges are ignored.

Crossings through, with correction above or following on the line, are observed.

The distinction between short and long caret marks are both regularized to a ʌ.

Gatherings to caret marks are reproduced on the page.

Marginal lineation, that is, two parallel lines down the side of an item, is reproduced and noted.

Information about colour of mark or deployment of pen, or pencil is noted.

Erasures which have rendered the text indecipherable are indicated by angle brackets round a blank space, that is, <   > .

Where deleted words and passages are recoverable, they are shown against a shaded background.

Doubtful or partially obscured readings are placed within angle brackets, that is, <word>.

Insignificant erasures and blotted-out letters or words are ignored.

Pagination

Items are numbered throughout the notebook as they occur on a specific page, with a letter indicating the position on page, 12e, 12f etc.

In certain cases linked items are separated and so numbered separately where there is a need to bring out their distinctive features, even though the items may be taken from the same source.

A double oblique stroke, //, indicates the end of a full manuscript page.

Headings

Incomplete underlinings of item headings are completed.

Item headings, not underlined, are left as they are and noted.

Centred lines between items, of varying lengths, deployed to divide one source from another, are reproduced.

Handwriting

Apart from the insertion of seven leaves near the end of the notebook, in a clearly identifiable third hand, entries are in two hands, predominantly that of Thomas Hardy himself, and in a small contribution in the hand of Emma. Of the notebook's 676 handwritten entries (there being 690 entries in total), at least 600 are in Hardy's hand. The remaining 76 are either in Emma's hand, or in both hands within the same entry, or in a hand or hands where identification is uncertain or, finally, in the hand of Florence Emily Dugdale whose contribution is confined to 10 pages taken from another notebook, and pasted into 'Facts' in 1909. Florence's hand, bold and consistent, presents no difficulties of identification, corresponding exactly with other surviving specimens of her handwriting. Discrimination between Hardy and Emma's hands, based, for example, on observation of their characteristic formation of individual letters, joining of words, slope of words and so on, has not so far produced a consensus of attribution. A further complication is the possibility that Emma's handwriting was influenced by her husband's. Yet the cumulative effect of lengthy passages in a single hand encourages recognition of some consistent individuality and therefore a distinction of hands. For example, Hardy's *d* is almost always distinct from Emma's, he tends not to cross *t* consistently, and the slope of his ascenders and descenders is irregular. (For further discussion of the characteristics of these two hands, see Dale Kramer, 'A Query Concerning the Handwriting in Hardy's Manuscripts', *Papers of the Bibliographical Society of America* (Third Quarter, 1963), 357–60, Lennart Björk (ed.), *LN*, i, xxxv–vi and Alan Manford, 'Emma Hardy's Helping Hand', in Dale Kramer (ed.), *Critical Essays on Thomas Hardy: The Novels* (Boston, MA: G.K. Hall, 1990), pp.100–121.)

The Notebook

(To be destroyed uncopied)

Facts
from Newspapers, Histories, Biographies, & other chronicles –
(mainly Local)

1a

<u>Condition of Rural England, temp. Hy VIII</u> : ——————————

The landlord leases land more & more frequently to capitalist farmers –

the class of yeoman arise – Farmer dependent on his hay & straw for his

winter keep. Cattle & sheep were fattened in summer & killed at its close,

their flesh being salted for winter use – "Summer is y-cumin in," meant

much more in those days than it does in ours on this account. Sheep

farming takes the place of agriculture – vast enclosures are made from

the common field, wh was the chief cause of Ket's rebellion in 1549 –

"The 15th cent. & the early years of the 16th were the golden age of the

English husbandman, the artisan, & the labourer." It was not till

after the Dissolution of monasteries that the roads went out of repair.

From review in Spec.of Thorold Rogers's Hist. of Agriculture.(c^t) //

Source: *Spectator*, 21 July 1883 (no. 2873): 938–9. This is a review of vols iii and iv (1882) of James Edwin Thorold Rogers, *History of Agriculture and Prices in England, 1259–1793*, 7 vols (Oxford, 1866–1902).
Note: *c^t*: cutting.

2a

Families of the ancient Saxon & Norman race – either extinct or

reduced to lowest fortune – Could one of those illustrious shades return to earth he might behold one of his descendants dancing at the lathe – another

tippling with his dark brethren of the apron...a fifth poaching upon the

very manors possessed by his ancestors.

Hand: ELH.
Text: no gap between this and subsequent item.
Source: Sylvaticus, pseud. (i.e. J.F. Pennie), *The Tale of a Modern Genius; or, the Miseries of Parnassus. In a Series of Letters*, 3 vols (London, 1827), ii, 128–9.
Note: John Fitzgerald Pennie (1782–1848) of East Lulworth, Dorset. TH probably consulted the copy lent to him by his Wimborne friend, the judge, H.T. Atkinson (*CL*, i, 111 fn.). If so, this and following items from Pennie were recorded at some time between late 1881 and December 1882 when TH returned *The Tale of a Modern Genius* to Atkinson (*CL*, i, 111), and were later entered in 'Facts'. For a discussion of Pennie's life and career see Glanville J. Davis, 'John Fitzgerald Pennie – "Sylvaticus"', *PDNHAS*, 118 (1996): 7–12. Michael Millgate has suggested that in writing *The Dynasts* TH could have been influenced by Pennie's *Britain's Historical Drama*, with its Preface (1832) (*Millgate, 1971, 316*).

2b

At Landulph – Cornwall – mural monument –

Here lyeth the body of Theodore Paleologus, of Pesaro, in Italy, descended

from ye imperial lyne of ye late Christian emperors of Greece, being the

sonne of Camilio, ye sonne of Prosper, ye sonne of Theodore, ye sonne of

John ye sonne of Thomas second brother of Constantine Paleologus the

8th of that name & last of y^t lyne of y^t reigned in Constantinople until

subdued by the Turks; who married w^t Mary ye daughter of William

Balls of Hadlye in Souffolke gent. & had issue 5 children...&

departed this lyfe at Clifton ye 21st of Jan. 1636.

Hand: ELH.
Text: y^t: in pencil. *that*: crossed through in pencil.
Source: Pennie, ii, 129.
Note: see Nikolaus Pevsner, *Cornwall (The Buildings of England)* (Harmondsworth: Penguin, 1951), p.73; but also A.R. Wagner, *English Genealogy* (Oxford: Clarendon Press, 1972), p.250.

2c

Poet, after much anxiety gets his epic printed – and at great labour to

himself calls round on his subscribers – but they

"absolutely swore to my face, when I presented them with their copies

that they never subscribed to the work or even heard of it."

Autobiog^y. of Pennie of E.Lulworth

Hand: ELH.
Source: Pennie, iii, 5.

2d

Louisa Durbach, German prodigy – Whilst watching her

cattle she wrote rude verses – in this she was accidentally assisted by a   //

                                                       contrived

neighbouring shepherd, who, although they were divided by a river, ~~continued~~

to lend her his whole library, consisting of R.Crusoe, The Asiatic Banise

(German romance) & the Arabian Nights.

Autobiog. of Pennie of L.

Hand: ELH.
Source: Pennie, i, 162.
Note: *Louisa Durbach*: Anna Louisa Durbach (1722–91), b. Silesia, poet whose work included the ode 'The Battle of Lowoschutz'. For Pennie she was an exemplar of 'what powerful obstacles true genius might ultimately surmount'. *Asiatic Banise*: *Die Asiatische Banise, oder Das blutig, doch muthige Pegu* (1689), by Henrich von Ziegler – an oriental romance much read in the eighteenth century.

3a

B, Smuggler, loved Mary W. – was the happiest of the happy whenever he

could obtain, which was but seldom, the hand of Mary in the dances on the

village green. But Mary was thoughtless & vain – a jilt. James W. the

officer of excise was her favoured beau (was this the Wallis, who lived at Lower House,
& whom g.f' knew?)

Smuggler was jealous. One evening he found her sitting on J.'s knee

at a little village party to which J. had been invited from strategem, that he

might not be on the look out to interrupt the landing, or send for the military

stationed in the next town for his service. B. entreated M. to quit the knee of

W. & come to him; but she obstinately refused. He then frantically exclaimed

"Mary, I cannot live to see you in the arms of another – I will end my existence!"

[Shall I end &c.] The unfeeling maid nodded her head & burst into a

fit of laughter. He ran to an adjoining stable. No one attempted to

follow him, either through fear, or a belief that he intended no violence.

Report of a pistol: ran: weltering in blood: expired. Buried by

moonlight – no priest – no bell.

The heartless M. went that evening to a merry junketting in

a neighbouring village. Played at forfeits, & b.man's buff, & romped

& laughed with the gayest there. On her way home was frightened by something   //

never went abroad alone again.

Life of Pennie.

Hand: ELH and TH.
Text: *(was this the Wallis…g.f' knew?)*: pencil insertion in TH's hand.
Source: Pennie, iii, 174–6.
Note: *B.*: Ben Roberts. *Mary W*: Mary Wilmot. The village is East Lulworth.
TH's interpolated insertion almost certainly refers to his paternal grandfather, Thomas Hardy (1778–1837), whose connivance in smuggling activity in the Bockhampton of the early 1800s would have made TH aware of the existence of James Wallis, the excise-man (see 'Memorandum 1', in *PN*, 8–9; *Millgate, 1982*, 8). See note to item 163a.

4a

Ball from musket passes close to lips of soldier – so close as to take

off the skin ~~of~~ from both.   ib.

Hand: ELH.
Source: Pennie, iii, 177–8.
Note: *soldier*: George Ford of East Lulworth, 'chief of the smuggling sea-gangs along the southern coast'.

4b

Girl who committed suicide – was buried on the hill where two roads

meet: but few followed to her unblest grave: no coffin: one girl threw

flowers on her. Stake driven through her body. Earth heaped round the

stake like an ancient tumulus. ib. (This is like M's description to me

of the similar burial on Hendford Hill, when she was a child).

Hand: ELH.
Source: Pennie, iii, 182–3.
Note: *Girl*: Jane Gilbert. *Hendford Hill*: S. of Yeovil, Somerset, mentioned in 'A Tragedy of Two Ambitions' (*LLI*) (*CS*, 416). *M*: TH's mother, Jemima; ELH is writing as for TH here. See also TH's note in 'Memoranda, 1': 'burial of suicides at cross roads abolished c 1830. (stake driven through it: between 9 & 12.) Times' (*PN*, 24); TH's 'The Grave by the Handpost' was based on this custom (*Brady*, 216). See also items 32f, 57a, 117a.

4c

Birth of a first born child – The running gossip, as she was called,

went from house to house to invite the female neighbours to be present –

& one stood on the stairs for the purpose of giving notice to another below,

who stood tap in hand ready to broach the barrel the moment the child

was born. No sooner were the glad tidings announced than the chimney

corner blazed from side to side with an immense turf fire – bowl brought forward & filled with toast & strong ale, spiced & sugared –

Dancing over three high, & lighted candles; she who was so unfortunate

as to knock either down forfeited the next draught.

Life of Pennie.   //

Hand: ELH.
Source: Pennie, iii, 187–8.

5a

The Daily News remarks on the lives of Scotch sheep-farmers in this snowy
                    1882
weather (Dec.7 ʌ), & the loss of their sheep in the snow. A more wretched

sight than a bleak Scottish valley, with its sour green hills, & cold steel-gray

burn, flowing in early spring past skeletons, & carcases of dead sheep, can

hardly be imagined...

A weary time, keeping 3 sheep alive at the cost of one. A hard life is that

of the sheep farmer in Sutherlandshire or Rossshire, with his long visits,

through choked-up glens, to the sheep of some starving upland farm...

Scenery of which all the familiar features are obliterated.

Hand: ELH.
Source: *DN*, 7 December 1882, p.5, col. 3.
Note: *Rossshire*: the original has 'Ross-shire'; ELH and TH, like other late Victorians, usually eliminated hyphens.

5b

Windsor October 3ʳᵈ 1792

...Anything so disgusting as the breakfast at Woodgates' Inn

[Woodyates] on the way from Weymouth I thank God I never saw before,

& never wish to see again – bad butter, Tea, Coffee, bread, &c; nothing to

touch but boil'd eggs which were so hard that I could not eat them. So

I returned to the carriage just as I got out, starved. "&c

"The Family of Geo III." Percy Fitzgerald. SR. 16.12. 82.

Hand: ELH.
Source: *Saturday Review*, 54 (16 December 1882): 796–7; review of Percy Fitzgerald, *The Royal Dukes and Princesses of the Family of George III: A View of Court and Manners for Seventy Years, 1760–1830*, 2 vols (London: Tinsley Bros., 1882).
Note: *[Woodyates]*: ELH's correction. ELH copied, verbatim, the review's quotation of a letter from Princess Elizabeth (1770–1840) dau. of George III, to Lady Harcourt (3 October 1792). In *The Trumpet-Major* the royal party 'change horses at Woodyates Inn' (ch. 11). Woodyates is mentioned in 'Incident in the Life of Mr George Crookhill' (*CS*, 516). See also *PN*, 131, *Life and Work*, 421–2. The inn (since demolished) on the Blandford–Salisbury road near the Dorset–Wiltshire boundary, was 'famous as a posting house in the old coaching days ... now much neglected' (Sir Frederick Treves, *Highways and Byways in Dorset* (London: Macmillan, 1906), p.182.); see also *Hawkins*, 96–7.

5c

At the Criminal Court of Innsbrück yesterday the trial commenced

of Baron von Pawel Rammingen...General Reinhardt...made an

enormous fortune in the service of a native prince in India – &c. P.M.G.

16.12.82.   //

Hand: ELH.
Source: 'Charge of Fraud Against a German Baron', *Pall Mall Gazette*, 36 (16 December 1882), p.8.

6a

Two brothers Wood, Robert & Edward. Their father bequeaths the

estate – half to one & half to the other. The younger, Edward, has the half

which includes the mansion – the best half. The elder emigrates to the

United States in 1834, marries a lady of Philadelphia – dies – leaves an only son & three daughters – Son inherits the estate, the half estate; in

England. Figure of King Geo III cut out on his estate. Hutch – Osm^n. II.505

Hand: ELH.
Source: *Hutchins*, ii, 505.
Note: *Two brothers Wood*: Robert Serrel and Edward Atkyns, sons of Revd R.S. Wood (b.1779) of Osmington, Dorset. *father*: Hutchins has 'grandfather'. *Figure of King George III*: George III on horseback, cut in the chalk of the downs 1 m. NW of Osmington *c.* 1808, on what was then Wood land. There are differing accounts of the origins of the Osmington White Horse. In *The Trumpet-Major* Anne Garland and John Loveday watch 'forty navvies at work removing the dark sod so as to lay bare the chalk beneath' (*Trumpet-Major, 1991*, 320). In the chronology of the novel this incident takes place in 1806; since a letter of 1808 refers to the cutting of the figure, TH's account is soundly based, see S. Briggs, 'An instrument from the equestrian figure of Osmington Hill', *PDNHAS*, 98 (1976): 63–4. *Hutch*: Revd John Hutchins (1698–1773), rector of Wareham and author of *The History and Antiquities of the County of Dorset* (1774; 4 vols, 3rd edn, 1861–74). TH owned and annotated this edition. There are entries from Hutchins in *LN*, i, items 584–98.

6b

Perth & Melfort – Earl of. The honours of this family were under

attainder from 1746 until reversed in 1853; his lordship's father, who,

but for this attainder would have been 13th Earl of Perth was Leon

Maurice, son of the 3^d Duc de Melfort (in France) – &c see Debrett.)

Hand: ELH.
Source: *Debrett's Peerage, Baronetage, Knightage, And Titles of Courtesy* (1878), p.493.
Note: the Debrett entry dates the attainder from 1716; the family had been Jacobites.

6c

At Yeovil – man has committed suicide after a week's bout of hard

drinking – His papers reveal him to be a temperance lecturer, & letters

were found on him congratulating him on the success of the movement

in which he was so active.   D.News. Dec. 30. 82.

Hand: ELH.
Source: *DN*, 30 December 1882, p.6, col.5.

Note: misread by ELH. The *DN* report reads: 'Yesterday a man, unknown, was found nearly dead with his throat cut, in the yard of the Half Moon Inn, Yeovil … He is in the hospital in a somewhat serious condition.' *Shepton Mallett Journal* reports (26 January 1883, p.4, col.1) that George Frederick Cook pleaded guilty to attempted suicide – 'the taste of brandy aroused the old craving'. He was discharged.

6d

European gentleman treated so successively by American oculist that

he left the oculist all his property, leaving ~~the~~ his daughter a pauper. She

wrote to oculist, who at once took measures to transfer it – going to

Europe & placing the whole of the property under her control.

Harper's Bazaar. Dec.82.   //

Hand: ELH.
Source: *Harper's Bazar*, XV, no.52 (30 December 1882), p.827, cols 3–4.
Note: *successively*: a mistranscription of 'successfully'. *Bazaar*: [*sic*].

7a

France in 1870. The Republican Opposition powerful – in the plebiscite, ¼

of the standing army (on which so much reliance was placed as an instrument

of coercion at home) voted against the Emperor. – An alarming sign – it

was decided by the Emperor's unofficial advisers that he must undertake

a war in order to recover his authority over the army & be able to cope

successfully with the Republican faction. To this scheme M. Emile Ollivier

was of course no party, as one of its objects was to dismiss him from office.

[he was Prime Minister, & too Republican at bottom for the Court party]

The decision was to fight Prussia, the candidature of Prince Leopold of

Hohenzollern to the throne of Spain, being seized upon as a pretext.

M. Ollivier assured the Chamber with perfect good faith that there
would be no war if the Candidate were withdrawn; & on the very day before
the war, he, (who knew little of what was passing at S[t] Cloud between
Emperor & his confidants) affirmed that he would resign sooner than
be responsible for an "aggression" upon Prussia. However his scruples
were overcome by the Empress. War declared.

They saw the prospect of a short sensational campaign, like that
against Austria in '59, to be followed by some high handed stroke of
home policy. Ollivier was then to be thrown aside "like a squeezed
orange. But three weeks after all was changed. Imperial armies
beaten – And then the Emperor surrendered at Sedan – At home a
revolution. The Emperor-Regent deposed, & a Provisional Governm[t]
formed.   (partly from Times, 2.1.83.)   //

Hand: ELH.
Source: *The Times*, 2 January 1883, p.5, cols 1–5, espec. col.3.
Note: from an obituary of Léon Gambetta (1838–82), French statesman.

8a

Suffocated – At Frome. Mr Randell, who keeps public h. on
Corsley Heath, employed a man named Barnes to clear out a large
vat used for brewing. R. left for a few minutes, & while he was
away B. got up to the vat to look in. He was overpowered by the
gases & fell. R. coming to his assistance also looked into vat, overpowered, & fell in. A man named Mines also went to their
assistance – similar fate. The 3 were taken out: R. & M. found

to be dead. Barnes is slowly recovering. Times. 4.1.83.

Hand: ELH.
Source: *The Times*, 4 January 1883, p.7, col.2.
Note: *clear out*: *The Times* report has 'clean out'. *Corsley Heath*: in Wiltshire.

8b

Marriage announcement – Scots Magazine 1772 (Harper's Bazaar)

"13 July. At Boston, Lincolnshire. Mr Wm Staines. He was so extremely

ill that he was obliged to be carried to the Church in a sedan Chair. He died

on the 16th, was buried on the 17th, & his widow was married again on the 30th.

Hand: ELH.
Source: 'Curious Marriage Announcements', *Harper's Bazar*, XVI, no.39 (29 September 1883), p.815, cols 1–3.

8c

– Henry Strubling, of Hempfield, Pennsylvania, lately visited the Antietam

battle-ground, where he had been wounded, & found a gravestone bearing his

name, an unknown body having been mistaken for his, as he was reported

killed. American Paper – Oct.20.83

Hand: ELH.
Source: unidentified.
Note: *Antietam*: near the Potomac in Maryland, the site of a battle in the American Civil War, 16–17 September 1862.

8d–[p.9]

Dramatic case. River Plate. Bank Frauds. D. News. Oct.17. 83 (cut)

Several striking scenes. Manager of Bank, with confederate — ~~passed~~
                                                           The audit
loses money in speculation – covers losses with securities in bank. ~~And it~~ comes

securities wanted – some of them are ingeniously released by confederate –   //

passed through the hands of the auditors – taken away by confederate – <u>others</u> released

by covering with those already passed &c. In the auditor's evidence he says

the securities were brought to him in bundles – then, more being wanted: – "When

you had ticked the last of the nine lots did Warden (the prisoner) say

anything to you ?" ∟ "He said he would go to the treasury (strong room) &

fetch the remainder of the securities – It was about half past one – He

went out of the room apparently for the purpose which he mentioned; &

he did not return." ∟ –"You waited some time & he did not return?"

∟ Yes…I waited some time…communicated with the chief book-

keeper…Mᴿ W. never returned. I never saw him again till he was in

custody."

Hand: TH and ELH.
Source: 'Trial at Queens Bench Court, Guildhall', *DN*, 17 October 1883, p.2, cols 1–6 (cols 2–3).
Note: *W*.: George Warden, one of two men accused of stealing and receiving securities belonging to the London and River Plate Banking Company. In the *DN* report the final sentence 'I never saw … in custody' is an adaptation of a question put to the witness (the accountant charged with carrying out the audit) by the lawyer for the prosecution: 'You never saw him again until he was in custody?' 'No'.

9a

Two of Washington Irving's nieces live in Sunnyside – it having

been left on condition that they bequeath it to some good man of the

name of Irving.   Am: Paper.

Hand: ELH.
Source: unidentified.

9b–[p.10]

Fraudulent bankrupt – D.C.C. Oct 25. 1883.

Butcher & Cattle dealer – sundry offences against the Bankruptcy laws

& the Debtor's Act of 1869. Gross turning over in the cattle business £40,000

a year. His process was to write down in his books bills as "paid, date

so, & so –" (after filing his petition for liquidation) so that when the

receiver came it was supposed the accounts were closed. Though the

money was still owed; thus should he be successful in purchasing   //

the business from the trusteess he would be able to collect debts that were the

property of the creditors. Entries had been taken out of his book with acid

– 12 months hard labour.

Hand: ELH.
Source: 'Alleged Fraudulent Bankrupt', *DCC*, 25 October 1883, p.3, col.4; p.4, cols 1–2.

10a

On Sunday a gentleman visitor observed a number of gulls hovering

over & pitching on something in the bay. With the help of a seaman he

took a boat & went to the spot, where he beheld the body of a fine big-

framed man in a state of very great decomposition, having probably

been brought in by the tide. They towed the body to shore & put it in a

store wrapped in a cloth. The parish authorities had a coffin at once

made for it, & then had it properly interred. <u>Swanage</u> news. D.C.C. 1.11.83.

Hand: ELH.
Source: *DCC*, 1 November 1883, p.5, col.3.
Note: this extract is copied verbatim.

10b

A boy – an itinerant fiddler – robbed by gipsies & left tied to a tree – the

perpetrators discovered, tried – boy assisted by the judge, & now in a

respectable position.   Life of Baron Martin. Times. Jan 10.83.

Hand: ELH.
Source: *The Times*, 10 January 1883, p.6, cols 1–2.
Note: from an obituary of Sir Samuel Martin, Baron of the Exchequer (1801–83).

10c

Great Robbery. Fifty thousand dollars in gold. Government money

which was being sent to the Pacific coast for naval expenses, has been

stolen. The coin was packed in a keg, which was dispatched across

the isthmus, & stolen from a vault in Panama. Another keg of

gold in the vault was left undisturbed.   D.C.C. 18.1.83.

Hand: ELH.
Source: *DCC*, 18 January 1883, p.10, col. 2.

10d

Dore was in Farringdon market – night – an appaling object   //

rose before him – rags & bones – croaking "I am a gentleman – a clergyman."

Dore took him home, & sketched him, preaching from a pulpit to a congregation

of other drunkards.   Times – 25. 1. 83.

Hand: ELH.
Source: *The Times*, 25 January 1883, p.6, cols 1–2, espec. col.1.
Note: from an obituary of Gustave Doré (1832–83), the illustrator and painter. *appaling* [*sic*] ...
took him home: *The Times* report has 'took him to his hotel'.

11a

Vermin. Hawks, jays, stoats, weasels, cats, rats, magpies, &c. Keeper

received 3^d or 4^d or 6^d a head for killing them. Field. Jan.20.83.

Hand: ELH.
Source: *The Field*, 61 (20 January 1883), p.90, col.3.
Note: *6^d a head*: TH's addition.

11b

Night – brewer driving home from fair – a flash of lightning revealed

that his vehicle was in the midst of a flock of sheep. He & his groom were

pitched out of the trap. Drover of sheep was drunk. The defence was that

brewer turned a corner suddenly, drove into the flock, killing two ewes,

injuring 15: a collie dog in rear of carriage rushed into flock. 8.2.83.

Hand: ELH.
Source: 'Salisbury: A "Smash" on The Road', *DCC*, 8 February 1883, p.10, col.3.
Note: a case of 'misadventure', the jury brought in a verdict 'for neither party'.

11c

A handsome well-educated woman is courted by a young American, son

of a millionaire – The latter is ignorant of spelling & grammar – He cannot

marry her because of his father, & she lives with him on the understanding

that they shall marry in future. She teaches him spelling &c. & in other ways
        He deserts her & marries another
educates him. ⋏ (Evidence of plaintiff. Breach of Prom. Miller v. Joy.) 14.11.83

Source: 'The Curious Breach of Promise Case', *DN*, 14 November 1883, p.2, cols 4–5.
Note: *DN* makes no reference to the plaintiff ('a milliner and perfumer at Bournemouth') as 'handsome' and 'well-educated', although the latter can reasonably be inferred from her lengthy testimony.

11d

    An engaged lady ill, is visited by her betrothed. He stays out on landing

smoking cigar, & talks to her as she lies in bed through open doorway.   ib. id.

Source: 'The Extraordinary Breach of Promise Case', *DN*, 15 November 1883, p.2, cols 7–8.
Note: *ib. id.*: i.e. same source, same story. This item is taken from a further report of the case recorded above (11c). The *DN* report reads: 'when I called her little girl said Mrs Miller was ill. I was about to leave, but she sent for me to go up to the landing and I sat there smoking a cigar and conversing with her'.

11e

<u>Victorious party</u> in lawsuit, hold the will against window pane, in faces of

other party driving past, flaunting it victoriously.   ~~Whalley~~ Priestman v. Thomas.
                               D.N. Nov 19.83   //

Source: 'The Extraordinary Will Case', *DN*, 19 November 1883, p.2, cols 7–8.
Note: TH appears to have misread this report, part of which reads: 'as they drove past the house of Thomas … he exhibited against the window a sheet of blue paper … the action seemed to say, "You think you have got the better of me, do you?"' This case, reported in detail by *DN*, began on 17 November and ended on 4 December 1883. See also items 12b, 13a, 14b.

12a

"<u>A sack was thrown</u> over my head & I was hustled into a house" Case

of a Swiss who was thus robbed of £80, which he had won by betting, & had

shown in public house.   D.N. Nov 19. 83

Source: 'Alleged Kidnapping of a Man Near King's Cross: An Extraordinary Story', *DN*, 19 November 1883, p.3, col. 1.

12b

<u>Pencil marks</u>, when apparently erased, will after a time reappear to some

extent. Will Case – Priestman v. Thomas. D.N. 23.11.83

Source: 'The Remarkable Will Case', *DN*, 23 November 1883, p.2, cols 7–8 (col. 7). See item 11e.

12c

Housebreaking implements – were displayed in court, consisting of a rope-ladder,

centre-bits, dark lanterns, silent matches, candles, skeleton keys, & other

articles of a like description. Housebreakers were Frenchmen – Policeman

collared one, & he slipped out of his coat, leaving it in policeman's hands.

D.N. Nov 8.83

Source: 'Daring Case of Housebreaking by French Men' (Report of Middlesex Sessions), *DN*, 8
November 1883, p.2, col.3.
Note: *centre-bits*: *DN* has 'centrebits'. Here TH reverts to the older hyphenated form.

12d

Woman obtains child of 7 months from its mother, by telling her that she wanted

a baby boy for a rich lady, to adopt & make her heir. Met the mother at rail[y]

station, paid her £5 – & took child, giving false address.   D.N. Nov 8. 83

Source: 'The Extraordinary Charge of Child-Stealing', *DN*, 8 November 1883, p.2, col.3.

12e

Man comes into house where woman (in this case his mother) is, sits down,

& falls asleep in chair. She does not like to wake him.   D.N. case

Source: *DN*, 22 November 1883, p.3, col.3.

12f

Man [stranger] enters house & sits there all day. Sunday, saying he is ashamed

to go out in his dirty clothes. Stays till dusk.   ib. //

Source: *DN*, 22 November 1883, p.3, col.3.
Note: *[stranger]*: TH's invention. This and the previous entry are from the *Daily News* report of the 'Liverpool Murder'. The report concerns the trial of Lewis Parry for the murder of Susannah Hatton. TH has extracted two aspects of the same report, and recorded them separately.

13a

Remarkable Will case – In which it is alleged that legatee forged will – in

this manner. Testator having made will in favour of natural son, slaps

breast pocket in presence of forger, in whose house testator lodges, & says

his affairs are settled. This will he always carries in a sealed leather case

in this pocket. He dies – forger is alone with dead body – goes to where

dead mans coat hangs, takes out the envelope, steams it, substitutes for

true will a false one which he, forger, has written on a pencilled letter

signed in ink by testator, & never sent.   D.N. Nov 20–23. 83

Source: *DN*, 21 November 1883, p.2, col.1; 22 November 1883, p.2, col.8; 23 November 1883, p.2, cols 6–7.
Note: this is a summary of the main events in a trial reported at length in *DN* (see items 11e, 12b and 14b).

13b

Man seduces young girl: then marries widow who keeps a public-house.

[young girl calls veiled, sits down, &c]   p^{tly} D.N.

Source: 'Breach of Promise of Marriage', *DN*, 23 November 1883, p.7, col.3.
Note: *young girl calls veiled, sits down, &c*: this insertion derives from a source other than *DN*. p^{tly} *D.N*: TH took details from another report (not traced).

13c

A terrible revenge. A man lives with woman; has children by her; treats

her brutally; leaves her; she has to keep children, & is reduced nearly to starvation. He marries another woman. They meet in a public house: she

asks him what he is going to do for her; he says nothing. She then throws

a quantity of vitriol in his face, severely burning him, & taking away the

sight of one of his eyes.   D.N. 23.11.83

Source: 'Throwing Vitriol', *DN*, 23 November 1883, p.7, col.2.
Note: the judge in this case states that the usual penalty would be penal servitude, but that in view of the circumstances the sentence is reduced to 12 months' hard labour.

13d–[p.14]

In 'Horrible London', (D.News) G.R.Sims describes some persons who have

recently passed through a common lodging house in one of the most notorious slums

in London = Two men who had been college chums at Camb. & met here

accidentally. One had succeeded to large fortune & kept pack of hounds. Also   //

~~A gorgeously dressed dandy, & a man in rags meet in wood~~

A physician's son, who by day sells fusees in the Strand. Also a clergyman

who had taken high honours: last seen in the Borough, drunk, followed

by jeering boys. Also a commerc^l tr^r Also a member of the Stock

Exchange, suffering from D.T. – removed to workhouse. &c. D.N. 23.11.83

Source: *DN*, 23 November 1883, p.5, col.5.
Note: *G.R.Sims*: George Robert Sims (1847–1922), journalist and playwright; his *Pictorial World* articles on London's slums were reprinted as *How the Poor Live* (1883). *DN* ran his graphic accounts of the housing of the poor in London on 8, 14, 19 and 23 November 1883, later published as *Horrible London* (1889). Sims gave evidence to a royal commission on housing in 1884. *A gorgeously dressed dandy, & a man in rags meet in wood*: there is no mention of this in the *DN* report. *fusees*: large matches. *the Borough*: London Borough of Southwark, S. of the Thames. *DT*: *delirium tremens*, a result of alcoholism. It is possible that reports of professional men reduced to poverty by drink or other causes were especially noted by TH, following the death of his friend Horace Moule (1832–73).

14a

A Parsee merchant in the City, sends 100 guineas to Ld Mayors poor box. The

merch^t , Mr D.P.Caina, has, with his wife, lived 13 yrs in London. Says that his

father has contributed £12,000 to the hospital at Bombay.   D.N. 24.11.83

Source: *DN*, 24 November 1883, p.2, col.6.

14b

Two men converse across fence, & their voices being raised, a third overhears.

Will Case. D.N. 24.11.83

Source: *DN*, 21 November 1883, p.2, col.3.
Note: see also items 11e, 12b and 13a.

14c

Signor Agostino Guiliano Susini, aged 60, An Italian by birth, & by occupation

an operatic singer, residing at Lambeth R^d run over by a hanson.   D.N.

Source: unidentified.
Note: *hanson* [*sic*].

14d

Tails cut off a number of a farmer's cattle – house broken into by men

with blackened faces.   Ireland. D.N.

Source: unidentified.

14e–[p.15]

Tragedy in Poole. Danish sailor Larsen, provoked by Poole lab-

ourers, &c idling at 11 p.m. in Poole street, stabs one of the latter,

Tom James, age 22 – height 6 ft 2 in to 4 in – Dr Vernede gives his

evidence…"He explained that one of the wounds – the one which caused

~~the~~ death had been occasioned by the knife passing through the unfortunate   //

man's left lung, & penetrating the heart. The doctor at this point searched in his

coat-tail pocket & produced a small paper parcel. Unfolding this with calm

deliberation he held up to view what appeared to be a dirty piece of chamois

leather. This he explained, as a shudder passed through the Court, is the

lung of the deceased through which the knife went. Later on in his evidence
                                        had
the doctor again ʌ recource to his pocket, & this time he produced a still

larger parcel. Again quietly opening it, he then presented to the shocked

gaze of the Court the heart of the dead man, & pointed out the hole in

it where the knife had penetrated. A thrill of horror pervaded the

place, one man had to hold on to the rail separating the audience

from the Court to prevent himself from falling through faintness, a

juryman who had dined but a short time previously, relieved

his stomach of its contents, & a general hissing ensued which was only

stopped when the Coroner threatened to have the Court cleared. The

doctor in the meanwhile calmly held up the heart, & described the

injuries with that nonchalance, which as a rule distinguishes the pro=

fession in matters of that sort…

"Frederick James, labourer, living at Parkstone, said: The body which

the jury has just seen is that of my son. He was 22 years of age. I last

saw him alive last Saturday night at ten minutes to five o'clock.

I left him at home when I went out. He was in the habit of drinking

too much occasionally, but never saw him quarrelsome in my life."

(Telegram. Nov 30. 83, & D.C.C. Nov 29. 83)

[In Telegram Nov 21. 84: is inquest on sweetheart of the above Tom James – Jane Dare, prostitute –
His death seemed to have preyed on her mind – took to drink – drowned herself (after kissing his likeness
in harbour – a couple of moans, a bubbling.]

Hand: TH: *Tragedy...unfortunate*; ELH: *man's 'left lung' ... my life*. TH: *(Telegram...Nov 29. 83)*
and *[In Telegram ... bubbling.]*.
Source: 'Frightful Tragedy in Poole', *Weymouth, Portland and Dorchester Telegram*, 30 November
1883, p.12, cols 1–4; 'Stabbing Affray At Poole Verdict of Manslaughter', *DCC*, 29 November
1883, p.4; 'A Sad End', *Telegram*, 21 November 1884, p.6, cols 2–3.
Note: *Larsen*: Wilhelm Gerson Larsen (18) was convicted of manslaughter: the inquest verdict was
'found drowned in the water of Poole Harbour'. *recource* [*sic*]. *Frederick James ... in my life*:
verbatim from *DCC*. *after kissing his likeness*: The *Telegram* has: 'she went into the house, and
taking down James' likeness kissed it and burst out crying. She then put it in her bosom. She
screamed out twice while out in the street'. *[In Telegram ... a bubbling]*: TH's addition (follows
development of story in the press). The *Telegram* reports that a local publican 'heard a splash in
the water, and also a couple of moans and he could see the water bubbling'.

16a

Onomacritus. "It is night...The darkness of the temple's inmost

shrine is lit by the ray of one earthen lamp...A venerable man stooping

above a coffer...What is he doing?...[imitating ~~one of~~ the old prophecies

in the coffer on a new sheet]...Suddenly a man's hand is laid on his

shoulder!...It is a rival poet who has caught him. (Herod. vii.6)

from A. Lang.

Source: Andrew Lang, 'Literary Forgeries', *Contemporary Review*, 44 (December 1883): 837–49
(p.839).
Note: Lang elaborated a sentence in Herodotus, *Histories*, vii. 6. *Onomacritus*: Athenian
priest/poet, 6th cent. BC.

16b

Princess Charlotte The princess was sent to Weymouth under a

strong guard of ladies whose watch never relaxed – [This was some

little time before her marriage with Leopold]   Molloy's Court Life.

Source: Joseph Fitzgerald Molloy (1858–1908), *Court Life Below Stairs, or, London Under the Last Georges 1760–1830*, 4 vols (London: Hurst & Blackett, 1882–83), iv, 250.
Note: *Princess Charlotte*: only child and heir presumptive (1796–1817) of Prince Regent (afterwards George IV), and Caroline of Brunswick. Having broken her engagement to the Prince of Orange, she was kept in seclusion before marrying Prince Leopold of Saxe-Coburg (1816); died in childbirth. *ladies*: amongst them Lady Ilchester. *Leopold*: Prince Leopold (1790–1865) lived for a time at Came House, near Dorchester after his wife's death (see *Frampton*, 303, and many references). In 1831 he was elected King of the Belgians. For Caroline of Brunswick, see item 151b. Molloy also wrote lives of Margaret (Peg) Woffington (from which TH quotes in item 143d) and Edmund Kean (see espec. item [218]a; *CL*, iii, 19, 28; vi, 248; *Life and Work*, 339–40.) After having met Molloy at the British Museum, in May 1885, TH wrote to ELH that 'he is an impulsive rather interesting Irishman. Shall we ask him to call?' (*CL*, i, 133).

16c

The horse Eclipse. Pre eminent – never beaten. Mechanism perfect – Yet
neither handsome nor well-proportioned.
⋏ compared with a table of the geometrical proportions of the horse he measured in height

$^1/_7$ more than he ought – neck $^1/_3$ too long, &c. Col. O'Kelly, the celebrated owner of Ec.

Hone's Table Book.   //

Source: William Hone, *The Every-day Book: And Table Book; or Everlasting Calendar of Popular Amusements, Sports, Pastimes, Ceremonies, Manners, Customs and Events etc.*, 3 vols (London: William Tegg, 1826–27), iii, (Table Book), 619–22.

f.9r&v are blank

19a

– Strong box. Wimborne Minster – 6 locks – keys kept by 6 persons – box

carved from solid wood.   Hutchins. 'Wimborne M.'

Source: Hutchins, iii, 208–9.

Note: f.10r–12v (pp.19–24) consist of three leaves, written out, at a different time, on separate sheets and tipped onto stubs of three removed leaves of the notebook. Since at the top of f.10r is a crossed through '77', at the top of f.11r is a crossed through '79' and the top of f.12r is a crossed through '81', it is likely that these pages were extracted from another notebook of substance, at least 81 pages long.

19b

kept
– Body ~~buried~~ in clamped coffin on window sill – not buried –   ib.

(it was the body of Antony Etricke – a humorsome man – had his tomb

made before he died – that he might be sure of not being put underground).

Source: Hutchins, iii, 218–19.
Note: *clamped coffin*: 'in the wall of the south chancel-aisle [of Wimborne Minster] … a coffin of thick slate, painted, clamped with iron' (*Hutchins*, iii, 218). *Etricke* [*sic*]: Anthony Ettricke (1622–1703), of Holt, near Wimborne, antiquary and friend of John Aubrey. *a humorsome man*: 'towards the latter end of his life grew very humorsome, phlegmatic, and credulous' (*Hutchins*, iii, 218–19). In the Preface to his *Dorset*, Hutchins referred to his own dependence on Ettricke's 'MS Collections' (*Hutchins*, i, vii–viii). Hutchins attributed Ettricke's burial 'in the wall' of the church to his 'having been offended with the inhabitants of Wimborne', and his vowing that he would 'never be buried in their church or churchyard' (*Hutchins*, iii, 218). From his time in Wimborne TH would have been familiar with the story of 'the man in the wall', but chooses to put his own construction on Ettricke's motives – 'that he might be sure of not being put underground'. On Ettricke, see James M.J. Fletcher, '"The Man in the Wall" at Wimborne Minster', *PDNHAS*, 37 (1916): 26–39; Anthony Powell, *John Aubrey and his Friends* (1948; rev. edn, London: Hogarth Press, 1988), pp.249–50. See also TH's 'At Shag's Heath: 1685' (*CP*, 752).

19c

– Etricke had a venture in a ship – it arrived safely in Portland

roads – he was persuaded it w^d not reach London – sold his venture –

his prediction was true – ship was lost.   ib. III. 219

Source: Hutchins, iii, 219.
Note: *Portland roads*: Hutchins has 'Portland Road'.

19d

<u>Old family</u> Habgood, tanner, <u>temp</u> Charles I. founded a charity

in Wimborne – [ancestor of the present Habgoods I suppose].   ib.

Source: Hutchins, iii, 250.
Note: *[ancestor of the present Habgoods I suppose]*: TH's addition. *Habgood*: Hutchins has: 'Robert Habgood, formerly a tanner in this town, about the 1st of December, 1642, settled two messuages and gardens in Wimborne in six trustees, for the better relief and maintenance of the poor of this parish'. *the present Habgoods*: TH probably had in mind Henry Habgood, of the Square, Wimborne, listed as Auctioneer and Appraiser (*Kelly's Directory of Dorsetshire* (1880), p.995).

19e

<u>Shaftesbury Legend</u> – People in Church during terrific thunderstorm – fell

on their knees – a man's wife showed him a cross on her body afterwards –

He examined himself, found he was marked in same way – & all the

congregation.   ib. Shaftesbury

Source: Hutchins, iii, 70.
Note: *Church*: Wells Cathedral. *man*: TH omits to say that this was Dr Still, the Bishop of Bath and Wells (1593–1608).

19f

<u>Town of great interest</u> & importance in Mediaeval times – 12 churches –
      shrines, pilgrims
monastery, ⋏ mansions, &c – Shaftesbury –   ib.

Source: Hutchins, iii, 3–24.
Note: *mansions*: derived from *mansiones* in one of Hutchins' extracts from a charter (p.24), in the now archaic sense of 'dwelling places'. TH drew on this note for his description of medieval 'Shaston' in *Jude the Obscure*, ed. Patricia Ingham (Oxford: Oxford University Press, 1985), Book IV, ch.1, pp.209–10.

19g

<u>Husband, to induce</u> wife to marry without settlement insists on her drinking

some liquid – ceremony of marriage gone through – she does not know what she

is doing –   Futcher v. Futcher – (cut.) 29.7.81.

Source: *The Times*, 29 July 1881, p.4, col.3.
Note: this is the first of a series of items derived from cuttings, presumably accumulated in Wimborne before TH's move to Dorchester. For a note comparing this item with Alec d'Urberville's use of a 'druggist's bottle', in the first edn of *Tess*, see *Tess of the d'Urbervilles*, ed. Tim Dolin (London: Penguin, 1988), p.72, and note 9 (p.415).

19h

Police lying in wait – fall asleep – their treasure gone when they wake – (cut.)

Source: unidentified.

19i

Doors closed up with masonry.   ib.

Source: unidentified.

19j

A clockwork movement to fire infernal machines. "Explosives at Liverpool". (cut)

Source: unidentified.
Note: the incident is attributed to Irish extremists.

19k

A colonels pension sequestered – he in poverty – Snow v. Bolton 29.7.81. (cut).   //

Source: *The Times*, 29 July 1881, p.4, cols 2–3.

20a

Gent. in boat with ladies – loses an oar – night – burns p. handkerchiefs. (cut)
                                   "An unpleasant adventure". 23.7.81.

Source: unidentified.

Note: this is a source for an incident in *The Well-Beloved*, ed. Tom Hetherington (Oxford: Oxford University Press, 1986), pt 3, ch.6, p.189.

20b

Boxes of silver plate in cellar – receivers of stolen goods – cut 26.5.80

Source: *The Times*, 26 May 1880, p.6, col.6.
Note: owner of a furniture shop convicted of receiving stolen property, 'in a hamper', covered with rugs.

20c

Unsound mind when she went through ceremony of marriage – void – cut 28.4

(76)

Text: *(76)*: in pencil.
Source: *The Times*, 28 April 1876, p.11, col.5.
Note: a successful petition for a decree of nullity of marriage, at Ashton, Lancs. (Wood, otherwise Harrison v. Harrison).

20d

‖ First husband alive – second husband in love with another – cut 28.4.76

Hand: TH.
Text: there are two vertical parallel line (red pencil) beside this item.
Source: *The Times*, 28 April 1876, p.11, col.3.
Note: Signor Vianesi, conductor of the orchestra at Covent Garden (the petitioner), prayed for a decree of nullity of marriage by reason of a previous and subsisting marriage of the respondent (Mrs Henderson) (Vianesi v. Henderson, otherwise Vianesi).

20e

Back turned – abstraction from a book.   cut 26.5.80

Source: *The Times*, 26 May 1880, p.6, cols 5–6.
Note: a former bank clerk forged two bills for £3000 each and got them cashed at a discount. They were payable by 28 Feb. He persuaded a clerk (contrary to orders) to show him the pass book where the bills were kept. 'When the back of the clerk was turned, he abstracted and destroyed the bills'. He absconded to the Cape of Good Hope but (via telegraph) was arrested on arrival. Only £28 recovered. Respectable family: seven years' penal servitude.

20f

<u>A night ride through a city</u>.   large cut. 21.4.76

Source: *The Times*, 21 April 1876, p.10, cols 1–2.
Note: from *The Times*'s Special Correspondent, an account of 'a night's ride round Stamboul', mod. Istanbul, formerly Constantinople.

20g

<u>Man is shot dead</u> by keeper in self-defence – drags body into thicket – tells

the doctor – thinks of the body: depressed – dog brings in the dead man's

glove – D^r & keeper go out at night to bury the man & read prayers ove< >

him – dig grave &c –The sense that (during important scenes in

the mansion) a dead man is lying in the park impresses reader –

                                                        Woodstock.

Text: *over*: word is obscured by tipping-in.
Source: Sir Walter Scott, *Woodstock; or, The Cavalier* (1826), chs 29 & 31.
Note: the action of *Woodstock* takes place after the battle of Worcester in 1651. The keeper, Joliffe, kills the Cromwellian spy Tomkins with a blow of his staff (not with a shot). The royalist parson, Dr Rochecliffe, helps bury the body. *important scenes in the mansion*: these involve the disguised Charles II, whose refuge at Woodstock Lodge was an invention of Scott's.

20h

<u>Glass painter</u>.

"Before the Reformation", says Aubrey "I believe there was no county or great

town in England but had glasse painters. Old Harding, of Blandford...

where I went to schoole, was the only country glasse painter that ever I

knew. Upon play daies I was wont to visit his shop & furnaces. He

dyed about 1643, aged 83."   Hutch . Blandford.

Source: Hutchins, i, 216.
Note: in copying Hutchins almost verbatim, TH retained Aubrey's spellings, but modernized

'beleive' and 'countrey'. This extract was used in 'Barbara of the House of Grebe' (*GND*), where Sir John Grebe refers to Edmond Willowes with whom his daughter had eloped. In the narrator's words, 'Willowes's father or grandfather was the last of the old glass-painters in that place [Shottsford-Forum, i.e. Blandford] where (as you may know) the art lingered on when it had died out in every other part of England' (*CS*, 231).

20i

<u>Paste the heads</u> of celebr^d char^{rs} into a book – Walpole's let: Vol 1

Source: *The Letters of Horace Walpole, Earl of Orford* (ed.) Peter Cunningham, 9 vols (London: Richard Bentley, 1857–59), i, xix.
Note: TH also took material from Walpole's 'Reminiscences of the Courts of George the First and Second', included in vol. i of Cunningham's edition (i, lxxxvii–clv) (items 20i–22c). TH used Walpole's *Letters* for *LN*, i, 355, probably in 1878–79. *Paste the heads*: in the preface to his edition, Cunningham noted that at the end of an evening of 'scandal' with Lady Suffolk, Walpole would write, and would also 'paste Faithornes and Hollars into his volumes of English heads', i.e. Walpole's large collection of engraved portraits of notables of earlier times. William Faithorne (1616–91) and Wenceslaus Hollar (1607–77) were prolific engravers and portraitists. *Walpole*: Horace Walpole, 4th Earl of Orford (1717–97), author, letter-writer, memoirist, connoisseur, youngest son of Sir Robert Walpole, 1st Earl of Orford and for 20 years chief minister. See also items 45b, 45c, 137c and Appendix Two.

20j

A christening in a bedroom.   ib. cxi

Source: *Walpole, Letters*, i, cxi.
Note: this refers to the christening in 1717 of an infant son of the Prince and Princess of Wales (later George II and Queen Caroline). Norman Page suggests that this item may be a source for the scene in *Tess* ch.14, in which Tess baptizes her baby, Sorrow (*Tess, 1988*, 99), see Page, *Thomas Hardy* (London: Routledge, 1977), p.152.

20k

Craggs caught his death by calling at gate of Lady Marsh, who was ill

of the small pox: told so by the porter, went home, fell ill of same distemp
                                                                  per
& died.   ib. cix.

Text: *per*: in pencil.
Source: *Walpole, Letters*, i, cix.

Note: *Craggs*: James Craggs the younger (1686–1721), politician, friend of Addison, Pope and Gay.
Marsh: the *Letters* has 'March'; Lady March was daughter-in-law of the Duke of Richmond.

20l–[p.21]

Sir R.W. ~~thre~~ is told that persons meditate his <u>assassination</u> – he laughs   //

forgets the warning. Man who gave it came next day & tells him that

though he scoffed at the warning he had nonetheless followed his advice –

Sir R. did not understand. "You did not come last night from the

House in your own chariot." Sir R. says he did – calls footman, who

informs him that when his carriage was called Col. C.'s came up first,

& Sir R. stepped in with Col. C. his own carriage returning empty. The

coachman remembered that 3 muffled men had looked into the empty

Chariot.   ib. cxiv.

Text: *laughs*: part of word is obscured by tipping-in.
Source: *Walpole, Letters*, i, cxiv.
Note: *Sir R.W.*: Sir Robert Walpole (1676–1745), 1st Earl of Orford, Prime Minister 1721–42,
father of Horace Walpole. *Col. C*: Colonel Churchill.

21a

<u>King (in Hanover)</u> sees a picture of a stranger in the robes & with the

regalia of the sovereigns of England! It is at the house of a German

nobleman, who has given the King shelter, the latter's carriage having

broken down within view of the house.   cxv.

Source: *Walpole, Letters*, i, cxv.
Note: *King*: George I.

21b

Sir R. Walpole, sitting alone one night with a Jacobite who sometimes

furnished him with intelligence: Jacobite suddenly puts hand into bosom

Text: item incomplete; lower half of f.11 is cut away.
Source: *Walpole, Letters*, i, cxiii (note 3).
Note: Walpole's text continued: 'and rising, said, "why do not I kill you now?" Walpole, starting up, replied, "Because I am a younger man and stronger."'

22a

The Prince is enamoured of Miss Bellenden – his gallantry not delicate

– takes out his purse & counts his money – repeats the enumeration – she

loses all patience. "Sir; if you count your money any more I will go

out of the room.   cxxiv

Source: *Walpole, Letters*, i, cxxiv.
Note: *Prince*: George, Prince of Wales, later George II. *Miss Bellenden*: Mary Bellenden, Maid of Honour to the Princess of Wales, m. John Campbell (1720).

22b

Miss B. owns to the Prince that she is privately affianced, but tells him

the wrong person as her lover. Married her lover privately lest Prince

sh^d throw any obstacle in her way – He never forgave her the trick–

always whispered harsh reproaches in her ear.   cxxv

Source: *Walpole, Letters*, i, cxxiv–cxxv.
Note: *tells him the wrong person*: Walpole wrote 'without acknowledging the person'.

22c

Howard goes into the quadrangle of St James's one night, & vociferously
                                    Princes
demands his wife (who has become ~~King's~~ mistress) [not legally his

wife. 1ˢᵗ wife's sister, who has married again]. Husband is < >determinᵈ

to reclaim her – when the Prince removes to Richmond husbᵈ forms

the project of seizing her on the road – she is sent early in morning cxxv

Text: 'is' is written over *cxxv*. The lower half of f.11v is cut away.
Source: *Walpole, Letters*, i, cxxv–cxxvi.
Note: *Howard*: Charles Howard, later Earl of Suffolk. *wife*: Henrietta Hobart (*c.* 1688–1767), later Mrs Howard, later Countess of Suffolk, mistress of George II and in later life an intimate friend of Horace Walpole. Pope's Chloe in his 'Epistle to a Lady: Of the Characters of Women', was, according to Walpole, 'meant for Lady Suffolk'. *[not legally his wife … married again]*: TH's interpolation. See Appendix One.

23a

A Princess (widow) has 5 children by her footman – nobody knows it till

after her death.   202

Source: *Walpole, Letters* (25 September 1742), i, 202.
Note: *Princess*: according to Walpole this was Eleonora of Guastalla, Italy.

23b

Daughter of the King pulled chair from under a countess who was

a favourite at court. King roars with laughter. Countess in revenge pulls

away his chair: he falls heavily. She is banished.   205

Hand: ELH.
Source: *Walpole, Letters* (8 October 1742), i, 205.
Note: *King*: George II. *Countess*: Countess Deloraine, governess to the princesses.

23c   Erased item f.12r (see Appendix One)

23d

Interesting character – Lady Sophia Fermor, afterwards Lady Granville.

Vol. 1. passim

Hand: ELH.
Source: *Walpole, Letters*, i, 75, 83, 298–9, 396–7.
Note: *Lady Sophia Fermor*: Lady Sophia (1721–45) dau. of Thomas Fermor, Earl of Pomfret. Walpole's mentions of her are not quite *passim*, but he makes numerous references to her beauty and brilliance. In 1744 she married John Carteret, Earl Granville (1690–1763), but she died in 1745 after giving birth to a daughter. Walpole wrote to Mann (11 October 1745) that it was 'very shocking for anybody so young, so handsome, so arrived at the height of happiness, so sensible of it … to be so quickly snatched away!' (*Walpole, Letters*, i, 396–7).

23e

Mysterious man – goes by name of Count St G. Owns that it is not his

right name – Sings – plays wonderfully on violin, composes, &c – Is called

an Italian, a Span^d – a Pole – a somebody who married a fortune in Mexico –

ran way with wife's jewels – a priest – nobleman – &c.   410.

Source: *Walpole, Letters* (9 December 1745), i, 410.
Note: *Count St. G*: Count St. Germain, under suspicion as a Jacobite spy.

23f

Large Parcel – contents unknown – opened – R.C. vestments &c. Vol II.16.

Source: *Walpole, Letters* (15 April 1746), ii, 16.
Note: *Parcel*: after the defeat of the Jacobite Rebellion in 1745, this parcel was found in the baggage of the military commander, the Duke of Cumberland, son of George II.

23g

Coiner. Widow left with children – did not know how to maintain &

educate them. Took to coining: used to buy old pewter pots, out of wh.

she made 3 pounds worth at a time – indicted her maid as an accomplice.
                    16–17

Source: *Walpole, Letters* (15 April 1746), ii, 16–17.

23h

Duchess of Manchester married a Mr Hussey privately – at last owned – 33.

Source: *Walpole, Letters* (3 July 1746), ii, 33.

———————

23i

(promoted to office of)

Weymouth Union – woman there: well educated : has been ∧ nurse: obliged

twice – 1ˢᵗ time forgiven –

to be discharged – drunk on doorstep ∧ – she goes back to the Union as a common

inmate – is the daughter of a late well known naval commander – D.C.C.

cut – Aug 11.81.

Source: *DCC*, 11 August 1881, p.4, cols 2–3.
Note: see also 13d, a further instance of TH's interest in degraded professionals of his own time.

23j

De Veres – Earls of Oxford – were once masters almost of this entire county –

~~Middlesex~~ but quite reduced – the last Earl's son died at a miserable cottage,

& another of the sisters besides Lady Mary Vere was forced to live upon her

beauty.   Walp. Let. Vol II. 118.   //

Hand: TH (but cited reference 'Walp. Let. Vol II' is probably in ELH's hand).
Source: *Walpole, Letters* (25 July 1748), ii, 118.
Note: *Middlesex*: was a mistake for 'Essex'. *last Earl*: Aubrey de Vere, 20th Earl of Oxford (1627–1703). With his death the earldom, created 1142, became extinct.

24a

Settlement – The Duchess of Somerset made a settlement of her

estate (derived from her own family) in case her sons died without heirs

male, on the children of her daughters –   137.

Source: *Walpole, Letters* (15 December 1748), ii, 137 (note 5).

24b

<u>Having to watch a sleeping old man</u> – Dk. of Somersets younger

daughter – it was feared he w^d leave nothing to her. Two or three

years ago he waked after dinner & found himself upon the floor;

she used to watch him, had left him, & he had fallen from his couch.

He forbade every body to speak to her: but yet to hear her with respect

as his daughter. She went about the house for a year, without anybody

daring openly to utter a syllable to her.   140

Source: *Walpole, Letters* (26 December 1748), ii, 140.
Note: *Dk. of Somerset*: Charles Seymour, 6th Duke of Somerset (1662–1748). Walpole's comment concludes: 'it was never known that he had forgiven her'.

24c

<u>Two young princes</u> (black) of Anamaboe go to the play – the play is s< >

like their own history that they can hardly bear it – one goes out. 14< >

Text: *so, 149* are partially obscured by tipping-in.
Source: *Walpole, Letters* (23 March 1749), ii, 149 (note 2, taken from J. Wright (ed.) *The Letters of Horace Walpole, Earl of Orford* 6 vols (1840)).
Note: *Two young princes*: the Yale edition of Walpole's letters notes that the African 'princes' were the son of a headman on the Guinea coast, W. Africa, and a companion, sent to England to be educated. (W.S. Lewis, W. Henry-Smith and G.L. Lam (eds), *Horace Walpole's Correspondence with Sir Horace Mann* (London: Oxford University Press; New Haven, CT: Yale University Press, 1960), iv, 40.) *the play*: *Oroonoko: a Tragedy* (1695), by Thomas Southerne, based on Aphra Behn's prose romance *Oroonoko; or, the Royal Slave* (1678). *so like their own history*: on his journey to England, the headman's son, like Oroonoko, had been abducted into slavery, though later ransomed. TH's source for their reaction to the play (at the Theatre Royal, Covent Garden, 2 February 1749) was not Walpole but, via Cunningham's edition, a note in Wright's edition of the *Letters*, derived from the *Gentleman's Magazine*, xix, 90 (1749).

24d

<u>Drinking & gaming</u> at Newmarket meeting – a bank bill was thrown down

& nobody claiming it they agreed to give it to a man who was standing by

15< >

Text: *155* is partially obscured by tipping-in.
Source: *Walpole, Letters* (3 May 1749), ii, 155.

24e

Lord B. Ld. R. & half a dozen more of White's Club take a house on

Richmond Green & come there every Saturday & Sunday to play at whist – 16< >

Text: *164* is partially obscured by tipping-in.
Source: *Walpole, Letters* (4 June 1749), ii, 164.
Note: *Lord B.*: Lord Bath. *Ld. R.*: a slip by TH; the person referred to is Lord Lonsdale.

———————

24f

The family (of Lenau-German poet) settled near Ofen, in a little house

that had once been a chapel, & which was situated in a dismal

graveyard. These melancholy religious surroundings did not fai< >

to make their mark upon the boy's impressionable mind – & sha< >

of this churchyard flit across his poems.   Cornhill

Text: *fail, shades* are obscured by tipping-in.
Source: 'Lenau', *Cornhill Magazine*, 44 (October 1881): 461–81 (p.463).
Note: *Lenau*: Nikolaus Lenau (1802–50), Hungarian-born German poet. TH entered an extract from
the same article in *LN*, i: 'the post-Goethean period produced at least a few poets – Heine the greatest
– But Lenau also deserves to be more widely recognised' (*LN*, i, 140 (item 1232) and note (p.374)).

24g

Lenau says he is to be married on a certain day – goes mad

on that day – Bride & mother, halting at an inn on the way to

him hear that "the poet L. has been put into a straight waistcoat.

ib. //

Source: 'Lenau', *Cornhill Magazine*, p.480.

25a

<u>Penalties for removing sheep</u> – At Hindon, W.G. summoned for ~~moving~~ ^{causing}

100 sheep ʌ ^{to be moved} from land in Dorset to the down in the adjoining parish of Tollard

Royal in Wilts without having obtained a removal licence. The shep^d was

charged with removing them. P.C. Briant proved the offence. W.G. fined £4

& costs. – Another man, bacon factor, 5 fat pigs from ditto to ditto, without a

licence, as required by the orders of the Local Authority; his man did it. £5.

D.C.C. 17.1.84

Source: 'Heavy Penalties', *DCC*, 17 January 1884, p.14, col.1.
Note: *Hindon*: small town in S.W. Wilts. where the case was heard. *Tollard Royal*: in Cranborne
Chase, on Wilts.–Dorset border. *W.G.*: William Goldier. See also item 54g.

25b

Col. Evans called. Cat came into room, passed behind him, & went out at

verandah door. Just as she was passing he turned round, grasped the arm

of the chair, & seemed to become quite rigid. I jumped up & shut the doors

on the cat, & he just avoided having a fit. He says the antipathy is inherited

from his mother, who would faint dead if a cat passes near her. He has done

his best to overcome it by having a kitten & trying to accustom himself to it, but

the attempt used so to exhaust him that doctors forbade his continuing it. He

says that more than once he has been found in a fit, & that he has no power

of keeping a cat away. He has tried to hit them with a stick, but his arm is

always paralysed, & he can neither hit them nor throw anything at them. C^d

not hit one should he fire at it. He always carries Strychnine & sugar pills

with him, & that is his only protection – he is able to throw down one of

these pills & the cat stops to eat it & dies. He always has a dog on his

bed at night who w^d not allow any cat to come near. This is the second

case I have met with.   (From Journal lent by Mrs Campbell.)   //

Source: unidentified.

26a

Murder witnessed by a boy of 9 & his little brother. Father & mother
                              with a friend
(not married) heard come in late, by the children in bed. Heard to dance

& sing. Father comes into same room where child^n are & goes to bed. Friend

comes up with him, & goes down again. Friend & mother remain below some

time. Friend comes up, cuts the father's throat quietly as he sleeps. The

children are afraid.   Police report 21.12.83.

Source: 'The Murder at Kennington', DN, 21 December 1883, p.6, col.4.

26b

Signing in her nightgown, under compulsion. Husband wants to borrow £30

Wife has separate estate. Lender will not advance except in joint names –
                              for £37
husband brings a promissary note ʌ signed by her, stipulating that the money shall

be repaid in 8 monthly instalments, "any one of which becoming due made the

whole due" (?) £32.10 advanced on it. Cross exam^n brings out that wife ill –

signed note in nightgown early in morning – threatened to knock head against wall if refused – to "spill someone's blood" – to forge her name – slapped her

face.   Police. D.N. 21.12.83.

Source: 'Curious Money-Lending Case', *DN*, 21 December 1883, p.6, col.2.

26c

Enticing a man out of doors to murder him – ~~the~~ One of the murderers

lets victim's horse out of stable – then goes & shouts outside his door that

his horse has got out. When he runs out to catch horse they shoot him.

Ireland – Telegram 14.3.84   //

Source: 'Extraordinary Murder Trial', Weymouth, Portland and Dorchester *Telegram*, 14 March
1884, p.7, cols 3–4.
Note: the case was heard at Sligo Assizes.

27a

Similarity of name François Thurot, roving from home, made the acq^{ce}

of an Irish smuggler bearing Thurot's family name of Farrell. (he had taken his
(his g.f^r being Irish – Capt. Farrell))
mother's name ᴧ . The Irishman told him he w^d find friends in the O'Farrells, who

were still a flourishing house in Connaught. Thurot started for Ireland with his

friend – they quarelled at the Isle of Man, & parted. Thurot never reaching the O'Fs.

Shep^n Mall^t Mag^{ne} 1883

Source: unidentified.

27b

Dog – fighting. Man owned bull terrier, wh. beat every dog of its size in

neighb^d. He fought it with a much stronger dog, wh. it beat after severe struggle.

As it lay panting on the ground he hounded upon it a young dog, saying his dog still had pluck for another battle. Feeble & lacerated his dog had for the first time to

yield. Owner so enraged at loss of match that he killed his dog.

Old D.C.C. Jan 5. 1826.

Source: 'Diabolical Cruelty', *DCC*, 5 January 1826, p.3, col.4.
Note: this is the first item taken from the files of *DCC* of the 1826–30 period, thus initiating the
central sequence of the notebook, begun by TH in mid-March 1884.

27c

Mail about to start; animals restive; upset coach: a gentleman killed:
                                        Manchester
he was a clerk in the banking house of Jones & Co, ʌ & had with him £100,000

for the use of the banks there.   ib.

Source: *DCC*, 5 January 1826, p.3, col.3.

27d

                                                                    s   d
Countryman sold woodcock to innkeeper at Barnstaple for 1 .. 6. watched

where the bird was deposited in larder: stole it: resold it.   ib.

Source: *DCC*, 5 January 1826, p.3, col. 4.

27e

Number of Spanish refugees begging in Dorset &c.   Feb 2.   ib.

Source: *DCC*, 2 February 1826, p.3, col.5.
Note: *Dorset*: *DCC* has 'going through the West of England'.

27f–[p.28]

Yeovil Glove trade – Its importance – evil conseq[ces] anticipated from the
     (i e Free trade)
measures ʌ about to be adopted by His Majesty's Ministers affecting the admission   //

of French gloves into this country are already seriously felt. If ministers

persist in such measures...ruin to honest tradesmen...& deprive thousands of

poor of means of subsistence. The trade has of late years much extended.

Within last 12 months skins dressed in Yeovil & neighb^d from 27000 to 30,000

by which not less than from £1400 to £1500 per week was distributed in

wages to men, women, & children...extending to villages 25 miles off. The country

peasant with 6 or 7/- a week was, as well as the town labourer, enabled by

earnings of wife & children in sewing gloves to obtain a comfortable subsistence.

The number of skins now dressed does not exceed 15000 or 16000 weekly, in

conceq. of this anticipated change of commercial policy. Many hands discharged.*

D.C.C. Feb 1826.

* Later on in the year – "The importers of Fch. gloves do not meet with the encouragm^t they expected." &c, D.C.C.

Text: *later on in the year...&c, D.C.C*: these additions in a smaller hand are appended at the bottom of the page, below item 28d.
Source: 'The Glove Trade', *DCC*, 9 February 1826, p.1, col.5. This is a letter to the editor [dated 7 February] from 'A Sincere Well-wisher for the Universal Prosperity of the Commerce of Old England'.
Note: *Yeovil*: town in Somerset. A *DCC* article in the previous week recorded that 'there is at present a great stagnation in the glove trade in this town; the manufacturers have put their hands on half work, and never, in the memory of the oldest person engaged in the business, has it been in so depressed a state. Petitions are in preparation, both from the manufactures and operatives, to the Houses of Parliament against the admission of French gloves' (*DCC*, 2 February 1826, p.4, col.5). Local deputations to the Chancellor were reported in March 1826 (*DCC*, 30 March 1826, p.2, col.5) and, again, in September 1828 (*DCC*, 4 September 1828, p.3, col.2). The situation was still grave in 1829 (see item 109b). See *Millgate, 1971*, 237–8.

28a

Man, farmer, in inn parlour is seen through window by woman in street

to pay for what he had from a pocket book of notes. When he comes out she accosts

him, accompanies him across ch. y^d where she thrusts her hand into his breast pock^t

& takes out notes.   ib.

Source: *DCC*, 30 March 1826, p.4, col.5.
Note: *woman*: Caroline Browning who was sentenced to 14 years' transportation.

28b

Attempt to poison by mixing arsenic in a parcel of sugar, & putting the parcel

among the groceries in cart of intended victims coming home from market.   ib.

Source: *DCC*, 30 March 1826, p.3, col.5.
Note: *cart*: of the Bideford carrier.

28c

Waggon returning from fair, full of persons: breaks down: many injured,

several being intoxicated.   ib.

Source: *DCC*, 30 March 1826, p.4, col.1.
Note: on the Greenwich Rd near New Cross, London.

28d

‖ – Wife pushes husband downstairs & kills him, he having come home drunk –   ib. ‖

Text: there are two vertical parallel lines (red pencil) beside this item.
Source: *DCC*, 27 April 1826, p.1, col.5.
Note: the inquest verdict was wilful murder.

29a

Abduction – by telling young lady her mother was ill. Then, on journey, telling

her that was only an excuse to prevent the schoolmistress, at whose school the

girl was, knowing the truth – that her father was in the power of some one,

& that by her secret marriage with abductor she will place him in a position

to help her father, i.e. by giving abductor power over her property.

Abduction of Miss Turner Ap[l] 6. 1826. D.C.C.

Source: 'The Abduction of Miss Turner', *DCC*, 6 April 1826, p.3, col.1.
Note: *Abduction*: Ellen Turner (*c.* 1810–31) dau. of William Turner of Shrigley Park, Cheshire, was abducted from her school in 1826 by Edward Wakefield (1796–1862), later a famous colonial statesman and publicist. In 1827 he was sentenced to three years imprisonment during which he conceived his scheme of planned colonization of Australia, and published, whilst still in prison, *Letter From Sydney* (1829). Miss Turner, an heiress, m. Thomas Legh of Lyme Park, who as magistrate had committed Wakefield for trial. See also items 48d, 49b, 63c. Her marriage to Wakefield at Gretna Green was annulled by special Act of Parliament (see A.J. Harrop, *The Amazing Career of Edward Gibbon Wakefield* (London: George Allen & Unwin, 1928), pp.22–63).

29b

Fatal Pugilism – "one of the men planted a right handed lunging blow on the

temple of his adversary, who fell & lived but 2 hrs.   1826. D.C.C.

Source: *DCC*, 6 April 1826, p.3, col.4.

29c

Elopement intercepted – young lady plans to elope with a young man, her neighbour,

to whom her father objects. She goes first, he to follow & meet her in London. Her

father misses her – goes to young man, & under threats makes him tell where

they are going to meet. Swan with Two Necks he says. He is then kept back

at home, while her father takes his place & meets dau. at the Swan.   ib.

Source: *DCC*, 27 April 1826, p.3, col.4.
Note: *Swan with Two Necks*: a famous coaching-inn in Lad Lane, London, 'opposite Milk Street, Cheapside' (John Lockie, *Topography of London* (2nd edn, London: 1816)). In the original report the father finds his daughter at a private lodging, not at the inn. There are numerous other stories of elopement in 'Facts', including items 45c, 79a, 120b, 120e, 133c, 143d, 175b.

29d

Highway robbery – Woman & son driving home. Man asks for a lift. He then knocks son out of cart, & robs woman.   ib.

Source: *DCC*, 27 April 1826, p.3, col.4.

29e

<u>Mechanic walking</u> along road towards Plymouth falls in with "a corporal's guard,

escorting a deserter". Walks & talks with corporal – tells him he has been a soldier –

(this untrue) – that he was once a sergeant in the 52^d, & enjoyed a pension of 15^d a day.

Soldier asks him for his discharge: he cannot produce it; corp^l handbolts him, & he is

committed to the county gaol till the reg^t has been communicated with.   ib. //

Source: 'Effects of Lying', *DCC*, 27 April 1826, p.3, col.5.
Note: *handbolts him*: handcuffs him.

30a

<u>Bankrupt</u>. A meeting of the Commissioners under the bankruptcy of M^r

Harvey of Launceston, banker, took place at the White Hart inn there, for

the purpose of his final examination. At the close of the proceedings M^r H.

laid his gold watch & pocket money on the table; but they were immediately returned

by the unanimous voice of the creditors present. The senior commis^n Mr Tonkin

addressed Mr Harvey & said he had been a commissioner for a number of

years but in all his experience he had never yet…more honourably…His

balance sheet was the most satisfactory that he had seen on any similar occ^n

& his creditors – a great many of whom were present – ought to feel perfectly

well satisfied with his conduct. The other comm^{rs} Mr B. & Mr F. coinc^{ded}

& the meeting…full of sympathy for Mr Harvey –   Old D.C.C. 1826.

Source: *DCC*, 27 April 1826, p.4, col.1.

Note: this item forms the basis of the bankruptcy hearing in *The Mayor*, ch.31. See also *Winfield*, 227–9, *Millgate, 1971*, 238–9.

30b

Erased item f.15v (see Appendix One)

30c

<u>Accident to a team of horses</u> near Sherborne – momentary negligence of the driver
   ploughing
who, ʌ near a boggy ditch gave wrong direction to horses, & the fore horse in making

a quick turn fell in, dragging with him the remainder of the team. Heads of

horses raised above the mire, by which means 3 of them were rescued from

suffocation; but the 4th a reliable colt worth 40gs. was taken out dead.   ib.

Source: *DCC*, 13 April 1826, p.4, col.5.
Note: *reliable*: *DCC* has 'valuable'.

30d

<u>Exchequer bills stolen</u> – eight for £100 each. Carried by thief in his umbrella.

Left his umbrella in coffee room of inn when he went to bed – it was supposed

to belong to somebody else – examined – bills fell out.   ib. //

Source: *DCC*, 13 April 1826, p.1, col.5.
Note: the theft of these bills 'in the pit at Astley's Theatre', is reported in the same issue, p.2. col.4.

31a

Spring gun – its contents struck knee of trespassing young man – gave him

lock-jaw, of which he died.   ib.

Source: 'Death by a Spring Gun', *DCC*, 13 April 1826, p.2, col.4.
Note: *DCC* adds: 'It is strange that landed proprietors, merely for the purpose of preserving bestial life, should persist in the use of measures by which human life is not only often endangered, but

sometimes destroyed. Such things ought not to be.' This item, together with item 32c, is a source for *Woodlanders*, see, in particular, ch.47: 'Once a keeper of Hintock woods set it on the track of a poacher, and afterwards coming back that way, forgetful of what he had done, walked into it himself. The wound brought on lock-jaw of which he died' (*Woodlanders, 1985*, 264–5). For the purposes of the novel TH conflated two reports, and substituted 'man-trap' for 'spring gun'.

31b

End of lotteries in England May 1826.   ib.

Source: *DCC*, 20 April 1826, p.1, col.1.
Note: see also items 31d, 38c. TH also makes reference to the 'state lottery' in the 'Trumpet-Major Notebook' (*PN*, 168).

31c

Four bags of wheat discovered by miller & his man outside mill door at 6.a.m.

when going to begin work – wonder whose they are – but they grind them.   ib.

Source: *DCC*, 13 April 1826, p.4, col.4.
Note: *mill*: Keinston mill, near Spettisbury, Dorset.

31d

Lottery.
"Carroll resp[tly] inf[s] the Public that by act of P. the Lottery to be drawn on Wedn[y]

3[d] May is the very last but one that can ever be submitted. L Twenty thous[d] gs.

can now be gained for a very few pounds...In this scheme all the popular

points of late Lotteries are retained...Six prizes of £21,000...All

to be decided in one day. Wed[y] 3[d] of May. Tickets & shares are now on sale at

"Carroll's Fortunate offices No 19. Cornhill"...A variety of numbers are also

selling by the following agents. [Here follows a list of Booksellers, Druggists,

Ironmongers, &c. in Dorset towns – e.g.Wey[th] Blandf.[d] .]

Adv[t] in Old D.C.C. Ap[l] . 20. 1826.

Source: *DCC*, 20 April 1826, p.1, col.2.
Note: *list*: in *DCC* the shops are named. See also items 31b, 38c. *Cornhill*: in Dorchester.

31e

<u>Supposed dead</u> – & devoured by cannibals on the coast of New Zealand – but
     (named Griffiths)
the young man ʌ arrived home a few days since at Devonport – He belongs

to the ship <u>Countess</u> of <u>Morley</u>, & in an affray with the natives he was left

as slain by his comrades, 2 yrs since. It seems that while preparing his body

for a sumptuous repast he recovered from their merciless belabouring – which

astonished the natives – Chief adopted him as son – was treated with great

kindness – escaped by swimming to a ship –   ib. //

Source: *DCC*, 11 May 1826, p.3, col.5.

32a

<u>Mistake</u> – Mr A. horsewhips Mr B., mistaking him for Mr C. an Italian

gentleman whom he much resembles – Duel &c.   ib.

Source: *DCC*, 25 May 1826, p.2, col.3.
Note: *Mr A.*: *DCC* has 'Mr. S.'.

32b

<u>Husband & wife quarrelling</u> – husband aims blow at wife – daughter rushes

between – is killed by the blow.   ib.

Source: *DCC*, 1 June 1826, p.3, col.5.

32c

<u>Gamekeeper treads upon</u> the wire of a <u>spring gun</u> which he has himself set, &

receives about 30 shots in the leg.   ib.

Source: *DCC*, 1 June 1826, p.3, col.4.
Note: this, together with item 31a is a source for *The Woodlanders*, ch.47, see note to item 31a, above.

32d

Young lady engaged to respectable cloth manuf^r at Leeds – he calls to see her

on his way home – the family have retired – a light in her room – he stands

upon a lower window sill to reach & speak to her [tap her w^w with walking stick]

She hears something – calls her father – he goes downstairs, & seeing figure of

man against the sky on w^w sill stabs through the glass at him with a sword &

wounds him mortally in abdomen.   ib.

Source: *DCC*, 1 June 1826, p.3, col.4.
Note: *[tap ... stick]*: Hardy's addition. See *Millgate, 1971*, 237.

32e

On Monday last the annual exhibition of the Maypole at Fordington attracted

a large concourse of people to the spot – weather unfavourable – but no lack

of merriment. Dancing on the green was kept up till a late hour –   ib. 1.6.26

Source: *DCC*, 1 June 1826, p.4, col.3.

32f

Felo de se. Privately buried at 10 o'clock at night –   ib.

Source: *DCC*, 1 June 1826, p.4, cols 4–5.
Note: see also item 4b.

32g–[p.33]

Sale of wife. Man at Brighton led a tidy looking young woman up to one   //

of the stalls in the market, with a halter round her neck, & offered her for sale.

A purchaser was soon found, who bought her for £2 30/- which he paid, & went

off with his bargain amid the sneers & laughter of the mob, but not before

the transaction was regularly entered by the clerk of the market book & the

toll of 1 shilling paid. He also paid 1/- for the halter, & another 1/- to the

man who performed the office of auctioneer. We understand they were country

people, & that the woman has had 2 chⁿ by her husband, one of whom

he consents to keep, & the other he throws in as a makeweight to the bargain.

                              ib. 25 May.1826 – from Brighton Gazᵗᵗᵉ

Source: *DCC*, 25 May 1826, p.4, col.2.
Note: *Sale of Wife*: the *DCC* report (from *Brighton Gazette*) opens with: 'A disgraceful exhibition took place in our market on Tuesday morning last'. This is the first of three reported wife sales in 'Facts' (the others being items 74b and 116b), sources for the memorable incident in *Mayor* ch.1; see *Winfield*, 225–7. *the woman has had 2 chⁿ by her husband, one of whom he consents to keep*: deletions in the manuscript of *Mayor* reveal that the Henchard family originally comprised two daughters, one of whom remains with Henchard, the other going with Susan. This extract 'thus bears a striking resemblance, both in outline and detail, to the earliest traceable phase of the plot of the novel' (*Winfield*, 227).

33a

Funeral passing inn. One of the bearers (women) suddenly left her station &

ran in to inn – The young lady was intoxicated.   ib.

Source: *DCC*, 25 May 1826, p.4, col.5.
Note: *women*: DCC has 'a female'.

33b

taking fright

Horse & small cart fall over bridge into stream – on account of the horse ⋏

becoming restive, & backing against bank – the man, wife, & young woman found

them⁵ in deep water – cart turned over & overwhelmed them – After sinking

& rising two or three times young w. found herself entangled with the horse,

clinging round his neck, the poor animal at the same time plunging & en-

deavouring to regain the land, wh. he so far effected as to enable the young

woman to catch hold of a small willow twig, from wh. she was immedʸ torn

by struggles of horse. Seized another – one of the reins entangled round arm –

cut the rein with knife – horse fell back & was drowned – only the y.

woman saved.   ib. //

Source: *DCC*, 25 May 1826, p.4, col.2.
Note: *deep water*: the river Medway, Kent.

34a

Suicide – Mr Cousins lent a set of swindlers his acceptances to bills amountˢ

to £89, for wh. in return they gave their acceptance at a shorter date –

when they became due, parties had decamped, bills dishonoured. Mr. C. followed

them to London...returned dejected, fatigued, & borne down by the feelings of

having been duped...advantage of his good nature...hung himself from tester

of bed by his cravat. Wife knew nothing of motive of his journey, or any

thing of the matter.   ib.

Source: *DCC*, 29 June 1826, p.3, col.5.
Note: *Cousins*: a coachmaker of Southampton.

34b–[p.35]

<u>Somerset Election</u>. Ilchester – (Hunt opposed Sir.T.Lethbridge.) <u>1826</u>.

The voice of Mr H. was heard long before he was seen – &c…At 10 the Sheriff

took his seat in the court house – called upon each of the poll-clerks…B., one of

them, objected to by M^r H on ground he kept the P.O.

B. (looking up at M^r H) That's another falsehood…

Sir T.L. (turning round & looking full in M^r H's face). What is that you.

say, Sir?…

   A number of voters stood forward & declared their readiness to take the oath

   M^r H; "Ay, they will do it without quivering the lip. There is not a man

┼in that group (pointing to the Huntites) who is not etc…what

do you think of that Sir T.?". Sir T. smiled, but made no observation

…Mr H. (looking contemptuously at Sir T.) They are no

slaves – they are not like your dependents. Mine are all honest men.

A voter; We are as honest as Sir Thomas, & are ready to take the oath

Mr H. These are honest faces, Sir J. No quivering here (Laughter in   //

which Sir T. joined.) It was said yesterday that no honest man would vote for Hunt.

A Voter: Any man who says, I am not an honest man is a rogue…

Sir T. The conduct of this person is most outrageous…

Sir T.L. looked sternly in Hunt's face, & said, this conduct is not to be

endured.

Sir T.L. smiled & turned away his head contemptuously…

(Here Sir T.L. & Mr H. looked at each other in so ferocious a manner that many of the spectators who were not aware that words

may be used long before blows are resorted to, expected immediate

violence.)

Sir T. to Mᵣ H. "How dare you direct such language to me?

Mᵣ H.: To you! Ye, ye (mimicking Sir T.L.) To you & the other

slave-driver.

Sir T. L.: It is useless to address the language which is current among

gentlemen to such a person...

One of the voters: We are as honest as he is. (looking towards Sir T.)

&c &c –

ib. June 29 1826

Mᵣ H. proposed three groans for Mᵣ W...The groans were loud & long.

Hand: TH *Somerset Election ... say, Sir?*; ELH *A number of voters ... looking towards Sir. T.*; TH thereafter.
Text: there is a line connecting 'ib. June 29 1826' to 'loud & long'.
Source: 'Somerset County Elections: Ilchester June 20th', 'Somerset County Elections: Ilchester June 21st' *DCC*, 29 June 1826, p.3, cols 2–3, *DCC*, 29 June 1826, p.3, col.3.
Note: *Hunt*: Henry Hunt (1773–1835), radical politician, imprisoned after the Manchester massacre ('Peterloo'), 1819. *Mr W*: a Mr Warren, solicitor. This item is a report of the fourth day of the poll at Ilchester in the County election; the final result of the poll was Dickinson, 1762 votes, Lethbridge, 1662, Hunt, 299. See *Millgate, 1971*, 238.

35a

<u>Passion</u> Young men fight about a young woman – one dies from excessive passion.

ib.

Source: *DCC*, 29 June, p.4, col.2.

35b–[p.36]

<u>Lady Erskine</u>. Fascinating straw bonnet makers apprentice – Lᵈ E. fell in love with

her – said his name was Mᵣ Thomas – & she consented to be his wife without knowing   //

anything of his rank and circum^s – Lived happily – he grew disturbed by

he dies –
her aberrations about the children ⌊ grew tired of her ⌋ – Separation – ʌ she

in poverty – w^d have been starved to death but for the kindness of strangers –

also her youngest child, because she w^d not part from him (though a provision for him,
as for the other three, if she w^d give him, or her, up.)   ib. July 27. 26

Source: *DCC*, 20 July 1826, p.1, col.5, and *DCC*, 27 July 1826, p.2, col.4.
Note: TH conflates two reports which give the cause of Lady Erskine's 'aberrations' as a 'puerperal disease'. *Ld E.*: Thomas Erskine (1750–1823), the outstanding advocate of his age, and briefly Lord Chancellor (1806–07). In 1818 he married at Gretna Green, his second wife, Sarah Buck, described in *DCC* as 'the daughter of a respectable tradesman…a girl of uncommonly fascinating manners'. A satiric cartoon of this marriage is reproduced in F.G. Stephens and M. Dorothy George (eds), *Catalogue of Political and Personal Satires … in the British Museum* 11 vols, 1870–1954 (London: The Trustees, 1949), ix, no. 13384. This entry is a possible source for 'Master John Horseleigh, Knight' (*CMT*), (see *Brady*, 184, 215 (n.83)).

36a

A gentleman bets £1000 ags^t a well known sporting gent^m that he will travel

as a wandering minstrel for 6 months, pay necess^y expenses, & save £100.

Has commenced his tour – A number of small bets on both sides.

ib.

Source: *DCC*, 27 July 1826, p.2, col.4.

36b

Window open. Hot weather – 2 Ladies go to bed leaving w. open. Thieves.

ib.

Source: *DCC*, 27 July 1826, p.2, col.4.

36c

Dorchester Races – Aug 15 & 16.

Source: *DCC*, 27 July 1826, p.4, col.2.

36d

Bread on Waters &c :___

(a person)

A few years ago ⋏ having all the manners of a gentleman but very much

reduced in life drew the attention of Mr Kinsman by frequently coming to

his shop for small bits of meat, from which, he entered into conversation with

him…great distress…supplied him with meat for twelvemonths

& became his friend in other respects…Man disappeared – six years ago –

It now turns out…very large property in Devon; at which place he died

a few months ago leaving Mr Kinsman the estate, worth £500 a year.

Mr K. will soon take possession.   ib.

Hand: TH: *Bread on Waters &c*; thereafter, ELH.
Text: there is a vertical line (pencil) beside this item.
Source: 'Remarkably Good Fortune', *DCC*, 27 July 1826, p.3, cols 1–2.
Note: *Bread on Waters*: TH's allusion to *Ecclesiastes*, xi, 1 – 'Cast thy bread upon the waters: for thou shalt find it after many days'. TH put 'after many days' in heading of ch.32 of *A Pair of Blue Eyes*, ed. Alan Manford (Oxford: Oxford University Press, 1985), p.340.

36e

Case of Doe on the demise of the Revd G. Wood v. Revd Morton Colson – in wh.

St Peters ch. is proved to have been a chapel to Trinity   D.C.C. July 27. 1826.   //

Source: 'Dorchester Summer Assizes', *DCC*, 27 July 1826, p.3, cols 3–5; p.4, col.1.
Note: *Doe*: a legal fiction, formerly used in cases of ejectment, i.e. recovery of possession of an estate. The case excited great local interest. *demise*: the conveyance of an estate. *St Peters, Trinity*: churches in High West Street, Dorchester.

37a

Men sent to pull down a cottage on moor – woman who lives there says "the first man who enters this house I'll chop down with this hook." Man takes

out unloaded pistol to intimidate her – she wounds him – taken into custody –

Tried at Assizes – His lp. asked the prisoner if any of her relations w^d be bound

for her future good behaviour – fortunate wound not fatal. She said she had

no friends in court...Acquitted – ib.

Source: *DCC*, 27 July 1826, p.4, cols 1–2.
Note: *lp*.: lordship.

37b

Country man sells 2 heifers at fair for £14. Coming home loses the notes –

those who find them will not let him have them unless he tells numbers – ib.

Source: *DCC*, 27 July 1826, p.4, col.4.

37c

Man, to rob another, knocks him off his horse at night with a rail, torn

from hedge. ib.

Source: *DCC*, 27 July 1826, p.4, col.5.
Note: *rail*: TH's underlining.

37d

Cobbett in his Register says his right arm was so much pulled & shaken

by salutations of the people...that next morning he c^d not lift it to tie his cr^vat.

ib.

Source: *DCC*, 13 July 1826, p.1, col.4.
Note: *Cobbett*: William Cobbett (1763–1835), journalist, essayist and politician. His *Weekly Political Register* published 1802–35. Cobbett was persistently belittled by *DCC*. This incident is recorded as taking place 'between Blackburn and Bolton'.

37e

The Brightonians are in the dumps from absence of his Majesty (Geo IV. had

decided to live there no more – pavilion sold &c.) Many buildings are

stopped in their progress – first rate houses let at £20.   July 13. 26.

Source: *DCC*, 13 July 1826, p.1, col.4.
Note: £20: *DCC* has '£30'.

37f

Narrow Lane – two horseman meet – heads of two rival county families – each

politely requests the other to go back – neither will. One takes newspaper from

pocket – reads it through from the "No." to "printed for &c". Occup^d 3 or 4 h^{rs}

sun gets low – "Will you lend paper to me when you have done." (Edin^g Obs^r)   ib. //

Source: 'The Point of Precedence', *DCC*, 13 July 1826, p.3, col.2.

38a

                          or in presence of def^t, plff handles him according to directions –
A horse – as long as, defendant handles him ∧ he is quiet & perfect.
              away   alone
directly he is taken ∧ to be managed by plaintiff ∧ he is incurably vicious.

                                                        ib. 13 July '26.

Source: *DCC*, 13 July 1826, p.3, col.5.

38b

Suicide – Climbs tree – along a lateral branch – flings himself of – head

is caught in fork –   ib.

Source: 'Singular Suicide', *DCC*, 13 July 1826, p.3, col.4.
Note: *of*: [*sic*]. The *DCC* report reads: 'On Wednesday se'nnight a poor fellow, named William
Hyde, of Hasfield, who had for some time been subject to fits of insanity, climbed up into a pear

tree, and making his way along a limb extending in a lateral direction, fixed his neck firmly in a forked branch, and then threw his body over, in which position he was discovered quite dead. An inquest was held upon the body on Thursday, before John Cooke, Esq., Coroner, when a verdict of Insanity, was returned.'

38c

Advertisement of last lottery: –
~~There~~ In a few days the Lotteries end for ever! L There will be no opp[y]

of getting a large fortune for a small sum after next Tuesday: on that

day the very last drawing to be allowed in this kingdom will take place.

Six matchless prizes of £30,000...will be drawn the 18th of this month –

Next Tu. – last & only drawing that will be allowed in this Kingd[m] after wh.

all Lotteries prohib[d] by Act of P. L Tickets & shares are now on sale" &c.

..."B. Harvey, Ironm[r]" &c.   ib. 13 July '26.

Hand: ELH: *Advertisement of last lottery ... In*; thereafter TH.
Source: *DCC*, 13 July 1826, p.1, col.1.
Note: see also items 31b, 31d.

38d

Advt.–
Turnpike Tolls to be Let. Notice is hereby given that the tolls arising at

the Toll gates upon the T.P.Rs...called or known by the names of Fordington

Moor Gate & Longbredy Gate will be let by au. to the best bid[r] at

the County H. in Dor. on Monday 14th Aug. next betw. h[rs] 12 & 2 in

the manner directed by act passed 3[d] y[r] reign Geo IV ("for regulating

T.P.R s") wh. tolls produced last yr. the foll[g] sums (that is to say)

L F.M.£621, L£. 386. L above the exp. of collecting them, & will be put

up at those sums resp[vely]...Best bidder...pay 1 month in adv[ce]   //

of the rent at wh. such tolls may be let, & give security with suffic[t] sureties

to satisf[n] of Trustees s[d] T.P.R. for payment of rest of money monthly.

J.T.King & Tho[s] Coombs. Clks. to Trustees of s[d] T.P.Rs. Dor. July 10 '26

Source: *DCC*, 13 July 1826, p.1, col.1.
Note: *T.P.R.*: turnpike road. *Fordington Moor Gate*: a turnpike gate on the N.E. outskirts of
Dorchester. *Longbredy Gate*: 7 miles W. of Dorchester, on the Bridport road.

39a

Great Heat – "Hills have caught fire in Scotland" – "burning several days."

200 sheep destroyed – forest of Mar on fire. Prayers in ch[s] for rain.

Haymakers fall dead – "visit[n] of God" – boy with[t] hat, brain fever.   ib.

Source: *DCC*, 13 July 1826, p.2, col.4, p.4, cols 2–5.
Note: this is a merged entry made up of: p.4, col.2 'hill-fires in Scotland'; p.4, col.4 'prayers for
rain'; p.4, col.4 'dead haymaker'; p.4, col.5 'visitation of God' ('dead in bed'); p.2, col.4 lad 'struck
by lightning'; p.4, col.5 case of 'brain fever'.

39b

Assizes – for stealing 3 cows – sentenced to death – Salisbury –   ib.

Source: *DCC*, 13 July 1826, p.4, col.5.

39c

School Adv[ts] The Rev[d]...who has been accustomed to the tuition of youth

for many years...a select number of Pupils... // Scholastic Duties of her

establishm[t] // Gent[n] designed for Mercantile pursuits...they are parlour

boarders...professional gent[m] of eminence in the departments of Fch. Dr.

Mus. Dancing &c...⌐ Terms...⌐ either of the accomplishments separately

4 gs...present vacation will terminate...   ib.

Source: *DCC*, 13 July 1826, p.1, col.3.
Note: this is a conflation of three separate advertisements on the same page of this issue of *DCC*.

39d

Epitaph (Some time since) in Herts – "Rem^ber me as you pass by ∟ As you are now

So once was I ∟ As I am now so you must be ∟ Therefore prepare to follow me". ib

(someone wrote under) – "To fol. you I'm not content ∟ unless I knew w. way y. went.") ib.

Source: *DCC*, 20 July 1826, p.2, col.3.
Note: *Herts*: Hertfordshire.

39e–[p.40]

Fortune Teller – Salisbury assizes – Ann Hill – aged 66, dressed in singular

fashion in some of the decayed finery of a century & half back – got a girls

clothes entirely away from her: w^d demand flannel petticoat – threaten to   //

take from her the power of speech & motion – girl takes it off – Another

time her apron & shawl, when walking out. Thus all her clothes &

money have been obtained under pretence of getting the girl a partner for life.

ib. July 20. 26.

Source: *DCC*, 20 July 1826, p.3, col.4.
Note: the following week *DCC* reported 'a petition, signed by not less than 95 respectable inhabitants of Malmesbury ... praying that his Majesty may be graciously pleased, in mercy to the public, to direct that Ann Hill ... be transported for her natural life' (*DCC*, 27 July 1826, p.3, col.1).

40a

The man made drunk to marry – The King v Brown, Waters & Masters –

("Salisbury assizes") dispute between rival parishes – the overseers of

psh. of Cranborne charging officers of psh. of Gamelan with a conspiracy to shift the maint^{ce} of a pauper from latter to former psh. The case: –

John Curdy, pau. of Cranb. was charged by pau. female of Gam. with

being father of a child about to become chargeable to psh. Hereupon officers

of psh. summoned J.C. before them, talked to him so alarmingly about

being sent to jail that partly by threats & partly by persuasion they got

his consent to make an honest woman of the girl. Lest he should cool

upon his rash promise they never let him out of their hands from that

time till the consum^n of the m^{ge}. They plied him plentifully with ale &

good cheer at a pub. h. & were not sparing in their own particip^n, so that

the unfort^{te} pau. was intox. when he took bride to ch. Conseq. was that

both partners became chargeable to psh. of Cranb. & hence the present indict-

ment for a conspiracy. (Proved that J.C. was not a pauper – parish not guilty.)

ib. July 20. 26.

Source: *DCC*, 20 July 1826, p.3, col.5.
Note: *Gamelan*: unidentified, but it is possibly a garbled version, taken down by a trial reporter in the Assize Court, of Gomeldon, near Porton, Wiltshire, N. of Salisbury, some 20 miles from Cranborne. *pau.*: pauper.

40b–[p41]

Coach upset.
Crofts v. Waterhouse. Coach leaves Salisbury – hill after crossing Avon.

driving down which the c. was upset. Defence – Cottages round which the

road turned sharply had been pulled down previous day ("They left S. at 1. a.m.   //
                             – road clear –
it was a fine starlight night, & the moon near its full – ʌ Upset at Harnham

Hill") also a fog. Coachman had been accustomed to keep his eye on gable

end of cottages – missing them he turned too quickly & went over foundations.

The turn was admitted to be dangerous – &c   ib.

Source: *DCC*, 20 July 1826, p.4, col.4.
Note: this provides a source for the accident in *The Woodlanders* (*Woodlanders, 1985*, 142), see
Millgate, 1971, 265, 401. *Harnham Hill*: S. of Salisbury on the Dorchester road.

41a

Wm Wheatley, "a respect^ble looking man of 50, with powdered hair &c.", charged with...

                                                                              ib.

Source: *DCC*, 20 July 1826, p.4, col.3.
Note: William Wheatley was charged with defrauding a prominent Weymouth hotelier, Jane Luce.

41b

Whipping a soldier – "Tiverton" – 2 Bat^n 32^d Reg^t passed through –

a court martial was held here on one of the men belonging to the band (before

Col. M.) for threatening the life of one of comrades. Sentenced to receive

150 lashes – which was executed ~~fr~~ on him at a short distance from the town.

                                                                    ib. (last page)

Source: *DCC*, 20 July 1826, p.4, col.5.
Note: see also items 82b, 94c, 144d, 158a.

41c

Transportation. "Portsmouth July 29." One hundred convicts were

removed from the hulks at this place to on board the Woodford, Chapman,

for Van Diemen's Land, also having stores on board for that colony.   ib. Aug 3.

Source: *DCC*, 3 August 1826, p.1, col.5.
Note: *Chapman*: the master of the ship.

41d

Night : threshing wheat. "Hampshire" – 100 sheaves of wheat thrashed in

field at midnight [spreading cloth &c] & wheat carried off by thieves.   ib.

Source: *DCC*, 3 August 1826, p.3, col.3.
Note: *[spreading cloth &c]*: TH's addition.

41e–[p.42]

Returned Soldier – "Exeter Assizes." Wm Dodd – 35 – Assaulting Sarah Ger

man – 21st July. Formerly a soldier in E. Indies – from wh. he returned 6 weeks

since. Acquired some property in India, & has succeeded to some patrimony

in this country – was married the day after the offence, & was apprehended   //

as he & his wife were leaving the Ch. Sarah G. pretty girl, apparently

innocent & artless, 15. Servant – Got leave from mistress to go to Moreton

Hampstead fair – a^{bt} 2 miles distant, her mother living close to the town of

M.H., & she was to sleep at mother's, & return to mistress at 7 in morning.

At the fair many hours – with another young woman, who afterw^{ds} left

her. At the Bell Inn there was dancing – went into dancing room –

About 2 in morning saw prisoner there – asked her in whisper to go with him –

she declined also in whisper. Was coming away – prisoner followed –

made her drunk from tumbler of spirits. He came out with her & s^d she

s^{hd} not go to mothers but to her master's. Took her arm by force &

led her in that direction. They passed by a fairing stall, fair still going

on; stopped to purchase a fairing for her master's children. Went onw^d

into fields…Arrived at mistress's in morning. – Witnesses for prisoner called – mother of his then sweetheart (now wife) her brother, & the waiter

of the inn were present, & took no notice of prisoner's conduct – he was

drunk...It came out that he had paid his addresses to sweeth[t] 16 years

ago, before leaving for Indies – She had been faithful to her promise to him

during 14 yrs. absence, & on his return, arrangem[ts] were made for marriage

which took place as above.   ib. Aug 3. 1826.

Source: *DCC*, 3 August 1826, p.3, cols 3–4.
Note: *fairing*: a gift obtained at a fair. TH omits all details of the alleged assault carried by the *DCC*
report.

42a

Fashions for August, of this period – Morning dress – pelisse robe of jacconot

muslin, embroidered – Pelerine cape – sleeves to fit the arm: scalloped em-

broidered muslin at wrist, turned upwards. Coral necklace: red silk slippers.

                                                                    ib. //

Source: *DCC*, 3 August 1826, p.3, col.2.

43a

Marine Costume for Seaside – India muslin dress – belt of celestial blue

riband round waist – collar cape – chemisette tucker – mancherons à la

Psyche of muslin edged with lace, to sleeves. gold bracelets clasped by emerald

brooch. White gros de Naples hat – crown adorned with large tulips, strings

celestial blue – amber necklace & earrings.   ib.

Source: *DCC*, 3 August 1826, p.3 col.2.

43b

<u>Races</u> – accident – Salisbury – In the last heat a farmer crossed the

course as <u>Hougoumont</u> was coming up. Horse struck him, & threw

rider to great distance – rider & horse seriously injured.   ib.

Source: *DCC*, 3 August, 1826, p.3, col.2.
Note: TH's attention was probably drawn to this item by the horse's name, Hougoumont, the chateau on the site of the battle of Waterloo which he visited in 1876; see *Millgate, 1982*, 183.

43c

("Exeter assizes")
<u>A sort of Jimmy</u> "Lopes v Andrews." ʌ The Tavy runs through

plaintiff's estate (along the side of it, apparently) – def^{ts} allowed to dig from their

side of river under it to other side, for lead ore. But Sir Manasseh Lopes

had no idea that they w^d dig so far: actually ran their shafts under till

he expected them to make appearance under drawing room w^{ws}...

Mr Selwyn called upon the jury (for the def^{ts}) to lay aside any prejudices in

favour of the worthy bart. (!) in justice to his clients: & if any of them had

observed the splendid hospitality & munificence at Maristow House, & had

partaken of its festivities, he entreated them at least to endeavour to forget circ^s

so likely to misl^d their judg^t. They might also be influenced by fact that

plaintiff had attracted pub. atten^n as a senator (!); but...bound to look at

case as between ordinary indiv^{ls}...On one occas^n the def^{ts} took the worthy

bart. in 6 oared boat to view works. In a moment of extravagance he gave

6^d to be divided among the 6 who had rowed him...   ib. Aug 3. 26. //

Source: *DCC*, 3 August 1826, p.3, col.5, p.4, col.1.
Note: *A sort of Jimmy*: probably slang: 'unauthorized entry'. *Sir Manasseh Lopes*: first baronet

(d.1831) of Maristow, on the river Tavy, S. Devon. *DCC* reports: 'the worthy baronet was to receive, as lord of the manor of Marystow, a tenth of the produce'. The verdict was for the plaintiff with 40s. damages. Both exclamation marks are TH's additions.

44a

Unworthy manager. "The King v. Wm Henry-Ellis." ("Exeter Assizes")

An indictment, charging prisoner with stealing cheese &c. prop^y Sarah New=

man. Had been for sev^l years in employ of Mr N. deceased, a grocer of

extensive business in Exeter: since M^r N's death had been in empl. of M^{rs} N.

who carried on business for benefit of self & 9 children. Mr N. had formed so

good an op^n of Ellis that he spoke of him in highest terms in his will –

& left him gold watch chain as a rememb^{ce}, observing that any more substant^l

proof of reg^d was unnec^y in conseq. prisoner being good circ^s (is a man of prop^{ty})

Losses discov^d by Mrs N. & eldest son – youth 19. Searching prisoner's mother's

house, where he lived, a quantity of property was found. Guilty – liable to

transp^n for 14 y^{rs}. [Here it is plain that Mrs N. set aside her own judgm^t

entirely, in trust in her husb$^{d's}$]

The defence was that there was a conspiracy against Ellis. Some shillings

were marked, put into till, prisoner seen to go to till & take out shillings; but

he had no intent^n of stealing them. ib. Aug 3. 26.

Source: *DCC*, 3 August 1826, p.4, col.1.
Note: *[Here ... husb$^{d's}$]*: TH's interpolation.

44b

Horse stealing – Very prevalent at this date – "Judges seem determined

to check the prevalence of the crime." ib.

Source: *DCC*, 3 August 1826, p.1, col.4.

44c

| Clergyman – said to have been an actor under another name formerly – at

| Covent Garden. Revd Thos Snow.   ib.

Text: there are two vertical parallel lines (pencil) beside this item. There is no space between this item and item 44d, below.
Source: *DCC*, 3 August 1826, p.4, col.4.
Note: this report is a continuation of an earlier one from *DCC*, 20 July 1826 p.2, col.1; see item 44d.

44d

Clergyman's secession – reason he gives is that, having doubts upon Inf^t

Baptism he engaged curate – Found that curate had far stronger obj^ns.

                              "Original notices"   ib. July 20. 26 //

Source: *DCC*, 20 July 1826, p.2, col.1.
Note: these details emerge from an exchange of correspondence between the Revd Thomas Snow and the Bishop of Bristol about Snow's secession from the Church of England over the infant baptism issue. Infant baptism was opposed by Baptist churches which believed in the baptism of adults as believers. For TH's interest in this question see 'Trumpet-Major Notebook' (*PN*, 180–81), and *A Laodicean* (ch.2) in which Paula Power refuses adult baptism by the church of which she is a member (*A Laodicean*, ed. Jane Gatewood (Oxford: Oxford University Press, 1991), pp.17–18).

45a

Blandford Races – August 2.   ib.

Source: *DCC*, 3 August 1826, p.4, col.4.

45b

General Garth – described as "an officer much beloved by the late King" –

Source: *DCC*, 3 August 1826, p.4, col.5.

Note: *General Garth*: Thomas Garth (1744–1829) was Equerry to George III. He rented Ilsington House, Puddletown, until his death. During these years the house was much used by the royal family en route for Weymouth. Widow Garland spots 'fractional parts of General Garth and the Duke of Cumberland' accompanying George III, the Queen and Princesses to inspect military manoeuvres, in *The Trumpet-Major*, ch.12 (*Trumpet-Major*, 1991, 104). See Appendix Two.

45c

– Tom Garth ? –
"Elopement" Capt. G. ⅄ son of Genˡ Garth; & Lady Astley. Both young.

She fled at 1 in morning withᵗ hat or bonnet…leaving everything, even

her purse & money behind her – so high minded was she, in conseq. of

having brought no fortune to husband. He rich: they poor.   ib. Aug 3

Text: – *Tom Garth ? –*, caret mark and the semicolon superimposed on dash after *Genˡ Garth*, are in pencil.
Source: *DCC*, 3 August 1826, p.4, col.5.
Note: *Capt. G*: Thomas Garth (b. 1800), adopted as his son by General Garth who was alleged to be his father. His mother was said to have been Princess Sophia, dau. of George III. Thomas Garth attempted to blackmail the Royal Family, see Dorothy Margaret Stuart, *The Daughters of George III* (London: Macmillan, 1939), pp.278–82. *Tom Garth ?*: added by TH. *Lady Astley*: wife of Sir Jacob Astley Bt., MP until 1837. A satiric cartoon of 8 August 1826, 'A Change of Performance at Astley's, or a pollution of Jacob's Ladder' is reproduced in Laurence Stone, *The Road to Divorce: England 1530–1987* (Oxford: Oxford University Press, 1990) (plate 15).

45d

A free & easy actor told me he had passed 3 festive days at seat of Marq.

& Marchˢˢ of – withᵗ any invitⁿ ; convinced (as proved to be the case) that

my L. & my Lady, not being on speaking terms, wᵈ each suppose the other had

invited him.   Reynold's Life & Times.   ib. Aug 10

Source: *DCC*, 10 August 1826, p.2, col.2.
Note: *Reynold*: Frederic Reynolds (1764–1841), dramatist and author of *The Life and Times of Frederic Reynolds, Written By Himself*, 2 vols (London: Henry Colburne, 1826).

45e

<u>Gipsy</u> – gets a woman to place £100 in notes, in a packet, in family bible,

for fortune telling purposes – calls to see it is done – changes packet for a

worthless one – when the woman examines it a long time after, gipsy never

reappearing, finds it does not contain her notes.   ib. Aug 10.

Source: *DCC*, 10 August 1826, p.3, col.2.
Note: this incident takes place 'about Preston', Lancashire.

45f

<u>Pugilism</u>. Man challenged to fight by a stranger. Is killed by stranger,

who is never known – proved that deceased was the aggressor.   ib. Aug 10.

Source: *DCC*, 10 August 1826, p.3, col.2.
Note: *Man challenged to fight by a stranger: DCC* has 'a man named Anderson, who met his death by fighting with a stranger'. The verdict was 'Justifiable Homicide by a person unknown'.

45g

<u>Dress of this period</u> – country – brown surtout coat, cord breeches, top boots –   ib.

Source: *DCC*, 10 August, p.3, col.3.
Note: this information about contemporary dress habits in fact derives from the report of an inquest on a drowned man, a watchmaker from Chalford. *DCC* reports: 'On Friday, as some fishermen were dragging their nets in the river Severn, about two miles below Gloucester, they rose the body of a man supposed to have been in the water eight or nine days. He was attired in a brown surtout coat, cord breeches, and top boots...' The verdict is 'Found drowned'.

45h

<u>Fire – wasp's nest</u> – burning the latter set fire to stubble field – ran to hedge –

thence to stacks – all the produce of farms for that year burnt –   ib. //

Source: 'Calamitous Fire', *DCC*, 10 August, 1826, p.3, cols 3–4.
Note: this took place on a farm between Beachley and Black Rock, on the Welsh side of the Severn estuary, S. of Chepstow.

46a

"Horse Stealing." The horse fair at Winchcombe, n^r Cheltenham –

desperate gangs of these ruffians – An experienced farmer suffered

an apparently respectable young man to jump into the saddle of his horse

on pretence of making trial of his paces, while he took charge of a showy

but worthless animal which was offered him in exchange – thief

gallopped off.

   Mr Jones took a valuable cob to sell – surrounded by a party of

confederates – their strategem to have the horse led down a lane to try

paces having failed, Jones was induced by a pretended purchaser to

enter the Inn on the pretext that it was not prudent to expose

money in fair...Jones running back to the Inn door found

the horse ~~for~~ had been ridden off by the "purchaser". He ran after – was

beset by a crowd of the thief's accomplices offering to purchase –

Breaking through he came within sight of ~~a~~ the stolen horse &
riding home,
rider. He overtook Mr Smith surgeon ʌ who assisted him in
(Mr S.)
pursuit, just as he ʌ had seized the bridle, & was about to secure

the culprit, an accomplice galloped up from a wood, & struck

him such a blow with a bludgeon as to fling him from his horse

& split his hat completely. Nothing daunted Mr Smith, having
on horseback;
recovered, intrepidly resumed pursuit ʌ aided by Mr Slater,
(on foot)
accompanied by Jones ʌ & two young farmers. Thieves were

so closely followed that their pursuers had them frequently in

until

view ~~the which~~ they reached Whichwood Forest – lost them

(Caverns there, it is said). (quot from <u>Cheltenham Chronicle</u>)   ib. Aug 10.1826. //

Hand: ELH.
Source: *DCC*, 10 August 1826, p.3, col.4.
Note: *Whichwood*: Wychwood Forest, N. of Burford.

47a

<u>Plantations on fire</u> – 10 acres of firs destroyed – sudden shifting of the

wind saved the owner's residence – supposed to be the work of an incend-

iary from being fired in 3 places. (It was a time of drought)   ib.

Source: *DCC*, 10 August 1826, p.4, col.2.
Note: *(It was a time of drought)*: TH's addition. See also item 39a.

47b

<u>Man accidentally kills</u> his son when chastising him.   ib.

Source: *DCC*, 10 August 1826, p.1, col.5.

47c

<u>Cuckoo – cuckoo</u> ! Some miners were employed in blasting rocks on the

banks of the Tarn when a cuckoo approached them & gave forth his

monotonous note. "For whom does he sing?" said one of the miners. – "Ｌ For

you probably Ｌ That can't be, as I am not married: but it is pps. for Peter"

Ｌ I defy him, s^d Peter for I know my wife to be virtuous. It is Brant? that

he is singing to. Ｌ Why sh^d you think so? s^d B. Ｌ Because every one says that

Cavalie is on very good terms with y^r wife...It is probable that they are

now together for you see he has not come to his work this morning. B. on hearing this [s^d nothing but presently] returned to village, & found door shut

knocked, but got no answer. Then climbed up to a window, & on getting into his

room saw C. & his wife jumping in terror from the bed. Seized knife, stabbed

C. Guilty wife tore her hair, beat her breast, & called on her h. to give her

the same death. [But] Brant molested her not. Gave himself up –   ib. Aug 10. 26

Source: *DCC*, 10 August 1826, p.4, col.5.
Note: *Tarn*: a river in the south of France.

47d

<u>Bather</u>, on returning to dress, finds pockets have been picked by a gent^n who

sat near his clothes reading.   ib. Aug 17

Source: *DCC*, 17 August 1826, p.3, col.1.

47e

Erased item f.24r (see Appendix One)   //

48a

<u>Theatre Royal Weymouth</u>. A melancholy charm attaches to it – when

we enter it our eyes are involuntarily directed to the once regal box: we

reflect how often that revered & almost idolized father of his people, the late

King has sat on that spot...wept at the fictitious sorrows of a Siddons, laughed

at the humours of a Quick...The whole of the dingy & tattered drapery of

cobwebs, which hung in such festoons, are entirely swept away – no

spiders dancing on their tight & slack ropes...as formerly –   ib. Aug 17. /26.

Source: *DCC*, 17 August 1826, p.4, col.3.
Note: *Siddons*: Sarah Siddons (1755–1831), actress, espec. in years 1774–1812. *Quick*: John Quick

(1748–1831), actor: the original Tony Lumpkin in Oliver Goldsmith's *She Stoops to Conquer* (1773).

48b

Travelling by kites. Bath to London: a large k. & a pilot: 18 or 20 miles an h.   ib. Aug 24./26

Source: *DCC*, 24 August 1826, p.1, col.5.
Note: *DCC* reported that two kites instead of horses were attached to a carriage, the Duke of Gloucester, in his coach and four, galloping to keep up. Another instance of travel by kite-power was observed a month later, 29 September 1826, by the Revd F.E. Witts, rector of Upper Slaughter, on the road from Gloucester to Cheltenham (see D. Verey (ed.) *The Diary of a Cotswold Parson* (Gloucester: Alan Sutton, 1978), p.67).

48c

Returned husb^d 27 years absent native village: met wife with 2^d husb^d :

would not interfere: preferred single blessed^s & lives on (apparently) alone

in same place.   ib. Aug 24/26

Source: *DCC*, 24 August 1826, p.1, col.5.
Note: *preferred single blessed^s*: TH's gloss on 'declared for single blessedness'. *in same* place: TH's addition. See *Millgate, 1971*, p.237.

48d

Identity concealed
~~Abduction — ruse~~ – Street to the court so crowded with persons waiting to

see the lady as to be dangerous for her: four ladies were therefore dressed like

her in every respect – mourning & thick veil – & when the four came out nobody

c^d say wh. was the real one – the 4 going in diff^t directions.   ib.

Source: *DCC*, 24 August 1826, p.3, col.3.
Note: *lady*: this was Miss Turner. See 'Abduction of Miss Turner' (29a). *four ladies*: there were three dressed like Miss Turner.

48e

Arrest hindered – A writ against a person…had been lodged with T., one of the

Sheriffs officers, & had by him been transferred to one of his men for execution.

Man accord^ly repaired to residence of party, knocked, was admitted. Advanced to

object of his pursuit: in act of making his caption with usual famil^r tap on should^r

he dropped down dead. Debtor made good his escape. ib. //

Source: *DCC*, 24 August 1826, p.3, col.4.
Note: *caption*: archaic form of 'capture'. *execution*: of the writ.

49a

Gambling – A servant loses £150 at a gambling table on the race course: then

pledged watch; lost: returned home & hung himself. Savings of years.
ib. Aug 24/26

Source: *DCC*, 24 August 1826, p.4, col.5.

49b

Flight of defend^t on bail. "Flight of Wm Wakefield" (Abduction of Miss Turner

ante p.29) Lancaster. Aug 21. At half past 9 Mr Justice Park took seat

on bench, & directed that the learn^d couns. engag^d for the prosec^n & the def^t, sh^d

informed arrival. 5 min. aft^ds Mr Brougham came into court & moved that

Wm W. sh^d be called upon his recognizances.
ce.
Mr R. the crier called def^t 3 times upon his recogniz of £2,000, but he did
of Macclesfield –
not appear. The sureties, D.Davies ʌ Doctor of divinity, Jno Cuthbert, of S., Kent,

were called upon 3 times to produce body of W.W., wh. they had undert^n to have

here this day, or to forfeit their recog^ces of £1,500.

Mr Justice P.: Is there any reason suppose def^t not in court? Probably

he is prevented appearing by the crowd.

Mr Brougham: Mr Denison, attorney for def^t says, my lord, that def^t

is not forthcoming.

Mr Just. P. (to Mr D.) Have you any reason to believe that def^t not be forthcoming?

Mr D. He will not appear my lord.

Mr J^{ce} P. Let the recogn^{ces} of W.W. & of his sureties Dr D. & Mr C. be estreated

Mr B. The def^t W.W. having absconded I have humbly to move y^r lp. for a bench

warrant against him.

Mr J. P. Let the warrant be prepared...Warrant made out.

ib. Aug 24. 1826 //

Source: 'Flight of William Wakefield', *DCC*, 24 August 1826, p.4, col.5 (continued from p.1).
Note: *def^t, sh^d informed arrival*: i.e. 'should be informed of his arrival'. *estreated*: a stage in the
process of forfeiture of sureities. TH refers back to item 29a, which summarizes an earlier *DCC*
report of this case. See also items 48d, 63c.

50a

Great distress & poverty in the country at this period (1826) – Suicides:

horse-stealing: highway robbery frequent. Talk of grant of pub. money necessary.

Source: *DCC*, 24 August 1826, p.4, col.4; 31 August 1826, p.1, col.5, p.2, col. 5, p.3, cols 3–4.
This is a general comment by TH arising from a series of reports on the state of trade and of
destitution at this time.

50b

Fall of Townsman. "Somersetshire". At Frome – several persons – formerly

considerable business-clothiers, & ranked among most respect^{le} tradesmen

of town – subsisting on parish allowance, wh. they obtain by breaking stones on the road. We are sorry that no hopes yet present thems^s of improve^t

in the commerce of this once active & thriving town. Those who wish to engage

in the woollen manuf^{re} w^d do well in engaging in that business at Frome,
                                            – poor rates exceed £1000 a month
as there are now upw^{ds} of 5000 out of regular employ. ⋏ Quot. <u>Bath Journal</u>.   ib.
(see also p. 53)

Source: *DCC*, 31 August 1826, p.3, col.3.
Note: *Townsman*: a term familiar to TH's contemporaries and a description which included TH
himself; for in 1884 *DCC* reported a Municipal Banquet at the King's Arms, Dorchester at which
the retiring Mayor 'entertained a large and influential gathering of his fellow-townsmen'; TH was
among the named guests (*DCC*, 13 November 1884, p.3, cols 2–3), at a time when he was at work
on *The Mayor*. TH's story 'Fellow-Townsmen' (*WT*), set in Bridport, was published in 1880.

50c

<u>"Cheddar"</u>: ~~Fair~~ <u>Priddy Fair</u>: Desperate Assaults & robberies : gangs of
                                      are employed in the   of
gipsies from Bristol: women related to them ⋏ conduct ~~the~~ E.O. tables, or other

low species of gambling. After nightfall resp^{ble} people who had been dining in

booths c^d not go outside. obliged to remain – &c.   ib. Aug 31.

Source: *DCC*, 31 August 1826, p.3, col.3.
Note: *Priddy Fair*: a notable sheep fair held at Priddy, in the Mendips, Somerset. *E.O.*: 'Evens
and Odds', a form of roulette, declared illegal by Parliament 1750, but persisting, especially at
fairs.

50d

<u>Depôt of stolen horses</u>.("Horse Stealing") At a p. house kept by a female, ~~the~~

the ostler concerned: the chief delinquent not yet caught.   ib.

Source: *DCC*, 31 August 1826, p.3, col.4.

50e

<u>Pugilism</u>. Fatal – by striking under ear – also a case where the

beaten man seizes a shovel & kills the victor by a blow on temple.   ib.

Source: *DCC*, 31 August 1826, p.4, col.5.
Note: TH refers to two separate but adjacent items.

50f–[p.51]

<u>Gentleman strolling musician</u>. – The Scotch military gent. who is playing   //
the bagpipes about the country for a wager of 1000 £ was at Lincoln on Mon.
said to be a Col. Macdonald: servant takes money; or as the paper says "receives the largess of the public".
6ft high: air of gent^n spectacles: like Lord C.: number of ladies interested & anxious to see: liberal to him: jean
or fustian dress – is it a trick?   ib. Oct 5.26

Text: the last two and a half lines of this item were evidently squeezed in after the next item had
been composed.
Source: *DCC*, 5 October 1826, p.4, col.4.
Note: *Lord C*: Lord Cochrane.

51a

<u>Jealousy &c</u>. Mr M. suspects improper intimacy between his wife

& Mr H. The wife's brother suggests that Mr H. call on Mr M. to

assure & prove to him that his suspicions are groundless, at an interview
                    – mutual –
at wh. are to be present M^r & Mrs M., with ʌ friends, &c. Mr H. goes

down from London to Birmingham accordingly. On the approach of M^r M.

however, Mr H. conceals himself in closet – Mr M. discovering him pulls

a pistol from pocket. &c – & is only just prevented murdering Mr H.   ib.

Source: *DCC*, 7 September 1826, p.3, col.3.
Note: *Mr M.*: Mr Madden, of Birmingham. *Mr H.*: Mr Harper, of London.

51b

<u>Decapitation</u> – Head of boy squeezed off by mill – father enters & sees his

son's body jumping about without a head! quot. fr. <u>Tyne Mercury</u>.   ib.

Source: *DCC*, 7 September 1826, p.3, col.3.

51c

<u>False sweetheart</u>. young lady staying at the house of her intended, near

Stroud, to be married to him, after a courtship of 3 years. On the morning

of the wedding she was missing from her room. Window close to canal: it

was thought she had drowned herself; young man distracted; canal dragged:

To the surprise of all at 9 o' clock the ch. bells rang out a merry peal, &

a messenger arrived to state that young lady was safely married to a <u>cousin</u>

of her intended, after a courtship in secret of 10 days (while staying here).   ib.

Source: 'Female Frailty', *DCC*, 7 September 1826, p.3, col.4.
Note: *False sweetheart*: TH's heading.

51d

<u>Stolen property returned</u> – The suspected man, a neighbour, being addressed
                                         (spoons.")(by fellow townspeople – notably Mʳˢ –)
as "Tom", &c; "now didst n' thee take my ʌ &c. ʌ After inward struggle – says
   ("and thee sh't have 'em again.")
he did – ʌ & gives all the property back to his neighbours – seems greatly relieved.

                                                                        ib. //

Source: *DCC*, 7 September 1826, p.3, col.4.

52a

 Singer –
~~Actress~~ – <u>mistress of Calcraft of Wareham</u>. Miss Bride: she succeeded

Mʳˢ Bellamy as his mistress. He leaves sums of from £5000 to £10,000 to his

children by these ladies – to Miss B. an annuity of £1,000, a sum of

£3,000, & another sum to expire on her death or marriage. She married,

& became M[rs] Lefevre.   ib. Sept 14. 26

Source: *DCC*, 14 September 1826, p.1, col.4.
Note: John Calcraft (1726–72), politician and army contractor. He bought Rempstone, near Corfe Castle, and the manor of Wareham, Dorset. *Miss Bride*: *DCC* reports her as 'the mother of Mr Calcraft the present member for Wareham', i.e. John Calcraft (1765–1831) who was MP for Wareham variously from 1786 to 1831. He committed suicide (see *Frampton*, 378). *M[rs] Bellamy*: see item 143d.

52b

Elusion. Gent. enters silversmith's – buys spoons, salt cellars &c – his elegant

gig waiting outside – asks shop keeper to allow his boy to accompany him to his

chambers, & will pay the bill. Gent. drives boy up obscure street – gets out

with the silver, telling boy to wait in gig. Does not return. Gig hired.   ib.

Source: *DCC*, 14 September 1826, p.3, col.3.
Note: *Elusion*: TH's own heading; the action of evading. OED cites *Far From the Madding Crowd* as illustration (Book 2, ch.16). *silversmith's*: *DCC* has 'goldsmith's'.

52c

Partially erased item f26v (see Appendix One)

52d–[p.53]

Horse dealers. one of Westbury, other of Wells. Agree to change horses i.e. "chop"

next morning the W[y] man's was found dead. He goes to Wells, & says he has   //

altered his mind; asks him to change again. After some conv[n] the other agrees, on

cond[n] he be paid 10[s] /- to boot. It is done. W[y] man then finds delivered to him

the dead body of his own horse, wh. has also died.   ib.

Source: *DCC*, 14 September 1826, p.3, col.4.

53a

<u>Tied to a Gatepost</u> by robbers, (money being taken) – found by a waggoner.   ib.

Source: *DCC*, 14 September 1826, p.3, col.4.

53b

<u>Frome</u>: does not recover from the depression like the towns in the north.

                    widening & levelling, a great improvem^t

400 weavers & shearmen are at work on t. p. roads $\wedge$, paid by fund, partly

contrib^d by London com^{ee} partly by opulent inhab^{ts}, partly by ratepayers.

They hope the ports will soon be open for all descriptions of grain...Population

of this once flourishing town consists about 13,000, 8000 of whom dep^t on cloth

manufacture.   ib. Sept 21/26.

Source: *DCC*, 21 September 1826, p.3, col.4.
Note: *shearmen*: craftsmen in the woollen trade. *t. p. roads*: turnpike roads.

53c

<u>Sherborne Annual diversions</u> – cudgel playing &c – terminated in favour

of the Dorset players – band on the stage played select pieces.   ib.

Source: *DCC*, 21 September 1826, p.4, col.2.
Note: *terminated ... Dorset players*: i.e. finished with the Dorset players winning.

53d

<u>The body of a rich Jew</u>, who died at hotel at Cheltenham, taken to London

neatly encased in lead on roof of one of own stage coaches at the contract price

of 5/- a pound.   ib.

Source: *DCC*, 21 September 1826, p.4, col.5.

53e

Horse painting – Farmer loses his horse – finds him in a field so

painted as to make it difficult to recognise him – black legs were white,

& marks put on forehead & other part.   ib. //

Source: *DCC*, 21 September 1826, p.4, col.5.
Note: *part*: *DCC* has 'parts'.

54a

Yellham Hill cutting made – 1826.   ib. 28 Sept.

Source: *DCC*, 28 September 1826, p.2, col.1.
Note: This is a reference by a 'traveller' in a letter deploring the surface of the recently realigned
Dorchester–Blandford road at Yellham, or Yellowham, between Puddletown and Dorchester, half
a mile from TH's birthplace.

54b

Game plentiful this year (1826) Exeter coach via Basingstoke brings to town each

journey from 200 to 300 head of game: on one 60 hares, 150 partridges &c –   ib.

Source: *DCC*, 28 September 1826, p.3, col.1.

54c

Dead – Woman comes on a visit to a friend – finds her dead and buried.   ib.

Source: *DCC*, 28 September 1826, p.3, col.1.

54d

                                                        Eagle
Cornish Wrestling – 2000 persons assemb^d bowling green ~~City~~ tavern City R^d to

witness the Cornish wrestling. The sport was finished by Warren a Cornish man

& Ab^m Cann the Devonshire Champion, who contended for 1st prize – 10 sovs. won by Cann – very muscular, ab^t 30. 2^d prize, 6 sovs. to Warren.   ib.

Source: *DCC*, 28 September 1826, p.3, col.2.
Note: See also items 82e, 106d. *Eagle tavern*: tavern in Finsbury, London; cf. the popular Victorian verse: 'Up and down the City Road/In and out the Eagle'. Abraham Cann (together with his brother James) appeared again at the Eagle tavern in April 1828 for a five-day tournament. *DCC* reported that the 'interest' generated by 'these rustic games' was 'convincing proof of their rising popularity' (*DCC*, 1 May 1828, p.3, col.2).

54e

Transported – Allen, conv^d manslaughter, Bucks assizes, 1825, has written home

from V. Diemen's L. States that he has (1826) £65 a year & board for managing a

farm.   ib.

Source: *DCC*, 28 September 1826, p.3, col.2.
Note: *V. Diemen's L.*: Van Diemen's Land, now Tasmania.

54f

Coach robbed – of parcel containing £1000 country bank notes –   ib.

Source: *DCC*, 28 September 1826, p.3, col.4.

54g

Gone down – Hindon market (Wilts – old clock) Some years ago an important

one – now on Thursday exhibited 42 pigs 2 baskets of butter 3 butchers stalls

The rates on small houses are more than the rent!   ib. Oct 12. 26

Source: *DCC*, 12 October 1826, p.1, col.4.
Note: *Gone down*: TH's heading. *(Wilts – old clock)*: TH's insertion. *rates*: refers to poor-rate. *Hindon*: S.W. Wilts., nr. Shaftesbury. *DCC* reads: 'Hindon market, which some years ago was a very considerable one, exhibited on Tuesday 42 pigs, two baskets of butter and three butchers' stalls. No corn, no other cattle, and not above 120 persons in the market. The fact is, that when there is no spirit, and few customers, there will be no inducement to offer produce for sale ... the landlord at the Lamb Inn in this town, who rents a posting and coach-house, scarcely worth £50 per annum, paid half a year's poor-rates a few days ago, which amounted to no less than £28. The rate is on small houses more than the rent. What is there in the north of England to equal this?'

This item relates to the deterioration of the fair at 'Weydon-Priors' (Weyhill) in *Mayor* (see item 117f for an 1829 report of the decline of Weyhill Fair). In fact *DCC* reported, the following week, that Weyhill Fair was experiencing an economic slump, similar to that of Hindon reported here: 'country sheep sold at 10s per head less than they would fetch at home' (*DCC*, 19 October 1826, p.4, col.3).

54h

The "Lady of a Noble Lord". Closes windows of house during day: night throws them

open – house illuminated – apart from husb^d – deranged –   ib. //

Source: *DCC*, 12 October 1826, p.3, col.2.
Note: *DCC* states that her derangement is the result of the death of an only child.

55a

A Drover – puts cattle into field close to inn he is going to stay at for the night.

swears at them because they won't go in: innkeeper reproachs, &c. –   ib.

Source: *DCC*, 12 October 1826, p.4, col.5.
Note: *DCC* also records that [the drover] 'answered … [the innkeeper] … by another oath, and instantly dropped dead before her face'.

55b

Wonderful sketches on a wall, when the people get up one morning at Turnham

Green. (skeletons &c. it seems; called Death's Doings): done by a young man out

of employ, at a very early hour, to divert his mind for dwelling on his wretched

situation [& to prevent suicide].   ib. Oct 10. 26

Source: *DCC*, 19 October 1826, p.3, col. 1, p.2, col.1.
Note: *Oct 10*: TH's error for 'Oct 19'. This is a conflation of two items partly concerning a review of R. Dagley, *Death's Doings* (1826). *&c.*

55c

Coffin used to convey smuggled liquor across public bridge, Aberdeen – borne by "a few decent looking men." [also in Dorset]. ib.

Text: *[also in Dorset]*: in pencil.
Source: *DCC*, 19 October 1826, p.3, col.2.
Note: *[also in Dorset]*: TH's addition. *DCC* records the following dialogue: 'they did not carry the dead?' 'Na, Na, ... They certainly had a dead weight, but it was three ankers o' guid Glenlivat whisky!'

55d

<u>Scarcity of News.</u> – 1750 <u>Leicester Journal</u>. – editor compelled to have the Bible "to help him

out", so great was the dearth of news. Began with 1ˢᵗ Gen. & got to 10ᵗʰ Ex. before anything

happened. ib.

Source: *DCC*, 19 October 1826, p.3, col.2.
Note: *DCC* reports that the editor 'extracted the 1ˢᵗ chapter of Genesis, and so continued the extracts in succeeding numbers as far as the 10ᵗʰ chapter of Exodus'. The journal 'was then printed in London and sent down to Leicester for publication!' *before anything happened*: TH's interpolation.

55e

<u>Treasure.</u> Woman begs man to meet her at 11.p.m. on down, with box & pickaxe –

there is buried treasure, [& she is not strong enough to dig]. ib.

Source: 'Extraordinary Credulity', *DCC*, 19 October 1826, p.3, col.4.
Note: *[& she is not strong enough to dig]* TH's addition.

55f

Honest principle – Mʳ Everell of Crockerton, Wilts, failed in 1815 as a clothier,

paying 5/- in pound; died shortly after leaving widow & children. Recently (1826) the
                                        – interest of dau's share to mʳ for life –
widow's brother died, leaving £20,000 between the 2 sons & the dau. of wᵂʰ The two sons have

paid their father's debt in full, leaving themselves only a few hundred pounds. ib

Source: *DCC*, 19 October 1826, p.3, col.5.

Excision from f.28r&v (see Appendix One)

56a

by police – (private clothes at this date) –
<u>Man addressed</u> in Dartmouth street ʌ – draws sword from cane – (night): it seems

that he had been cautioned by slip of paper through keyhole against attack, &

this was his reason for carrying sword stick. (Qʸ who was going to attack?)   ib.

Source: *DCC*, 19 October 1826, p.3, col.5.
Note: *addressed*: TH wrote this over his initial 'attacked'. *(private clothes at this date), (Qʸ who was going to attack?)*: TH's interpolations.

56b

<u>Next door neighbours</u> – put up their tickets in their wwˢ each defaming other –   ib.

Source: 'Extraordinary Occurrence', *DCC*, 21 September 1826, p.1, col.3.
Note: this concerns two women summonsed for 'keeping a disorderly house', in Brighton. The next-door neighbour, a solicitor, put a placard in his window – 'beware of the brothel-house', whereupon the women placed a retaliatory placard in theirs denouncing his 'infamous libel'.

56c

<u>Resurrection-men</u> – Barrels of bodies, supposed to be buried, found on board

vessel going to Scotland – they were for the anatomical schools: salted in.

(reason of these doings was that at this date medical schools were not supplied

from hospitals, as in France.)   ib.

Source: *DCC*, 19 October 1826, p.3, col.4.
Note: *Resurrection-men*: also known as 'body snatchers'. The illegal trade in corpses for the use of anatomy schools was effectively stopped by the Anatomy Act of 1832. See items 61a, 90a, 192e. *(reason ... France)*: TH's addition.

56d

<u>Smokers'</u> [song] quaint lines.

decrie	Who lives more frugally

All daintee meats I doe <   > ∟ which feed men fat as swine ∟ He is a frugal man

         I   Have

than I   < > need no dripping-pans or crocks ∟ hath no

<   > ∟ That on a leaf can dine! ∟ <   > ∟ <   >

    wet   my   <   > my

greased hands to wipe < > larder is a littel box, ∟ < > kitchen is a pipe!

<   >)   <   >   ∟ <   >   ib.

                  I keep my raw meat in a box   <   >

Source: *DCC*, 26 October 1826, p.2, col.1.
Note: this ditty in praise of smoking is recorded by *DCC* as follows: 'All daintie meats I do defie // Which feed man fat as swine; // He is a frugal man indeed // That on a leaf can dine. // He needs no napkin for his hands // His finger ends to wipe, // Then keeps his kitchen in a box //And roast meat in a pipe.' It is not clear whether TH has another ditty in mind for comparison, or whether he wants to improve on the original.

56e

Dead Passenger – Methodist preacher on journey to chapel to preach – is

taken ill on hill near Sherborne – sits down – asks driver of cart to let

him ride – gets up – when driver turns to ask him how he feels he is dead.

                                                 ib. Oct 26.26.

Source: *DCC*, 26 October 1826, p.3, col.2.
Note: *DCC* quotes the carter asking the preacher 'how he did'.

56f

Capt. Begg – shot sheriffs officer about to arrest him: escaped; & lived about

England in disguise, & in privation: has at last called at army agents, & been taken.

                                               ib. //

Source: *DCC*, 26 October 1826, p.3, col.2.

Excision f.28r&v (See Appendix One)

57a

Cross-road burial "A recent alteration in the law has abolished the practice

of burying in the high road in cases of <u>felo</u> <u>de</u> <u>se</u>. The body is now allowed to be

consigned to ch.y^d...A verdict of Suicide committed in a sound state of mind"

was returned, & an order issued for her interment the same night...But the

hurried interment & the omission of the funeral service together with the hour

at which it must take place (between 10 & 12 at night) are circumstances

sufficiently appaling to the country people. (The girl was a young man's

sweetheart, who sent him for arsenic, for no apparent reason).   ib.

Source: *DCC*, 26 October 1826, p.3, col.3.
Note: *appaling*: [*sic*]. See also items 4b, 32f, 117a; TH's 'The Grave by The Handpost' (*CMT*);
'Memoranda 1' (*PN*, 24).

57b

                                        (Tamar).
Floating candle – Woman's child falls into river ⋏ & is washed away: she

is told by neighbours that if she sticks a candle in a wooden bowl & sets it afloat,

with a recommendatory prayer to St Nicholas, the bowl will stop over the corpse.

The candle drifted against a boatload of hay & set it on fire, the flames of which

communicated the fire to her house, & it was burnt to ashes.   ib.

Source: *DCC*, 26 October 1826, p.3, col.5.
Note: *(Tamar)*: river separating Devon from Cornwall.

57c

Drowned – another pulled out – Child drowned in the sea near Christchurch –

In drawing for body of child the body of a <u>man</u> was brought ashore.   ib.

Source: *DCC*, 26 October 1826, p.4, col.2.

57d

<u>Public houses – late at night</u>. Whereas...P. Houses in the town (Wey[th])

are kept open at late hours in the night or early in the morning...Notice...that

...after 11 at night for any other purpose than reception of travellers...&c –   ib.

Nov 2. 26.

Source: *DCC*, 2 November 1826, p.1, col.2.

57e–[p.58]

<u>Bank-Notes</u> ("Snow & others") – Action of Ss, Fleet St. bankers against   //

Ls, Doncaster bankers, to recover value of £200 £100 & £50 B. of E. notes.

Ss. in conseq. of illness of a clerk, sent porter to collect money amounting

to £3000 in various sums, in London. Returning from B. of E. was hustled

& robbed. Loss advertised: as Doncaster races were about to commence it

was conjectured that an attempt might be made to get rid of such property

there: banks of the town apprized by letter & handbills. But def[ts] received

the notes. Mr G. clerk in def[ts] bank stated that they in daily habit of

receiving several £200 B.E. notes. If they did not know the name of the

party, the course was to enter in a book "received of strange gent[n]." Sometimes

the name is asked. The practice is to take nos. of notes when they are remitted

to London. During the race time there is no time for taking such minute

partic[rs] ~~of~~ as gent[ns] names...The notice respecting the stolen notes was on a

table in the office: the no[s] of them were not entered.

Another clerk states that in his bank they do not take names of parties

paying in notes provided they take the local notes in exchange.

B. of E. clerk says, might be 2 notes same no, & am[t] but diff[t] dates.

nos. run from 1 to 20,000 – then begin afresh.   Verd. Plaintiff.   ib. Nov 2. 26.

Source: *DCC*, 2 November 1826, p.2, col.5.
Note: *Ss*: Messrs Snow & Company, bankers. *Ls*: Messrs Latham, Tew & Co. *G*: Gee, a clerk.

58a–[p.59]

Fraudulent Bills of Ex: ("Savage v. Rich.") Savage accepts bill for £1000.

…The defence set up was that def[t] having occ[n] ab[t] 3 y[rs] since to raise

money, a sum of £2,500, consented to accept bills to am[t] of £15,000

in 15 bills of £1000 ea. These bills were to be accepted by him for benefit

of a man named Rowe in Cornwall: they were negotiated by M[r] Beare   //

of London, on cond[n] that he sh[d] receive 5 p.c per ann. as commission for

the trouble he had taken. This was stated by Beare himself, who gave evidence.

L[d] C.J. s[d] it was an infamous transaction – L Beare s[d] he had lost

& not gained by it. L Def[t] has accep[d] – 8 only of them; disposed of them

with Rowe – afterw[ds] sent to get them returned as he had received nothing

for them. Rowe how[r] made various excuses, & the bills were finally put

(who had failed)

in ag[st] def[t] L It then appeared they had passed through house of Hobson, ⋀

& had come to Savage, who claimed to recover on it. L It was contended

for def[t] that bill been obt[d] fraud[ly] & that Hobson ought to have known,

& that if pl[ff] did not know he sh[d] have inquired. Plaintiff s[d] he

had been ignorant of manner in wh. bill had been drawn.   Verd. Pl[ff].   ib.

Source: *DCC*, 2 November 1826, p.3, col.1.
Note: *Ld C.J.*: Lord Chief Justice. *did not know*: *DCC* has 'did not know the same, yet they should not have taken a bill to such an amount without some enquiry'.

59a

<u>Blind Giant</u> – His dimensions had attracted cupidity of an exhibitor, who
Age 19.
had barely allowed him necessaries & kept him a sort of prisoner. ʌ   ib.

Source: *DCC*, 2 November 1826, p.3, col.4.
Note: *His dimensions*: 7 feet 2 inches. This is the basis of TH's 'At a Country Fair' (*MV*, *CP*, 504) in which a blind giant is led by a dwarf.

59b

"<u>Bligh v. Wellesley</u>" – adultery – Naples, Genoa, Paris, &c.   Nov 9. 26.

Text: this and the next three items (59c, 59d & 59e) have no space between them.
Source: 'Bligh v Wellesley', *DCC*, 9 November 1826, p.2, cols 3–5, p.3, cols 1–4.
Note: this and the following three items are all derived from five and a half columns of report in *DCC* of an action for damages against the defendant, William Long-Wellesley, nephew of the Duke of Wellington, brought by Captain Bligh for the seduction of his wife, Helena Bligh. Bligh was awarded £6000; he died in 1828 (see item 93a). William Long-Wellesley (1788–1857) m. Catherine Tylney-Long, the richest heiress in England, in 1812. Included in her estate was Athelhampton which therefore became a Wellesley property before being sold by Long-Wellesley's son in 1848 to the wealthy farmer, George James Wood (see J.R. Doheny, 'Thomas Hardy's Relatives and Their Times' in *Thomas Hardy Yearbook* 18 (1989), 5–80 (pp.56–7), rpt in *THFH*, i, 47–81 (pp.56–7)). Long-Wellesley's sensational marital history is described by Elizabeth Longford, *Wellington: Pillar of State* (London: Weidenfeld & Nicolson, 1972), pp.250–57. After completing his reading of *DCC* for 1829, TH returned to this issue of *DCC* 1826 in item 120e, to make, with the assistance of ELH, the longest single entry in 'Facts'. Memories of Wellesley's pursuit of Miss Long at Draycot, near Chippenham, Wilts., were recorded by Francis Kilvert: *Kilvert's Diary 1870–1879*, ed. William Plomer (London: Jonathan Cape, 1944), pp.229–31. See also Tim Couzens, *Hand of Fate: The History of the Longs, Wellesleys and the Draycot Estate in Wiltshire* (Bradford-on-Avon: ELSP, 2001).

59c

<u>Dog wh. barked at visitors</u>, banished from Mrs Bligh's room (she slept apart).   ib.

Source: *DCC*, 9 November 1826, p.3, col.2.

59d

Pin stuck in shutter by l.maid – found next morning on ground: boot track –   ib.

Source: *DCC*, 9 November 1826, p.3, col.2.
Note: *l.maid*: lady's maid.

59e

Nightdress – plain one, an ornamental one substituted by Mrs Bligh.   ib.

(vide <u>post</u> p.93)
& after –

Text: *& after –* : in pencil.
Source: *DCC*, 9 November 1826, p.3, col.2.

59f

Soldier ("Accid[ts] & offences") Lisbon – condemned to be shot – reprieve comes

to officer morning of execution – with a view to a salutary effect officer says nothing

when cap over victim's face officer turns to take reprieve from pocket: the poor

fellow dropped his handkt. wh. the shooting party understood as a signal to fire: &

fired –   ib. //

Text: there are two vertical parallel lines (pencil and red pencil) beside this item. The final line of this item is below the last ruled line of the page.
Source: 'Extract from private letter from Lisbon', *DCC*, 9 November 1826, p.3, col.4.

60a Erased item f.30v (see Appendix One)

60b

Sets fire to his house to defraud insurance Co.: had increased his insurance

from £600 to £3000 – sentenced to death.   ib.

Source: *DCC*, 9 November 1826, p.4, col.4.

60c

Escape from jail. ("Accid[s] & Off[ces]") Four notorious off[rs] escaped Glasgow jail.

Blacksmith, one of them, by means of an implement like a military screw-key,

wh. he had got in a W.C. had at his leisure taken off plate from lock

inside, & removed a spring, so that he c[d] remove bolt. But as the door

opened & locked in usual way the turnkey had no susp[n] . Another in same

cell; & they began open[ng] by breaking away a portion of stone by wh. they

got a strong iron bar from door head. With this they opened door of their

cell…found way from cell to day room – mounted table – thence to

roof of prison – bound their blankets & sheeting to lightning rods, descended,

& made escape: came down oppos[te] Market Inn – watchmen had gone home.

ib. Jan 18.27

Source: *DCC*, 18 January 1827, p.1, col.5.
Note: *W.C.*: water-closet.

60d–[p.61]

Farmer's Will not as he intended – ("Game v. Fryer") Farmer at Shapwick

wrote to his lawyer two days before he died…"Mr F[r] I have been looking into my will

& am very uneasy: I hope it is an error of my reading: my will is that my

b[r] James shall have my property. If, please God, I live till Monday I will //

come to Wimborne. I promised James, & he has worked with me. None of the

rest are entitled to it. If the will do say that the property is to be parted it

is not my will: it is a mistake." He died Monday morning, & did not go.

(Fryer the lawyer was joint executor). The admission of these papers (the letter)

(& codicil)

would revive an antecedent will in favour of James. The other brothers con-

       & cod[l]

tended that the letter ⌄ was a fabrication – But the judge pronounced for them.

ib. Feb 1. 1827

Source: *DCC*, 1 February 1827, p.3 cols 1–2.
Note: *Shapwick*: village near Wimborne, Dorset. *pronounced for them*: i.e. in favour of the papers'
authenticity.

61a

Body snatching on large scale – Man takes house the back w[ws] of which

open over one of the largest ch. y[ds] of Bath – & carries on his operations at

night – £12 per head paid him by anatomists –   ib. Feb 7.

Source: *DCC*, 8 February 1827, p.4, col.3. See also item 56c.

61b

Robbery of Dover Mail – A regular gang…learned that a large quant[y] of diam[ds]

were expected from Paris. They endeavoured to secure all places inside & outside the

mail, but there were two inside places otherwise engaged. They, however, placed some

of the most active of the gang outside; & at Canterbury the best opp[y] of getting hold

of the d. presented itself. The Paris bag was, as is the custom, on the top of the coach
          ⌄wh. con[d] no dia[s] & it was this they pitched upon. Feb 15. 27.
& it contained the diamonds…great value. There was however another bag, the Neapolitan,⌄

Source: 'Late Robbery of the Dover Mail', *DCC*, 15 February 1827, p.3, cols 3–4.
Note: *Neapolitan*: bag containing letters from Naples.

Excision from f.31r&v (see Appendix One)

62a

Thieves – in tree overhanging road, with hook attached to rope – fling hook on

in early winter morn^{ing}   Devizes   half
sack of wheat in waggons passing ⋏ to wheat market ⋏ – waggoner ⋏ asleep – 22.2.27

Source: *DCC*, 22 February 1827, p.3, cols 4–5.
Note: *waggoner*: *DCC* has 'carter'.

62b

<u>Waxwork show</u>. Dk of York lying in state: negroo, &c. Caught fire by people pressing.

ib.

Source: *DCC*, 22 February 1827, p.3, col.4.
Note: this incident took place at Bath Fair. *Dk of York*: Frederick, Duke of York, died 5 January 1827. *negroo*: TH's word. *DCC* has 'a poor Indian … who was shown in the same caravan, was almost suffocated'.

62c

<u>Bideford Fair.</u> (Feb^y). Cattle numerous: full of pleasure hunters: a ball at the rooms.   ib.

Source: *DCC*, 22 February 1827, p.3, col.5.

62d

<u>Fight at Andover.</u> £100 a side. Town crowded by the attendance of a numerous train

of the fancy & patrons of the ring. Men arrived evening previous: spot selected

a mile from town. Stage executed 6ft high, 24 ft square, ring formed by placing

60 waggons, wh. afforded an excellent view for spect^{rs}. Fine science displayed.

B. thrown over ropes, but he descended in a wagon beneath: 10th round a

heavy blow dealt by C. on right of B.'s neck, & laid him prostrate. Another

fight on same stage afterw^{ds}. 10,000 persons present, highest satisfaction – ib.

March 1.
ib. ~~28 2~~. 27

Source: 'Fight at Andover between Dick Curtis and Barney Aaron for £100 a side', *DCC*, 1 March 1827, p.4, col.3.
Note: *the fancy*: keen followers of sport, esp. pugilism.

62e

Timber sale, very large, in New Forest (Lyndhurst).　　　　　March 8. 27　　　　//

Source: 'Advertisement New Forest, Hants. To Be Sold By Auction', *DCC*, 8 March 1827, p.1, col.1.

Excision from f.31r&v (see Appendix One)

63a

Stolen – out of the Stable of Mr John Bennett, Basket-maker in the

Parish of Ruishston, near Taunton, on Saturday night, or early on Sunday

morning, the 25th of February, A Bright Bay Pony Horse, about thirteen hands

high, white face, blind in the right eye, has a long gray hog mane and short tail

two white feet behind, collar mark on the neck, saddle marks on the back,

halter mark behind the ears, & a D burnt in the near shoulder. Whoever will

bring the same to the said John Bennett shall receive Ten Guineas Reward

on conviction of the offender; but if found in any person's possession, after

this public notice, they will be prosecuted according to law. Feb 27th 1827.

Hand: ELH.
Source: 'Stolen', *DCC*, 22 March 1827, p.4, col.4.
Note: *Ruishston*: now Ruishton, Somerset. *long*: not in *DCC*'s description of the horse's mane.

63b

Hoped to win mistress's daughter – man in service of lady 11yrs saved

£200 with a view to win the dau. whom he loved. She rejected him, &

he then murdered her – [eve of her wedding day].   ib. March 29. 27

Text: [eve of her wedding day]: in pencil.
Source: 'Horrid Murders', DCC, 29 March 1827, p.3, col.5.
Note: DCC reports: 'there is reason to fear that the constancy with which she had resisted his approaches instigated him to an act of diabolical revenge'. [eve of her wedding day]: TH's interpolation.

63c

Abduction. Trial of Wakefields for abⁿ of Miss Turner – evidence of the

Gretna Green blacksmith verbatim.   ib. March 29. 27

Source: 'Lancaster Assizes', DCC, 29 March 1827, p.4, cols 3–5.
Note: Gretna Green blacksmith: David Laing, who conducted marriages in return for fees and gifts. See also items 29a, 48d, 49b.

63d–[p.64]

The Naval Officer ("Devon & Cornwall – Exeter assizes") action brought by

naval officer to recover £30 fr. overseers of parish in Devonport, unjustly appropri^ted

by them to their own use. Landing at that port from a cruise took up quarters with

a female who, proving enceinte she laid to his account by anticipation a bastard   //

child. As he was a "stranger" the parish officers "took him in" – in other words

agreed to take £30 to cover the expenses of maintenance &c., wh. being assented

to by plaintiff the £30 was paid to the overseer. When the lady was confined

however the child proved to be dead born, whereby parish saved all exp^ces

the lady having paid the accoucheur herself. Action brought to get back money.

                    ib. Apˡ 5. 27

Source: DCC, 5 April 1827, p.3, col.4.

64a

Husband & Wife – In 1778 Mr Morris married. In 1788 he & his wife

separated, he being quiet & rather parsimonious; she being gay & extravagant,

& both having property. When separated they became better friends than

when they lived together: he sent her presents, & they frequently visited. In

1793 Mrs M. had a son – & since it was possible her husband c^d be the

father he was assumed to be, notwithstanding a favourite footman, who became

a Captain in Army. ib. Ap^l. 12.27

Source: 'Shrewsbury Assizes – Morris v Davis' *DCC*, 12 April 1827, p.3, col.3.
Note: this is a case of a (successful) claim for legitimacy by the son in the light of the law relating to the presumption that the husband, if alive, must be taken as the father. As far as it goes TH's summary is correct, although it does appear that he found the law dubious.

64b

Dozing – man has desk put on table before fire at inn, to sort his papers.

Falls half asleep – has an indistinct sense that somebody came in & took

notes from desk. ib. Ap. 19.

Source: Report of Lent Assizes – Taunton, *DCC*, 19 April 1827, p.4, cols 3–4 (col.3).

64c

‖ Boy stolen, & sold to a sweep for 1/6 (to be used as climbing boy. ib. 26

Text: there are two parallel lines (red pencil) beside this item. There is no closing bracket after 'boy'.
Source: *DCC*, 26 April 1827, p.3, col.2.
Note: *DCC* reports a 'pawning', rather than a sale. *climbing boy*: *DCC* has 'sweep'. The accused is sentenced to seven years' transportation.

64d–[p.65]

Notorious Horse stealer – "Blue Jemmy" – at Ilchester (executed) – had stolen more than 100 horses. Came to Crown & Anchor Misterton, with a horse. Landlord

having heard his fame as a horsestealer went & looked at horse – was offered him   //

did not buy, but

at £25, afterw^{ds} £19 – much less than value. Landl^d ʌ privately cut 3 notches in

mane of mare. Following day a handbill was left at house, offering reward for the

recovery of a mare that had been stolen. Landl^d pointed out direction in wh. the

prisoner went. Finding himself pursued prisoner left horse concealed in a pit

...Prisoner has been brought to bar 19 times –   ib. May 3. 27

(He stole a horse belonging to W. Keats's father: grazing in Bockⁿ Lane –)

Text: *did not buy, but,* caret mark, *(He stole a horse ... Lane –),* in pencil.
Source: 'Execution of James Clase better known by the name of Blue Jemmy, and Wm. Hewlett',
DCC, 3 May 1827, p.3, cols 3–4.
Note: *(He stole a horse ... Lane –):* TH's addition. *'Blue Jemmy'* or 'Blue Jimmy': James Clase who
was hanged, aged 52, having been brought to the bar nineteen times for horse-stealing. William
Keates was a near neighbour of the Hardys in Higher Bockhampton (see *Millgate, 1982,* 24; *Life
and Work,* 94.) TH indirectly alludes to the theft by Clase of one of Keates's horses in his note to
'A Trampwoman's Tragedy': '"Blue Jimmy" ... was a notorious horse-stealer of Wessex in those
days, who appropriated more than a hundred horses before he was caught, among others one
belonged to a neighbour of the writer's grandfather' (*TL, CP,* 199). The trial of James Clase is the
source for Florence Dugdale [and Thomas Hardy], 'Blue Jimmy The Horse Stealer', written in
1910; (see Pamela Dalziel (ed.), *Thomas Hardy: The Excluded and Collaborative Stories* (Oxford:
Clarendon Press, 1992), 337–42.) Dugdale's principal sources were reports of the Somerset Lent
Assizes from 1825 and 1827 in the *Taunton Courier and Western Advertiser* for 30 March 1825
and 11 April 1827 (which she had 'been at some pains to hunt up ... at the British Museum' (*CL,*
iv, 114) and the *DCC* report of 3 May 1827 (Dalziel, pp.338–41). The story was heavily dependent
on these reports of the trial: the narrator foregrounds one of its sources when referring to the 'tepid
and unemotional account' of Clase's execution in 'the ... old *County Chronicle*' with its 'laconic
heading, "Execution, Wednesday, April 25, 1827" (*DCC,* 3 May 1827)'. Dalziel suggests that 'Blue
Jimmy' is 'constituted more largely of plagiarized newspaper paragraphs than of original
composition by either Dugdale or Hardy' (p.342) – paragraphs on which Dugdale drew with a
literalness fully justifying Hardy's subsequently recommending the piece to the *Cornhill* not as a
story but as a 'record' (*CL,* iv, 114). The isssue of *DCC* for 3 May 1827 which includes this report
(not found by Dalziel) survives in the Dorset County Library. For a report of the execution in the
Salopian Journal see G. Stevens Cox, '"A Trampwoman's Tragedy", Blue Jimmy and Ilchester Jail',
Thomas Hardy Year Book, 1 (1970): 82–5.

65a

The Burning Cliff – A long description of it in the papers about this time (spring '27).

(&Aug.'27)

Source: *DCC*, 19 April 1827, p.2. cols 1–2, 2 August 1827, p.4, col.2.
Note: *Burning Cliff*: at Holworth, 2 miles E. of Osmington, Dorset. This spectacle of apparently spontaneous combustion provoked widespread comment and correspondence in *DCC* for over a year. See *inter alia*, 'Burning Cliff at Holworth' (*DCC*, 28 August 1828, p.2, col.2). The cliff in Ringstead Bay, Dorset, is still known as 'Burning Cliff'. There is a contemporary engraving of the phenomenon at Weymouth Museum, dated April 1827.

65b

Mrs Coutts's maiden name was not Mellon, but Entweesel: her father kept the

post. office at Cheltenham for many years – quot. fr. Morning Herald. June 28.27

Source: *DCC*, 28 June 1827, p.1, col.4.
Note: *Mrs Coutts*: a *canard* about the widow of Thomas Coutts, banker (1735–1822), formerly Harriot Mellon, actress. In 1827 she married the 9th Duke of St Albans.

65c

Nightingale – at Lincoln – people assembled night after night to listen to the

bird as it sang in an adjoining garden. Owner of garden shot it on its perch,

disliking trespassers.   17. May 27.

Source: *DCC*, 17 May 1827, p.4, col.3.

65d

Putting on Clock – on fast Day, in France, that he might eat sausages an

hour sooner.   ib.

Source: *DCC*, 17 May 1827, p.3, col.1.
Note: the impatient man is an innkeeper.

65e

<u>At public house</u>. n^r Crewkerne – Daughter of the late Baker, the well known

Somersetshire conjurer – has been staying there a fortnight in course of her

travelling through the Western counties, with a male compan^n. She affects to

cure halt lame & blind by a charm – & to counteract effects of witchcraft.

May 24. 27

Source: 'Caution', *DCC*, 24 May 1827, p.4, col.3.
Note: *Baker*: mentioned by TH in a letter to Herman Lea (*CL*, iii, 264).

65f

<u>Man of 50 Christened</u> – preparatorily to being married – at Burton

Bradstock.   Feb 15. 27   //

Text: this item is entered below last ruled line of page.
Source: 'Christening Extraordinary', *DCC*, 15 February 1827, p.4, col.2.
Note: *Man of 50*: his sponsors 'not so old as himself'. *Burton Bradstock*: Bridport, Dorset.

66a

<u>Inquest</u> – clergyman enters, & shows coroner a bill for 40 quarts of ale

furnished the deceased between Thurs. morn. & Sat eveng. Landlord & wife

reprimanded: (the man was drowned through returning home intoxic^d.   ib.

Source: *DCC*, 24 May 1827, p.4, col.3.

66b

<u>Auction</u>. In Dorchester market pl. Seven cast troop horses belonging to

H.M's 4th Drag^n gards. Apply Regm^l Serj. Maj. at Barracks. – May 31. 27

Source: *DCC*, 31 May 1827, p.1, col.2.
Note: *cast*: i.e. no longer fit. *gards*: [*sic*].

66c

Old woman who kept a small shop, & always pleaded extreme poverty – asked

to subscribe for relief of...Surprised, she s[d], that they sh[d] think of calling upon

her, when she was almost starving. Such was the effect upon her of the idea that

people supposed her to be possessed of money that she was taken ill, & died. On

removing a stone in shop...upwards of £1000 in floor.   May 31
                                                              ~~June 14.~~ 27

Source: *DCC*, 31 May 1827, p.3, col.4.

66d

One day's courtship – First saw e. other Sat. morn[g] . Married Sun morn[g].   ib.

Source: *DCC*, 31 May 1827, p.3, col.5.
Note: this incident is cited by Kristin Brady as a source for TH's story 'A Mere Interlude' (*CMT*),
(*Brady*, 172).

66e

Grocers, Butter factors &c. of Weymouth, Dorchester &c. obtain their goods from London

by Smacks wh. sail fr. Carpenter Smith's wharf, London every ten days, & every ten

days from Wey[th] A commodious cellar at the old bridge foot for accommodation

of all goods. (Adv[t] .)   June 14.27

Source: *DCC*, 14 June 1827, p.1, col.3.
Note: *Smacks*: light coastal vessels.

66f

Wanted a number of tailors...6 months certain. Regim[l] Q. M[r] D.Barracks.   ib.

Source: *DCC*, 14 June 1827, p.1, col.2.
Note: *Regim[l] ... Barracks*: Regimental Quartermaster, Dorchester Barracks.

66g

<u>Packets</u> from Southampton to Havre once a week –   ib. //

Source: *DCC*, 14 June 1827, p.1, col.3.
Note: *Packets*: vessels carrying mail.

67a

<u>Road Waggon</u> of Messrs W. & C. carriers, of Sherborne left the office on way to

London on Tuesday even[g] with two female passengers. On Pontington Down it

suddenly stopped; & the women missed the waggoner. Supposing him to have gone

into some p.h. & in momentary expec. of his return they remained till daybr[k]

when they determined to return to Sherborne – distance of ¼ mile they perceived

waggoner across road dead, wheel passed over him.   ib.

Source: *DCC*, 14 June 1827, p.4, col.2.
Note: *W. & C.*: this is intended to stand for 'Woolcott and King' carriers. *Pontington Down*:
Poyntington, N. of Sherborne, Dorset. *p.h.*: public house.

67b

<u>Cudgelling, wrestling</u>, &c, at Lambert's Castle fair as usual –   ib.

Source: *DCC*, 14 June 1827, p.4, col.2.
Note: *Lambert's Castle*: an Iron Age hill-fort N. of Lyme Regis, West Dorset, in use for horse-racing
until recent years.

67c

Sea Mark Fair – On Horn Hill, n[r] Beaminster – 1st Tu. in Aug. Cattle, sheep, Horses,

Cheese &c –. Diversions in Handbills.   July 19. 27

Source: *DCC*, 19 July 1827, p.1, col.2.
Note: *Horn Hill*: N.W. of Beaminster, West Dorset, with a view of the sea 10 miles away. This item
is a conflation of a notice, *DCC* 19 July 1827, p.1, col.2 and a brief report from the same issue p.4,
col.1.

67d

Returning home she met a young man of her acquaintance who made

her intoxicated, & took her to a brothel, where she passed the night with him.

On her return home she seemed in very low spirits, & declared she would

never see her father again.   ib. Aug 2. //

Source: *DCC*, 2 August 1827, p.3, col.2.
Note: *DCC* reports that 'the deceased threw herself into the Surrey Canal'. The woman was Ellen Logan of Camberwell, S. London. She had been unsuccessful in seeking 'a position as a housemaid': her resultant 'low spirits' seem to have helped the inquest jury bring in a verdict of 'insanity'.

Excision from f.34r&v (see Appendix One)

68a

Stone thrown by boy: strikes another in forehead: not expected to live.   ib.

Source: *DCC*, 23 August 1827, p.3, col.3.

68b

                    (see post)
Howarth the Burglar – at large in the extensive woods round Pen Pits

near Bourton. Called at a lonely cottage near the wood last Wedn^y...

horseman passed – he immed^{ly} fell flat in ditch...cottage woman alarmed

at his extraord app^{ce}...placed a jug of water within a short distance of

him [retired & watched – he came out from bushes] & she then had an

opp^y of observing him particularly...He continues with^t hat, coat or

shoes...black plaster across nose...handbills 100 gs. reward.   ib. Aug 23. 27

Source: *DCC*, 23 August 1827, p.4, col.4.
Note: see also item 69a. *Pen Pits*, or 'Penselwood Pits': shallow excavations on the wooded border of Dorset, Wiltshire and Somerset, over some 200 acres, variously explained as prehistoric defences

or worked-out quarrying. The Dorset Natural History and Antiquarian Field Club (of which TH was a member) visited the pits in 1883 (J.S. Udal, 'Dorset Collection' (n.d.), ii. 37–8).

68c

Cranborne Chase – particulars concerning – extent – deer – habits of villagers

plan for disenfranchisement.   ib. Aug 23. 27

Source: *DCC*, 23 August 1827, p.3, col.3.
Note: a highly compressed summary of a *DCC* report of 'a public meeting of the Proprietors of land in, and bordering on, Cranborne Chace', which extended from Dorset into Wiltshire and Hampshire. A proposal was made by the owner of the Chase, Lord Rivers, to dispose of his rights in return for an annuity of £1,800 per annum. The report suggested that the stock of deer was 15,000: 'in times of scarcity of food they make inroads into all the surrounding lands'. The sole right to these animals was vested in Lord Rivers. *habits of villagers*: clandestine killing of the deer. Eventually the Chase was disenfranchised by Act of Parliament with effect from 10 October 1830; see Desmond Hawkins, *Cranborne Chase* (London: Victor Gollancz, 1980), pp.77–85.

68d

Blandford Races – Dk of Wellington present – balls, &c –   ib.

Source: *DCC*, 23 August 1827, p.4, cols 1–2.
Note: *Blandford Races*: Blandford, N.E. Dorset, with its racecourse and Assembly Rooms, was a social centre for the many landed proprietors in the neighbourhood. *Dk of Wellington*: Arthur Wellesley, 1st Duke of Wellington (1769–1852), soldier and statesman (victor at Waterloo (1815)), was currently Commander-in-Chief (appointed 1826). He was Prime Minister from the following January (1828) until 1830. His connections with Dorset developed after his receiving from Parliament the gift of the house and estate of Stratfield Saye, in neighbouring Hampshire, which had been sold to Parliament by George Pitt, Lord Rivers, in 1817. It had been a property of the Dorset Pitts for 200 years. The ball on the second night was in the Duke's honour – 'there were upwards of 400 in the room'. See also items 108d, 120e, 191b.

68e

Gaming-table at Haldon Races, nʳ Exeter. Handsome marquee – 39 chances

to 1 in favour of the table keeper (?) Wine & porter handed about free of expense   //

Text: the conclusion of this entry is cut off by the excision from this page.
Source: *DCC*, 20 September 1827, p.3, col.5.
Note: *table keeper (?)*: presumably the holder of the bank.

Excision from f.34r&v (see Appendix One)

69a

Howarths, burglars, of Frome. – carried it on for 16 yrs. Gave capital entert[ts]

to their neighbours – were very generous – prayer-meetings at their house – Sheep

& calves innumerable have been stolen by them. No suspicion as to how they

had the means to live so comfortably. Robbed churches – wife of one had a

silk dress made out of clergymans gown, & passed him wearing it. She also

had a bonnet made from the velvet of the pulpit cushion – drank sacra-

ment wine, & used the chalice as utensil.   ib. Sept 20. 27

Source: *DCC*, 20 September 1827, p.3, col.3.
Note: see also item 68b.

69b

Dorchester races – Ball in evening, attended by elite of neighb[d].   ib. Oct 4.

Source: *DCC*, 4 October 1827, p.4, col.1.
Note: *elite*: TH's own word for what *DCC* described as 'upwards of one hundred and seventy ladies and gentlemen of distinction and fashion'. The 'Ball' was at the King's Arms, Dorchester.

69c

Escape from prison – At locking up time in even[g] the turnkey looked into P's

cell & saw him, as he supposed, sitting on side of bed; but the prisoner had conceived

a successful plan of deceit, by dressing up a brush with his pillow, cap, & outer garments,

while he himself was concealed in one of the outhouses; he had also divested the bed

of his blankets, & during the day had worn them round his body; with these he formed a rope, & attaching a heavy weight of stones to one end, he slung it over

the wall, & the counterbalance being sufficient, he had no difficulty in gaining the

summit & lowering himself by a similar process on the other side into the

adjoining Bridewell garden & thence into the high road. He has not yet been

retaken. (This occurred at Exeter) ib. Oct 11.27

Hand: TH: *Escape ... the prisoner*; ELH: *had conceived ... retaken*; TH: *(This occurred at Exeter)*.
Source: *DCC*, 11 October 1827, p.3, col.5.
Note: this is either a rare example of ELH taking over the summarizing of an item from TH for direct transmission into the notebook, or an instance of her continuing the transcription from his existing notes.

69d

Lover – gets over wall one eveng to meet sweeth^t in her garden: drops into

water butt up to neck – &c. ib. Oct 18 //

Source: *DCC*, 18 October 1827, p.2, col.3.

70a

Govr of Preston Prison discharged for intoxication, serving out raw beef to

prisoners, & playing at cards with a convicted prisoner. ib.

Source: *DCC*, 18 October 1827, p.2, col.5.
Note: *Preston*: town in Lancashire.

70b

Man transported for life reappears in village in Hampshire – having returned

from Botany Bay in an unknown way. Was retaken. ib. Oct 18.

Source: *DCC*, 18 October 1827, p.3, col.4.
Note: *Botany Bay*: in New South Wales, Australia, a name in general use for Australian convict settlements.

70c

<u>Coaches</u>. King's Arms Dorchester – (by W. Oliver) – Times: "Royal Mail"
                              morning
from London ¼ past 9. ʌ (to Exeter –). to London (fr. Exeter) 4½ p.m. (½ hʳ stoppage

each way at Dor.) "Royal Clarence" from Swan with 2 necks Lad Lane London

every morning at 7: arrives at 12 at night. at Dor., on way to Exeter. Passes

through D. on return journey at 11. p.m. "Magnet" London & Weymouth.

<u>up</u>; ¼ before 6 every morning through Dor.; down; 8.p.m. through D.

"Southampton & Plymouth" 3 times a week: through D. about 1, up & down.

"Commercial" – South. & Weyᵗʰ 3 times a week. Down 6 p.m. up. 9.a.m.

"Royal Dorset" – Weyᵗʰ & Bristol (through Yeovil &c) Mon.Wed. Fri. ½ past

8.a.m. to B. Tu .Th. Sat. 6.p.m. to W.

"Royal Regulator" Dor. & Weyᵗʰ leaves Dor on arrival of London mail – &

returns in time to catch it.

Also "Duke of Wellington"– Weyᵗʰ to Bath – via Cerne & Sherborne.

Source: *DCC*, 13 December 1827, p.1, col.2.
Note: information taken from an advertisement: 'King's Arms Inn, Dorchester. Royal Mails and General Coach Office. W. Oliver respectfully announces to the Public the time of arrival and departure of the ROYAL MAIL & OTHER COACHES, viz.'; TH has summarized two notices (in the same column) and inserted extra information regarding arrivals, departures and stoppages in Dorchester.

70d

<u>Count D'Orsay</u> – Lady Anne Harriet, youngest dau of Earl Blessington

was married last week at Paris to young Count D'Orsay.   ib. Dec 24. 27

Source: *DCC*, 27 December 1827, p.2, col.4.
Note: *D'Orsay*: Alfred, Comte D'Orsay (1801–52), son of one of Napoleon's generals. *Lady Anne*

Harriet: Harriet Gardiner (1812–69), dau. of the Earl of Blessington's first marriage. D'Orsay and Harriet soon separated. After the Earl's death in 1829, D'Orsay became the lifelong companion of the Earl's widow, his second wife, Margaret, Countess of Blessington (1789–1849), author, who at Gore House, Kensington, was hostess to many writers and artists. D'Orsay was a successful amateur painter, sculptor, and man of fashion. For D'Orsay see Countess of Cardigan, *My Recollections* (London: Everleigh Nash, 1909), p.154, and G.H. Gronow, *Reminiscences and Recollections* (London: Smith Elder & Co., 1862), pp.222–4. TH's old friend Anne Thackeray, later Lady Ritchie, recalled from her childhood her father, Thackeray, sitting with D'Orsay, 'the most splendid person I ever remember seeing' (H.T. Fuller and V. Hammersley (eds), *Thackeray's Daughter: Some Recollections of Anne Thackeray Ritchie* (Dublin: Euthorion Books, 1951), pp.55–6. See Michael Sadleir, *Blessington/D'Orsay* (London: Constable, 1933).

70e

Qy. by the same man?

<u>Abduction</u> of a man's 3 daughters successively ⋏ – one marries – one dies –

one is recovered.   ib. //

Text: *Qy. by the same man?* and caret mark, in pencil.
Source: *DCC*, 27 December 1827, p.2, col.4.
Note: *Qy. by the same man?*: TH's addition. *Qy.*: query. From the facts as reported, three daughters could not have been abducted by the same man, although two could have been.

71a–[p.74]

<u>Coach Robbery</u>. Brookes v. Pickwick & others.

Mr Erskine opened the pleadings. This was an action brought by Dr Brookes

against the proprietors of a coach running from Bath to Exeter, for the recovery

of the value of a trunk lost on defendant's coach.

Mr Sergeant Wilde stated the case. In the month of September last plaintiff &c

his family booked themselves to go from Bath to Exeter by the Regulator coach; after

the coach had arrived at Taunton, the coachman was asked by Dr Brookes if his

luggage was all safe; the coachman said it was; but on arriving at the New

London Inn, at Exeter the largest trunk containing goods to the value of

nearly £200, was missing. He would call witnesses to prove that it was owing
to gross negligence on the part of the proprietors, which occasioned this loss.

Isabella Frances Brookes, the daughter of the plaintiff deposed that her
father was Rector of Horton, in the county of Gloucester; was at Bath on the
12ᵗʰ of September last with her Father, was booked by him to go by the
Regulator Coach to Exeter; her father took three places inside; went to the
White Hart, Bath on Wednesday Sep.13. paid the fare & went by the coach;
they had three trunks & some other small packages, recollected the largest
of the trunks contained linen and jewellery; started from Bath at 8 o'clock
in the morning & reached Taunton at 3 o'clock in the afternoon; the
passengers stayed & dined there, the coachman came in & said the coach was
changed there, her father requested the coachman to see the luggage changed
from one coach to the other, & the coachman said he would, took some
refreshment & returned to the Coach, & the coachman then said that   //
the luggage was sccurcd, viz, three trunks on the top of the coach; the coachman
said the boot was not large enough to contain them. A porter brought up
the trunks into the room at the New London Inn; they did not get the large
trunk for five weeks after, in Bath; it was then empty. After her father
had arrived in Cornwall some days, he returned to look after the trunk which
had been lost.

Cross-exam: by Mʳ Mereweather: The luggage was taken in at the Castle & Ball
Bath; did not look up to see if the trunks were on the coach; did not look up
at all; did not know that the porter. etc.

Re-exam: Before they went from Bath they were staying at the Castle Ball.

Thomas Braddick exam: by Mr Serj: W.: was employed at the C. & B.

as porter; remembered D^r B's family being there in September last; they

were going by the Exeter coach; assisted in putting the luggage into the boot;

to the best of his receollection there were a portmanteau & two trunks; believed

the one produced to be one of them, the three trunks were the first things put into

the boot.

Miss B. re-exam: The trunk produced was the one put into the boot.

T.B. cross exam: Had been sent once or twice before by D^r B's family to

the White Hart; went to the W.H. & desired the coach might go down to

the C. & B.; the coach went down; there were eight articles of luggage

which filled up the boot. D^r & his family got in at the W.H. The horse

keeper drove the coach down; had often been at the W.H. had seen notices

but never examined them, had received bills of the clerk; had read about   //

the coaches, but did not take particular notice of the bottom; had examined

the notices since, when he was examined at the W.H., but did not before understand

them as he was but a poor scholar.

Mary Tautton examin: Found the trunk about a mile from Taunton on

the Exeter road empty in Sep. last.

Mr M. said the defendants were individuals who were not over-fastidious

to resist any legal claims arising out of the general discharge of the duty they

owed to the public; but on some occasions they would not do justice to

themselves if they did not resist the demands made upon them, & this case was a great hardship upon them. His learned friend had endeavoured to give

a complexion to that case which the sober judgement of the Jury would

not warrant, when he stated that there was a gross negligence on the part of

the defendants, or the persons who belonged to them. The luggage was stated

to have been put on the coach; but no one that belonged to the coach saw it;

& somehow or other it was lost. What were the circumstances of the case?

Dʳ B occupied the whole of the boot &...

    John Hobbert exam: Was bookkeeper at the W.H. in Sep. last: knew

Dʳ B. the plaintiff. remembered his coming to the W.H.on the 12ᵗʰ Sep;

he took three places at the time; the plaintiff was in the office five minutes

there was a painted board in the office [The board was here produced; it

was about 4 fᵗ square] The board had on it. "Take notice, the proprietors

of this coach will not be answerable for any package above the value of

£5, if lost or damaged, unless as such & paid for accordingly." That   //

notice was in a conspicuous place, & it was almost impossible to avoid

seeing it. Did not know that parcels of any particular value were ~~not~~

paid by themselves; considered luggage under the care of passengers themselves

    Mʳ Justice B. Are you in the habit of taking up passengers at other places?

Yes, sometimes.

Do you always act up to the notice, as it respects the value of luggage, without

being paid extra for it? I never recollect its being done but once.

    James Batt. attended at the coach at Exeter at the new London Inn;

recollected Dʳ B. & his daughters coming; he said his trunk contained linen;

did not say anything of jewels. Dr B. sent on a note by the Bath Mail

guard the next morning, saying that the trunk was lost.

Verdict for plaintiff   ib. Ap^l 12th 27.

Hand: ELH.
Source: *DCC*, 12 April 1827, p.4, col.4.
Note: *Pickwick*: Eleazer Pickwick, landlord of the White Hart Inn, Bath and sometime Mayor of Bath.

74a

<u>An artificial hand</u>, which can be made to open, close &c, & wear glove.

                                                                              ib.

Source: 'Mechanical Hand', *DCC*, 13 December 1827, p.2, col.2.

74b

<u>Selling wife</u>. At Buckland, n^r Frome, a labr^ing man named Charles

Pearce sold wife to shoemaker named Elton for £5, & delivered her in

a halter in the public street. She seemed very willing. Bells rang.

                                                                    ib. Dec 6. 27

Source: 'Disgraceful Occurrence', *DCC*, 6 December 1827, p.4, col.4.
Note: the second of three reported wife-sales, recorded in 'Facts', on which TH drew for the episode in *The Mayor of Casterbridge*, ch.1 (*Mayor*, 1987, 11–15). See also items 32g and 116c. (See *Winfield*, 227; *Millgate, 1971*, 241–2). DCC reports the incident as follows: 'On Thursday, at Buckland, near Frome, a labouring man, named Charles Pearce, actually sold his wife to a shoemaker of the name of Elton, for the sum of £5, and delivered her in a halter in the public street. Pearce has been married some years, and they have a family of 5 children now living, the youngest of whom is to go with the unnatural mother, who seemed very willing that the sale should take place! The bells rang several peals on the occasion, at the joint expense of the parties.'

74c

<u>Soldier's Wife</u>. Wife of private in 3^d reg^t Foot guards residing in York Street

Westminster, hung herself in her own appartm^t . She & her husb^d in great distress, receiving parochial relief for their two children; but being informed

that it would cease, & that she would be sent to Nottingham her native   //

place, which would cause separation from husband, she became melanch[y].

During her husband's absence, who left home that morning dejected & penni-

less to go on duty, she committed this act.   ib. Dec. 13. 1827

Source: *DCC*, 13 December 1827, p.2, col.5.
Note: the *DCC* report does not explain why a private in the Guards should have been in need of parish relief.

75a

Horse stealing extra[y] Auctioneers's man of Shepton Mallett was riding

along Polden hill: met by a man who begged to be allowed to ride behind

him, a request which was kindly complied with. Fellow no sooner got up

than he pushed the man off, & rode pony away. But the horse belonged

to a third man, & was seen in Bridgwater; & returned to owner.   ib. 20.' 27

Source: *DCC*, 20 December 1827, p.3, col.3.
Note: *extra*[y]: i.e. extraordinary: TH's addition. *Polden hill*: S. of Glastonbury, Somerset.

75b

Deaf and dumb – the whole family, 5, of a poor labouring man –   ib.

Source: *DCC*, 20 December 1827, p.3, col.3.
Note: this item is referred to by Cullen Brown (*Cullen Brown*, 87).

75c

Coining – Masons pulling down house find moulds of coiners – unknown.   ib.

Source: *DCC*, 20 December 1827, p.3, col.5.
Note: the house was in Falmouth, Cornwall.

75d

<u>Load Bridge</u>. & Ilchester. "At these two places the river Parret is navigable

where water carriage may be procured to the several ports in the Brist. Chan^l.

Halstock is also distant 12 m. fr. Bridp^t Harb^r where the timber may be

shipped to the several ports & building yards in the British Channel."

   Extract from adv^t – of sale of Oak Timber at Halstock.   ib. Dec 20. 1827

Source: *DCC*, 20 December 1827, p.4, col.4.
Note: *Load Bridge*: mentioned by TH in his note to 'Vagg Hollow' (*LLE, CP*, 649). *Ilchester*: town
in Somerset. *Halstock*: W. Dorset village on edge of 'Woodlanders' country. *Bridp^t Harb^r*: in *The
Woodlanders* Melbury speaks to Grace about his Port-Bredy [Bridport] Harbour bonds: 'We have
a great stake in that harbour, you know, because I send off timber there' (*Woodlanders, 1985,* 67).

75e

<u>Babies mixed</u> – ("Curious mistake") Day or two ago a lady named

Harman, residing Hackney R^d next door to estab^t ~~for~~ of the Refuge for

the Destitute called on a friend Mrs Ubrick of Cornhill & stopped to dinner –   //

After wh. her friend endeav^d persuade her stay tea but she refused on

ac. of child being left at home. Mrs U. suggested sending maid servant for

the infant, & she was sent. But instead of knocking at Mrs H's door,

knocked at door of Refuge; & on the serv^t coming down the girl duly asked
                                                                to a friends,
for child to take to its mother. The matron of the estab^t had gone out ʌ & girl

at once thought she had sent for her child – gave it to applicant, who took

it to Mrs H. On Mrs H. putting infant to her breast she gave a violent shriek,

& declared that the child did not belong to her, & that it must have been changed

during her absence from home. During the interval the mother of the little

creature had returned home, & on being told her baby had been sent ~~for~~ to her by the girl who had called for it she ran about in state of distraction. Mrs H acc[pd]

by servant – hastened back – girl pointed out where she had brought baby from,

Mrs H. restored little creature to broken-hearted mother.   ib. Dec 27. 1827

Source: 'Curious mistake', *DCC*, 27 December 1827, p.2, col.3.

76a

Horse stealing – trouble & expense if the laws are appealed to – Two farmers

lost two horses – stolen out of fields – tracked to main road – inferred they had

been conveyed to London. Went to L. made enquiries at stables, inns &c

left descript[n] at police offices…received inform[n] that the horses had been

stopped. Had to attend twice in L. at trials of thieves – altogether 4
          (£10 to £15 each journey)
times to L. ʌ then attorney's bill of £34, horses' keep 25gs. Expenses

altog[r] £200. One horse worth £15 the other £20.   ib.

Source: *DCC*, 27 December 1827, p.2, col.5.

76b

Smallpox very prevalent in Sherborne, & in Bodmin jail ib. & later.

Source: *DCC*, 27 December 1827, p.4, col.2 and *DCC*, 3 January 1828, p.3, col.4.
Note: the first report announces 'that the small-pox, which for many months has been prevalent in Sherborne, is now rapidly disappearing', the second 'We are concerned to state that [the small-pox] has appeared amongst the prisoners in the county jail at Bodmin, where three persons died of it last week'. See TH's 'The First Countess of Wessex' (*GND*) and *Cullen Brown*, 87.

76c

Weipperts & Harts sets of Quad[s] performed at ball, Wey[th].   ib. //

Text: this item is entered under last ruled line of page.
Source: *DCC*, 27 December 1827, p.4. col.2.
Note: *Weipperts*: John M. Weippert (1775–1831), composer of dance music, especially the

quadrille, and leader of a popular band. His 'admired Tyrolese Quadrilles' were advertised in *DCC* (28 August 1828, p.1, col.4). At the Dorset County Ball, Blandford, 'Weippert and his unrivalled band attended' (*DCC*, 12 November, 1829, p.4, col.2). See TH's 'A Gentleman's Epitaph on Himself and a Lady, Who Were Buried Together', ll.7–8, 'To guide her with accents adoring//Through Weippert's "First Set"', with its note 'Quadrilles danced early in the nineteenth century' (*LLE, CP*, 584–5).

77a

Woman gets her living by finding fossils at Lyme – grand specimens of the

lizard tribe – sends them everywhere – to America, having many orders

thence –   ib.

Source: *DCC*, 27 December 1827, p.4, col.2.
Note: *Woman*: Mary Anning (1799–1847), celebrated discoverer of the ichthyosaurus. The report reads: 'Miss Mary Anning of Lyme, has several orders for the grand specimens of the Lizard tribe, to be sent to America for Museums there. It is to be hoped that after the late severe gales some of their remains may be disclosed, to reward her for the constant and unremitting assiduity which she applies in searching for them.'

77b

400 gs. found behind mantelpiece, pulling down house –   ib.

Source: *DCC*, 27 December 1827, p.4, col.4.
Note: *gs.*: guineas. *DCC* has 'Joiner … employed … to remove a mantelpiece'.

77c

Two strangers arrive at inn – eat their supper, & retire to same bedroom early.

Presently one comes down & leaves house – the other is found to be (murdered).

                                                                                              ib. Jan 3. 28.

Source: 'Murders at Barnet', *DCC*, 3 January 1828, p.2, col.5.
Note: *DCC* refers to 'a most barbarous murder', 'a most extraordinary murder'.

77d

<u>Guard of coach & poachers</u> – He desired them to get him large basket of game, wh.

they did, & charged him £1 for it: he paid them & they divided money. When he

reached London (from Mere) he found it packed only with hay &c –   ib.

Source: *DCC*, 3 January 1828, p.3, col.3.
Note: 'Memoranda 1' (*PN*, 15–16), gives an account of a mail-coach guard who took game and
dairy products on the London coach, near Higher Bockhampton.

77e

<u>Father scolds</u> newly-returned-home daughter, 21, handsome, virtuous, for remain

ing so late (in bed) a quarrel at breakfast, & he strikes her with his open

hand. She immed^{ly} left the house, (& hastened to Harnham Bridge (Salisbury)

where she jumped into river – young man saw her, tried to save her, but c^d not).   ib.

Source: 'Melancholy Suicide', *DCC*, 3 January 1828, p.3, col.3.
Note: *young man*: DCC has 'a man'.

77f

<u>Workmen & master</u> – he discharges all except one: jealousy of the rest, & hate,

(leading to his murder).   ib.

Source: 'Atrocious Murder', *DCC*, 3 January 1828, p.3, col.4.
Note: TH does not record the particularly gory details of this murder.

77g

(at Navarino)

<u>Man</u> (sold^r) <u>loses both arms</u> – ʌ after amputation is heard singing – asked why.

says he is trying what he can do at ballads – no other means left for a living.

          ib. //

Source: *DCC*, 3 January 1828, p.3, col.4.
Note: *Navarino*: a sea-battle between Turkish-Egyptian fleet and British allies, S.W. Pelopennese, Greece, 1827. *DCC* records the soldier's words: 'I am trying what I can do at ballad-singing, now I've lost my arms', and that he eventually died of his wounds, aged 21.

78a

& pocked-marked

<u>Impostor</u> in blue frock coat, speaking in feigned voice ʌ ...Carries a book "allowing

him to solicit the benevolence of any of the inhab^{ts} of this kingdom for 90 days

in conseq^{ce} of the loss of all his property amounting to £3500, the vessel of wh.

he was supercargo having foundered at sea on her passage from St John's New

Brunswick, in Aug. last." &c. In the book are the names of many ladies

& gent^n with sums attached.   ib.

Source: *DCC*, 3 January 1828, p.4, cols 1–2.
Note: *supercargo*: an officer on a merchant ship whose function is to superintend its cargo.

78b

<u>Method of setting house on fire, after an interval</u> – left candle touching wainscot.   ib.

Source: *DCC*, 10 January 1828, p.3, col.2.

78c

<u>Forger writes</u> to Mr Martin the lithographic <u>engraver</u> & printer in Holborn, to

induce him to assist in producing forged notes.   Jan 10. 28.

Source: 'Singular Charge of Forgery', *DCC*, 10 January 1828, p.3, col.2.

78d

<u>Floods</u>. Salisbury cath^d & Wells, floors overflown – c^d have no service –   ib.

Source: *DCC*, 10 January 1828, p.3, cols 2&3.

78e

17

<u>Miner in debt</u> leaves village in Cornwall. Returns ⋏ years after, & pays all his

debts: does not tell how he has acquired the money.   ib.

Source: *DCC*, 10 January 1828, p.3, col.5.

78f

<u>Lad</u>, apprentice, in surgery of 14 – steady – then goes to bad, associating with

improper females of the town – drowns himself –   ib.

Source: *DCC*, 10 January 1828, p.4, col.3.
Note: *DCC* reports that the apprentice 'had given way to improper indulgences; had associated
with idle characters, both male and female'. The coroner 'forcibly commented upon the gross
misconduct of several girls of the town [Wareham] – naming those with whom the deceased was
connected'.

78g–[p.79]

<u>Brothers</u> – "Kings Arms Inn, Dorc^r – Wm Oliver, deeply impressed with the

most grateful feelings for the firm & liberal support he has so long received at the above Inn

begs to inform the nobility, gent^y com^l trav^{rs} & pub. gen^{ly} that in conseq. of frequent   //

indisposition he has taken his brother Francis Oliver (for several years maitre d'hotel to the

Earl of Liverpool & Ld Rivers) as a partner in his business: & W^m & Fr.O. join in

respectfully soliciting" &c.   ib. Adv ^{t} Jan 17. 28.

Source: *DCC*, 17 January 1828, p.1, col.3.

79a

<u>Elopement</u> – Heiress of 19, Gloucester, with lad same age, son of resp^{ble} boarding h. keeper.
                                                                                       ib.
very handsome lad, living near her father's house.

Source: *DCC*, 17 January 1828, p.3, col.4.
Note: *DCC* refers to the heiress as 'possessing considerable personal attractions and a fortune of nearly £20,000'.

79b

(Borough)
<u>Quarter sessions</u> ʌ Thoˢ Amey was indicted for an assault on John H. It

appeared from the evidence adduced that on Christmas eve (1827), H., who belongs

to the B. band, was in the kitchen of the Phoenix Inn with the remainder of the

band. Whilst there a set of mummers from Fordington came to the door, & one

of them knocked the drum-stick out of the hand of H., who was then standing outside

the door. As he stooped down to pick up the drum stick he was struck on the head

by A. with a wooden sword with such violence as to knock him down. He then

went into the street where he was knocked down several times & much bruised.

A. denied positively that it was he who had struck H...In considⁿ...good charʳ...fortnight.

ib.

Source: *DCC*, 17 January 1828, p.4, col.2.
Note: *John H.*: John Hardy (1803–66?), TH's uncle and resident of Higher Bockhampton who, by the 1840s, was living in the less desirable area of 'Cuckold's Row' in Fordington (see Charlotte Lindgren, 'Thomas Hardy: Grim Facts And Local Lore', *THJ*, 1 (3) (October 1985): 18–27 (pp.21–2)). *B.band*: Bockhampton band. *Phoenix Inn*, formerly an inn, High East Street, Dorchester (until 1973); see 'The Dance at the Phoenix' (*WP*, *CP*, 43–8). *DCC* reports that 'the Court, in consideration of [Thomas Amey's] former good character, were disposed to treat him with lenity, and he was therefore sentenced to imprisonment for one fortnight'. See also item 81b for a further report of the fracas between the Bockhampton band and Fordington mummers on Christmas Eve 1827.

79c

<u>The 4ᵗʰ Royal Irish Dragoon Guards</u> – very popular in D...Balls &c. Mrs...gives

a grand ball & supper to the officers, & other ladies & gentⁿ. The band serenade the officers at their lodgings in the town New Year's morn.   ib. passim.

Source: *DCC*, 3 January 1828, p.4, col.1 and *DCC*, 17 January 1828, p.4, col.4.
Note: TH has conflated two reports. *Mrs*: Mrs Bayles-Wardel.

79d–[p.80]

<u>On highway</u>. Mr B. of Bridgwater attacked – eveng – 2 fellows – one seized h.

by bridle – other laid hold of stirrup-leather & with many imprec^{ns} demanded money. //

Mr B. freed himself fr. former by striking him across arm – then spurring his

horse dragged latter consid^{ble} dist^{ce} until disengaged by stirrup giving way.   ib.

Source: *DCC*, 17 January 1828, p.4, col.4.
Note: *Mr B.*: Mr Blackford. *Bridgwater*: town in Somerset.

80a

Man walking home at night falls over a man lying across road: the latter turns

out to be drunk: the former, having dislocated shoulder by fall, lies there.   ib.

Source: *DCC*, 17 January 1828, p.4, col.4.

80b

                                                                        "Dk of Wellington"
<u>Coaches Antelope</u>, Dor. "Royal Clarence". "Magnet" – London. "Toms's ʌ Bath

& Weyth. Tu. Th. & Sat. 9 a.m. to B. Mon. W. Sat. 5 p.m to W.

"John Bull" Bath & Weyth M. W. F. 9^1/$_2$ a.m. to B.: ret. Tu W. & Sat. 5. p.m.

The "Independent" South^m & Wey^h M.W. F^r 9 a.m. up (via Wareham &c) T.Th. S 5^1/$_2$ pm
                                                                        down.   ib.

Source: *DCC*, 24 January 1828, p.1, col.3.
Note: a conflation of two notices in the same column. *Antelope*: a major Dorchester coaching-inn, at N. end of Cornhill; it continued to trade as an inn/hotel until the 1990s. '*Royal Clarence*', '*Magnet*': coach names.

80c

Fast Coach. said to have changed horses in 34 seconds – no less than 7 persons engaged in

the operation – ib.

Source: *DCC*, 24 January 1828, p.2, col.5.

80d

& keeping the Kings Head
Coach. Action by coach proprietor, residing at ʌ Thatcham, on road Bath to London.

Def.ᵗ is proprietor of York House Bath. & is also coach proprietor. Plff has stabling

behind him for 100 horses, & being abᵗ retire fr. business he disposed of his shares

in the Regulator, Express, Defiance & Marlb. Sⁿ coaches for the considⁿ of £2250,

with the condⁿ that the coaches shᵈ stop as heretofore at Kings Hᵈ & give time to

passʳˢ to breakfast dine or sup. Breach of contrᶜᵗ was that no longer stopped

– inn & stabling greatly reduced in value – defence, accomⁿ bad. Verd. plff d. £800

Source: *DCC*, 24 January 1828, p.2, col.4.
Note *Marlb. Sⁿ*: DCC has 'Malborough coaches, as well as a branch coach to Swindon'. *Verd* …
£800: verdict for plaintiff with damages of £800.

80e

Ring, containing watch – wh. struck hours on finger of wearer – worn by Anne of Denᵏ.

Feb 21. ib. //

Source: 'Mechanism', *DCC*, 21 February 1828, p.2, col.1.
Note: *Anne of Denᵏ*: Anne of Denmark (1574–1619), married to James VI of Scotland, later James
I of England.

81a

Lady escapes detectives. "Bow St. officers outwitted" – they come down to country village where she has taken cottage – she sees them from w^w answers

door (slipping on cap) saying that the lady is not at home – steps out at back, leaving

them in parlour...they see her in street – she slips into a boarding h. where unk^n

& says she is followed by two suspicious looking men – shelter her – they are shown in

when they inquire for her describing dress – room empty.   ib. Jan 24. 28.

Source: *DCC*, 24 January 1828, p.3, col.3.
Note: *(slipping on cap)*: TH's addition.

81b

Bock^n Band – Ford^n Mummers. Jno.Lock, Joseph Lucas Jas Burt & Geo

Burt were indicted (Dorset Epiphany Sess^{ns}) for creating a riot on 24th Dec

(1827) & assaulting James Keats & Wm Keats. Hostility between Fording^n mummers

& B. Band because the latter had sprung up as rivals to former, & plucked

from them a portion of their laurels, & profits. This hostility ripened till on

Xmas eve it reached to what may be termed a "battle royal".

Jas. Keats sworn: Is one of the B. band: knows Lucas & G.B.: they were

with the mummers on Xmas Eve. J.L. & Jas B. are Ford^n mummers. About

10, witness was passing between Swan B^{ge} & Greys B^{ge} with rest of band,

quietly homewards: followed by prisoners & a dozen others. Witness & a man

named H. were carrying the drum when L. came up, s^d he w^d break drum

& pulled off coat – wanting to fight. G.B. also wanted to fight H. Witness

& H. attempted to get away, but foll^d by whole of mum^s & others, amounting

~~then~~ to about 100 who came up & surrounded the band. Witness received a

severe blow on body, one on back of head, gash in foreh^d with sword – &c.

W.Keats, Chas K. & John H. corroborated, & proved assault on W.K.

Guilty of riot & assault. J.B. 6m. hard l. G.B. J.L^k & J.Lu. 3 m. hard l.

ib. Jan 24. 28. //

Text: the final two lines of this item are entered below the last ruled line of the page.

Source: 'Dorset Epiphany Sessions', *DCC*, 24 January 1828, p.4, col.2.

Note: *Jno.*: John Lock. *Jas. Keates*: James Keates (which TH has silently corrected from Joseph). *H.*: John Hardy, TH's uncle (see item 79b). William Keates is referred to by TH in item 64d (see *Millgate, 1982*, 24, 61). William, James and Charles Keates were near neighbours of the Hardys in Higher Bockhampton. *Swan^{bdg}*, *Grey's ^{bdg}* are the two bridges to the east of Dorchester, the Swan (or Town) bridge is at the entrance to the town, whereas Grey's bridge is a stone bridge within the town boundary but further east – 'fairly in the meadows', along the London road (see *Mayor, 1987*, 223). *L.*: Lucas. *hard l.*: hard labour. *Dorset Epiphany Sessions*: the court of justices for the County of Dorset, meeting at Epiphany, i.e. 12 days after Christmas, presided over by the liberal-minded magistrate, D. Parry Okeden of Turnworth, Dorset. This *DCC* report is reproduced verbatim by Millgate who describes it as 'a historical episode of which [TH] had apparently been unaware at the time of writing *Under the Greenwood Tree*' (in 1871) (*Millgate, 1971*, 59–60), but it is virtually certain that TH had known about this incident since boyhood; he indirectly alludes to it in conversation with William Archer in 1901 when he recalled that 'sometimes the mummers of one village would encroach on the traditional "sphere of influence" of another village, and then there would be a battle in earnest' (William Archer, 'Conversations with Mr Thomas Hardy', *THFH*, iii, 27–50 (p.35).) With its two bridges and two 'bands' of men, this item is suggestive of the carefully observed socially differentiated groups of working people in *The Mayor of Casterbridge* (see, in particular, chs 32, 36 and 39). See also item 79b. This item is cited by Cullen Brown (*Cullen Brown*, 266).

82a

New Year.

Admiston Hall. Jas. G. Balston Esq. ʌ 100 persons from neighb^g villages

sitting round his hospitable board...country dancing kept up...fine old

fashioned hall in wh. they were assembled...Repast over, music's strains again

summoned the happy villagers to join the mazy dance...late hour. ib. Jan 31. 28

J.G.B. kept mistress ⁄ & children at New Mill cottage. Mrs Beasant was one – she had
(– Dibbin by name)   "a fortune" from her father –

Text: *J.G.B. ... from her father*: in pencil. There are two vertical parallel lines (in pencil) beside this item.

Source: *DCC*, 31 January 1828, p.4, col.3.

Note: *Admiston Hall*: Athelhampton House, near Puddletown, Dorset, variously known locally as 'Admiston' or 'Adminston' (as in *DCC*), a 15th-century manor house well known to the Hardys; from the 17th century it was owned by the Longs of Draycot, Wiltshire. For its ownership by William Wellesley, nephew of the Duke of Wellington (through his marriage with Catherine Tylney-Long in 1812) see note to item 59b. *J.G.B. ... from her father*: an insertion by TH in pencil. *Jas. G. Balston*: a well-to-do farmer and tenant at Athelhampton. In 1798 he was listed as 'yeoman' in the Dorset Militia (Index to *Dorset Militia Ballot Lists 1757–1799*, 2 vols (Somerset and Dorset Family History Society, 1999), ii, 19). His 'great hospitality' at Athelhampton was recalled by Lucia Boswell-Stone, *Memories and Traditions* (London: Richard Clay, 1895), p.47. TH's interpolations on Balston, his mistress and their daughter, imply a long-standing familiarity amongst the Hardys (transmitted to TH), with Balston's tenancy of Athelhampton, as well as with the Wellesley connexion. This item is a source for TH's story 'The Waiting Supper', written by the end of 1887. He placed some of its action at Athelhampton, first referred to as 'Eldhampton Hall', and later, in the revision of 1913, as 'Athelhall'. The 'fine old-fashioned hall' of *DCC* appears as the 'fine open-timbered' roofed hall in the first version of the story (*CS*, 556). James Balston was a tenant of the Longs at Athelhampton. In 'The Waiting Supper', Christine Everard marries a James Belston whilst her true lover is Nick Long. She steers her inexpert partner, Belston, through the 'maze' of the dance (559), which had been 'mazy' in *DCC*. *New Mill cottage*: in Puddletown.

82b

Whipped – Ambrose Whitmarsh, Shaftesbury – stealing quantity of potatoes – one

month (at Epiphany sessions) & once whipped. Was whipped in the Park at

Shaftesbury, 2000 spectators being present.   ib. Feb 6. 28.

Source: *DCC*, 24 January 1828, p.4, cols 2–3 and *DCC*, 7 February 1828, p.4, col.1.
Note: this is a conflation of two reports. See also items 41b, 94c, 144d, 158a.

82c

New Theatre (built by Curme) opened [in North Square Dorchester?] Feb 25. 28

on a Monday, by Mr Lee, with the play of "John Bull" –   ib. Feb 28. 28

Text: there is no space between this and the following item (82d).
Source: *DCC*, 28 February 1828, p.4, cols 1–2.
Note: (*built by Curme*); [*in North Square Dorchester?*]: TH's interpolations. *Lee*: Henry Lee (1765–1836), theatre manager and impresario, connected with Dorset playhouses since the early 1790s, and author of *Memoirs of a Manager; or Life's Stage with New Scenes*, 2 vols. (Taunton: W. Bragg, 1830). *John Bull* was a comedy by George Colman the younger (1762–1836), produced 1803, published 1805. Charles Curme, the architect son of Curme, a builder, had financed the building of the theatre himself (*DCC*, 13 December 1827, p.4, col.2). The location of this theatre

of 1828 (known as the Loyalty Theatre) is unlikely to have been in North Square. It was most probably situated behind the S. side of High West Street, just E. of Trinity Street, on a site which from the 1880s until as late as WW2, was occupied by Messrs T. Godwin, china merchants. TH repeated the error during the course of three contributions (over the pseudonym 'History') to a correspondence in *DCC* (May–July 1902); see *Life and Work*, 340; *Public Voice*, 176–80. The question was debated as to the site of the Dorchester theatre in which Edmund Kean performed in 1813. TH remained convinced that Kean had played at the High West Street site (see his letter to Harley Granville Barker, 28 April 1924 (*CL*, vi, 248); see also Khinlyn Fern, 'Visitors' Book for the Loyalty Theatre, Dorchester', *PDNHAS*, 121 (1999): 145–50). However A.M. Broadley was able to establish in 1912 that there was another theatre in North Square erected for Henry Lee by Henning, which preceded the Loyalty Theatre ('Dorchester and Its Theatres: A Satisfactory Solution', *DCC*, 7 March 1912, p.14, cols 1–2), pasted in by TH as item [219]a; see also items [217]a, [217]b, [218]a, [218]b. The most thorough account of the Dorchester theatre to date is by Ann Sheridan, 'Circuit theatres in Dorchester and Bridport, 1793–1843', *Theatre Notebook*, 53 (1) (1999): 19–40, where she suggests that 'Henry Lee's second Dorchester theatre (at North Square) remains the most likely venue for Edmund Kean's performance' (p.29).

82d

"The celebrated Miss Foote" engaged during March – she plays the part of

Letitia Hardy in the Belle's Stratagem – Rosalind – &c.   ib. March.

Source: *DCC*, 20 March 1828, p.4, col.4.
Note: *Miss Foote*: Maria Foote (1797?–1867), actress, later Countess of Harrington. *Belle's Stratagem*: by Mrs Hannah Cowley (1743–1809), first produced, Covent Garden, 1780, published, 1782. This play is one of a list of plays and comic operas of the period entered (by ELH) in *Trumpet-Major Notebook*, p.76, (*PN*, 162). Henry Lee engaged Miss Foot for three nights, 13–15 March 1828: she acted in *Belle's Stratagem* and *The Weathercock* on the 13th, she 'personated' Rosalind and Zephyrina on the 14th and Violante and Muggy McGilpin on the 15th. The following year *DCC* reports that Miss Foote is 'traversing the provinces with her usual success', playing to 'crowded houses' at Leamington and Derby (*DCC*, 20 August 1829, p.2, col.3).

82e

Wrestling – Wrestlers from all parts – commence Easter Tu. & continue 3

days – Devonshire against the northern counties (the matches to take place at

Leeds.) Among the Devon men are the giant Jordan & Cann the champion.

Wrestling will t. place on stage 5½ ft. from ground & covered with turf.

Restaurateurs will pitch tents &c.   ib. Ap. 3. 28

Source: *DCC*, 3 April 1828, p.4, col.4.
Note: see also items 54d, 106d. Cann and a brother, James, wrestled in London later that month (see note to item 54d). This event took place in Haigh Park, Leeds.

82f

<u>Long engagem^t</u> Scotch youth & damsel (Elgin) – attachment – 1794 – separated &

marriage forbidden by their relations. Ten years passed; union again nearly achieved,

when doomed to disapp^t. Twenty more years – mutually constant, & in uninterrupted

corresp^{ce}. Then married. W^d it not have been better to wait till death &c.   ib. 10. //

Source: *DCC*, 10 April 1828, p.2, col.2.
Note: *W^d... death &c*: additional comment by *DCC* (not by TH). This item is a probable source of TH's story 'The Waiting Supper' (*CMT*) (see *Brady*, 179–80); see also TH's 'Long Plighted' (*PPP*, *CP*, 140).

83a

<u>Women's War</u> – Miss Hamerton, mill^r & dress^r Cheltenham charged

with robbing Miss Davis her lodger. Asserted her innocence, & made counter-

charge – in conseq. latter committed House of Correction. Subseq. informⁿ how^r

induced police to apprehend Miss H. again. Tried for robbery of her old lodger

– 7 years – During trial pleaded her innocence, but in vain: hung herself

in Gaol night after trial. She was an interesting young woman, consider^{ble}

beauty – & respect^{bly} connected. (vide post)   ib. Ap^l. 17. 28

Source: 'Fatal Effects of Despair', *DCC*, 17 April 1828, p.3, col.4.
Note: *7 years*: i.e. seven years' transportation. *vide post*: refers to item 93b which summarizes a charge against Miss Davis by Miss Hammerton, pursued even though she was dead.

83b

<u>Turning out of house</u>. Village of Littleton Drew. Wilts – Robt Browne had

lived in house more than 9 yrs. & only paid land^d £6 – yearly rent being £10.

Landl^d wished naturally to get him out – told him if he w^d pay 1 yr's r. & leave

he w^d give him remain^r. B. w^d not: then l. offered to cancel the whole if

w^d quit within a week; rejected by B. Land^d then took legal measures to

eject him, & after proceedings were instituted constable parish called assist

in exec^n of ejectment. Knowing his man, c. took 2 others: entering premises

B. met them with dagger – stabbed both men employed   ib.
[It transpires at trial that B. was enraged at seeing his wife put out of the house].

Source: 'Dreadful and Fatal Affray', *DCC*, 17 April 1828, p.3, col.4.
Note: *DCC* reports Browne's trial and conviction at the Wiltshire Assizes (31 July 1828, p.3, col.4).
[It transpires … house]: TH's addition.

83c

Cider trade – 12,00 hhds. cider shipped last week at Torquay for London

Dublin, Brighton, South^n & Yarmouth.

Source: *DCC*, 17 April 1828, p.3, col.4.
Note: *12,00*: *DCC* has '1200'. *hhds.*: hogsheads, casks for holding liquor to the liquid measure of 52.5 gallons.

83d

Enmity – A young man's term as tenant comes to an end – he finds that his

enemy has taken lease of property to succeed him: on that account he will

not turn out – & a scuffle ensues –   June 5. ib. //

Source: *DCC*, 5 June 1828, p.3, col.2.

84a

The farmer – Honest Essex farmer attended Rumford Market – met person who claimed his acq^{ce} & mentioned circ^s that convinced farmer must have

met before. The farmer sold his beasts, retired with his old acq^{ce} to a p.house

drank freely tog^r & both proceeded on their respective horses tow^{ds} Chelmsf^d.

On road stopped to bait horses – more to drink – farmer too much inebriated

to proceed further that night. Slept in a double bedded room – early in

morning, farmer still asleep, friend dressed himself in his clothes, in

the pockets of wh. was his money, paid expenses, proceeded to stable, &

was ready to mount farmer's horse, worth 40gs. leaving his old animal.

Just as leaving f. awoke, finding friend, money & clothes gone, got hastily

up in clothes left for him, & came down to prevent escape of other. Knave

succeeded in convincing landlord & servants that the f. was impostor (both

being strangers.) The villain proposed they sh^d ride together to Chelmsf^d

where his identity c^d be proved. Farmer perforce agreed, & mounted knave's

old horse. On way it became so lame (the thief having driven nail in

foot), that it c^d scarcely walk, thief applied spur & escaped.   ib. Ap.^{l} 24.28

Source: 'Most impudent Robbery', *DCC*, 24 April 1828, p.3, col.2.
Note: *Rumford*: now modern Romford, Essex. *bait*: to give fodder and water to a horse on a journey. See also item 97a, and the alternative ending to 'Incident in the Life of Mr George Crookhill' (*LLI*) (Ray, 253–5).

84b

<u>Winning horse, or favourite, roasted alive</u> – Stable – night before race – doing

up the horses the boy had ignited straw with candle – horse seen enveloped

in flames on opening stable door –   ib.

Source: *DCC*, 24 April 1828, p.3, col.2.
Note: *DCC* reports the horse 'entered for the great handicap gold cup at Liverpool'.

84c

<u>Eccentric farmer</u>. Friend to vermin: 60 rats seen feeding at his pig-troughs:

& he kept up a hot-bed of manure for snakes.   ib. May 1.28 //

Source: 'Singular Taste', *DCC*, 1 May 1828, p.3, col.4.

85a

<u>Cider</u> – Prospect of a poor crop of apples – price of cider rapidly advancing –   ib.
    1000 hhd[s] retailed in Yeovil in 6 weeks.

Source: *DCC*, 1 May 1828, p.3, col.4.
Note: *hhd[s]*: hogsheads, see item 83c; *1000 hhd[s] ... weeks*: does not appear in this *DCC* report.

85b

<u>Murder of Maria Martin</u> – Corder, with whom she had been intimate, induced

her to meet him, in male attire, at a barn of his, called the red barn – that

they might go on to Ipswich & be married. She went, & was never afterwards

seen. Her mother had a dream that the girl was buried in the barn – search,

& the body was found. Corder was apprehended at his house at Ealing,

n[r] London – had married a young wife whom he obtained by adv[t]. They

kept a ladies boarding school. On officers' arrival he was found in parlour

with 4 ladies at breakfast, in dressing gown, & had a watch before him by
       'minuting'
which he was ~~timing~~ the boiling of some eggs.

Source: *DCC*, 1 May 1828, p.3, col.2.
Note: there are further reports in *DCC*, 15 May, 1828, p.3, col.2; *DCC*, 14 August 1828, p.2, cols 3–5 (sentencing of Corder). *Maria Martin*: Maria Marten 'of the Red Barn', victim of the notorious murder, May 1827 and the subject of a famous melodrama. *Corder*: William Corder (1804–28) was tried and executed at Bury St Edmunds, Suffolk, August 1828. See also item 137b.

85c

Fire – Merry making of villagers in a barn, Cornwall – candle falls unobserved

through chink in floor – barn burnt down &c.   ib. May 8 28

Source: *DCC*, 8 May 1828, p.3, col.4.
Note: there were no human fatalities, but four cows were burnt to death.

85d

22 Uncles – young man's funeral attended by.   ib.

Source: *DCC*, 15 May 1828, p.3, col.3.
Note: the man was John Bayley of the Castle Inn. 'His remains were attended to the family vault at Whatley [a village, W. of Frome, Somerset], by twenty-two uncles'.

85e

Wife drowned in a brook, quite near her husband, who, however, was unconscious

of her danger until ~~lost~~ too late. Nevertheless he is looked on with suspicion –

which preyed so much upon his mind that he destroyed himself.   ib. June 5. 28.

Text: there is a single vertical line (red pencil) beside this item.
Source: *DCC*, 5 June 1828, p.3 col.2.
Note: *DCC* reports that 'several malignant reports were … circulated against him'.

85f–[86]

40:
Guilty wife – White, baker, Southampton ʌ informed that his friend & neighb[r]

Macdonald, 23, is too intimate with his wife, 35. Doubting the fact, yet unhappy   //

at the report, he determined if possible to ascertain truth. Told wife he was

going some distance, & sh[d] not return till late. Went out, privately got back

secreted himself in lumber room behind parlour, boring hole through part[n]

with gimlet. Here he remained 3 h[rs] & was witness to his worst susp[ns].

As M. left W. stabbed him in neck, & he died. Manslaughter. Heavy

Rain at M's funeral – but 1000 spect^{rs}, & his mother fell in a fit. The

woman least concerned, occasionally showing herself at shop door.   ib. July 3.28.

Text: there is a single vertical line (red pencil) beside the first two lines of this item.
Source: 'Shocking Affair', *DCC*, 3 July 1828, p.3, col.3.

86a

<u>At a party</u> – Ann Morris, fine young woman of 18, at wedding party at the

Castle Inn Blackburn – remained till 3 in morning dancing, music being

rendered by Hughes, 67th foot, who played on his bugle, having obtained permission

of commanding officer. It is not known if he became acquainted with her during

the evening. She left the Castle, accomp. by $\wedge$ other y. women (they were all

factory girls) & went towards her lodgings. They agreed that as it was

late they w^d not go to bed, but w^d change clothes, & then w^d be ready begin

work in factory: the two having done this they went to Ann's lodgings; but she

had not changed her clothes, & they found her crying in yard. Inquired cause

of her grief, but she did not return satisf^y answer. All three then went out

tog^r to have a walk before they began work, & as they passed through the street

they met the bugleman, who spoke to Ann, & after some conv^n walked with

her into the fields, leaving the other two (who saw no more of her: he & she were

afterw^{ds} seen by canal by other persons – he with arm round her neck, she struggling

to get away: seen floating in canal, he running off; took his red jacket off...)

                                                    ib. July 31.28 //

Source: 'Mysterious Occurrence', *DCC*, 31 July 1828, p.2, col.5.

87a

Magistrates 1828. Sir J.W.Smith: Sir R.C.Glyn: Sir M.H.Nepean: Archdeacon

England: H.Bankes: W.J.Bankes: F.J.Browne: J.H.Browne: T.B.Bower:

J.Bragge: T.H.Bastard: J.B.Garland: R.P.Glyn: G.T.Jacob: B.L.Lester:

J.Michell: W.M.Pitt: E.M.Pleydell: W.Pitt: H.Seymer: C.B.Wollaston:

R.Williams: Revd H.F.Yeatman:

Grand Jury – Most of the above. & C.Spurrier: T.Banger: Aug^s Foster.

Source: 'Dorset Summer Assizes', *DCC*, 31 July 1828, p.3, col.1.
Note: this report of the Dorset magistracy in the 1820s, one of many in *DCC*, is representative of the bench of the time, drawn almost exclusively from the landed and propertied families, including not only the old-established gentry like Browne of Frampton, and the more recently landed families, such as the Glyns, but also the Anglican clergy such as Archdeacon England and the Revd Henry Farr Yeatman, the lawyer, C.B. Wollaston (half-brother of the landlord and magistrate James Frampton) and Benjamin Lester, a wealthy Poole Newfoundland trader. *Grand Jury*: substantially the body of magistrates for the county to whom the judge's charge was addressed at the opening of the Assizes, and whose function it was to determine whether there were cases to answer.

87b

The bay gelding – white streak on face & on white leg. Saw him in stable at $^1/_2$ p.

10 at night, missed him next morning about $^1/_4$ p.4. (Farmer Dean's evidence). Carrier

Grayer says he met prisoner leading a horse, & bought it of him in p.house near

Salisbury. Good char^r given prisoner – sentence of death recorded.   ib. July 31:28

Source: *DCC*, 31 July 1828, p.3, col.1.
Note: *DCC* reports that the judge told the prisoner that 'his case should be taken into consideration', i.e. a possible reprieve.

87c

Going to Hang-fair – Three young men of Bridport walk to Dor. to see man

hanged, & steal money from warehouse of sack manuf^{rs} to pay expenses. A great deal of it is in <u>copper</u>, & they bury it.   ib.

Source: *DCC*, 31 July 1828, p.3, col.2.
Note: *Hang-fair*: a fair held at a time of a public execution. In 'The Withered Arm', Gertrude Lodge is thought to come to Casterbridge for 'hang-fair' (*CS*, 66), see also *The Woodlanders* (*Woodlanders*, 1985, 57). *Three young men ... steal money*: one man was given 14 years, the other two were given seven years' transportation each.

87d

<u>Cutting out panel of door</u> – to effect entry.   ib.

Source: *DCC*, 31 July 1828, p.3, col.2.

87e–[p.88]

<u>Imposture – well done</u> "Bath. 21 Feb 1828. ⌊ The bearer, Lieut. Henry Treymayne

a retired officer was with his wife & 6 ch. late occup^g apart^{ts} at Mr K's brother,

when the melancholy fire at 3 o'c. on morn^g Xmas day wh. commenced at York House

& included in its destr^{ve} career the adj. premises, whereby Lieut. Tremayne lost the

whole of his furniture, & all the wearing app^l of his helpless fam, wh., together with   //

a large sum in bills wh. he had withdrawn from the funds to fulfil his agreement

for purchase of small freehold mansion in this neigh^d on Thursday following

which the whole of his losses exceeded five thousand pounds – ⌊ We undersigned

being 2 of HM's J. of the peace for City of Bath & C. of Somerset have investig^d

the above case, wh. proves Lieut Treymayne perf^{ly} correct: we therefore strongly

recommend his unfort^{te} situ^n to those who may be humanely inclined to

assist the really deserving & unfortunate.   G.H.T / Chas. C.

   The bearer of the above called on gentleman in adjoining county – &

obtained money...14 y^{rs} transp. (for this & another offence). July 31. 28.

Source; 'Obtaining Money under false Pretences', *DCC*, 31 July 1828, p.3, cols 3–4.
Note: *K*: Knight. *G.H.T* / *Chas. C.*: George Hayward Tugwell and Charles Crook, Bath magistrates.

88a

<u>Poor Law</u> – Agric. servants &c, who live 12 months with a master, if single

must almost for certain gain a settlement, whether born there or not, or else the

farmer must be under the necessity of discharging before the end of year, or

resort to some subterfuge.   ib.

Source: *DCC*, 31 July, 1828, p.4, col.3.
Note: *settlement*: right to parish relief based on evidence of residence. This item is 'From a Correspondent' who discounts anxieties about a clause in a Bill on the Poor Laws, currently before Parliament, which prevents a man 'gaining a settlement by servitude or hiring'.

88b

<u>Coach struck by Lightning</u>. Burton-in-Kendal – scene awful – gent[n] sitting on

hind part of coach opposite a lady, whom he asked to lower her umbrella (probably

the object of attraction) On recovering from shock, wh threw him from seat, the first

object...view...was lady hanging backwards, countenance livid, no animation,

bonnet, cap, gown &c burnt – umbrella shivered to atoms – flesh torn from her

thighs – no hope of her recovery. 2 wheel horses & off-side leader killed – driver

& guard unhurt.   from Kendal Chron.   ib. Aug 21.28. //

Source: *DCC*, 21 August 1828, p.2, col.1.
Note: *Burton-in-Kendal*: village between Lancaster and Kendal, in Cumbria. *wheel horses*: horses nearest the carriage wheels.

89a

Horse purchase – Bristol fair – saw a delightful animal £40... ~~got home~~ $\wedge$ after ‹an hour or so›

One said "look at his hock, sir; there's something like a pudding." Another "why look

sir, his hock is as big as his head sh^d be." Reaching Somerton on way home

& being anxious to have the opinion of the ostler, asked him what he thought of

his horse. "Oh, sir," s^d ostler looking at him knowingly "there's only a screw

loose." Others told him it w^d not last above 3 months.   ib.

Source: 'French v King', *DCC*, 21 August 1828, p.3, col.3.

89b

Poisoned by mushrooms – gathered in a shady lane under trees – father & son ate

heartily – 5 hrs after, sick & uncomfortable, then vomiting & purging – convulsions

– death, former in 46 latter in 36 hrs. – medical aid not called in till the poison

had taken effect.   ib.

Source: *DCC*, 21 August 1828, p.4, col.2.

89c

Finding Bank note. Journeyman brickl^r passing along road to Sydenham fr.

Greenwich – piece of paper on some road stuff beside path. Two persons ahead must

have passed the spot. To his utter aston^t £1000 B. of E. note, nearly new, & with^t

endorsement or other mark upon it. Went to work with the treasure in pocket; in

even^g mentioned it to some respec^ble persons; who advised him to take it to the

Bank – did so next day – explained how he came possessed of it. He was desired

to leave note with cashier, that necess^y steps might be taken to find owner: if identified, he w^d be entitled to a salvage of $^1/_8$th if not claimed in 12 months

he would have it returned. No claimant has yet come forw^d. Meanwhile a defaulter

clerk at Greenwich Hospital is missing – He has been in the habit of lending money

to various persons &c.   ib. Sept. 4. 28. //

Source: *DCC*, 4 September 1828, p.2, col.3.

90a

Regent Street beauty – Miss Verrey, the Swiss confectioner's daughter whose personal

attractions have been so mischievously exaggerated, died of fever on the M. evening,

brought on by the annoyance she had been for sometime subject to – Only 17. –
Buried at St Georges, burying-ground, Bayswater – body attempted by resurrectionists.
                                                              ib. Oct 16. 28

Source: 'The Regent-Street Beauty', *DCC*, 16 October 1828, p.2, col.3.
Note: *Buried … resurrectionists*: not in *DCC*; this is evidently a later addition by TH. *resurrectionists*: body-snatchers; see item 192e. *St George's*: St George's, Hanover Square which owned a burying ground in Bayswater, W. London. This item is the source for TH's 'The Beauty' (*LLE*, *CP*, 616–17; *CPW*, ii. 513–14). His note to the poem is identical with this 'Facts' entry up to the point of 'sometime subject to', but omits 'Only 17' and adds 'London paper, October 1828'. This was correct in so far as the report derived from a London newspaper, but it had been read by TH in *DCC*.

90b

Multitudinous murders – There is in one of the prisons at Bremen a

female in bloom of youth & very handsome, charged with having poisoned 65 persons

amongst whom were three husbands & five lovers. The motives of those crimes

were love jealousy amb^n or avarice. One was a physician, who having pro-

nounced the cause of death in victim was himself poisoned next day. Poison

found concealed in the hairpapers of her head. Courrier des Tribunaux   ib.

Source: *DCC*, 16 October 1828, p.2. col.3.

90c

<u>Silk cloak stolen</u> – Mrs Bridge calls on J.J.Lambert Esq. Dorchester, &

leaves her silk cloak in the hall. Man steals it & takes it to Reynolds the

pawnbroker to be pledged. ib.

Source: *DCC*, 16 October 1828, p.4, col.2.

90d

<u>Book Hawker</u> – carries a pack: at Beaminster offers books for sale at

the Greyhound – man does not want the books he shows, but a Ready Reckoner –

Hawker produces the R.R. – he was from Exeter. ib.

Source: *DCC*, 23 October 1828, p.3, col.2.
Note: this is a successful appeal against conviction under the Hawker's and Pedlar's Act for trading
without a licence.

90e

                    – (in out of the way villages) –
Illicit cider shops ⋏ selling cider without licence – £10 fine. ib.

Source: *DCC*, 23 October 1828, p.4, col.4.
Note: *(in out of the way villages)*: TH's addition. See item 167f.

90f

<u>Wife deserts husband</u> for another man – is, in turn, abandoned by him –

poisons herself – was wife of resp[ble] stonemason of Colchester.   Nov 6. 28.   //

Source: *DCC*, 6 November 1828, p.2, col.4.
Note: *DCC* speaks of her 'fit of despair at her destitute situation'.

91a

<u>A General robbed</u> by 2 nephews of his wife, of gold coins – ib.

Source: *DCC*, 6 November 1828, p.2, col.4.

91b

Field of Waterloo, few days after battle – desc. by Rev[d] D[r] Rudge, F.R.S. Rector

of Hawkchurch.   ib. Nov 6. 28.

Source: *DCC*, 6 November 1828, p.2, cols 2–3.
Note: *Rev[d] D[r] Rudge*: James Horace Rudge (1785–1852), rector of Hawkchurch, a village then in
Dorset, now in E. Devon. Rudge writes of the 'house and garden of Hougoumont where the battle
commenced', now 'in a state of ruin' ('Original Correspondence: Description of the Field of
Waterloo by James Rudge'). Although not printed until 1828, Rudge's account, in a letter to a
friend, was written in Brussels a 'few days after the battle'.

91c

J.Abbott, labouring under impression of his wife's inconstancy, cuts her throat;

but she does not die. At his trial she comes forw[d] & with great earnestness,

pleads for mercy for him. He faints in court.   ib.

Source: 'Old Bailey Sessions: Case of Abbott', *DCC*, 6 November 1828, p.2, col.5.

91d

Mail – accident to – soon after changing horses at Bagshot on way from. L.

to Dor. Morning extremely foggy & dark – horses bolted – ran away at full speed

for nearly 3 miles – no outside passenger – coach full inside – the glasses were let

down, & everyone kept his place expecting momentary destruction, as the coach was

freq. on 2 wheels for many yds. together. Coachman with presence of mind, ran

the 2 leaders against one of the large waggons going the same way: they fell,
                                                 one of
completely separated themselves from coach, wh. went over ʌ them – other was mutilated

much blood on ground: left them there, & coach proceeded with a pair. All night coaches liable to accident – reins broken in effort to stop. ib. Nov 13. 28

Source: *DCC*, 13 November 1828, p.4, col.2.
Note: TH was misled by the opening sentence of this item which referred to the coach from London; the report is of a coach travelling from Poole to London.

91e

<u>Group of pedestrians</u>, seemingly tramps, stop a carrier & ask if he carries

passengers – he refuses – they strike him, rob van &c.   ib.

Source: *DCC*, 13 November 1828, p.4, col.2.
Note: *Group of pedestrians, seemingly tramps*: this is TH's addition as *DCC* simply reports that the carrier was 'stopped by two men and a woman'.

91f–[p.92]

<u>Double-bedded room</u> – China-dealer returned to bed in room he shared with an   //

itinerant corn-extractor, at Half Moon Inn Sherborne. The latter did not

retire till between 12 & 1 – in the morning it was discovered that he had

decamped soon after retiring, leaving the house door open, taking watch,

seals, £16, & other property of his fellow lodger. The fellow is about 5/6

in height, with dark hair, & has lost 2 teeth in front.   ib.

Source: *DCC*, 13 November 1828, p.4, col.1.

92a

"<u>The King, & God bless him</u>" was drunk with enthusiasm, & 4 times 4 (Dinner)

Source: *DCC*, 13 November 1828, p.4, col.3.
Note: a Taunton dinner by the Constables of the Borough, the King's health being followed by 'the Duke of Clarence and other branches of the Royal Family, 3x3'.

92b

Cheese impostors – Two fellows on Monday offered for sale some worthless cheese

out of wh. they pretended to bore a sample, but substituted some of better quality.

They were all "young men with frocks, & travelled in a light green spring cart,

with a fierce bulldog."   ib.

Source: *DCC*, 13 November 1828, p.4, col.3.
Note: *frocks*: long coats.

92c

Burglar – Coxley Pound Inn, n^r Wells – stage waggon arrived at ¼ past 4.a.m.

driver rapped at door to arouse ostler for the purpose of taking the horses from

the waggon. The burglar, hearing the noise looked from the window, & was questioned

by the waggoner's lad if he was the ostler. He replied "Yes", & adroitly added

that if the boy w^d proceed to take out the horses he w^d come to his assistance

immediately. The boy proceeded to do this; the burglar jumped out of the

window [at back] to escape; tearing off a piece of the tail of his coat, &

dropping a tankard, silver, & taking another, with wh. he decamped.   ib. //

Source: *DCC*, 13 November 1828, p.4 col.3.
Note: *adroitly*; *[at back]*: TH's additions. *dropping … taking another*: DCC has 'taking with him
a new plated tankard, which he probably mistook for a silver one'.

93a

Bligh v Wellesley. (ante p.59) A letter from Paris states that Capt. Bligh,

the late husband of Mrs Helena Bligh (now Wellesley) died on the 15th ult.

at Valence, on his way to Nice.   ib. Nov. 20. 28.

[N.B. Capt. Bligh was an invalid – wife & he occupied separate rooms after but were fairly happy till   (abroad)

they had been married some little time – ʌW. met her at a friend's house ʌ &

an intimacy arose – he entering her room at night by wᵂ – she divorced.]

(vide post. p.120)

Text: (*vide post. p.120*): in pencil.
Source: *DCC*, 20 November 1828, p.2, col.5.
Note: [*N.B. Capt. Bligh … she divorced.*]: this passage is derived from the full report of 9 November 1826 (see 120e). See also items 59b, 59c, 59d, 59e.

93b–[p.94]

p.83

Women's War – (vide ante.) Mary Davis v. Capper – Action brought

against a magistrate of county of Gloucester for false imprisonment…

M. Davis, plff., was a woman in a decent situation in life: she boarded with

a young woman of the name of Hammerton in Cheltenham. She was in

receipt of a small income, & on the 20ᵗʰ Nov. last had shown her annuity

in a box to Miss H. The next night an alarm was given that the

house had been robbed & her box, containing notes & cash, stolen. No sus-

picion was entertained of Miss H. until some days after, when part

of the property stolen from the plff. was seen in her possession. Davis

then brought a charge against her before Mʳ Capper the magistrate,

& was bound over to appear at the sessions. Miss H. was convicted,

& the same night hanged herself. Mary Davis soon after went to

reside at house of a tradesman in Cheltenham; & the same evening

Russel, a police officer, took her in custody upon a charge of robbery

preferred by Miss Hammerton some time before the latter was found guilty.

When taken before the defendant (magistrate) it appeared that H. had   //

supported her charge by the production of a letter purporting to be written

to Mary Davis by an accomplice in the imputed robbery (of Miss Hamerton).

It turned out to be a fictitious letter, & was supposed to be the invention

of Miss H. Mr Capper asked the plff. who it came from: the old lady

said she did not know. The magistrate then observed that her memory would

be refreshed by a short residence in prison, & comm^{ted} her for further exam^n

for 14 days.   Action illegal &c   ib. Nov. 20. 28

Source: *DCC*, 20 November 1828, p.2, col.5.
Note: *(vide ante.)*: TH notes his earlier summary of this case on p.83 (item 83a).

94a

Going to draw water by candlelight &c.   ib.

Source: *DCC*, 20 November 1828, p.3, col.3.
Note: the report concerns two children going to a well for water; their candle blows out and one
of them falls into the well to his death.

94b

Lady returning to Cheltenham from Bath stopped at village of Oulpen –

her carriage being placed in a barn for security. In morning, door found

wrenched open, & the imperial of the carriage taken away, containing jewellery

&c, to the amount of £2000 – Imperial found in a wood, rifled of its contents

…In the boot of the carriage was £1000 worth of plate wh. escaped notice of

the depredators.   ib. Nov 20. 28

Source: 'Extensive Robbery', *DCC*, 20 November 1828, p.3, col.3.
Note: *Oulpen*: now Owlpen, near Stroud, Gloucestershire. *imperial*: a case or trunk for luggage,
usually to fit a carriage or coach.

94c

Great Fire at Cerne: <u>Man whipped at Sturm^r Newton</u> for stealing pigs: <u>trees planted</u>

from bottom of Dor. to G.Bridge & T.P.G. ib.

Source: *DCC*, 20 November 1828, p.4, col.1.
Note: this item appears to cover three separate reports from the same column of this edition of
DCC. *Cerne*: Cerne Abbas, Dorset. *Sturm^r Newton*: Sturminster Newton, Dorset. *G.Bridge*: Grey's
Bridge (see note to item 81b). *T.P.G.*: turnpike gate. See also items 41b, 82b, 144d, 158a.

94d

<u>Dorchester Tradesman's dinner</u>. Kings Arms (annually). Thos Gould Read Esq.
– Present Revd G.Wood. W.Elliot. J.Stone Cols Halyburton & Bower – Maj Garland &c
in chair ⋏ Toasted 'a native of the town who had greatly disting^d hims^f at Bat. of
Col. Bower who came
Waterloo where he was severely wounded – Major Garland. Also ~~ib. Dec 4. 28~~ who came
forw^d in time of danger, at head of Dorch^r Volunteers – The gall^t col. ret^d thanks: s^d honour conferred
upon them by late Maj^y when at Weyth by attending in person with mem^s of R.Fam. at consecration of their colours
a greater hon^r than had been conferred on any other vol. corps in kingdom. //

Source: 'Dorchester Annual Dinner', *DCC*, 4 December 1828, p.4, col.2.
Note: *Col. Bower*: see *Boswell-Stone*, 56–8. *late Maj^y*: George III. *DCC* reported the speeches made
at this dinner (for nearly a hundred guests) at length. The chairman, Thomas Gould Read, toasted
'Prosperity to the Town of Dorchester'. With 'pride and pleasure, he had long witnessed the gradual
and rising prosperity of his native town, which he attributed not only to the good conduct, industry
and exertions of the inhabitants, but to the harmony and unanimity in which they lived, and which
he sincerely hoped would long continue'. He 'proposed the "health of the King" with 4 times 4,
which was drunk with the greatest enthusiasm'. See *The Mayor of Casterbridge* (*Mayor, 1987*,
33–43). See also Millgate (*Millgate, 1971*, 238) and item 92a.

95a

<u>Advertisement</u> – "<u>A Blakeman</u>, with feelings of gratitude, returns her sincere

thanks to the Ladies of Weymouth & its vicinities, who have so very liberally

countenanced her since her first soliciting their Favours and begs to assure them

nothing shall be wanting on her part towards the continuance of that Patronage

which it will be her constant pride to merit. A. B. at the same time begs to say, she will be ready on Tuesday. Nov. 25. with a Fashionable Selection of <u>Parisian</u>

<u>& London Millinery Dress Cloak Models</u> &c. She would also particularly

direct the attention of Ladies to the last new mode in Velvet Hats, <u>likewise</u>

<u>are elegant new style of walking Bonnet, particularly adapted for Morning calls</u> &c.

Wanted immediately, an Improver & Indoor <u>Apprentice</u>. Four or

five <u>respectable</u> young persons could also be taken as out-door <u>Apprentices</u>."

Hand: ELH.
Source: *DCC*, 20 November 1828, p.1, col.2.

95b

<u>A Revd Gentleman of pugnacity</u>. Charged with an attempt to extort £2000 by sup-

pressing a work in the press in wh. the amours of Ld Plymouth were treated of. &c.

The Earl procured a warrant for apprehⁿ of Revd Gentⁿ – he was secured – conveyed

in chaise – allowed to walk some distance with constable, arm in arm. Knocked

down constable, swam the canal &c.   ib. Dec 18. 28

Source: 'Committal of a Clergyman', *DCC*, 18 December 1828, p.2, col.4.
Note: *a work*: the book in question contained details of 'amours of Plymouth and those of Lady Hamilton'. The clergyman was the Revd Heaton de Crespigny, who was eventually apprehended at Market Harborough, Leicestershire on the point of hiring a carriage to London; subsequently committed to Leicester gaol.

95c

<u>Lunatic who continually escaped</u> – a flat ring of iron prepared for him 6½"

across the outside, & 3½" in internal diameter – "Bodmin Lunatic asylum" deeply

engraved on it: it was case hardened, & secured with 4 counter sunk rivets

on his right ankle. With this on his leg he escaped.   ib. Jan 29. 29 //

Source: *DCC*, 29 January 1829, p.2, col.5.

Note: *DCC* refers to 'the ingenious lunatic James Parsons'.

96a

<u>Hoard</u> – Eliz[h] Warner, head chambermaid, King's Arms, Dor. having been of

economical habits, had amassed £200 in gold, wh. she kept in a small

box in her bedroom. Went to her hoard to change a ten-pound note, when

to her consternation money had disap[d]. Fellow-maid had married a private

5th Drag gd[s] lately, now stationed here – had slept in same room &c. Feb 5.29

<u>v. post</u> p.111

Source: *DCC*, 5 February 1829, p.4, col.1.
Note: see also item 111c.

96b

<u>Son of a farmer</u> marries widow of a labourer. He takes a dislike

to her, & she goes to service. He calls on her one evening to arrange

matters...she accompanied him into the grounds...he shot her (Ireland)

(It was deliberately done – he decoying her out on purpose).   Feb 26.29

Source: *DCC*, 26 February 1829, p.2, col.4.

96c

<u>Stranger in a white hat</u> enters tap room of inn, sits down & remains there

all day without calling for anything to eat or drink (He has no money).   ib.

Source: 'Death from Starvation', *DCC*, 26 February, 1829, p.4, col.3.
Note: *inn*: at Odd Down, Bath.

96d

"<u>Died</u>...At Swanwich, on the 15th, Dairyman Masters, aged 88 yrs, leaving behind him a numerous progeny, viz 9 sons & dau's; 8 sons & dau's in law,

49 grans[ns] & dau's, 11 g'sons & dau's in law: 21 g.g'son's & dau's: 2 g.g'sons

& daus in law; making in the aggregate 100 persons."   ib.

Source: *DCC*, 26 February 1829, p.4, col.3.
Note: *Swanwich*: older form of Swanage, Dorset, persisting well into the nineteenth-century.

96e

Dress 1829. Travellers (commerc[l]) Bk c[t] & waistc[t], crape hatband, drab

breeches & gaiters, age about 40. dark complex[n] A younger one, blue coat,

black waistc[t] drab breeches & gaiters, dark complex[n] full blk eyes. They had

a large bundle with them. (Teignmouth)   ib. //

Source: *DCC*, 5 March 1829, p.3, col.4.
Note: *Bk. c[t] & waistc[t]*: black coat and waistcoat. *They had a large bundle with them*: TH's words. This is not an item about fashion *c*. 1829, as TH treats it, but of two con-men on the run; the description of their clothes is designed to jog the memory of a *DCC* reader. This source contributes to a description of the clothing worn by Edmond Willowes in TH's 'Barbara of the House of Grebe' (*GND*): 'A blue coat, murrey waistcoat, and breeches of drab set off a figure that could scarcely be surpassed' (*CS*, 233).

97a

Gent[n] comes from Inn in Oxford St. intoxicated – falls down – is seen by the landl[d]

to be picked up by a soldier, & assisted on his way. Gent[n] reaches his house, in

company of soldier, who talks familiarly to half-senseless gent[n] before latter's family.

A bed is made up downstairs for the gent[n] & another in same room for soldier.

The ladies of the house then retire. Next morning the gent[n] is found dead – &

his clothes &c. are gone. Soldier taken into custody as a deserter the same day,

having on the clothes of Mr Neale (the gent[n]).   ib. Ap[l] 2. 1829

Text: there are two parallel lines (pencil) beside this item.

Source: 'Supposed Murder', *DCC*, 2 April 1829, p.3, col.2.
Note: see 'Incident in the Life of Mr George Crookhill' (*LLI*) (*Brady*, 149; *Ray*, 253–5). Ray cites an interesting alternative ending (at the foot of the final leaf of the MS) whose style is remarkably similar to a typical 'Facts' item and whose content has elements in common with item 84a; see also items 29e, 91f.

97b

<u>Stern irascible gamekeeper</u> – Pedlar trespassing: as he does not move off very

quickly (he had entered park to slide), the g.keeper s^d to deceased (pedlar) "What

is it you say, you saucy rascal?"&c. Took out the barrels from the stock of his

gun...Struck him with the double barrel, as he sat on the wall...blow fell on head,
 fracturing skull
& ⋏ killed pedlar...One of the party s^d to the keeper, "you have killed the man." He said,

"I hope not. I did not intend to hit him so hard." The g.keeper, in defence, admitted

that he did wrong in striking the man; that he had no intention of doing him an

injury. Good char^r – Transported for 7 y^{rs} .   ib.

Source: *DCC*, 2 April 1829, p.3, col.3.
Note: in the *DCC* report there are three people involved – the pedlar has an assistant who is killed by the gamekeeper. The pedlar is alive to give evidence against him.

97c–[p.105]

<u>Attempt to murder</u> – <u>William Kennedy</u>, aged 19, a private in the 5th Dragoon

Guards, quartered in Dorchester Barracks, was placed at the bar, charged with

shooting at the Rev Henry Willoughby, on the night of Friday the 28th November

with intent to murder him.

Mr Barstow for the prosecution, addressed the jury, stating the circumstances

of the case, & then proceeded to call the following witnesses.   //

"The Rev. Henry Philip Willoughby: – I am a clergyman, residing at Dorchester:

on Friday 28th Nov. last, I dined with my brother at Weymouth, & was returning

home in the evening on a light grey horse. The horse walked nearly the whole distance;

on arriving at the top of Ridgway hill I perceived a man walking on the left-hand

side of the way. I was also on the left-hand side; when I came up to him I turned a

little to the right; he stepped forward & without saying a word fired a pistol.

My body was inclined towards him for a short time which enabled me to see

from the flash of his pistol, that he wore the dress of a soldier. I distinctly

saw a red jacket with a dark collar, but the light was so momentary

that I could not discover his countenance. The instrument he held in his

hand had a great deal of brass on it. I felt myself wounded; & my horse

being terrified, galloped towards Dorchester with such speed that I do not

think more than a quarter of an hour could have elapsed before I arrived

at Dorchester which was about a quarter before ten.

By the Court – The light as so instantaneous that I could not ascertain

whether the instrument used was a pistol or a carbine. I left my brother's

about half past eight. It was very dark. I was much exhausted from

the wound.

Mary Purchase – I was with the prisoner on the night of ~~the~~ Nov. 28, and

left him a little after eight. I heard the barrack-trumpet sound about

seven o'clock; & asked him if he was not going to the stable; he said he

had a pass & should not go in until 4 o'clock in the morning.

M[r] Jas. Devenish – I live at Weymouth, & was travelling on the   //

Magnet Coach from Dorchester to Weymouth on the night of Friday the 28 Nov.

I was on the box: the coach had lamps. On arriving at Moncton Hill I saw

a soldier standing in the road in the uniform of the 5th Dragoon Guards, a

part of which regiment is quartered at Weymouth. I particularly noticed the

yellow stripe down the trousers. The time there was a little after nine. The

coach arrived at Weymouth about ten.

Thomas Gaulton – I am a carrier between Dorchester & Weymouth. I remember

being on the road on the night of Friday 28. Nov. About half past eight I met

a soldier about a mile from Dorchester, towards which place I was coming. I

had previously seen another soldier at Broadway, going towards Weymouth

about six o'clock. When I met the soldier near Dorchester it was starlight & I

was sufficiently near to see that he had on a red jacket & a soldier's cap.

Christopher Kellaway – I was on the road about half past eight, & saw a

soldier about one mile & a half from Dorchester. I spoke to him & he did

not answer. It was very dark, so that I could not distinguish his features.

John Maccane, sergeant in the 5th Dragoon Guards, belonging to that part

of the regiment quartered at Weymouth; – It is part of my duty to go the

round to see that all the men are in the barracks. On the night of 28. Nov. last

I went the round at half past nine, & found every man in the barracks. I

was called up that night between ten & eleven.

Michael Tyning, sergeant major of the troop of the 5th Dragoon Guards

quartered at Weymouth: – The Roll was called over on 28 of Nov.

at half past eleven. One man named William Ruth was missing;   //

& on search being made for him he was found in a house of ill-fame at Weymouth.

He had not leave of absence.

Sergeant Maccane recalled – When I went the rounds at half past nine William

Ruth was in the barracks.

The Rev. John Morton Colson – I am a clergyman living at Dorchester; on

the night of Friday Nov. 28. I went to bed soon after nine; & was called up a

few minutes after ten on account of an alarm respecting Mr Willoughby. In

consequence of what was said to me, I went immediately to the barracks & was

there about a quarter past ten where I saw Lieut. Griffith.

John Griffith, a Lieut. in the 5th Dragoon Guards: I am Adjutant of the de-

tachment quartered at Dorchester; on the 28th Nov. the prisoner showed me a pass

about six o'clock in the evening. About a quarter past ten that night, the Rev. M^r

Colson came to the barracks, & told me that the Rev. Mr Willoughby had been

shot by a soldier, in consequence of which I immediately had the roll called, &

every man was found there excepting the prisoner. I afterwards examined the

armoury & found that the arms belonging to the prisoner were missing; ten

rounds of ball cartridge are allowed to every man, & five rounds belonging to

the prisoner were missing; as was also the powder of the other five rounds.

Directions were then given to place men inside the barrack wall. I know the

wall which divides the yards from Mr Henning's hay yard; about a

dozen men were placed under that wall, in order to prevent any one coming

over the wall. The prisoner came in about half past eleven perfectly

regular. There was a regimental order that no man should pass the   //

barrack gates without his sword. The prisoner could not have gone out of the barracks without his sword. The men leave the stables at a quarter past eight.

The last trumpet sounds at nine o'clock. There is also a trumpet call for the

men to go to the stables at a quarter before seven. I searched the prisoner &

found nothing on him; on being asked where his pistol was he said he

knew nothing at all about it, but thought it was on the armour rack in his ^room

By the Court – The arms are inspected once a week: & it is expected that every

man should keep his arms clean. Any man may leave the barracks from

eight o'clock until nine. There are eight men in each room & one arm rack in

the room. Saturday is the day for examining the room. Every person in the room

has access to the whole of the arms.

William Boyd, regimental sergeant major of the 5th Dragoon Guards: – I was

called up on the 28th Nov. about half past ten, & was directed by the Adjutant to

go round the rooms & call the roll, when I found every man there except Kennedy

who came in about 12, & was immediately taken to the guard house. He was

dressed in his stable jacket; blue overalls, boots & spurs, forage cap, sword &

belt. The blue overalls had a yellow stripe on the side. The jacket had on a

green facing & a green collar. On searching his room I found his pistol & five

rounds of ammunition were missing. On being asked by the Adjutant where

his pistol was, he said it was on the above rack that day, but he knew nothing

more of it. Every soldier is furnished with ten rounds of ammunition which

he keeps in his valise, to which every man in the room has access.

John Cusac, sergeant of the troop to which the prisoner belongs. It is my duty //

to inspect the arms of all the men of my squad every morning. I saw the prisoner's pistol in its place between seven & eight o'clock on the morning

Of the 28th Nov; it was then quite clean. I inspected the prisoner's ammunition

bag the next day, & found five broken rounds & five were missing. I gave

the bag up afterwards to M[r] Coombs on the examination of the prisoner.

By the Court – I had not seen the ammunition bag since the previous Saturday

when it was in regular condition.

Richard Amey – I was a watchman of Dorchester on the 28th Nov. last;

I saw Kennedy that evening about half-past ten passing through the market

place. I had heard of a gentleman having been shot that night, & said to the

prisoner "You are doing wrong by being out of barracks at this time of the night

as it is after hours, & the roll is going to be called." I told him that a serious

accident had happened, & that a parson had been shot, & a soldier had done it.

I am sure the prisoner is the man. The prisoner replied that he had a pass, until

~~nine~~ one o'clock; & shewed me the pass. I saw something in his right hand

which looked like a pair of trowsers rolled up; it appeared nine or ten

inches in length; but I cannot say exactly, as he was some distance from me,

he had neither sword nor belt. I saw him in the guard-room the next morning

with several other soldiers, amongst whom I identified the prisoner.

By the Court – He held the parcel in his right hand as if he wished to hide it from me

M[r] Henry Jacob: – I live at Dorchester; on the 1st Dec. last, I searched

for a pistol: there is a wall dividing the barrack yard from M[r] Henning's

hay yard; there was a heap of straw under the wall and on M[r] Henning's side.   //

There are folding gates at the entrance of the yard, through which persons must pass to obtain access to the yard. There is no difficulty in doing this from the Sherborne road, & a person

going through the market, up the back street, & Glyde-path hill, would come into the

Sherborne road. I do not think there would be much difference in the distance whether a

man went that way or up the main street to the barracks but I should think the front

street rather nearer than the other. The top of the straw heap was on a level with the top

of the wall. On searching the straw I found a pistol almost close to the wall,

imbedded in the straw; but so near the top that a person on the other side could

get it without difficulty. I took the pistol to Mr Henning's house for the purpose

of examining it; when a piece of tow being put in, the pistol was found foul, the

tow coming out very black. The pistol appeared to have been recently discharged,

& several grains of powder fell from the ł lock. The touch hole was very foul, but

but the other parts of the pistol exhibited nothing material. I marked my initials

on it & Mr Manfield then took it. It was afterwards given to Mr Coombs

in my presence.

Mr George Henning corroborated the evidence of Mr H. Jacob. It appeared to him

that the pistol had been recently fired, & partly cleaned.

Mr W.D.Tapp: – I am a surgeon, residing at Dorchester; I was called up on the

night of Friday 28th Nov. & extracted a ball from him which had entered on the

left side just below the region of the heart, & passed across the chest, & lodged in

the right side. On the following day I gave it to Dr Cooper. The wound was

a very dangerous wound; & Mr Willoughby remained in danger from ~~infl~~

inflammation for several days.   //

C. Cooper M.D. – I live at Dorchester. On Sunday I received a ball From Mr Tapp which I afterwards handed over to Mr Coombs.

Mr T. Coombes produced the ball, the canvass ammunition bag & the pistol

Sergeant Cusac recalled: – the prisoner was sometimes in the habit of using his

pistol in the riding-school; witness found the ammunition, right in the morning

& believes the prisoner was afterwards in the riding-school, but does not know

whether he fired. They do not use ball cartridge in the riding-school, & the

powder they use there is delivered out by the quarter-master. Passes are seldom

granted to so late an hour as one; but the prisoner was very anxious.

The pistol was then identified by Cusac as the prisoner's. The ball extracted

from Mr Willoughby was then ascertained by Cusac to be similar to the pistol

balls of the regiment; & on being compared was found to ~~be~~ correspond with the others.

The prisoner in his defence, denied his guilt; & said he was quite unable to

account for his pistol & ammunition being missed; he had not seen his

ammunition since the previous Saturday, but saw his pistol the day on

which the crime was committed, about 12 o'clock, every man in the troop

had access to his pistol & ammunition. He then called

Jane Masters who deposed as follows – My husband keeps the Wood &

Stone public-house in this town; I saw a soldier & Mary Purchase pass through

my kitchen between seven & eight o'clock on Friday evening the 28 Nov. I do

not know that the prisoner is the man. They staid about half an hour.

I know they were gone a few minutes after eight.

Mary Purchase, being recalled, said she left the W&S. a few minutes after 8 with the ⋀ prisoner //

_____

<u>In the confession of the prisoner</u> previous to his execution, he says that

on coming to the archway of the market, when the watchman caught hold of him

by the left arm, he had his pistol in his right hand, loaded & cocked with his finger

on the trigger, & if the watchman had tried to deter him he w^d have shot him

dead on the spot. That he unloaded his pistol at bottom of North Walk, went tow^ds

barrack wall to throw it over, but finding the place was alarmed he concealed

the pistol in a rick of hay in Mr Henning's straw yard. Saw two watchmen

but they retired or he w^d have shot them: that he ran round by Friary mill

to Marketplace, & up high street to barracks, that upon coming to barrack

gate he was seized by Lieut Griffiths, who examined his person & dress. That

he had practised pistol at the rats – &c, &c –

(It is reported that when, after his trial he descended from the dock

to the subterranean room where Jack Ketch was, as usual, assisting to

keep charge over the prisoners, he flew at him saying, "you are the chap

who is going to do the job for me – but you shan't" – & would have killed him

there. The officers of the reg^t wanted to shoot him, or at least not to

have him hung in regimentals. But as he had been condemned by the

civil law their request was not granted. The reg^t shortly afterw^ds left D.)

ib. March 19. & Ap^l 2. 29

Hand: ELH: from beginning of item to *a few minutes after 8 with the prisoner*; TH: *In the confession of the prisoner ... Apl. 2. 29.*
Text: *but but*: [sic]; in paragraph beginning 'Mr Henry Jacob'.
Source: 'Attempt To Murder', DCC, 19 March 1829, p.3, col.2, p.4, col.1; DCC, 2 April 1829, p.4, cols 1&2.
Note: *(It is reported that ... afterw^ds left D.)*: TH's addition cannot be traced to these DCC reports: he may have gleaned the details from another source, or relied upon oral transmission. *tow*: a length of fibre used for cleaning guns: a pull-through. *Moncton Hill*: near Winterborne Monkton,

S.E. of Maiden Castle. *Jack Ketch*: traditional, colloquial name for hangman (Jack Ketch executed Duke of Monmouth in 1685). *Wood and Stone*: formerly an inn, Durnover Street, Dorchester, dating back at least until the early 1820s, with no further record of it after 1871. William Kennedy was hanged at Dorchester gaol on 28 March 1829. The length of this item is partly explained by the interest of TH and ELH in the topography of Dorchester, especially as their own house in Shire-Hall Place (off what is now Glyde Path Road) was central to the area of Kennedy's movements revealed at the trial. TH and ELH knew of this case (and the *DCC* report of it of 19 March 1829), as far back as 1878–79, since the 'Trumpet-Major Notebook', compiled during these years, records the following: 'D.C.Chronicle. Thursday March 19 1829//Trial of Kennedy for shooting at Rev. H. Willoughby'. (*PN*, 168). The trial is also recalled by Boswell–Stone (*Boswell-Stone*, 54–5) (for TH's entries from this source see items 198a–202a). Boswell-Stone records that, according to Mr Clemetson, the gaol chaplain, 'Kennedy did not mean to kill Mr. Willoughby, but a man to whom he owed a grudge, who also rode a gray horse, and had gone to Weymouth that day … we thought he was one of Kennedy's own officers' (54–5).

105a

Six valuable horses – property of M[r] B. of Brentford, died a week ago by poison

supposed to have been intent[ly] mixed with their food – the sweepings of the manger having

been thrown into cowyard were eaten by one of cows wh. died in few days. Value of

horses & cow £200.   ib. Ap. 16. 29 //

Source: *DCC*, 16 April 1829, p.2, col.5.

106a

Forged notes – forger visits 31 tradesmen in Devizes & with each managed to

deposit a forged £10 note – mostly persons of his own trade – a grocer.   ib.

Source: *DCC*, 16 April 1829, p.3, cols 2–3.
Note: *DCC* reports that John Bailey, a grocer, attempted to pass forged £10 Devizes bank notes; the 31 tradesmen were at Bath.

106b

Van Diemen's Land – man goes there to see his wife who was transported as

a receiver of stolen goods.   ib. Ap. 23. 29.

Source: *DCC*, 23 April 1829, p.4, col.5.
Note: *Van Diemen's Land*: modern Tasmania. *man*: a notorious criminal, Ikey Solomons, who, having escaped from Newgate, was rearrested on reaching Van Diemen's Land.

106c

Magnet Coach – Weymouth to London in 15 hrs. 2 coachmen only. Leaving

W. every morning at ¹/₄ to 5 arriving White Horse Cellar same evening at 8.

Saracen's head at 9. Leaves latter at 5 in morning, W.H.C. at 6.   Adv^r

Source: *DCC*, 23 April 1829, p.1, col.4.
Note: *White Horse Cellar*: a coaching inn in Piccadilly, C. London, mentioned in *The Dynasts* Part Third, V.vi. *Saracen's head*: a coaching inn, Snow Hill, City of London.

106d–[p.107]

Wrestling at St Thomas (Devon) Match between J.Cann of St T. & W. Hill,

Okeford, with Messrs Roach & Southcott, as trier, Mr Baker of Okef^d being umpire.

The terms were the best 2 out of 3 fair back falls, fair shoe & padding, with 10

minutes time between the falls. At the outset Hill's hold was by the right hand

only, firmly grappling Cann's left collar: whilst the latter held him at the

collar with the contrary hand, his right gently feeling his antag^{sts} spare arm

at the wrist. Hill planted the first toe, & made free use of the right, whilst

Cann crossed him with his left. As a school specimen – & it would be difficult

to conceive of it as anything more – nothing c^d be finer than this, nor J.Cann's

peculiar & very super^r mode of play displayed to greater advantage, he had

the fore hand, & kept it, his opponent not appearing very anxious to endeavour

to take it from him. At the end of 15 minutes Hill seemed rather uneasy at

the gripe of the wrist, & freeing his hand aimed to make good his hold at   //

Cann's right collar: this was resisted & a fine rally took place, which ended

in 15 min. in Cann's going down on his knees. The seizing at again setting to,

was precisely as before, but an immed^te attempt to make good being made, a

smart rally again took place, & at end of ab^t 21 m^tes C. was again on his knees.

From this time there c^d be no doubt which way the match w^d end. C was

evidently giving H. a lesson, & at the end of 26 minutes delivered his man by the

left fore hip as fine a turn as ever was seen. H. inst^ly complained of

injury to shoulder, & though the second turn was commenced he was powerless

& at end of 2½ m. gave in.

   Between Webber, baker of Exeter, & Esworthy – W's Cann-like skill as-

tonished those who beheld it; whenever in danger he locked himself to his

antagonist, & all the efforts of such a veteran as Esworthy were in vain exerted

to lift him. The both turns after severe contest were in his favour; in

the last he turned E. a complete summerset, & put him down spinning on

his head like a top; wh. the latter allowed to be a fall.   ib. Ap.30.29.

Source: 'Wrestling at St. Thomas', *DCC*, 30 April 1829, p.3, col.4.
Note: *St. Thomas*: a parish and district of the city of Exeter. *The seizing at again*: DCC inserts comma after 'seizing'. The both turns: [*sic*]. This item provides a source for the wrestling episode between Henchard and Farfrae in *The Mayor of Casterbridge*, ch.38. The wording of the scene shows several close resemblances to the *DCC* report: compare 'the terms were the best 2 out of 3 fair back falls' ('Facts') with 'it was a wrestling match, the object of each being to give his antagonist a back fall' (*Mayor of Casterbridge*); 'At the outset Hill's hold was by the right hand only, firmly grappling Cann's left collar: whilst the latter held him at the collar with the contrary hand, his right *gently feeling* his antag^sts spare arm at the wrist' (F), 'At the outset Henchard's hold by his only free hand, the right, was on the left side of Farfrae's collar, which he firmly grappled, the latter holding Henchard by his collar with the contrary hand. With his right he endeavoured to get hold of his antagonist's left arm' (M); 'Cann … delivered his man by the left fore-hip as fine a turn as ever was seen' (F), 'He instantly delivered the younger man an annihilating turn by the left fore hip, as it used to be expressed' (M); 'in the last he turned E. a complete summerset' (F), 'Henchard contrived to turn Farfrae a complete somersault' (M). TH followed with interest the progress of Cann, a champion wrestler of the day (see items 54d and 82e). In this item the cross-

currents of masculine aggression and feminine tenderness are suggested by the action of the muscular Cann *'gently feeling* his antagonist's arm' (*DCC's* italic), reinforcing the view that Henchard's feelings for Farfrae are mildly homoerotic. Certainly it is through typologies of gender that TH conveys the full force of Henchard's remorse and guilt once the wrestling-match is over: 'So thoroughly subdued was he that he remained on the sacks in a crouching attitude, unusual for a man, and for such a man. Its womanliness sat tragically on the figure of so stern a piece of virility' (*Mayor, 1987,* 274).

107a

Street door left open – Coat missed – found at pawnbroker's – has been pledged

by a woman in a black gown – papers in pocket, as when taken; so probably

carried there at once.   ib.

Source: 'Caution to Housekeepers', *DCC*, 30 April 1829, p.4, col.3.

107b

Countess of Derby – formerly the celebrated Miss Farren, died at Knowsley on 23[d]

inst. The elegant & accomplished manner in wh. she represented Lady Teazle won

the heart of her noble lord, forming an hon[ble] attachm[t] wh. has lasted through a long life.

                                                                            ib. //

Source: *DCC*, 30 April 1829, p.4, col.4.
Note: *Miss Farren*: Elizabeth Farren (1759?–1829) m. (1797) 12th Earl of Derby. Farren and the Earl were the subject of caricatures by Gillray. *Knowsley*: the seat of the Earls of Derby near Liverpool. *Lady Teazle*: a character in R.B. Sheridan's *The School for Scandal* (1777).

108a

A young lady about 25, full face & fresh col[r] called at jeweller's shop, Bath,
                    looked at
(in evening) ~~obtained a~~ gold watches: ordered him to send 4 to a house she

named, not being able to make up mind. At the door she met the person

entrusted with the watches, selected one (with a cut coral brooch & a locket –

from another jeweller). It was found that the inhab^{ts} of the house knew

nothing of her.   ib. May 21.29

Source: *DCC*, 21 May 1829, p.3, col.3.

108b

<u>Kicking at a wrestling match</u> – a barbarous practice…The bare foot, or

thin pump only sh^d be used: padding the legs w^d then be uncalled for.   ib.

Source: 'Wrestling', *DCC*, 21 May 1829, p.3, col.3.

108c

<u>Convicts</u>. Coaches from Dorch^r & Exeter, to Plymouth, laden with convicts this

week, for their new residence on board the hulks. (they had been sentenced to

transportation for 7, 14 yrs &c)   ib.

Source: *DCC*, 21 May 1829, p.3, col.4.
Note: *(they had been sentenced … 14 yrs &c)*: TH's addition. See *Life and Work*, 222–3.

108d

<u>The Premier's property</u> – The Duke of Wellington is in treaty for another estate to

add to his Hampshire property. Some idea may be formed of the extent of his Grace's

property in Hants when it is stated that its circuit will be at least 30 miles, & that

an avenue to the house may be formed upwards of 8m. in length.

                                    ib. 28 May. 29. quot fr <u>Windsor Express</u>.

Source: *DCC*, 28 May 1829, p.2, col.3.
Note: *Duke of Wellington*: the current Prime Minister; he formed his first ministry in January 1828. *Hampshire property*: Stratfield Saye. See also item 68d.

108e–[109]

Dk. of Cumberland's son – It has not as yet been noticed by any n. paper that

a son of his present R.H. the Dk of Cumb^d. departed this life at Hammersmith

5th Nov. last. The name borne by his R.H's son was George Fitz Ernest, & some   //

few years ago this illustrious personage was well known in fashionable circles

at Ramsgate &c. For the last 2 yrs & more the deceased had lived at an

humble though pleasant villa in Webb's Lane, Hammth , & in conseq. of afflictions

both bodily & mental, the Dk. had placed as a guardian over him & his affairs

the Revd Dr Clark. Died suddenly, after rising early in morn^g & was buried

in the "Post Mortem" retreat of H. Ch. 33 years of age. followed to grave by Col.

Thornton, Dr Clark & his immed^{te} attendants.   ib. 20 May 29.

Source: *DCC*, 28 May 1829, p.2, col.3.
Note: TH mistakes the date of this entry. *Duke of Cumberland*: (1771–1851), fifth son of George III. *Hammth*: Hammersmith, W. London. *The Revd Dr Clark*: James Stanier Clarke, Royal Chaplain. *H.Ch.*: Hammersmith Church. See also Claire Tomalin, *Mrs Jordan's Profession* (1994; London: Penguin, 1995), pp. 162–3.

109a

Love & Suicide – Two lovers after wandering in the forest of Montmorency go to

restaurateur's of the village; & while the house resounded with the music of a

wedding wh. was celebrating below they each perpetrated self murder by firing

a pistol at their hearts. The noise of the merrymaking prevented the pistols

being heard. She 17; he 22: he was married.   Fch. paper.   ib.

Source: *DCC*, 28 May 1829, p.2, col.5.
Note: *Montmorency*: in Val d'Oise, N. of Paris. *restaurateur's*: TH reproduces the redundant apostrophe from *DCC*.

109b

Gloving. The situation of the unfortunate poor who used to find employment

in the glove manuf^y Yeovil, & adj. districts is very distressing; & when we

look at extent of import^n of foreign gloves we see little prosp. of imp^t. The

quantity imported this year to end of Ap^l is 24, 813 doz. wh w^d have given empl^t

for 100 days to 1000 w. & ch^n in the sewing, & prop^{te} number of men & boys in

dressing & preparing the leather.   ib.

Source: *DCC*, 28 May 1829, p.3, col.3.
Note: *w. & ch^n*: women and children. *prop^{te}*: proportionate. See item 27f on the Yeovil glove trade
as an index of the local economy in the late 1820s.

109c

West of England Bank robbery. It appears that the cash & securities

were deposited in an iron safe placed in strong room at back of banking house   //

the key of which was always kept in drawer in bank counter. The strong room

was secured by a lock with four bolts, & an iron bar let down from the room

above into rings fastened in the inside; & over the top of the bar was a trap door

with a lock. This room was occupied by Mesdames Hearn & Braund (?).

Mr M. the principal clerk was gen. the person who fast^d the t.d. &

let down bar. He was indisposed, & it devolved on the other clk to close the

bank. He stated before Mayor & Alderm^n W. that on Sat. aft. ab^t 4 M^r

M left. & about 5 he, having struck his balance made all safe went upstairs

let down bar & locked t.d. as usual. Monday m. found lock of t.d forced &c,

locksmith called &c. All the cash, B of E. notes, other notes, & bills, gone

& on examining the book in the chest in wh. the cash balance was daily struck it was found the leaves for a month past had been torn out.

...R.Davy, late <u>master of work house</u>, sworn as constable... ib.

Source: *DCC*, 28 May 1829, p.3, col.5.
Note: W.: White. M.: Matthews. *bar*: these references in lines 5, 8, 11 are 'bolt' in the original.

110a–[p.111]

<u>Procession</u> of conveyances laden with persons afflicted with the Kings evil

passed through Sturm^r Newton on way to Hazlebury $\wedge$ where resides a man
near

named Buckland, who has attained a reputation for curing, in a miraculous

manner, the King's evil, at his yearly fair or feast. Exactly 24 h^{rs} before

the new moon in month of May every year, whether it happens by night

or day, the afflicted assemble at the doctors residence, where they are

supplied by him with the hind legs of a toad enclosed in a small bag,

(accomp. with some verbal charm or incant^n) & also a lotion & salve of the

d^{rs} preparation. The bag is worn suspended from the neck, & the lotion   //

& salve applied in the usual manner until the cure is completed, or until

the next year's fair...the app^{ces} of many showed that they moved in resp^{ble} sphere of

life. ib. May 28.29.

Source: 'Curing the King's Evil', *DCC*, 28 May 1829, p.4, col.2.
Note: *King's evil*: scrofula, a tubercular condition of the neck-glands, traditionally believed to be cured by the Royal Touch. *Hazlebury*: Hazelbury Bryan, village near Sturminster Newton, Dorset. *Buckland*: John Buckland, a 'white witch' or 'cunning-man'. Buckland and his toads are mentioned by J.S. Udal, *Dorsetshire Folk-Lore* (1922; Guernsey: Toucan Press, 1970), p.216. TH had already noted (*c.* 1876) reports of a 'wizard' and his 'toad fair', active in this part of Dorset (*Life and Work*, 115). Not long after entering the above item in 'Facts', TH wrote of Henchard in *The Mayor of Casterbridge*, seeking out a 'weather-prophet', and asking, 'Cure the evil?', with the reply, 'That I've done ... if they will wear the toad-bag ...' (*Mayor*, 1987, 187). See also item [203]b, and *Cullen Brown*, 87.

111a

Road accident – "As we came opposite S. lane the horse attempted to turn

into it: deceased pulled the left rein to keep horse tow^{ds} Taunton, when it

broke, & other horse became unmanageable & set off full speed: thought I heard the

other rein snap – jumped out of carriage – followed on & found deceased

thrown out – horse jammed between posts at a t.p.g.   ib.

Source: *DCC*, 28 May 1829, p.4, col.2.
Note: *t.p.g.*: turnpike gate.

111b

                    (on foot?)
Man being conveyed in the custody of J. F., tythingman of Cutcombe (Somerset)

& his assistant to Wilton house of correction on a charge of burglary.

Prisoner endeavoured to escape by leaping over bridge into water (11 o'c. at

night), & was drowned. He was not handcuffed, a circum^{ce} wh. the jury re-

probated in strong terms, when the constables informed them that there was

not a pair of handcuffs or a constable's staff in parish of Cutcombe.   ib.

Source: *DCC*, 28 May 1829, p.4, col.3.
Note: (*on foot?*): TH's interpolation. *tythingman*: a parish peace-officer or petty constable, charged
with maintaining law and order. *Cutcombe*: W. Somerset. *Wilton house of correction*: in Taunton.

111c

Alice C. (v. ante p.96) who was tried & convicted at the last assizes (Dor) stealing

money fr. ch. maid, Kings Arms, & on whom judgm^t of death was recorded, was

removed from our jail on Sunday last, on board the Lucy Davidson, transp^t ship,

lying in river Thames, her sentence having been commuted to transp^n for life. July 2. 29

Source: *DCC*, 2 July 1829, p.4, col.2.
Note: *Alice C.*: Alice Conroy. See also item 96a.

111d–[112]

Almost wholly erased item f.56r&v (see Appendix One) //

112a

<u>Farmer eased</u> of his money by being advised to put it in safer pocket, as he

the rogue, is doing. ib.

Source: *DCC*, 9 July 1829, p.3, col.3.

112b

<u>Escape from Dor. gaol</u> by three men, who made a breach in wall of cell by removing

bricks, tearing bedding into strips for ropes to scale boundary wall – ib.

Source: *DCC*, 9 July 1829, p.4, col.1.

112c

A <u>"Fair-house"</u> – Prosecutor deposed that he kept the fair-house at Toller

Down. The fair closed in May, & on locking up the house he left in it a

quantity of bottled beer, cups & saucers, glass, & many other articles. Aug 13. 29

Source: *DCC*, 13 August 1829, p.3, col.2.
Note: '*Fair-house*': house for entertainment of gentry etc. at a fair. *Toller Down*: near Toller Gate, at the junction of Dorchester–Crewkerne road and road from Evershot. The view from here to Wynyard's Gap was one of TH's favourites, see TH, 'Which is the Finest View in Dorset?', *The Society of Dorset Men in London Year-book, 1915–16*, pp.31–2; reprinted in *PW*, 232–3, *Public Voice*, 369–70.

112d

<u>Thieves in dress of livery servants</u> at Taunton races, & were thus enabled to rifle

carriages without detection.   ib.

Source: *DCC*, 13 August 1829, p.3, col.4.

112e–[113]

                              stopped a short time
Robber shot by traveller…He had ~~baited his horse~~ at Birdlip, (on the road

between Gloucester & Cirencester) & baited his horse, & come onward, when about

a mile from Breech Pike a kind of presentment of probable danger, caused by

the lateness of the hour & lonely road, induced him to take a pair of pistols from

his pocket, which he cocked & laid on the seat of the gig close beside him. He   //

had not done this many minutes when, arriving near a grove of firs by the side

of the road, two men, (who by their voices he believes to be Irish) rushed forth from

the plantation: one seized horse's head while the other came to side of gig & com-

manded him to stop: both were armed with reaping hooks. Much alarmed he

s^d "D – it , what do you mean?" & at same moment seized one of his pistols, wh.

missed fire, on wh. robber aimed a blow at him with reap-hook & cut his hand –

he discharged other pistol, robber fell. Horse rendered furious by discharge

of pistol reared plunged & ran away. (He is a commercial tr^r & had about him

nearly £400.)   ib. Aug 13, 1829

Source: *DCC*, 13 August 1829, p.3, col.4.
Note: *Breech*: a mistake by *DCC* for 'Beech Pike' on the Gloucester–Cirencester road, near
Elkstone.

113a

Horsewhipping her lover – Malster courts young lady – breaks off with her,

"feeling he does not want a wife" Her brother & his friend come to malt house, b^r says will you sign this, holding up a paper in one hand, & a horsewhip

in the other. He refused to sign, & the b^r struck him with whip – Maltster

thereupon summons him for an assault – & the b^r has to pay.   ib.

Source: 'Summary Punishment for the fickleness of a lover', DCC, 13 August 1829, p.3, col.2.

113b

<u>One pound notes</u> – The withdrawal of one pound notes is severely felt by farmers

(at Dorchester fair, August 1829 – they were withdrawn from cir^n this year).   ib.

Source: DCC, 13 August 1829, p.4, col.1.
Note: *cir^n*: circulation.

113c–[114]

<u>The apple county</u> –Traveller by coach ~~fr~~ through Salisbury, Dor. & on

to Exeter, says, "As we approach the great apple country the sounds of cheerful-

ness and gratitude are heard. The vintage of the Arcadian counties has seldom

been hailed with gladder hearts than are now universal in Devonshire, by   //

the contemplation of the luxuriant orchards. Even the solitary trees which are met with

in gardens, or before the peasants door, appear almost encumbered by the rosy clusters.

The only qualification wh. this gen. feeling admits is derived from the fear that

there will not be a suffic^t supply of vessels to contain the cider.   ib. Aug 13. 29

(the paper for June 4 says that the apples in the orchards are gen^{lly} well set, & promise
        having sustained but slight injury from frost
abundant crops ʌ – & for third week in May that the orch^{ds} present a beautiful spectacle

the trees being literally covered with blossom – sheets of blossom &c)

Source: 'The great-apple country', DCC, 21 May 1829, p.4, col.1; DCC, 4 June 1829, p.4, col.3;
DCC, 13 August 1829, p.4, col.1.

Note: *by the contemplation of*: DCC has 'excited to joy by the contemplation of'. *having sustained but slight injury from frost*: there is no reference to injury from frost in any of the reports, but *DCC* notes 'the present genial weather succeeding to a long prevalence of cold' (21 May 1829, p.4, col.1). TH here reproduces snatches of conventional pastoral writing threading through these *DCC* reports, e.g. 'the budding beauties of the orchard, long restrained, have at length broken their cerements, and burst into a sheet of blossom' (*DCC*, 21 May 1829, p.4, col.1). His description of the 'cider country' in *The Woodlanders* (chs 19 & 28) eschews this approach.

114a

How to sell a horse. In Smithfield a horse dealer sold to farmer a rank

roarer, worth about £2, as a sound horse. When farmer got home he found

that instead of having 4 blk legs, as he thought, 3 of them were white, & were

painted; & what he had mistaken for horse's tail & foretop came off, having

been cleverly affixed to trappings. Horse had travelled over ½ kingdom in the

hands of this purchaser, who w^d buy it back at a consid^ble sacrifice. The

false tail was affixed to a linen strap.   ib. Aug 27. 29

Source: 'How to Sell A Horse', *DCC*, 27 August 1829, p.3, col.2.
Note: *farmer*: DCC has 'an old countryman'.

114b–[115]

Marriage Portions – mortgaging same – Thos Harris left in 1797 to the

parishes of Cloford & Nunney, Somerset £2000, the int^st to be annually

disposed of among such women, natives of the parishes, as sh^d have been

m^d during the preceding year in those parishes, the sums to be distrib^d

by ministers C.Wardens &c. It has sometimes happened (the Commissioners

state) that no m^ge has t. place within the year preceding in the parishes,

to entitle any persons to the bounty, in wh. case the div^ds are accumul^ted   //

until an applicant present herself who is entitled under the will. She then receives the <u>whole</u> amount of the accumul^d div^{ds}. This charity has, in the

opinion of the Rev^d – the curate, a tendency to produce mischievous effects.

Besides its gen^l tendency to produ^{ce} immorality, young persons have been induced

thereby to marry at a very early age to entitle thems. to the bounty;

& in some instances they may have been known to anticipate the sum by mortgaging

the same before marriage.

ib. from Comm^{rs} concerning Charities (20 vols. folio) vol III, p.317

Text: there are two vertical parallel lines (pencil) beside final two lines of this item.
Source: DCC, 27 August 1829, p.3, col.2.
Note: *Rev^d –* : the Revd J. Ireland. *(20 vols. folio)*: 20 folio volumes resulting from the labours of the 'commissioners concerning charities'.

115a

<u>Sad romanticism of a young girl</u> – Daughter of Mr Marshall of Hassal-

grove Farm, aged 17: tied up a bundle & gave it in charge to a young

man who was at her father's house on a friendly visit for the afternoon,

saying he was not to open it till he got home, as it was a present for his

sisters (supper time arriving & the girl not appearing about the house)

the bundle was opened, & it contained a number of trinkets usually worn

by her: these circ^s created an unpleasant suspicion in the minds of all

present; when a diligent search was immed^{ly} made all over the premises

& during the whole of the succeeding night, without effect, till on Monday

morn^g ab^t 10 she was found in a deep pond, about 2 or 300 yds from house

quite dead, with her legs tied, her hands tied behind her, & a handk^f tied

over her eyes...distress of family...no reason can be assigned.   Aug 27. 29

Source: 'Distressing Event', *DCC*, 27 August 1829, p.4, col.3.

115b–[116]

Convict transported – The notorious Robinson, sent^{ced} at last Devon Assizes to be   //

transp. for life, was on Wedn^y morning sent off per coach, to be put on board the

Captivity hulk, at Devonport, preparatory to his voyage to N.S.Wales –   ib. 17 Sept.29

Source: *DCC*, 17 September 1829, p.3, col.3.

116a

Escaped Convict. B.H. seen drinking in a p.h. in Bath – he being an escaped

c. from N.S.Wales since 1828. Convicted assizes 1827, & sent^d transp. life

Officers pursued the prisoner in post chaise from Bath to Chippenham: ultimately

secured – dressed as a sailor, will take his trial –   ib.

Source: *DCC*, 17 September 1829, p.3, col.2.
Note: *B.H.*: Baynham Helps.

116b

stock – ⌐

River Parrett flooded – [stitches of corn] endangered, & barley –   ib.

Source: *DCC*, 17 September 1829, p.4, col.3.
Note: *stitches*: strips. TH conflates two reports from the same column.

116c

Sale of Wife – at Stamford – fellow sold her "for 2/- wet & 2/- dry" – delivered

her to the purchaser on the market hill in a halter; after wh. the trio retired to

a p.house to quaff the heavy wet.   ib. Oct.1.29

Source: *DCC*, 1 October 1829, p.3, col.2.

Note: by the side of this note are the words, in pencil, 'used in The Mayor of Casterbridge' which may be in TH's hand. This is third of three wife sales which TH recorded in 'Facts' (see also 32g and 74b) and on which he drew for the wife-sale episode in *The Mayor*, ch.1. See *Winfield*, 227. *DCC* reports the incident as follows: 'A most disgraceful scene took place at Stamford on Friday last: a fellow sold his wife for 2s. wet and 2s. dry, delivered her to the purchaser in a halter on the Market-hill; after which the trio retired to a public-house to quaff the heavy wet!'

116d

d

Paupers – Apply at Worcester house of Industry for relief (man & wife) at 3 a mile

Woman & 2 ch. also applies, having a pass for 3½ a mile. Passes found to be

forgeries – the man & wife had received £2.15.6, & the woman & children £3.9.8.

Their route had been from Carlisle to Kidderminster – the latter being the last

place where they obtained relief. The system of forged passes is carried on

largely. Near Basingstoke lately one of these passing strangers addressed some

lab^{rs} turnip hoeing, wondering how they c^d be constant to work, when they might

get a pass, & travel at pleasure. "We see all sights" s^d he. "live well, go where

we like, own no master, & get handsomely paid." Such at a time of gen^l depression

among honest men is the flourishing state of beggary!   ib. //

Source: *DCC*, 1 October 1829, p.3, col.3.

117a

Felo de se. privately buried in Avington Ch.y^d without the rites of Xtian

burial, at 11 o'c. the same night –   ib.

Source: 'Suicide', *DCC*, 1 October 1829, p.3, col.4.

Note: *Avington*: near Hungerford, Berkshire. The burial of this cook-maid still observed the traditional treatment of a suicide. See item 57a.

117b

Honey-stealing…is becoming prevalent in some villages near this town (Taunton)

A clandestine burning of bees belonging to 3 individuals of Cheddon. Honey

was all taken away, & empty hives replaced in their former situations to

prevent suspicion of the loss.

Source: *DCC*, 1 October 1829, p.4, col.3.
Note: *Cheddon*: Cheddon Fitzpaine, Somerset.

117c

Landlord obtains a white rabbit, & puts earrings in its ears – says it is

the witch…   ib.

Source: 'A Hoax!', *DCC*, 1 October 1829, p.4, col.3.
Note: *DCC* notes that 'the landlord reaped a golden harvest from the credulity of the public'.

117d

Tender thief – Last week Mrs Oxford, late Mrs Allen, of the Carriage Inn

Coombe Down, received a ring wh. was stolen from her 12 years since, inclosed
                                    [man]
in a note from the person who stole the ring. [Handsome woman prob^{ly}]   ib.

Source: *DCC*, 1 October 1829, p.4, col.3.
Note: *Coombe Down*: outside Bath. *[man]*; *[Handsome woman prob^{ly}]*: TH's additions.

117e

Eliza Leach, fine young woman, about to be married. Banns pub^d, wedding

dress made, day fixed, when Willis wrote to her that he c^d not marry her.

It turned out that he married another woman on the day fixed. [Probably

had wavered between the two]   ib. Oct 15. 29

Source: 'Melancholy Suicide', *DCC*, 15 October 1829, p.2, col.4.
Note: there is no mention of suicide of Eliza Leach by TH. *[Probably ... the two]*: TH's own gloss is concerned with the man's predicament, rather than with Eliza Leach's.

117f

Erasure f.59r (see Appendix One)

117g

Weyhill Fair – By 12 o'c only 40 waggons had passed through Andover gate –

in former, abundant years, 400 horses have passed it by same hour.   ib. //

Text: this item is entered below the last ruled line of the page.
Source: 'Weyhill Sheep Fair', *DCC*, 15 October 1829, p.2, col.5.
Note: *Weyhill*: 3 miles west of Andover, the site of an ancient, prominent week-long fair in October. *DCC* reported that 'The number of sheep penned on Saturday was unusually large ... the sales however were very few, and nearly half the quantity penned were driven home again ... Some comparison may be drawn between this and past years, when at twelve o'clock on Saturday only 40 waggons had passed through at Andover gate, and by the same time in former abundant years upwards of 400 have passed it'. See also, item 54g for the decline of Hindon market. This is one of several items in 'Facts' which depict trading fairs of the S.W. region as indexes of the state of the local economy. In the same issue *DCC* reports that at a Sherborne fair, in common with 'almost every fair during the last year', the supply of goods outstrips demand, with 'a dull sale at ruinously low prices' (*DCC*, 15 October 1829, p.4, col.2). Weyhill is a key location for TH as 'Weydon-Priors' in *The Mayor of Casterbridge*, (chs 1–3) at which fair Henchard sells his wife, Susan. See William Greenslade, *Degeneration, Culture and the Novel 1880–1940* (Cambridge: Cambridge University Press, 1994), pp. 61–2.

118a

Burglar's & forger's execution – After hanging the usual time the bodies

were taken into Newgate, & will be delivered to their friends this evening. Oct 22.29

Source: *DCC*, 22 October 1829, p.2, col.4.

118b

Hatchment over shop – widow of tradesman near Tott^n C^t R^d has placed

above front of shop a hatchment to memory of late husband.   ib.

Text: there are two parallel lines (pencil) beside this item.
Source: 'The March of Refinement', *DCC*, 22 October 1829, p.2, col.4.
Note: *hatchment*: a tablet showing the coat of arms of the deceased. *Tott^n C^t R^d*: Tottenham Court Road, C. London.

118c

Sinking of the Dolphin Hulk – full of convicts – moored in Thames – they

were got out – some tried to escape –   ib.

Source: *DCC*, 22 October 1829, p.2, col.5.

118d

Plan of horse stealers is to transfer the stolen horses from one part of England to

another, travelling with them at night, & resting at some obscure place during

day, altering horses by docking, trimming &c –   ib. Oct 29. 29

Source: 'Horse-stealing', *DCC*, 29 October 1829, p.2, col.3.

118e

Benefit societies on the old system – suicide – severe shock on conseq. of breaking

up of B.Soc of wh. he had been member 35 yrs, expecting certain provision in

his old age from the funds, instead of wh. he had only received 25/- as his share on

the dissolution of the soc.   ib. Nov 5 29.

Source: *DCC*, 5 November 1829, p.2, col.3.
Note: a report of an inquest after a suicide.

118f–[120]

Escape of 12 Convicts. 9 in morning Albion coach took up as passengers 12

convicts from Chester, sent^d to transp. life for various offences, & who were to be

forw^{ded} to Portsmouth, for wh. purpose a Portsmth coach was to meet them at the

Bull & Mouth, London. Coach had no other passengers. 9 p.m. coach reached Birm^m

when a new coachman & guard relieved the former ones, & the c. proceeded to Elmedon //

when the c's partook of some refresh^{ts}. After having gone on 4m. to Meriden the guards

atten^n was arrested by hearing one of the convicts filing the chain attached to

his handcuffs. With^t apparently noticing the noise he continued to apprise the

keeper of the circ^{ce}, & he then took the guard's situation behind, the guard afterw^{ds}

riding with the coachman. With this alter^n everything became quiet & there were

no appearances of an attempt at escape. The coach now approached Coventry,

through wh. it passed, & after it had proceeded 9 miles to a sequestered part of

the road, where trees extend on either side upwards of 6 miles & not a house

near, in an instant 4 of the c's seized hold of coachm. & guard (at same

moment stopping the horses) & succeeded in fastening both of them with cords & straps

at same time stating that they did not intend to injure them nor rob the c.

but that they were determ^d at every hazard, to regain their liberty, for

they had rather suffer death than be transp. for life. While this scene was trans-

acting in front of coach 5 other c's seized keeper behind, secured him, & rifling his

pockets obtained keys of the handcuffs. Noise and confusion outside was signal to

remaining convicts within: instantly the keeper was laid hold of and confined,

& having got poss^n of his handcuff keys also, they lost no time in manacling him. Convicts then descended, endeav^d extricate thems. from their fetters,

a work wh. occupied them some time, & in wh. notwith^s their violence & ingenuity

they made little progress. While thus engaged they were alarmed by noise

of coach appoaching...made its app^{ce}...they rushed to fields, although

most of them were still fastened by legs – night dark...made escape before
  (a Liverpool)
other ∧ coach came up, by wh. time g^d & c.man had extric. thems. & unbound

keepers. Having communic^d circum^s to the L.pool coachman – the Ch.   //

coach was taken to Dunchurch, where the 2 keepers, one still handcuffed, set off to

Coventry to get assistance. Before L.pool coach came the c.s had detached

the horses, to make use of them in their flight.   ib. Nov 12. 29

Source: *DCC*, 12 November 1829, p.2, col.3.
Note: *Elmedon*: Elmdon, and *Meriden*: both between Birmingham and Coventry. *Dunchurch*: near Rugby. *Ch. coach*: Chester coach.

120a

Young man in Church renovating monument – comes down ladder &

marries young woman.   ib.

Source: 'All in his Day's Work', *DCC*, 12 November 1829, p.2, col.4.
Note: the ceremony over, he mounted the ladder and recommenced his work. The expected bridegroom did not turn up.

120b

Landlady who had eloped with young man lodging at the inn asks her husband

when in court to forgive her, since it was the only crime she had ever been

guilty of. To this he agreed & the prisoner (in custody for stealing landlady's

wearing apparel) was discharged.   ib.

Source: 'Love and Mercy', *DCC*, 12 November 1829, p.3, col.3.

120c

Capt. Andrews resigns office of <u>Master of Ceremonies,</u> Wey[th]. Bishop offers as Candidate.

Nov 19.   ib.

Source: *DCC*, 19 November 1829, p.4, col.2.
Note: *Wey[th]*: Weymouth, a fashionable resort at that time. *Bishop*: Mr J.M. Bishop.

120d

<u>Comm[l] traveller returns home unexpec[ly]</u> – goes to bed – wife says she has spasms –

sends him out for brandy – in paying for it he tenders what he supposes to be

a shilling, but change for a sov[n] is given – finds he has 14 more, instead of

shillings – has on strange pair of trousers – rushes home – his own breeches gone.   ib.

Source: 'A Funny Occurrence', *DCC*, 19 November 1829, p.2, col.4.
Note: *breeches gone*: i.e. worn by escaping lover.

120e–[131]

<u>Bligh v. Wellesley</u> – (see pp 59 & 93 ante –) C[t] Com. Pleas, bef. L.C.J.Brett

M[r] D.F.Jones opened the pleadings. The declar[n] charged deft. with having

assaulted & debauched the wife of the plff. Deft. pl. "not guilty" – & thereupon

issue was joined. M[r] Serj[t] Vaughan (with whom were M[r] Serj Wilde &   //f.61r

M[r] D.F.Jones) conducted the ~~el~~ case for the plff. He said –

...Plff was M[r] Tho[s] Bligh, & the deft[t] M[r] W., both of them gent[m]

of noble birth, & connected with the first families in the kingdom. M[r] Bligh

had been in the army, but from ill health, unfortunately, acquired in service of

his country, had been obliged to retire from it some few years ago. He was the son of Mr Shadwell Bligh, who was a gent^n of consid^le landed est^s in

Ireland & a near relation of the Earl of Darnley. With respect to the defendant, he scarcely

needed to mention his name; & he assured the jury that if he did mention it, it was only to instruct

them to dismiss from their minds, as far as possible, all that they might have heard rumoured

or seen published, to the prejudice of his general character; for be that character what it

might, the defendant must stand or fall that day by the merits of the case which

might be proved in evidence against him. Though it might be difficult to discard

from their recollection what was passing in the world, & forming the subject of its

daily conversation, still he was sure that such respectable men as he then had

the honour of addressing would bring to the consideration of the present issue a

mind perfectly untainted by anything which they might either have heard

or read against the defendant, no matter whether it had taken place either in

or out of a court of justice. The defendant was the eldest son of Lord Mary=

borough, the nephew of the Duke of Wellington & of the Marquis Wellesley

~~all~~ as they must all be aware, the heir to a very considerable fortune. With

respect to the lady whose affections he had seduced from her husband, she

was the daughter of Colonel Patterson, an officer who had served in India

with great credit for many years, & who had returned to England with a   //f.61v

modest competency. She was a lady of great beauty and numerous accomplishments

to whom the plaintiff after some acquaintance and with the consent and approbation

of her father was married in the course of the year 1815. On that subject he would

beg leave to say one word and it should be one word only in consequence of a

circumstance which had been stated when application was made to put off the trial of the present cause. The marriage of the plaintiff to Miss Patterson took place

he repeated in 1815; but without the knowledge of the plaintiff's father. In consequence

of some doubts arising at to its legality, which was of great importance, as not only

a fortune might eventually fall to the issue of the marriage, the ceremony in order

to make assurance doubly sure, was re-performed two years afterwards in the

presence of both his & her relations. If then any inference were to be drawn from the

double celebration of the marriage ceremony in this case, it was an inference highly

favourable to the plaintiff's case; for it afforded evidence that the affection which

led to the first marriage continued unimpaired between the parties to the time

of the second. Indeed, if ever there had been a marriage of affection, such was the

marriage between the plaintiff & his wife; for it was strongly objected to by

Captain Bligh's father, & was not at all sanctioned at the time by any of his

relations. The first object of Captain Bligh after his marriage was, if possible

to reconcile his family to it; & being very anxious to make a permanent provision

for his lady, he used active measures to prevail upon his father to resettle the

family estate, – which was settled in the final instance upon himself. After

waiting some time he succeeded in effecting the object of his wishes. In the

year 1819, the estate which had been settled on him was resettled in order   //f.62r

to enable him to make a jointure to his lady. He must now tell the jury, that when

the marriage between these parties first took place Captain Bligh resided with

Colonel Patterson. Shortly afterwards he joined his regiment, which at the close of

the war in 1815, formed part of the army of occupation in France, & resided with his

wife sometime in that country. They then came back to England, where he fell into a state of ill health, which at this moment, was so little repaired that there was no

chance of his enjoying a long period of life. He was then advised by D[r] Baillie

to go to the south of Europe, in order to try whether his health might not improve

by residence in a milder climate. In this state of things, he went, in the year 1821 to

Geneva. He left that place & wintered in Nice. From Nice he proceeded to

Genoa, & from Genoa he went to Rome, where he passed the winter of 1822.

the defendant's
In the next y[r] he went to Naples & there it was that commenced ~~his~~ adulterous

intercourse with M[rs] Bligh. In spring of '23 the plff. was joined at Rome

by his b[r], M[r] Ed. Bligh, & his family, & from Rome they went together, as he

had told them, to Naples. They took a house in that city, & during their resid[ce]

in it the acq[ce] of plff. com[ced] with def[t]…M[r] W. had, just before, married

a lovely & accomplished lady, who had put him in poss[n] of what it was no

exag[n] to call an immense fortune. Immense as it had been, it was, however,

deeply incumbered before M[r] Well[y] went abroad. Those of her estates in wh.

he had only a life interest were in conseq. put to nurse; & she was left

to support herself & fam. on a revenue of £5,000 a year wh. had been

set aside for her pin-money. She went to the continent with that in-

come, & he joined her there, for the purpose of living upon her property,   //f.62v

whilst his own was out at nurse. M[r] & M[rs] Wellesley happened to be at Naples at the

same time with Captain & M[rs] Bligh. They were introduced to each other at the house of

M[r] Hamilton the British minister by his sister M[rs] Maxwell. An acquaintance

followed that introduction; they visited each other; & the consequence was that the

defendant, after seeing M[rs] Bligh, became passionately fond of her, paid her great attention, & finally accomplished his base purposes, in seducing her affections

from her husband, & in making himself the master of her person. At the time that he

committed this outrage upon the domestic happiness of the Cap$^{t.n}$ B. Mr W. was living in

apparent harmony & on the very best terms with his own wife; & what formed a

singular aggravation of M^r W's guilt was this – that from the moment in which he

obtained the gratification of his own wishes by the seduction of his friend's wife

he made his own wife an innocent instrument to her own dishonour, causing her

to act upon all occasions as the friend & protectress of the woman with whom

he was himself carrying on an adulterous intrigue. The parties he had before said

met at Mr Hamilton's where they were introduced to each other by Mrs Maxwell.
From that
∧ moment M W. cherished by every artifice in his power the acquaintance he had
           Cap^n
formed with ~~M^r~~ B. Considerable intimacy took place in consequence between

them, & Mr W. was admitted to all the hospitalities of Cap^{tn} B's house & table.

He was admitted for a length of time without any suspicion of his motives being

either incorrect or dishonourable; but at last his attention to M^{rs} B became so

marked, his language so unguarded, & his whole conduct so extraordinary

that it could not escape notice that he had an object in view which no

honourable man would think of pursuing – namely that of making an   //f.63r

inroad on the domestic happiness & chastity of his friend's wife. Cap^{tn} Bligh became uneasy

at the defendant's visits, & remonstrated against them to his wife. A lady, too, of high rank would

that day be called before them, to prove that she had given M^{rs} B a friendly caution not

to see M^r W on any account in private & to decline his visits as they had become of a suspicious

character...The health of Cap^{tn} B. was very infirm. At certain regular periods of the day he was in the habit of riding or going out, for the sake of exercise, & it was observable

that Mr W. always paid a visit to Mrs B. at those hours, when he was certain that

her husband would not be found at home. It was observed also that Mr W. was

peculiarly anxious to make up parties for M^rs B; & amongst other parties was one

to visit the crater of Mt Vesuvius. To this latter party Cap^tn B. decidedly objected

on the ground that he was not in a situation to attend his wife upon it; for it was

a night excursion, as excursions to Mt V. generally are, for the purpose of seeing the

eruptions to the best advantage. M^rs B, however, declared that she would go; &

the discussion ended in Cap^n B's brother accompanying her on the excursion. The

defendant accompanied her also; & from the evidence – & M^r W's own conduct, he

believed there could be no question that the guilt of the parties was consummated

about the time of that excursion. In a very short time subsequent to it, it became

necessary for Cap^n B. to lay an interdict, or to threaten it, on M^r W's visits, & at

the very moment when he expressed his intention to do so, a determined resistance was

offered to it by the lady. Nay more she assigned as a reason for eloping from the

house after her husband on the 31 July that he objected to the visits of Mr W. – visits

of so suspicious a nature that any man who had permitted their continuance would

have rendered himself accessory to any guilt which his wife might have contracted //f.63v

by it. When that elopement ᴧ where did the jury suppose that the lady sought shelter?
                              took place

He would prove that on the night of that day she was seen in a retired shrubbery; walking

with Mr W. & hanging upon his arm – that she took lodging at an hotel in the im=

mediate vicinity of the house in which he was residing – that he was in every sense

of the words her adviser & counsellor – & that he even dictated her letters & managed her correspondence. He would likewise prove to them that M^r W took her more im-

mediately under his ^own protection – that he persuaded his wife to take her into his own house

as a part of the family, for the avowed purpose of maintaining her character, but for

the real purpose of facilitating the adulterous intercourse which he continued with

her for months – & that he even went to the length of insisting with the British minister

that she should be received with the other English visitors at the court of Naples. He

ought here to inform the jury that Mr Hamilton, who was bound to take care that

no improper person should be admitted under his auspices at the Court where he

was representing the King of England, & felt himself under the necessity of desiring

that the liberty that had been given her to visit there should be withdrawn, & had

intimated to her, that if she attempted to intrude her presence there any more, he

must order her to be excluded, in as much as her character, from her connexion with

the defendant, had rendered her no longer fit to visit or reside with decent society

By his influence over his wife's mind he had made her consider that such a decision

on the part of Mr Hamilton was a gross calumny on the character of Mrs Bligh

& could therefore call upon her to receive his paramour into her house, in order to

vindicate his honour, which he represented to be endangered so long as M^{rs} B's

innocence was not asserted. He would prove to them that Mr W. had done   //f.64r

all this by the handwriting of M^r W himself, the correspondence which had passed between

them, he thought, would be sufficient to convince the most incredulous…M^{rs} B continued

to be an intimate of M^{rs} W's mansion until their departure from Naples on the 5th Oct.

On that day M^r & Mrs W. set out from Naples for the purpose of pursuing their route

to Paris. When they arrived at Florence, the proceedings of Mr W. assumed a character the most extraordinary. M^{rs} B resided at Florence, as she did at Naples, in the same

hotel with Mrs W. The whole party stayed there from the 15 Oct. to the 31. December, at

which time M^{rs} W's eyes were fortunately opened to the real state of the connexion

existing between her husband & Mrs B. She then saw that it was no longer

consistent with the honour of any party that Mrs B. should remain the inmate of

the same hotel with herself & her husband, & she communicated that opinion to M^{rs}

B. accompanying it with a strong recommendation that she should immediately

pursue her own way by herself to England. Mrs W. had at first every reason to

believe that her recommendation was attended to; but she subsequently discovered

that Mrs B. had remained in the same hotel with her at Florence from the 31st

Dec. to the 11th of the following April. And for what purpose, he would ask the jury

had she so remained, except to indulge in the adulterous connexion to which he

had before alluded? Mrs B. left Florence on the 11th April & M^{r} W he would

prove, proceeded to the South on the 12th They would not be surprised at hearing

that by this time, Mr W. satiated with the luscious banquet which he had enjoyed

so long, & having his passion cooled by ⟨the⟩ long residence which the lady had made

under his roof, was anxious to get Mrs B. to return to England, & this he

effected by giving her a promise that he would shortly follow her. He would   //f.64v

read to them letters of Mrs B. in which she reproached the defendant with the non-

fulfillment of his promise in delaying at Florence & in which she entreated him to

follow her immediately to Paris. He complied with her intreaties he followed her

to Paris; he continued with her at that place the intercourse which he had commenced

at Naples, having craftily arranged that M^{rs} W, should always be a day's journey behind him on the ground that he could so make a better arrangement

for her lodgings. He passed for some time at Paris under the feigned name of Smith,

but at that place his connexion with Mrs B., began at length to be so open & notorious

that it became necessary for Mrs W. to believe the interference of her friends to effect a

separation from her husband. They would find that Lord Maryborough had gone to

Paris, to interfere on hr behalf – that a separation took place between her & her husband

that she returned to England with his father & that he remained at Paris. Whilst

matters were in this condition, Mr W. wrote a letter to his wife which he would

neither call justificatory nor exculpatory, giving her an account of what

occurred between himself & M^{rs} B, & stating what his own conduct had between

towards that lady from the time she left Florence down to the moment of his writing

to her (M^{rs} W). It was so extraordinary a letter that he would beg leave to call

their particular attention to it. He would take the account which it contained

to be either true or false, because, either in a moral point of view or in any other

point of view, it was of little importance whether the circumstances it detailed

had really occurred, or were only matters of pure invention. After informing

his wife that it had been his intention to give a friend the statement he was

then going to make to her, in order to let him communicate it to her at some future //f.65r

period as a justification of his own conduct he proceeded in the following strain: –

'However, upon reflection, I have resolved to send it at once to you, especially after that

which occurred to me last night, or rather at daylight this morning. I shall give you the

statement without comment. I hope it will cause you to reflect deeply, & will induce

you to refrain from acts of precipitation. So soon as Mrs B. quitted your residence at

Florence I endeavoured by all the means in my power to persuade her to seek the

assistance of her father. I frequently pressed her upon this point which produced

certainly an aberration of mind; & in a fit of insanity she attempted her life, & nearly

succeeded in destroying herself. She took poison. The physician who attended her at

Florence Dr Dooers was fully satisfied of her insanity, & strongly recommended me

to use towards her the mildest conduct. I persuaded Mrs B., upon our leaving Florence

to precede us by a day. The day she quitted Florence, I wrote to her father, stating her

having done so, of my intention to delay my journey to Paris, to give him time to meet

his daughter at Paris, where I implored him to exercise his authority as a parent, to

remove her to his protection; & I added the physician's opinion of her deranged state

of intellect. I went as you know to Leghorn, where I stayed to carry my purpose

into execution. Mrs B. heard at Genoa of my not having come on the road to Paris

She came back to Florence. From there she went to Pisa, where she wrote to me to

come to her. I refused, & at length persuaded her without having seen me to

proceed upon her journey to Paris on my promising to follow her. I did so, in

order that she might not escape her father. I arrived at Paris: I found her

there but not her father. The day of my arrival at Paris I wrote to Shawe, to

beg he would urge his father to see her. I repeated to Shawe that I found her   //f.65v

intellects quite decayed, & begged he would so acquaint her father. Mr Daly wrote to a

friend of her father's, for the inspection of the father, at my instigation, a statement of

his belief of her deranged state of intellect. The physician who attended her" – [And

here, gentleman, I must remind you, that she passed at Paris under the feigned name of

Smith. The physician will tell you that the connexion continued in that place almost as unblushingly as it continues to be carried on up to the present hour at which I have

the honour to be addressing you. Whether it commenced at Naples at the time & under

the circumstances I have mentioned to you, you may, perhaps, doubt, though I cannot

but that it was carried on at Paris, & that it continued to be carried on down to the

hour no one can doubt...] "the physician who attended her, Dʳ Laffen, did the same

I took the best legal advice opinion in France as to my power either to place her in

confinement as a maniac, or send her to her parents. I found I had none. My

frequently urging her to go to her parents increased her mental malady, I feared

the worst consequences. I waited upon a celebrated French mad doctor, & con:

sulted him upon the course I had better pursue, to persuade her to go to England.

He, without hesitation, gave me the advice to treat her with the greatest kindness

to endeavour to lead her by assiduity & attention, & he assured me of her intellects

being really impaired, & that she found me the object of her affections. I should

have said, I had adopted this course for about six or seven weeks. From time

to time I saw the mad doctor who gave me directions as to my proceedings.

Two days before Lord Maryborough arrived at Paris, Mᴿˢ B. had promised

to go to her father. Her intellects were greatly improved, & I was seeing an opening

to a termination of ~~to~~ the dreadful anxiety which hung over me when you   //f.66r

took the step you did." [Now, continued the learned serjeant, we are not inquiring into the

correctness of the circˢ...but did it mitigate the guilt of Mʳ W. that...

he was anxious to have her confined as a lunatic..."My resolution", proceeds

Mʳ W. "was to have remained at Paris till her father came to her. But

I lost my temper, & too rigidly urged the fulfilling of her promise to me to go home...It produced the most violent effects...I put her under the care

of Mr Hyde...I travelled night & day to this place, having taken every

possible precaution that she should not discover me. How she escaped from

her keepers I know not; but she burst into my room this morning at

daylight...made two attempts on her life...I called in a physician

...he says she cannot live." So much the letter, written 25th July.

On the 15th Mrs W. had formally separated from her husband, his intrigue

with Mrs B. having become so notorious that it was impossible for her to

live with him any longer...He must now inform them that in conseq.

of the ill health of Mr B. he & Mrs B. had for some time before the

elopement slept in separate beds...

   Mr W. took lodgings for Mrs B, and in the name of Mme Ronset

at the house of Mrs Parker, Seymour Place, New Road for the avowed

purpose of her lying-in there...

   Mr Scarlett, for the deft...It was proved that the tempers of

husband & wife were violent, that they frequently wrangled...This tender

husband Mr B. who seduced his wife before marriage, never occupied the

same bed with her after the first 11 weeks...

   Judge briefly summed up – Verdict for Plff. Damages £6,000.

Old D.C.C. Nov 9. 1826.   //f.66v

Hand: TH: *Bligh v. Wellesley ... landed est* in'* (f.60v–61r); ELH: *Ireland ... moderate competency* (f.61r–61v); TH: *She was a lady ... had been stated* (f.61v); ELH: *when application ... he left that* (f.61v–62r); TH: *place ... property* (f.62r); ELH: *whilst his own ... not enquiring into the* (f.62v–66r); TH: *correctness of the circ* ... Old D.C.C. Nov. 9. 1826 (f.66r–66v).

Source: *DCC*, 9 November 1826, p.2, cols 3–5, p.3 cols 1–4.

Text: *From that* (f.62v, 1.16): TH's addition, in pencil. *took place* (f.63v, 1.1): TH's addition, in pencil.

Note: exceptionally, in the case of this lengthy item, folio numbers have been entered in rh margin for ease of reference. *Brett*: TH's slip; the judge was 'Best' (f.61r). *conduct had between* (f.64v, ll.15–16): i.e. 'conduct had been between'. *put to nurse/out at nurse* (f.62r, l.20, f.62v, l.1): estates rented out for income, including Athelhampton, let to J.G. Balston (see item 82a). For the context of this action for damages (to the report of which *DCC* devoted about one third of its usual news-space) see note to item 59b. *DCC* reported that the adulterous relationship took place in 1823, and that a child (a boy) was born to Mrs Bligh, Wellesley the father. 'When the verdict was delivered a tumult of applause was heard in the court' which was 'excessively crowded'. *Duke of Wellington* (f.61r, l.19): see item 68d.

132a

Picking up with a stranger ("Charge of conveying money to convicts")

Howard has permit to see his nephew, a convict in Portland Prison.

Mʳ H., according to his counsel, is a gentleman in good position. Coming

down he met with Montagu, ticket of leave man, gentlemanly, who knew

Mʳ H's nephew. Both Catholics, & they went on to Portland together, Montagu's

ostensible errand being to see the priest, for whom he had acquired a friendship

during his incarceration. It turns out that Montagu's errand was to

place tobacco, money, &c in a shed where the convicts worked.

D.C.C. W.Gazette cutting, &c. May 9 84.

Source: 'The Case of Trafficking With Convicts At Portland Prison', *DCC*, 15 May 1884, p.5 cols 3–4, p.6, col.1.

Note: *ticket of leave man*: prisoner released on parole.

132b

Interesting ladylike girl marries Capt. Bell, after knowing him only a week

or two. Honeymoon trip to Dublin. He dies suddenly. She telegraphs to his mother, at an address he has spoken of – There is no mother – no "Capt.

Bell" in army list. She doesn't know who he is.   Cut D.N. 22.5.84

Text: the last two lines of this item are entered below the last ruled line of the page.
Source: *DN*, 22 May 1884, p.3, col.1.
Note: *Interesting ladylike girl*: the *DN* report has: 'daughter of a most respectable woman'. *There is no mother*: the report states that the recently married wife of the deceased 'telegraphed twice to his mother … but received no reply'. *no 'Capt. Bell' in army list*: the report states only that the widow was unable to establish his military credentials through enquiries via her brother. The verdict of the jury in this case was that 'the person calling himself Captain Alex William Bell died from natural causes, but we have not before us sufficient evidence to show that the deceased was Captain Bell'.

132c

Young man puts up at pub. h. at Barnsley for a night – the servant

took his fancy – licence obtained – married next morning. Old D.C.C. 14.1.30

Source: 'Short Courtship', *DCC*, 14 January 1830, p.2 col.5.
Note: in late May/early June 1884, TH started taking notes from the old DCC file for 1830, but his work on the issues for that year was protracted over at least five years, to 1889, or 1890.

132d

Purse in pocket – man writes to daily papers as instance of uncertainty

of circum[l] evidence, that at theatre…empty purse…placed in his pocket.

ib.

Source: 'Circumstantial Evidence', *DCC*, 14 January 1830, p.2, col.4.
Note: *theatre*: Drury Lane Theatre, London.

132e

Distress in the Medical Profession, particularly country practitioners, in

an unparalleled degree. Long journeys – improbability of being paid – Great numbers

have embarked for America & the settlement on the Swan river.   ib. //

Source: 'Distress of the Medical Profession', *DCC*, 14 January 1830, p.4, col.4.
Note: *Swan River*: site of the city of Perth, W. Australia.

133a

<u>Bibles & paupers</u> – Edith Simcox in article 19th Century for June '84

says that Bible societies who produce bibles for the poor at 1/- & 6[d]

send people to the slums by making them work at ruination prices

to keep up their supply at that cheap rate.

Source: Edith Simcox, 'Eight Years of Cooperative Shirtmaking', *Nineteenth Century*, 15 (June 1884): 1037–54 (p.1054).
Note: *Edith Simcox*: Edith Simcox (1844–1901), essayist and political activist. The article tells the story of Simcox's involvement with women workers in one of the worst of the sweated trades, 1875–84. The passage in question reads: 'For the moment the religious and charitable world is interested in the denizens of the slums; but will that world bear to be told that the slums are peopled by those whom they themselves help to send there? What about the shilling bibles and sixpenny or penny testaments which it is supposed to be a good work to disseminate? The women who fold and sew these books must live in slums, with the rest of the vast army whose life amongst us is a slow death upon starvation wages' (pp.1053–4). This argument is echoed in the criticism levelled at Christianity by socialists such as Ernest Belfort Bax and Edward Aveling at this period. *ruination prices*: TH's version of 'starvation wages'.

133b

<u>Disguise</u> – Bonaparte used to perambulate Paris in disguise, during the

Consulate (according to Bourriene), to learn the opinions entertained of him by

the commonalty – driven out of shop by old woman for speaking disrespect[ly]

of himself.   D.C.C. Jan 28. 1830

Source: *DCC*, 28 January 1830, p.2, col.2.
Note: *Bourriene* [*sic.*]: Louis A. Fauvelet de Bourrienne (1769–1834), Bonapartist diplomat, at one time intimate with Napoleon as his secretary, author of *Mémoires de Monsieur de Bourrienne … sur Napoléon Bonaparte*, 10 vols (Paris, 1829–31). It appears that this report in *DCC* was derived from the French (1st edn) of the *Mémoires*, iv, 37. See also item 191c and *LN*, i, item 1528.

133c

Elopement. The dau. of a gent. of large estates in Shropshire recently

eloped with the footman – pursuit too late to prevent marriage –   ib.

Source: 'Singular Elopement', *DCC*, 28 January 1830, p.2, col.5.
Note: the couple managed to get to Manchester where they were married.

133d

Winter, severe weather – A woman, labourer's wife, has large family, &

several children ill, & without food. She goes out & steals a piece of beef

from butchers stall in Poole – Has been known as rep[ble] woman for years.

one month's imprisonment –   ib.

Source: 'Poole Quarter Sessions', *DCC*, 28 January 1830, p.4, col.3.
Note: *A woman*: Jane Willis. *rep[ble]*: respectable. TH's own heading is apposite since numerous items in this issue concern the effects of the appalling winter weather (including heavy snow drifts), the consequences for the poor, and the acts of charity which their plight aroused in the region (e.g. the distribution of coal, bread and flannel). *DCC* reported that 'the Chairman in delivering the sentence, admonished the prisoner that although in such seasons as the present every one must feel for the misery of the poor, still no distress could justify the commission of a felony'.

133e

Coming out of prison – As Berryman comes out of Exeter jail (in for 12 months

for passing counterfeit coin) in high spirits at the prospect of enlargement,

they are suddenly damped as he approaches the entrance & sees the well known

face of Howard, whose errand he guesses is to himself. The instant he emerged

that officer seized him – charge of bigamy.   ib. //

Source: *DCC*, 28 January 1830, p.4, col.3.

134a–[p.135]

<u>Chaise in Sea</u>. It is our painful task to record a most melancholy &

awful accident attended with the loss of three lives. On Friday last about

the hour of ten at night, cries for help were heard on the beach at Starcross

which after continuing a short time ceased, all was again still & no further

notice taken of the circumstance. On the following morning about 9 o'clock

something wearing a strange appearance was discovered full a half

mile from the shore; immediately boats were procured & put off for the

purpose of ascertaining what it could be; on their arrival they found

a chaise & two horses swampt. The people immediately set to work

to extricate the chaise & on opening the blinds (all of which were up)

they were horror-struck at finding it contain the bodies of two well-

dressed men. At that time they must have been in the water twelve

hours, all hopes therefore of recovery were gone, & nothing remained but

to bring them ashore which, together with the chaise was accordingly

done, the horses were dragged ashore shortly afterwards, altogether

presenting the most melancholy appearance that perhaps was ever

witnessed. The driver has not been found & is supposed to be carried

out to sea. The unfortunate persons are, Mr Lipscombe of the Marine

Hotel Teignmouth & his relative Mr J.Ponsford, the former about

45, the latter a young man about 18 years of age. To account

for the catastrophe is impossible, the oldest inhabitants of the town

cannot recollect a similar circumstance happening on a spot

to all appearance void of danger. Many of our readers will be   //

able to recollect the place, it being that part of the beach, midway

between the slope at the end of Starcross & Cockwood bridge.

It is conjectured the driver (who from all accounts was perfectly

sober) must have fallen asleep (those inside from the blinds

being up had doubtless composed themselves also) & the horses

instead of taking the road along the beach to the right, had gone

towards the sea. It was almost low water at the time & the horses

having nothing to check them, continued the same route until they

came to one of the channels of the river, where, the bank shelving

almost perpendicularly, the horses lost their footing & were plunged

into deep water. Mr Lipscombe has left a wife & six children to

lament his loss. On Sunday at 12 o'clock an inquest was held on
                    M^r
the bodies by Gribble of Ashburton when nothing transpired to

throw further light on the subject, the evidence went merely to state

that the chaise was found nearly half a mile out in 12^{ft} of water

with the pole erect, & just the head & tail of the grey mare were

seen with her fore leg over the other horse's neck, & her hind leg over

the pole, not a rein or trace broken, the blinds were up; the post boy

was unmarried & had not been found, the chaise past Starcross

twenty minutes after ten, the watches were taken from the pockets

one stopt at half past 10, the other 20 minutes after 11 o'clock.

                                                                    ib.

Hand: ELH
Source: 'Melancholy Accident', *DCC*, 28 January 1830, p.4, col.4.
Note: *about* (l.20): ELH's addition, otherwise she copies verbatim from the report. *Starcross*: at the mouth of the river Exe, S. Devon. *pole*: a long wooden shaft fitted to the fore-carriage and attached to the yoke or collar of the horse, serving to guide and control the vehicle (OED).

135a

Mask – boy puts it on knocks at door – terrified young servant into fits,

likely to be subject to them for life   ib. //

Source: 'Danger of Sudden Fright', *DCC*, 28 January 1830, p.4, col.4.
Note: DCC notes the 'terrific looking mask'. This is a probable source for a grim incident in 'The Winters and the Palmleys' (from 'A Few Crusted Characters') in which a young boy, 'frightened … into fits' becomes a drivelling idiot, and dies 'soon afterwards' (*LL1, CS,* 509).

136a

<u>The Old Queen of Portugal</u>. Enjoyed extensive means of mischief;

& exercised them. Died on the 7th at age of 54 – the victim of her dis-

solute habits & ravenous passions. The scandalous Chronicle of the court

of Lisbon records more causes of her premature decay than we are willing

to notice…The pretended penance & prayers – the devotion & retirement of the

latter years of her life – however edifying to her confessor, could not be expect[d]

to repair the ravages wh. early & long-continued profligacy had made upon

her constitution. Some curious stories are told of the means employed by

the doctors & divines who surrounded her deathbed to prolong the life of

this worthless princess. Medical skill confessing defeat they sent for a little

miraculous image…Her hopeful son Miguel was anxious that her life

might be preserved a few days, chiefly that he might enjoy a hunting ex-

cursion wh. he had projected at Peinheiro, & he was not a little displeased with <u>our Lady</u> for allowing his m[r] to die on the 7th inst[d] of 10th, when

he w[d] have been ready for the event. Quot. from <u>Times</u>. D.C.C. 4.2.30

Source: *DCC*, 4 February 1830, p.2, col.2 (from *The Times* 25 January 1830, p.2, cols a–c).
Note: *Queen of Portugal*: Carlotta Joaquina.

136b

<u>The Eagle</u>. On F. week an eagle was shot in neigh[d] of Bridgewater by

man in pursuit of wild fowl. Wing only being broken, bird escaped, & seated

itself on summit of tree – dislodged by a 2[d] shot from a stranger who happ[d]

to be near. The monarch of the air, pps with intent[n] inflict summary ven-

geance, alighted on arm of his assailant – & w[d] probably have amply avenged

himself had not the man dexterously seized him by throat, & notw[g] the repeated

& violent blows from powerful pinions of enraged bird held it till rescued from

perilous pos[n] by 1st sportsman. Bird secured by binding pinions. 8ft tip to tip of wings   //
                                                                                            ib.

Text: the final line of the item is entered below the last ruled line of the page.
Source: *DCC*, 4 February 1830, p.3, col.3.

137a

Married woman left in charge of mansion – husband lives at their

cottage – he breaks in & robs the house [she not knowing of his intention –

& only guessing it was he?] It was in Pulteney St. Bath –   ib.

Text: there are two vertical parallel lines (pencil) beside this item.
Source: *DCC*, 4 February 1830, p.4, col.3.
Note: *[she not knowing … it was he?]*: TH's addition. The *DCC* report varies considerably from
TH's account: 'Mr Templeman [of Pulteney Street] went to Lyme … leaving Mary, the wife of John
Chidgy, in charge of the house and furniture … on returning home, Mr Templeman found that his
house had, during her absence, been robbed of property to the amount of £30 in value: and it was
discovered that John Chidgy had sold several of the articles missing to several persons in Bath.

Chidgy, finding he was suspected, absconded from Bath.' He is arrested at Chipping Sodbury, Glos, armed, and brought in custody back to Bath where he is committed for trial at the next assize and transported for seven years (*DCC*, 8 April 1830, p.2, col.2).

137b

<u>Murder of Clergyman</u> planned by several villagers, because he was obnox

ious to them by rigid manner in wh. he exacted his tithes, &c. Murder carried

out by one named Hemming. Hemming soon after disappears – It is

found years after that a reward being offered the planners feared H. w^d

not withstand it – & murdered him in barn – Skeleton found there, a

2 ft rule beside it. He was carpenter –   ib.

Source: 'A Parallel to the Polstead Murder', *DCC*, 4 February 1830, p.4, col. 4 and 'Adjourned Inquest on Hemming the Murderer', *DCC*, 11 February 1830, p.2, col.3.
Note: for the Polstead Murder (of Maria Marten) see item 85b. According to the second *DCC* report Richard Hemming was discovered at 'Oddingley, near Worcester' through the confession by Thomas Clewes who claimed that he was present at the murder, but was not the perpetrator. TH here combines the two reports. *DCC* also reported ('The Oddingley Murders', 25 March 1830, p.4, col.3) that the accused were discharged, 'the principal felon ... being now dead'. Church bells rang when the news reached Oddingley.

137c

<u>The late Genl Garth</u> – formerly of the Kings Mews, London, & late of Ilsington

House Piddletown – all persons having any claim or demand &c Adv.   ib.

Source: *DCC*, 4 February 1830, p.1, col.3.
Note: for details of Garth see also item 45b and Appendix Two. Garth fell into debt in his later years (see Jeremy Musson, 'Ilsington House, Dorset', *Country Life* (12 June 1997): 158–63 (pp.158–9); John Newth, 'Ilsington', *Dorset County Magazine* (May 1992): 12–14). Lady Dorothy Nevill, born a Walpole, spent much of her childhood at Ilsington in the 1830s (see her *Under Five Reigns* (London: Methuen, 1910), ch.1): she and TH were acquaintances. *Piddletown*: the original name for Puddletown; still designated Piddletown as late as 1848 (*Kelly's Directory*). Puddletown began to be adopted as a prim alternative from mid-century (see *Harrods Postal and Commercial Directory of Dorsetshire and Wiltshire* (1865)). While the 1891 census designates the town as 'Puddletown', 'Piddletown' remained in common use down to the late 1920s. An attempt (by Dorset County Council) to reinstate 'Piddletown' in 1955–56, was

seen off by powerful local opposition; see *Dorset Evening Echo* (14 December 1956), *Western Gazette* (22 February 1957).

137d

Frozen to death – Smuggling galley 4 men in it frozen to death, picked

up in Chale Bay, Isle of Wight, supposed to have drifted from coast of Sussex.

ib. 11.2.30

Source: *DCC*, 11 February 1830, p.3, col.4.

137e

market
Severity of Weather – 2 men coming from Salisbury ʌ in a light cart; cold took

such effect on one that if journey had not terminated he w^d have perished.   ib.

Source: *DCC*, 11 February 1830, p.3, col.4.

137f

Legacy Lost. A poor turncock is, with his brothers, left a legacy by a relative

who dies in Canada. The solicitor's son, clk in office of his father who received the money

on the part of the turncock, absconds with it. "A misappropriated legacy." D.N. (cuttings)

July 28. 84   //

Source: *DN*, 28 July 1884, p.3, col.6.
Note: *turncock*: a water-supply worker.

138a

Forgery – Consol office, Bank Of E. a person obtained the div^ds on

£66,000 Consols by personating the real holder, & counterfeiting his signature. The amount thus obtained was £990, & the forgery was not disc^d

till the true claimant, Thos Hudson, presented himself as usual to sign for

his dividend. The money was taken out chiefly in notes of £50 each

of wh. only one has come back to the bank, so that the offender will

prob^ly be detected. Loss falls on Bank. Old D.C.C. Feb 25. 30

Source: *DCC*, 25 February 1830, p.2, col.2.

138b

30

<u>Missing snuff box</u> – 18 y^rs ago ~~13~~ of E. of Mr Edgcumbe's tradesmen

dined at the Cremill Passage Inn, nr Devonport. One of party missed a

silver snuff box, high value. All denied the theft: gen^l search proposed –

but the gem had disappeared. Years rolled on – every member of that

resp^ble society considered it a personal misfortune, & at each of the

succeeding annual festivities the incident was adverted to. Last Tuesday

a little boy knocked at owner's door, delivered parcel wh. he s^d a

gent^n had given him in street – long lost treasure – tarnished by time.   ib.

[E. says the inn is where you land at Mr Edgcumbe on the beach]

Source: *DCC*, 25 February 1830, p.3, col.4.
Note: *E. of Mr Edgcumbe*: Earl of Mount Edgcumbe who lived in a fortified Tudor mansion overlooking Plymouth Sound. *Cremill Passage Inn* (in Cornwall) faces Devonport across the mouth of the river Tamar. *[E. says ... beach]*: information derived from Emma.

138c

<u>A roper</u> of Okehampton, returning to Exeter – horseback, very brisk pace –

extremely dark – pole of Ld Graves's carriage – precipitated under feet of horses – death instantaneous –   ib.

Source: *DCC*, 25 February 1830, p.3, col.4.
Note: the verdict at the inquest was 'Accidental Death'. The roper, William Dustin, left a widow (pregnant) and three young children. *pole*: see note to 134a.

138d

"Beer-flavour" Publicans used it, with water, increasing the quantity of beer

by $^1/_3$ – deleterious composition – defraud revenue to enormous extent.   ib.

                                                                                      //

Text: the final line of this item is entered below the last ruled line of the page.
Source: 'Adulteration of Porter', *DCC*, 25 February 1830, p.4, col.4.

139a

Mr Toms, propr. of Dk. of Wellington Coach – proceeding in a 4 wheel phaeton

from Weyth to Revels Inn – Descending hill near Dogberry Gate, splinter bar

pressed on hocks of horse, wh. was a large one – animal commenced kicking,

& became quite unmanageable – Two women in cottage by road saw the

horse galloping away, & Mr Toms standing in the vehicle, pulling hard –

but before they came to the door vehicle was upset – Mr T. on ground –

horse on him. Body removed to Revels Inn. "Accidental death"

Proprietor of "Dk of W." 20 years – & very seldom did he omit personally

accompanying it.   ib. id.

Source: 'Melancholy And Fatal Accident', *DCC*, 25 February 1830, p.4, col.1.
Note: *Revels Inn*: the present Lower Revels Farm, E. of Lyon's Gate, is on the site of the former inn, then on a coach road; referred to as 'Reveller's Inn' in *The Woodlanders* (*Woodlanders*, 1985, 156). *Dogberry Gate*: Dogbury, N. of Minterne Magna. *splinter bar*: 'A cross-bar in a carriage ... which is fixed across the head of the shafts, and to which traces are attached' (OED).

139b

Melancholy man – moody attitude over fire – had been a month

writing a letter, wh. he w^d attempt to do, & suddenly crumple it up –

ib.

Source: 'Distressing Suicide', *DCC*, 25 February 1830, p.4, col.1.
Note: Lieutenant George Andrews, Dorset Militia, aged 60, cut his own throat. According to one witness he exhibited 'a gloomy and melancholy picture of mental abstraction'. The verdict of the inquest was 'temporary derangement'.

139c

The Revd John Russell – After dinner & the days sport, he mounted

a hack, & starting from Stock, shaped his course as best he could for

Bath, hoping to reach that city…fifty odd miles…before the inns & stables

were all closed for the night. At Warminster, however, he found it ex-

pedient to leave own horse behind him, & hire a fresh one – landl^d supplied

him with "a rare goer" – "w^d carry him like an infant in a cradle" – "Bring

him out", s^d Russell…Dark…never did R. undergo such a bumping

as on the ribs of that hack. Bath – long after midnight – White Lion open –

"Feed him well", s^d R. to owner as he groped his way out of yard – …

Next day he discovered the horse had no hair on mane or tail – Life.   //

Source: E.W.L. Davies, *Memoir of the Rev. John Russell and his Out-of-door Life* (1878; new edn, London: Richard Bentley & Son, 1883), pp.123–7.
Note: *The Revd John Russell*: The Revd John Russell (1795–1883), 'the sporting parson' who bred the 'Jack Russell' terrier. *Stock*: Stock House, near Sherborne, Dorset, home of Revd Henry Farr Yeatman, another sporting parson and a local magistrate noted for his conservative views on wages and poor relief (see Barbara Kerr, *Bound to the Soil: A Social History of Dorset* (1968; East Ardsley, Wakefield: E.P. Publishing, 1975), p.98).

140a

Diabolical cutting of rope – during night, at Royal Oak Dorch[r]

while M[r] Tolbort was repairing pump in well – 70ft deep – when stepping

into bucket, found that somebody had cut 3 strands out of 4 of wh. the

rope was composed.   Old D.C.C. Mar. 18. 1830.

Source: *DCC*, 18 March 1830, p.4, col.3.
Note: *Royal Oak*: inn, High West Street, Dorchester. According to *DCC*: 'had it been not
discovered that instant, Mr Tolbort must have been precipitated the whole depth of the well'.

140b

Forbidding the banns – Cattistock : ch. crowded to suffocation, the con-

gregation expecting it to come off – Forbidden by a rival who had the fair

one's previous promise. After service, however, the rivals of the lady went

to Fox & Hounds Inn, to submit the case to the court of Bacchus – a few

jugs of ale, & a reconciliation took place, the lady going back to her

original lover – The second one lachrymose & mortified – acclamation

of assembled crowd – Blushing bride endeavoured to hide her face, but from

corner of eye there beamed a token of delight at the adventure.   ib.

Source: *DCC*, 18 March 1830, p.4, col.3.
Note: *Cattistock*: near Maiden Newton, W. Dorset. *expecting it to come off*: TH's phrase for
DCC's 'expecting that on the publication of the banns of an intended marriage, it would be
forbidden by a rival'.

140c

Two women, E. Loosemore & M. Loosemore: stealing 2 heifers – at

Mariansleigh – E. was dressed in male attire at time of robbery, & was com-

mitted under the name of John Hill. A.L. a labourer on the roads deposed

that he saw the prisoners with the heifers, wh. appeared to have been very much overdriven, & in conseq. of M^r K's (owner's) man asking him respecting them

he took the prisoners into custody on their returning the same road next day.

They sold the cattle in Exeter market – (about 17 miles off apparently).   ib. 25.3.30 //

Text: there are two vertical parallel lines (pencil) beside the first four lines of this item.
Source: *DCC*, 25 March 1830, p.3, col.4.
Note: *Mariansleigh*: village in N. Devon, near South Molton. *A.L.*: TH's transcription of Abraham Greenslade, labourer. *(about 17 miles off apparently)*: TH's addition.

141a

Waylaid – Man walking from Blandford to Honiton – overtaken

by two men – go into public house & drink together at Milborne St

Andrews. They say they are going to Exeter. Walk on together.

A mile or so from Milborne they attack him with his own stick –

stuff his mouth with mud to stifle his cries, & leave him for dead,

after picking his pocket, taking watch &c – He comes to himself – reaches

Piddletown – finds one of the men in bed there. Old D.C.C. Ap^l 1. 1830

(Notice the custom of walking long distances in those days)

Source: 'Robbery and Brutal Outrage', *DCC*, 1 April 1830, p.4, col.3.
Note: *Piddletown*: see item 137c. *(Notice … those days)*: TH's addition.

141b

To Tanners – To be let – an old-established yard at Yetminster &c.   ib.

Source: *DCC*, 8 April 1830, p.1, col.2.
Note: *Yetminster*: village in N.W. Dorset.

141c

Driving home – from Priddy Fair – "was driving a mare of my own – but having got out of my road (was drunk) I gave up the reins & whip

to my compan^n – he drove – I retained my seat, on the side for driving.

ib. Ap. 8.

Source: *DCC*, 8 April 1830, p.3, cols 3–4.
Note: *Priddy*: village in the Mendips, Somerset (see item 50c). This lengthy report contains details
of the injuries to the passengers and damage to the cart, all omitted here.

141d

Man leaves all his property to his servant instead of to his [wife &] family.

(He was taken dangerously ill, & confined to bed for a long time, during wh. the

servant Elizth Hicks paid him great attention)…His sister used him

badly…He was seized with a paralysis wh. deprived him of the use of

his right side & of his speech with the exception of certain words, such as

"yes", "no", "dear", & "dammy".   ib. Ap^l 15.
               (by his nephew)
Will disputed ʌ – signed with left hand on account of paralysis: had formerly

had a child by servant when living at his original home in Somerset – left there,
                    (including nephew)   time
& lived with friends ʌ at a distance for some ~~years~~ : made will in their favour:
                                        (who was either now married – or after will)
was taken ill: returned to original home, sent for his old servant ʌ : made will in <u>her</u>

favour, witnessed by clergyman attorney & medical gent^n (later paper – May 18. 30). //

Text: there are two vertical parallel lines (pencil) beside the last eight lines of this item.
Source: *DCC*, 15 April 1830, p.4, col.4; *DCC*, 13 May 1830, p.3, col.3.
Note: *dammy*: DCC has 'd-n ye'. *May 18*: TH's error.

142a

Watchmen in 1830 – Poole Robbery of Bank – slates taken off roof & a

rope used to let robber down – "We hope the police will soon be put on a more effective plan & the Commission of the nightly watch of this town will now see

serviceable

the necessity of putting that establishment on a more ~~effective~~ footing: the present

plan of the watchman resorting together at a house on the quay, & only sallying out

to call the hour of night, & then returning to close quarters again, cannot afford

any security. We w^d recommend that the w. be appointed to diff^t stations, & each man

be const^ly walking his beat.   Old D.C.C. Ap.29 '30

Source: *DCC*, 29 April 1830, p.4, col.2.
Note: *police*: at this date a term applied to the watch.

142b

Skeleton of an infant found behind plastering of roof –   ib. May 5. 30

Source: *DCC*, 6 May 1830, p.3, col.4.
Note: *May 5*: TH's error.

142c

<u>Oaktree</u> – G.G. killed – tree falls on him; unexpectedly blown down by sudden

gust of wind while he was engaged in felling it. Verd: Acc. Death.   ib.

Source: *DCC*, 6 May 1830, p.3, col.4.
Note: *G.G.*: George Gibbons.

142d

<u>H.H. a marine</u>, discharged, travelling to his native place in Wilts – Slept

Sat. night at Phoenix Inn, in same room with a waggoner. On Sunday morn.

at 5 he took waggoner's breeches from under his head while he was asleep –

& robbed him of 3 sov^s & some silver – drank – died.   ib.

Source: *DCC*, 6 May 1830, p.3, col.4.
Note: *H.H.*: Henry Hewlett. *Phoenix Inn*: in Hartley Wintney, Hampshire. The verdict at the

inquest on the marine was that he 'died from excessive drinking' (in prison, after his arrest).

142e

<u>Man borrowed gun</u> of neighbour, without telling him why he wanted it. Neighb^r

hears it is to shoot his brother (borrower's), who being owed money by borrower of gun
& bailiff in possession,
⋏ exasperating borrower of gun against his b^r. When neighb^r learnt this he went to

get back gun – in the struggle was shot.   ib. //

Source: *DCC*, 6 May 1830, p.3, col.4.

143a

Wife deserted, supports herself & child by copying documents at the record office

& the B. Museum.   D.N. 12.11.84

Source: *DN*, 12 November, 1884, p.7, col.4.

143b

<u>Father goes out with child</u>; comes home without it; has left it in pub.

house, & forgotten where.   ib.

Source: *DN*, 12 November 1884, p.7, col.4.

143c

At a cattle-fair at Edinburgh yesterday a bull rushed at a woman and catching her
upon his horns, bore her aloft through the excited crowd of spectators. The woman,
though half dead with fright, maintained her position for a considerable distance, and
was at length thrown over the animal's head on to the green sward. She escaped with
only a few bruises. 12.11.84

Text: pasted-in newspaper cutting (2 x 6.7 cm). 12.11.84, added by TH (in ink).
Source: *DN*, 12 November 1884, p.7, col.5.
Note: this item is the first cutting from a newspaper or periodical to be pasted into '*Facts*'. *bull
rushed at a woman*: in *The Mayor of Casterbridge* a bull 'too savage to be driven', threatens the

safety of Lucetta and Elizabeth-Jane until tamed by Henchard (*Mayor*, 1987, 205–6).

143d–[p.144]

<u>Lord Tyrawley, Miss Seal, Lady Mary Stewart</u> &c. Miss Seal eloped

from boarding school with Ld T. & lived with him at Somerset House. Obliged

to go to Ireland, where he found his affairs so desperate on account of an

unjust steward that he was obliged to look for a wife possessing wealth –

& chose Lady M. Stewart, Dau. of E. of Blessington, with £30,000.

L^d Bl^n had heard of Miss Seal. Wrote to her, informing her of the con-

templated marriage, & asking if reports were true. She in a rage sent to him

L^d T's letters, including one she had not opened (wh. contained a confession

of the intended marriage from him, & stated the bride was ugly: necessity, &c.)

Ld B. in a fury – forbade his dau. to see Ld T. But she had privately

married him. He refused to give her a guinea, whereupon the bridegroom

demanded & obtained a separation from wife, & was sent as minister to

a foreign court.

Miss Seal became an actress. Her lover forgave her; pressed her   //

to join him in Lisbon. At last she consented – & Ld T. placed her

in the family of a British merchant there, where he occasionally visited

her. Here she met with an English gent[n] named Bellamy, who,

unacquainted with her situation & struck with her charms, solicited

her hand. She refused, till it came to her ears that Ld T. had an

intrigue with a Donna Anna, when, in a fit of jealousy, she accepted

Bellamy, married him, sailed with him for Ireland, & in a few months presented him, to his infinite surprise, with a daughter. He

abandoned her. L[d] T. gave instructions to have her taken care of.

Molloy's Peg Woffington

Source: J. Fitzgerald Molloy, *The Life And Adventures of Peg Woffington With Pictures of the Period In Which She Lived* (London: Hurst & Blackett, 1884), pp. 218–23.
Note: *Lord Tyrawley*: James O'Hara, Lord Tyrawley (*c.* 1682–1773), Irish soldier. *a daughter*: George Anne Bellamy, actress and later mistress of John Calcraft, politican; see item 52a. For Molloy see item 16b.

144a

Hand lacerated dreadfully by gun bursting – thumb had to be removed.

Old D.C.C. May 13 30.

Source: *DCC*, 13 May 1830, p.4, col.2.

144b

Gentleman Bagpiper, the – stays at "Wood & Stone" inn – question if a

gent[n] after all. Calls himself Capt. Barclay, or Col. Stewart – got between

One & two pounds at Salisbury – only 6/- odd at Dorchester.   ib.

Source: *DCC*, 13 May 1830, p.4, col.2.
Note: *'Wood & Stone' inn*: see item 97c.

144c

A troop of the 3[d] Dragoon guards arrived at Taunton on Tuesday, & the

following morning marched on their route to Exeter –   ib.

Source: *DCC*, 13 May 1830, p.4, col.4.

144d

Whipped – J. Gray & J. Blacker, notorious char[s] were publicly whipped by the hangman of the county through the market of Shepton Mallet, pursuant to

their sentence at the last sessions: G. for stealing a quantity of clothes, & B.

for stealing sacks & some flour.   ib. //

Text: the final line of this item is entered below the last ruled line of the page.
Source: *DCC*, 13 May 1830, p.3, col.3.
Note: see also items 41b, 82b, 94c, 158a.

145a

Princes – Precautions against family impoverishment. – "It appears

from an acc^t of Viennese soc^y now publishing in Paris that there are

no less than 70 Arcd^s & Archd^{sses} belonging to the House of Hapsburg

who all marry into the Royal Caste, from a clan among thems^s & do not

associate on intimate terms even with the highest nobility. Who maintains

all these Princes & Princesses? They have we presume all claims upon

the patrimonial estate of the House of H., & the estate is larger, but the

subdivision is becoming extreme. If the number of claimants sh^d in 50

y^{rs} be doubled...the family with either be compelled to give up its pretensions

to solitude & mate with millionaires, or to pass a rule like that of

some Dutch families that only a certain number shall marry; or to

instance the example of the Delhi Princes, who all lived together in the

great palace, some of them upon allowances barely sufficient to

sustain life."   Spec. Dec 20. 1884

Source: *Spectator* (20 December 1884), p.1687, col.2.

145b

A skilful workman, who had discovered the art of making glass

malleable, carried a specimen of it to Tiberius, who asked him

if he alone was in possession of the secret. He replied in the

affirmative; on which the tyrant ordered his head to be struck

off immediately, lest his invention sh[d] have prove injurious to

the workers in gold, silver & other metals.   Petronius, (notes to Sha
                                                    Pericles p.232)   //

Source: *The Dramatic Works of William Shakespeare* (ed. S.W. Singer), 10 vols (1826; London: Bell
& Daldy, 1856), ix, *Pericles*, p.348, n.11. This was the edition of Shakespeare owned by TH
(*DCM*).
Note: *making glass malleable*: from *Pericles* IV.vi. 142–3, 'crack the glass of her virginity, and make
the rest malleable'. *Petronius*: Petronius Arbiter (d. A.D. 66), Roman author of the *Satyricon*, sect.
51 of which is cited by Singer. TH's page ref. is not explained.

146a

Cure of hydrophobia – "D[r] George Vaillant of New York has recently pub-

lished a paper on the properties of simata cedron as a positive cure for

hydrophobia, a substance long known to Southwestern trappers as an anti-

dote to snake poison & other venom."   Harpers Bazar – Jan 10. 1885.

Source: *Harper's Bazar*, XVIII, no.2 (10 January 1885), p.27, col.3.

146b

Balaclava Charge – "Sir George Wombell saw Capt. Nolan hit by

the shot which killed him. Though killed the body for some little

time maintained its balance on the horse, & was carried past my

informant with its arms extended, the horse going at full gallop.

A minute after it fell to the ground."

Yates's <u>Recollections</u>

Source: Edmund Yates, *Edmund Yates: his Recollections and Experiences*, 2 vols (London: Richard Bentley & Son, 1884), i, 80.
Note: Edmund Yates (1831–94), prolific novelist and journalist, editor of *The World, Temple Bar, Tinsley's Magazine*, associate of Dickens. See P.D. Edwards, *Dickens's 'Young Men': George Augustus Sala, Edmund Yates and the World of Victorian Journalism* (Aldershot: Ashgate, 1997).

146c

<u>Her Sunday clothes</u> – Sarah Goodling, 10, dau. of a seaman belonging to

the Preventive Service, at Port Wrinkle, Sheviock, Cornwall; was ordered by

her father to wear her everyday clothes on Sunday as a punishm[t]...suicide.

Old D.C.C. May 20. 30

Source: 'Extraordinary Suicide', *DCC*, 20 May 1830, p.3, col.4.
Note: TH pinpoints the emotional crisis, but not the cause of death which was an overdose of laudanum.

146d

<u>A valuable horse</u> – nearly destroyed...from the effects of a few sprigs of Wolf's

bane, or Monks hood – (aconitum Napellus) wh. it had eaten –   ib.

Source: *DCC*, 20 May 1830, p.3, col.4.

146e–[147]

<u>Importation of Bristol thieves</u> for Caerleon Fair...The St David steamboat

left the Hotwells, Bristol, about 12, for Newport. Had not proceeded far down the

river when a gent[n] missed his pocket-book. Alarm given – Capt. stood on

paddlebox, & stated to passengers in plain terms his belief that he had 50 thieves   //

on board...threats from the "prigs"...silenced them by saying he would put them ashore.

The time of crossing was spent by them in all sorts of gambling. Intelligence was

conveyed to Caerleon, where a large fair was to be held next day...Twenty spec[l]

constables sworn in.   ib.

Source: *DCC*, 20 May 1830, p.3, col.4.
Note: *Caerleon*: near Chepstow. *prigs*: petty thieves.

147a

A small farmer at Motcombe has raised £700 of £800 by frugal conduct – He

joins the Methodists or Ranters – Lends his money to them to build a chapel.

Interest is paid out of the pew rents. His advances were not repaid. It much

affects him – he murders his child.   ib.

Source: *DCC*, 20 May 1830, p.4, col.1.
Note: *Motcombe*: near Shaftesbury, N. Dorset. *Ranters*: also known as Primitive Methodists whose
revival movement in the early 19th century led to their separation from the Wesleyan Methodists,
though later reunited. *DCC* (1 June 1830, p.4, col.2) printed a letter by an itinerant preacher and
steward of the Society of Primitive Methodists at Shaftesbury which attributed the farmer's crime
not to 'religious enthusiasm' (as reported by *DCC* on 20 May 1830) but to 'an hereditary disease
in the family'. TH again refers to the Motcombe farmer in item 173a. J.O. Bailey suggests that TH
may have drawn on both items for 'The Church-Builder' (*PPP, CP,* 170), *Bailey*, 183–4.

147b

Driving their cart home to Poole, 11 or 12 p.m. after having been to Lymington

to sell Newfoundland Cranberries – a man gets up – gets out – takes horse's head

threatens the men with a pistol if they do not drive up a lane. He has 2 dogs.

                                                                                                       ib.

Source: *DCC*, 20 May 1830, p.4, col.2.
Note: *Lymington*: coastal town in Hampshire. *Newfoundland*: Poole was the chief port trading
with Newfoundland.

147c–[148]

Fortune left to his manserv^t Thos Southwood Esq. with other extensive

property, was Lord of the Manor of Taunton Deane, purchased a few years

ago of the Bp. of Winch^r, the rights & privileges incident to which M^r S.

realized with keen solicitude. Eccentric habits – Dress plain – Domestic ar-

rangements most frugal – dined with serv^{ts} in kitchen – insisted upon

a quiet, cheerless, & uniform administration of household. Aversion to

female sex inexplicable – many anecdotes thereupon – Never married –

few relatives, & those very distant – Expendit^{re} slight in compar^{son} with his

magnificent income. Was reported a few years ago that his splendid

//

property w^d be left to Ld Gifford a distant relative, now dead. But by a

recent will the bulk of his freehold & pers^l estates, estimated at lowest

at £100,000, is beq. to Mr Robt Mattock his serv^t – 33 yrs, having

been placed at an early age in Mr Southwood's family as a parish ap-

prentice by the overseers. M^r M's parents are both still living in obscur-

& near

ity, he has several relatives in ⋏ Taunton, filling humble stations – M^r M.

had not contemplated his fortune, his whimsical benefactor having merely

intimated, at time of making will that "he had left him something comfortable

s   s

but whether it was 5/- or 10/- he sh^d not say" Legacies to other persons

am^t to about £15,000, including provisions for other domestics, & some

estates of the ann^l. value of £600 are devised to a respectable but

distantly related family at Wellington.   Old D.C.C. May 27. 30

Source: *DCC*, 27 May 1830, p.3, col.3.
Note: *beq.*: bequeathed.

148a

In Husband's absence. Jane Phillips, seaman's wife, leaves her infant

under rick – Had become pregnant during husb[ds] absence, & wished

to conceal her guilt from him.   ib.

Source: *DCC*, 27 May 1830, p.3, col.4.

148b

Cider. Farmer sends his man to Plymouth from neighb[d] of Kings-

bridge, with 12 hhds. of cider to dispose of them to best advant[ge] Man

spends the money.   ib.

Source: 'Suicide rather than encounter his employer', *DCC*, 27 May 1830, p.3, col.4.

148c

Jewels. Box of Jewellery stolen from L[d] South[ns] mansion Leicestersh.

Found buried in field by lab[r].   ib. //

Source: 'Singular Recovery of Stolen Property', *DCC*, 27 May 1830, p.2, col.4.
Note: *L[d] South[ns]*: Lord Southampton of Quorndon Hall.

149a

"The Cook's revenge" – Having being punished for a trivial offence by the Monks

of the Convent, he mixed opium with the sauce for supper, & they were soon

fast asleep. Shaved their beards – they w[d] not go out in public.

Ext. from Sidney Anecdotes   ib.

Source: *DCC*, 27 May 1830, p.2, col.1.
Note: *Monks*: bearded Capuchins of the Franciscan Order. *Sidney Anecdotes*: DCC is quoting a
story of 1761 from *Sidney Anecdotes* by Charles and Ambrose Sidney, of Glastonbury (1830?).

149b

Incendiarism – A woman confesses to setting fire to several houses.   ib.

Source: *DCC*, 27 May 1830, p.4, col.1.
Note: the woman, Iddy Still, was 'charged on her own confession with having set fire to several houses in the neighbourhood of Shaftesbury'. Six weeks before her committal *DCC* expressed 'our conviction that the conduct of the woman could be attributed to nothing but insanity', a judgement 'fully confirmed' by her demeanour since her committal. With evidence of her 'mental aberration' care is needed to 'prevent her from committing self-destruction'.

149c

Cider – Crop a failure, after the superabundant crop of last year – blossom

as good as then, but at time of the young fruit setting it was observed that

an insect had lodged in heart of bud. One farmer who made 300 hhds.

last year, does not expect to make one. Same in Hereford & Devon. –

ib. (Somerset)

Source: *DCC*, 27 May 1830, p.4, col.3.

149d

Cudgel Playing – At Taunton; this almost obsolete game was revived.   ib.

Source: *DCC*, 27 May 1830, p.4, col.3.

149e

Petition from Glastonbury against the punishm^t of death for forgery.   ib.

Source: *DCC*, 27 May 1830, p.4, col.3.
Note: this is only one of numerous similar petitions from all over the West Country, reported by *DCC* during these months.

149f

King George IV. The King's will...some dispositions have been made which will never, out of delicacy to the objects of his care, be made

public. We believe that many annuities have been paid to indi-

viduals, through the medium of one great house, of which those most

intimately acquainted with his Majesty's private affairs in other respects,

are ignorant. At the origin of some of these we shall not hint further

than to say that it was the object of his mature life to comfort those

who might otherwise have suffered from the errors of his youth.

Quot. from "Morning Paper" in D.C.C. June 17. 30.   //

Text: the final line of this item is below the last ruled line of the page.
Source: 'His Majesty's Annuitantes', DCC, 17 June 1830, p.2, col.3.
Note: George IV was at this point just alive; for his death see item 150e.

150a

Diamonds…will, it is expected, shortly become less scarce…The late

Burmese war has put into British possession some rich mines of those gems.

ib.

Source: DCC, 17 June 1830, p.2, col.2.
Note: late Burmese war: first Burmese War 1823–26.

150b

Money from India. Lord Combermere is said to have realized

£140,000 by the capture of Bhurtpore, & by the Indian Campaign.

Text: there are two parallel vertical lines (pencil) beside this item.
Source: DCC, 17 June 1830, p.2, col.4.
Note: Lord Combermere: Sir Stephen Cottam, first Viscount Combermere and Field Marshal (1773–1865): acting for the East India Company, he captured and destroyed the citadel of Bharatpur (Bhurtpore) in 1826.

150c

Sir R. Graham, bart, of Walbrook, has presented a petition to his Majesty,

in wh. he claims the title of Earl Annandale & Hartfell, Viscount

Annan, & Baron Johnstone of Lockwood, &c. The King directed the

petition to be forwarded to the house of Lords, & their Lps have referred

the same to a Committee of Privileges.   ib.

Source: *DCC*, 17 June 1830, p.2, col.4.

150d

Binegar fair. Immense supply of horses.   ib.

Source: *DCC*, 17 June 1830, p.4, col.3.
Note: *Binegar fair*: near Wells, Somerset, noted for its four-day Whitsun fair. In TH's 'A Tragedy of Two Ambitions' (*LLI*), Halborough and his 'gipsy wife' are on their way to 'see Mis'ess's friends at Binegar Fair' (*CS*, 408). The reference to 'Binegar Fair' in the first edition of *A Pair of Blue Eyes* (1873; Harmondsworth: Penguin, 1998, p.92), was omitted from the Wessex Edition of 1912.

150e–[151]

Death of Geo. IV. The physicians retired at 10 p.m. with directions to the

two pages, & Sir W. Waller, that if any change occurred they were to be

called. At 3. Sir W.W. became alarmed at the change in the King, who had
   signified by finger that he   his eye became fixed, lips
waked, & ʌ wished to be lifted up: while preparing to raise him ~~the change~~
quivered – Eau de cologne –
~~was noticed~~, changes in his whole appearance: instantly summoned the phy[ns]
                   no relative or friend present
& surgeons; but his M. expired in about 10 minutes. ʌ After having performed

the last duties to the illustrious deceased Sir H.Halford & Sir Math[w] Tierney

left the castle together; the remains were given in charge to M[r] O'Reilly

the surgeon, & M[r] W. the head page, who had been ever since keeping   //

watch over the corpse, one sitting on each side of it. At about 7 it was

announced by M^r O'R. to all other members of the household that they were

at liberty to enter the room & view the body. About one hundred persons,

half of whom were not of the establishment entered the chamber at $^1/_2$ past 7

& were permitted to touch the right hand of H.M. as he lay on the couch

on which he died...After this orders were given to prepare a mahogany

shell... The shell is to be lined ~~wh~~ with white gros de Naples, & is to be

stuffed with wool...   ib. July 2 1830

Source: *DCC*, 1 July 1830, p.2, cols 1 and 2; p.4, col.3.
Note: *Death of Geo. IV*: George IV died on Saturday 26 June 1830. This item is a conflation of
two reports: the interlined additions are from the second report 'Latest Particulars', which reads:
'The page next him instantly proceeded to raise His Majesty, according to the motion which he
signified by his finger ... the attendants at once assisted the King with sal volatile, eau de Cologne,
and such stimulants as were at hand.'

151a

<u>Load of treasure</u> – at time of Geo IV's birth we were at war with Fce.

& Spain; & the Hermione Sp^{sh} frigate, laden with treasure, & one of the

richest prizes of the war, had recently been captured; & at the moment that
                                   (August 12. 1762)
the Pk. & Tower guns announced the birth of a prince ʌ numerous waggons,
                                        down
laden with the treasures of the prize, passed up St James's St. in front of

the palace, on their way to the Bank amid the cheers & huzzas of an exulting

populace, & in presence of the King & great officers of State.   ib.

(£800,000 worth: in 21 waggons – v. <u>Walpole</u> IV)

Source: 'Life and Reign of George IV', *DCC*, 1 July 1830, p.2, col.2.
Note: *passed down/up*: DCC has 'up St James's St.'. (*£800,000 ... IV*): TH adds from *Walpole,
Letters*, iv, 14: 'I have not even told you that the treasure of the *Hermione*, reckoned eight hundred
thousand pounds, passed the end of my street this morning [Arlington Street] in one-and-twenty

waggons.' (Letter to Sir Horace Mann, 12 August 1762 [letter 804]).

151b–[152]

Arrival of Caroline of Brunswick – Scene – ~~on entering on the 30.th Dec. 1794~~ ~~her Serene Highness left the c.t of Brunswick~~ In 1794 the Dk. of York, com-

manding the army in Flanders, became acq. with his uncle the Dk of Brunsw^k

who commanded the Prussian army; & to his court and family he was introd^d.

The accomp^s of Pcess Caroline made impress^n on him – communicated his   //

feelings to P^{ce} of Wales & King. Formal proposals from King for a marriage.

The Duke immed^y consulted his daughter: mother did not strive to conceal

her happiness & delight. Pcess. received the intelligence with composure –

indifference. Admitted that her family w^d be elevated; heart unmoved.

Did not withhold her consent, for although she had heard of the Prince's follies

she had also heard of his virtues. But she c^d not love him. Her affec^{ns}

had been fixed on a young German prince to whom she c^d not give her

hand. On 30th Dec.1794 she left the court of Brunswick attended by

mother, & numerous & splendid retinue – did not, on account of war, embark

till 28 March 95 – came over, landed Greenwich – left Greenwich drawn

by 6 horses, one of King's coaches. Before 3 she alighted at St James's, &

was introd^d to her apartments. Prince agitated on entering palace, but

on being intro^d he saluted her. Dined together – afterw^{ds} visited by King

Queen &c – At 11. the prince retired – & the princess was left with Mrs

Aston.

  Lady Jersey, who had been present the greater part of the interview, & who had been charged with being on terms of intimacy with the Pce, appeared

to be displeased at those attentions wh. the P. of W. had paid to his

destined wife. To this lady her Serene Highness had most imprudently

owned her attachment to a German P[ce] : according to Lady J. she s[d]

she loved his little finger better than P. of W's whole body. She after[wds]

denied the words, but admitted that she had referred to a former attachment.

ib. //

Source: 'Life and Reign of George IV', *DCC*, 1 July 1830, p.2, cols 2–3.
Note: *Caroline of Brunswick*: Caroline of Brunswick (1768–1821), m. Prince of Wales, later
George IV (1795), but, though Queen, was excluded from coronation (1821). *Lady Jersey*: Frances
Twysden (1753–1821), dau. of an Irish bishop, m. Earl of Jersey (1770); sometime mistress of
Prince of Wales. See item 175c.

153a

Lightning – Explosion like a discharge of artillery – M[r] Mayo of Lewell's

young son came down from his bedroom in attic – passing door of his brother's

room saw him lying on bed – found to be dead – elec. fluid came down the
                                           (the brother)
chimney, loosening bricks & struck M[r] M. ⋏ who was dressing, & threw him on

the bed where he was found.   ib.

Source: 'The Weather', *DCC*, 1 July 1830, p.4, col.2.
Note: *Lewell's*: near West Stafford, E. of Dorchester.

153b

Man also struck driving in a horse & cart.   ib.

Source: 'The Weather', *DCC*, 1 July 1830, p.4, col.2.
Note: *Man also struck*: on the road from Blandford to Dorchester: he 'providentially escaped
unhurt', 'on the same morning'.

153c

<u>Illegitimate, but bearing title</u>   Many years ago Earl Poulett

contracted an unfortunate marriage; marrying someone far beneath
                                        (Visc^t)
him in station. Six months after the marriage Lord ʌ Hinton was born.

No doubt by the law of this country a child born in wedlock was legi-

timate. In consequence of the circumstances of the child's birth L^d P.

had cut off the entail of the estate, as he had a perfect right to do. More

than that Viscount Hinton had had notice to the effect that not one penny

w^d be left him, as Earl P. did not consider that he was his son. Hinton

was a clown at the Surrey theatre – utterly impecunious.

<u>Times</u>. Cent^l Crim^l Court – 15.3.86

Cont^d:–

– <u>500</u> settled on him, or his son [in pity?] by Duchess of Cleveland.   ib.

Source: *The Times*, 15 March 1886, p.10, cols e–f.
Note: *[in pity?]*: TH's addition. With no child of her own, Grace, Dowager Duchess of Cleveland
(d.1883), distantly related to the Pouletts, settled £5000 on Hinton's son who became a tea-planter.
TH was mistaken in recording '500', but was probably correct in suggesting 'in pity'. This report
is from prosecution evidence in trial of William, Viscount Hinton and others on charge of obtaining
property under false pretences.

153d

– Letter from Earl Poulett, (Times 19.3.86) explaining that it was his

predecessor, the late Earl, who with his eldest son then alive made a re-

settlement of the estates by deed of entail in 1853, barring "the person now

calling himself Viscount Hinton" from ever inheriting them. "It is under this deed I

hold them, & at my death they go to my son by my third wife, Wm Jno. L. Poulett born 1883, & failing his attaining 21...they pass to the male heir of the late Col. Somerset...' //

Source: *The Times*, 19 March 1886, p.14, col.a. (Letter from Earl Poulett, 'Hinton St. George, Crewkerne, March 17').
Note: *Wm Jno. L. Poulett*: William John Lydston Poulett.

154a

Jewels

The question of the sale of the French Crown Jewels will very shortly

be brought before the senate for decision; the Bill for this purpose

having already passed the Chamber of Deputies...The chief articles

will be preserved, on account of their hist^l or artistic interest –

e.g "Regent" diamond (valued 12 million francs)...&c – A large

engraved ruby, which figured in the order of the Toison d'Or of Louis XVI, &c

Formerly there existed near the Louvre, a building called the "Garde

Meuble" of the Crown, where the furniture, jewels, &c, belonging to the

sovereigns were deposited...The Crown diamonds were contained

in a chest of drawers in one of the apartments.

In the disorders attendant on the Fch. Rev^n a great robbery of

these jewels occurred in 1792...The great treasures stolen

by these robbers & not recovered contained about one thousand carats

of brilliants & roses of various sizes & qualities. Four remarkable

objects have disappeared from the Treasury; the "Sanci" diamond –

the magnificent opal, known as the "Burning of Troy", wh. belonged

to Josephine; a fine brilliant that Nap^n wore at his marriage &

wh. it is s^d he lost at Waterloo; a blue diamond of the rarest weighing 67 carats;

perfection, stolen in 1792 ⋀ supposed to be the blue diamond in

the Hope Collection weighing 44¹/₈ carats by the French, purposely reduced

to disguise its identity. &c, &c.

'The Crown Treasures of France' – Graphic 27.3.86   //

Source: *Graphic*, 27 March 1886, p. 335, cols 1–2.
Note: TH noted in spring 1887: 'Passing through Paris, they went to see the Crown jewels that chanced just then to be on exhibition, previous to their sale' (*Life and Work*, 204). This issue of the *Graphic* contains a portion of ch.27 of *The Mayor of Casterbridge*, then being serialized.

155a

Jewels –

...The prisoner, a Frenchman, after being remanded...had to pass

along a passage to the cell allotted to him in House of Detention. A

pail of water was standing in the corridor...diamonds found in the

bottom of the pail concealed in a glove belonging to prisoner. Had secreted

them in the fingers...   Times – 27. 3. 86.

Source: *The Times*, 27 March 1886, p.12, col.b.
Note: *House of Detention*: in Clerkenwell, C. London; it makes a brief appearance in the opening chapter of George Gissing's *The Nether World*, ed. John Goode (1889; Brighton: Harvester Press, 1974).

155b

"Capt. Gronow's Recollections & Anecdotes"

– A lady lends money to a Jew money lender, who pays her 15

per cent. The money lender (named King) lends it to her son, charging

him 80 per cent.

Source: Capt. R.H. Gronow, *Reminiscences ... being Anecdotes of the Camp, The Court, and the*

Clubs, at the close of the last War with France (London: Smith, Elder and Co, 1862), p.187.
Note: Rees Howell Gronow (1794–1865), soldier and memoirist, wrote four volumes of memoirs of which *Reminiscences* was the first. TH read this and also the second volume, *Recollections and Anecdotes* (1863). Gronow, who had been at Eton with Shelley ('my friend and associate') served in Spain and at the battle of Waterloo (*Reminiscences*, 91–108).

155c

– Byron, when he went boating at Brighton, was gen^{rly} accomp^d

by a lad, who was said to be a girl in boy's clothes.   ib.

Source: Gronow, *Reminiscences*, p.210.

155d

– Capt. Hesse – gen^{rly} believed to be a son of the D^k of York, by

a German lady of rank. In early youth he lived with the D.

& Duchess of York. When he was wounded at Vittoria a royal

lady wrote requesting that he might be carefully attended to – a watch,

with her portrait, was forwarded…The Prince Regent afterwds

demanded back the watch & letters, sending Ld Keith to Hesse's

lodgings for them…He gave them up, thinking to obtain the princes

friendship…Prince refused even to receive him.   ib. //

Text: there are two vertical parallel lines (pencil) beside the final two lines of this item.
Source: Gronow, *Reminiscences*, 217–18.
Note: *Hesse*: 'formerly of 18th Hussars'. *Vittoria*: battle in Spain (1813) at which Wellington decisively defeated the French. The lady wrote through Wellington. *Keith*: Admiral Lord Keith.

156a

                    plans to accompany
– Mr Bradshaw ~~following~~ the actress Miss Maria Tree from Bath –

to Birmingham – under assumed name of Tompkins – arrived at

B. by the wrong coach (not knowg there were two, & that she had

taken the other) he found that his luggage had gone on to Manchester,

his money being in his trunk. Went to Bank – explained his position –

showed letters proving himself to be Mr B. – & the banker s^d he

w^d write the necessary letter & cheque, & send the money over to

his hotel. Cashier makes his app^{ce} : asks for Mr B. : is

told there is no such gent^n – only a Mr Tomkins. &c –

ib.

Source: Gronow, *Reminiscences*, 230–32 (the whole episode extends to p.234).
Note: *Tompkins*: Gronow has 'Tomkins', corrected in subsequent references in the item. Maria Tree (together with her sister) was an admired vocalist and actress of the period. At Birmingham, Bradshaw's inability to explain away his alias makes him an object of suspicion. Followed and detained, he is forced to 'send to the fair charmer of his heart to identify him, which she readily did as soon as [her] rehearsal was over'. Bradshaw's explanation for his presence in Birmingham won her over and marriage resulted.

156b

Jewellers – Bridge & others were patronized by the great – obtained

large sums of money from enamoured clients for jewellry for

their ladies.   ib.

Source: Gronow, *Reminiscences*, p.234.
Note: *Jewellers*: 'Hamlet, and Rundell and Bridge' are the jewellers mentioned. *enamoured clients*: including Lord C, who presented to Madmoiselle Le G. a present of jewels, valued at £30,000.

156c

A lady of the Terpsichorean tribe – fascinated many noblemen –

got jewels from them – purchased an estate with their proceeds,

on which she lived in old age (in France).   ib.

Source: Gronow, *Reminiscences*, p.236.
Note: *A lady of the Terpsichorean tribe*: a dancer, Mlle. Noblet, 'this fair daughter of Terpsichore', received £80,000 from Lord Fife.

156d

The pig-faced lady – believed to be the daughter of a nobleman in Grosv[r]

Square – during illuminations at the peace a pig's snout was said

to have been seen looking from the window of a carriage under < > poke-

bonnet.   ib.

Source: Gronow, *Recollections and Anecdotes, being a second series of Reminiscences by Capt. R.H.Gronow* (London: Smith, Elder & Co., 1863), pp.111–12.
Note: *under poke-bonnet*: Gronow has: 'protruding from a fashionable-looking bonnet'. An 'absurd' and 'ridiculous' story – 'the general belief of everybody in London'.

157a–[158]

Malibran & Grisi – Maria Malibran was still in the zenith of

her fame when Giulia Grisi made her appearance on the stage in

Paris. She was not at that period of her life the consummate actress

she afterwards became, but trusted a good deal to the power of her

personal attractions, as well as to the singularly fine compass & sweet tones

of her beautiful voice, to insure the applause of the public.

Malibran was, on the contrary, the soul of music. She was a grand

being; that small slight woman, with flushed cheeks & ardent expressive

eyes, consumed by the love of her art, & that one passionate attachment

which seemed woven into her soul, a part of her very being. I really

believe that this blind idolatry for the man who afterwards became her husband was the cause of the kind of frenzy with which she clung

to her fame as an artist. She felt instinctively that she had been

sought because she was celebrated & that the applause which she elicited

was the fuel which fed the flickering flame in De Beriot's heart.

There can be no doubt that the dread that in losing the one she might

fail to keep the other, fastened on her heart & killed her.

Poor Malibran! Grisi's new-born fame was a cankerworm

eating into her very soul; & I truly believe not from a mean feeling

of envy, but for the reason that I have assigned...

...At one of the concerts at L – House Malibran & Grisi were to

sing a duet. M. did not make her app^ce – waited consid^ble time, & then

the noble & courteous host supplied her place by an inferior artist, & Grisi   //

had all the honours of the even^g. In the midst of her triumph the

Diva walked in, flushed with anger, her fine brow lowering & her

full lips compressed. L^d L – with scrupulous urbanity advanced

tow^ds M. & made her a thousand apologies for having begun without

her on acc^t of lateness of hour. She catching sight of rival wreathed

in triumphant smiles, saluted him with a volley of abuse, to wh. he

kept bowing politely till he had darted out of room.   ib.

Hand: ELH, then TH from: *At one of the concerts ... darted out of room.*
Source: Gronow, *Recollections*, pp.198–200.
Note: *Malibran*: Maria-Felicia Malibran (1808–36), Spanish mezzo-soprano. *Grisi*: Giulia Grisi (1811–69), Italian soprano. *De Beriot*: Charles de Bériot, m.1836. violinist. See also note to 161c.

(Old D.C.Cs)

158a

Publickly whipped in the market Place, Bridport, & a year's hard

labour – for picking ^a pockets.   July 22. 1830

Source: *DCC*, 22 July 1830, p.3, col.2.
Note: Charles Downs Gale, picked pocket of William Pike (£4 18s) and was sentenced 'to imprisonment with hard labour for one year and to be once publicly whipped in the Market-place, Bridport'. See also items 41b, 82b, 94c, 144d.

158b–[159]

Cows clandestinely removed. Insolvents debtors court – Two Stalbridge

Farmers G.Dawe & J. Barrett – The insolvent had rented since 1821 Gibbs

Farm of Marquis of Anglesea at £420 per ann. Paid regularly till 1828

when they fell in arrear: At Mich^mas 1829 owed £486, at wh. time £50

was paid off, & a notice to quit on the ensuing Lady Day was given by Barrett –
                    & assured the steward Mr Castleman of their perfect solvency –
Promised shortly to reduce the arrears ^ : on that very day 20 heifers secretly

removed, & other property secreted. Upon Mr C. hearing of this, wh. was on

the 2^d Feb he levied a distress on the farm for £500, & took possession

of all the property – the insolvents having absconded...Traced 12 milch cows –
                                                                          ts.
& 18 beasts were concealed at a friend's farm. In Feb. Mr C. arrested the insolv.

& they gave bail...M^r C^ke for the insolvents contended that his clients had   //

suffered from oppression...The Chief Commissioner adjudged them

8 calendar months imprisonment.   ib.

Source: *DCC*, 22 July 1830, p.3, col.3.
Note: *M^r C^ke*: Mr Cooke.

159a

Funeral of Geo IV. "The Royal Body." "His late Most Sacred Majesty."   ib.

Source: 'Funeral of George IV', *DCC*, 22 July 1830, p.3, cols 3–4.

159b

Poacher – found in park, armed, with intent to take or destroy game – The

prisoner's defence was that the farmers & gentlemen had a spite against him,

because he had <u>been</u> a bit of a poacher – Seven years transp[n] (Salisbury

Assizes)   ib.

Source: 'Salisbury Summer Assizes', *DCC*, 29 July 1830, p.4, col.3.
Note: *Poacher*: Richard Young, found in Clarendon Park.

159c

Stealing a mare – same assizes – death recorded.   ib.

Source: 'Salisbury Summer Assizes', *DCC*, 29 July 1830, p.4, col.3.

159d

Scandal. "Whereas I, John Roe, of Stoborough, Dorset, fisherman, have

raised and circulated a scandalous report, tending to the injury of the char[r]

of Unity Hood of S. aforesaid, single woman, without any cause or

reason for so doing, for wh. conduct a prosecution was directed to

be commenced against me, but wh. the s[d] U.H. has kindly consented

to forego on my paying her the sum of £5 & all expenses, & thus

publicly ackn[ing] & declaring that such report was false, & with[t]

the least found[n] , & I promise never to be guilty of the like again

Witness my hand this 10th dy of July 1830.   John Roe.

Wit^s J.Gillingham, Wm Hood."

ib. Adv^t Aug 5. 30 //

Source: *DCC*, 5 August 1830, p.1, col.2.
Note: this is an advertisement on page 1 of *DCC*. *Stoborough*: village near Wareham, Dorset. *Wit^s*: witness.

160a

King of Gypsies. "Royal Death – the K. of the G., Wm Lee,

died last week at Sevenoaks in Kent at the age of 105 y^{rs}. He

was well-known in different parts of the country by his periodical visits.

ib.

Text: this item and the one below (160b) are bracketed together (pencil).
Source: *DCC*, 5 August 1830, p.2, col.3.
Note: *died last week at Sevenoaks*: Lee (and his tribe?) would have travelled here during the summer for the hop-picking.

160b

Robbing a boy. Jefferey Foot, a remarkably intelligent lad of 11

(son of Revd Lundy Foot) stated that – 3 after^n – 18th May – returning

home – prisoner jumped through hedge – laid hold of his right arm –

took everything from pockets – held what seemed a pistol to head – if

he made any noise w^d blow brains out – took off shoes – said he w^d have

his coat too – w^d not part with coat – Cart was heard – prisoner told

him to go home, & think himself very well off that he was not shot.

Verdict of guilty – "Sent. of Death recorded".   ib. Dorset assize.

Source: 'Dorset Summer Assizes', *DCC*, 5 August 1830, p.3, col.1.

160c

Renan's grandm^r , having suffered during the Terror with a

priest, among others, heard years after of his coming back

to the neighb^d. She went to see him, thinking he w^d feel

as warmly as she in consideration of their past sufferings

together. On the contrary he was cold, did not ask her

to stay, or take so much as a glass of water, though she

was nearly fainting from having walked so far.   <u>Renan</u>

Source: Ernest Renan, *Recollections of My Youth* (trans. C.B. Pitman, revised by Madame Renan) (London: Chapman and Hall, 1883), p.94 (translation of *Souvenirs D'Enfance et De Jeunesse* (1883), pp.103–4).
Note: *Renan*: Ernest Renan (1823–92), French scholar, historian of religion and critic, best known for his *Life of Jesus* (1863). TH noted eight extracts from this work in *LN* (items 1387–94, i, 175–6) as well as other extracts from Renan: (items 1187–8, i, 131–2; items 1278–9, i, 147).

160d

<u>Cellar of Snuff</u>. His late Majesty's (Geo IV's) – sold to a purveyor for

£400.   Old D.C.C. Aug 12. 1830   //

Source: *DCC*, 12 August 1830, p.2, col.3.
Note: the stock weighed 'sixteen hundred weight'.

161a

"The Misses Fitzclarence" (King W^m IV's bastards) visit Vauxhall –   ib.

Source: 'Vauxhall', *DCC*, 12 August 1830, p.2, col.3.
Note: '*The Misses Fitzclarence*': they were amongst the 10 children of the Duke of Clarence (later William IV) and Mrs Dorothy Jordan, actress and his partner of many years. After separating,

Clarence made offers of marriage to the heiress Catherine Tylney-Long, but in 1812 she married William Wellesley (see item 59b and note). *(King W^m IV's bastards)*: TH's interpolation. *Vauxhall*: Vauxhall Gardens, popular London pleasure gardens in Lambeth, S. of the Thames (closed 1859). For the Fitzclarence children see Tomalin, *Mrs Jordan's Profession* (1995).

161b

Duel – Capt. Helsham fully committed for wilful murder of Lieu^t Crowther,

...stood 15 paces apart – C. fired first – H. after a distinct pause

of four or five seconds – Witnesses 200 y^ds distant. The pause is the

feature on wh. the friends of the deceased depend. London news.   ib.

Source: *DCC*, 12 August 1830, p.2, col.4.

161c

(Dean of Worcester)
Poor Miss Paton – Bp. Of Rochester ʌ revokes permission granted for

use of Worcester Cath^d for approaching Musical Festival if Miss P.

be allowed to sing. [What had she done?]   ib.

Source: *DCC*, 12 August 1830, p.2, col.3.
Note: *Poor Miss Paton*; *[What had she done?]*: TH's interpolations. *Miss Paton*: Mary Ann Paton (1802–64), leading operatic soprano of the 1820s. In 1824 she married Lord William Pitt Lennox (1799–1881), fourth son of the 4th Duke of Richmond. The marriage was dissolved in 1831. *Bp. Of Rochester*: Hon. George Murray (1784–1860), Bishop of Rochester, 1827–54 and Dean of Worcester, 1828–54; in the latter capacity he controlled the use of Worcester Cathedral. He was elder brother of the Revd Edward Murray, vicar of Stinsford 1823–37. *Musical Festival*: the Three Choirs Festival, dating from the 1720s, held annually, ever since, in one of the cathedrals of Gloucester, Hereford and Worcester; but at this period referred to as 'the Meeting'. *Poor Miss Paton ... [What had she done?]*: by 1826 Miss Paton was not only reported as being received 'in the highest circles as Lady Lennox' (*DCC*, 10 August 1826, p.4, col.4), but was performing as lead soprano under Weber in the first performance of his *Oberon*. In 1829 she was praised for her performance at the Three Choirs Meeting at Hereford Cathedral. But by 1830 she had separated from her husband Lord Lennox and was living openly with the Covent Garden singer Joseph Wood, whom she later married. The news reached *John Bull*. Bishop Murray (also Dean) was provoked to announce to *John Bull* that if Miss Paton's invitation to sing at Worcester were taken up he would close the Cathedral to the Meeting (*Berrow's Worcester Journal*, 12 August 1830, p.3, col.3); the invitation was at once

withdrawn. Bishop/Dean Murray was the grandson of a Duke, his mother was a Lady-in-Waiting at Court and his sister Caroline had married the 3rd Earl of Ilchester. Mary Paton was no longer acceptable 'in the highest circles'. By August 1830 Bishop Murray was organizing the most ambitious occasion in his time as Dean of Worcester – the presence in September, in his Cathedral, of the heir-presumptive to the throne, the 11-year old Princess Victoria, then staying with her mother the Duchess of Kent at Malvern. All went well; Miss Paton was excluded, Madame Malibran (see item 157a) sang, the Bishop/Dean preached and after the service he 'and Lady Sarah Murray entertained upwards of 300 of the nobility and gentry ... at a sumptuous Banquet in The Chapter-room, where they had the honour of meeting the Duchess of Kent and the Princess Victoria' (*Berrow's Worcester Journal*, 16 September 1830, p.3, cols 2–3). Miss Paton and Joseph Wood had immediately fought back. According to the *Worcester Journal*, 'Mr Wood states that offers of country engagements for himself and Lady Wm. Lennox were pouring in so fast that he could not say when he should be able to return to London!' The paper comments: 'are we to infer that profligacy renders theatrical performers more attractive?' (12 August 1830, p.4, col.4).

161d

Funeral of Mrs Weld. Mother of his Eminence Cardinal Weld – remains

arrived at Wareham – met by more than 30 of the tenantry of estates

of Jos.Weld Esq. Lulworth Cas. St Mary's bell tolled while funeral

procession was passing through town – Formed in following manner – Two

mutes on horseback L Mr Weld's stewards L Tenantry 2&2 on horseback.

L Hearse with body L Mourning coaches with sons L Private carriages of

the family L two mutes L Procession extended nearly ½ a mile...

    Lulworth Castle – body borne into the Catholic Chapel – where it remained

before high altar all night – Buried 9 a.m. with all the ceremonies

of Romish Ch. Rev^d Mr Montardier, Chap. of the family at Lulworth,

preached sermon. High mass having been celebrated, body conveyed

to family vault beneath chapel.   ib. //

Source: *DCC*, 12 August 1830, p.4, col.2.
Note: *Cardinal Weld*: Thomas Weld (1773–1837), of Lulworth Castle, Dorset. The Welds were a noted Catholic family. After the death of his wife Thomas Weld entered the R.C. priesthood,

becoming Cardinal in 1830. *Jos. Weld*: Joseph Weld (1777–1863), head of the Lulworth estate following his brother's entry into the priesthood. *St Mary's*: parish church of Lady St Mary, Wareham, Dorset. *mutes*: professional mourners. See item 166a.

162a

Market price for a seat in Parl[t] for whole term £7000, or £1000

a year – on the authority of L[d] Durham.   ib.

Source: *DCC*, 12 August 1830, p.2, col.3.
Note: *Market price*: DCC reports that 'we have it in the public prints, given, as they assert on the authority of Lord Durham'. *L[d] Durham*: John Lambton, first Earl (1792–1840), MP and Whig minister.

162b

Election expenses – Last Leicester elections £19,000, £10,000, £16,000 –

The corpor[n] £16,000 : in all £61,000...Cockades of £5 each – at Stafford –

China of Camelford Voters wrapped in £1 notes. L[d] Grosvenor for Chester £70,000.

Source: *DCC*, 12 August 1830, p.2, col.3.
Note: the expenses at the Leicester election were incurred by Mr Evans, Otway Cave and Sir Charles Hastings, respectively.

162c

Shaftesbury – Scots Greys called from Blandford: 4 days election: votes –

Penrhyn 169, Dugdale 145, Knowles 121 (loses).   ib.

Source: *DCC*, 12 August 1830, p.4, col.1.
Note: *Scots Greys*: before their arrival, 'the mob had broken the windows of the Grosvenor Arms Inn', at Shaftesbury. Cavalry troops (as distinct from local militia) were brought in to quell popular unrest.

162d

Supposed murder on Chillington down – M[r] Stuckey builder of Chard riding home – left Chillington at 10 p.m. Horse found without rider –

also hat & stick, with marks of blood: spot notorious: near < >

"Windwhistle Inn." (Cf. Murder, broad day, P.Hinton down).   ib.

Source: 'Mysterious Circumstance', DCC, 12 August 1830, p.4, col.4.
Note: *Supposed murder*: there are further reports on this case in DCC , 19 August 1830, p.4, col.3;
26 August 1830, p.4, col.4; 2 September 1830, p.4., col.4 (reports the discovery of the body).
Chillington down: on the road from Crewkerne to Chard, Somerset, the highest point of which is
Windwhistle, see 'A Trampwoman's Tragedy': '"Windwhistle" high and dry' (stanza 4), and TH's
prefatory note to his poem (*TL, CP*, 196, 199). *(Cf. Murder … P.Hinton down)*: TH's
interpolation; a separate incident whose source has not been traced.

162e

Walking with constable to gaol – Village near Gloucester – Horse stealing –

Conveyed before a neighbouring magistrate – remanded to gaol for further

exam^n On way jumped into river – drowned –   ib. Aug 19. '30

Source: 'Singular Circumstance', DCC, 19 August 1830, p.3, col.2.
Note: William Jones and Jos. Sneed arrested at Over, Gloucestershire. While crossing Maisemore
bridge over the Severn 'Jones threw himself into river and drowned'.

162f

Exeter mail – reins of one of the leaders got under its tail – When

coachm^n endeavoured to clear it the leaders turned agst hedge, coach upset.

Taunton coach passed rendered assistance.   ib.

Source: DCC, 19 August 1830, p.4, col.2.

162g

Dark night. Shaft of waggon enters breast of ridden horse, when

latter was passing between former & a gig passing it.   ib. //

Source: DCC, 19 August 1830, p.4, col.4.

Note: there is a pencil mark in l.h. margin, 'used in "Tess"', which it might be thought was made by TH. However in a personal communication Michael Millgate suggests that 'the note is not in TH's hand but was evidently inserted by an irresponsibly browsing modern reader … the marginal note does not appear at all in my xerox, which dates back to the early 1970s or even the late 1960s'. Together with the erased item 117f, this report provides key source material for the accident to the Durbeyfield's horse, Prince, in *Tess of the d'Urbervilles* (Pt.1, ch.4), with its devastating consequences for the Durbeyfield's haggling business and for Tess personally (*Tess, 1988*, 36–7). (See *Winfield*, 226, *Millgate, 1971*, 265, 400). It is worth quoting in full: 'As Mr. Wm.Cabble of Kingsbury Episcopi was returning from Crewkerne market, on Saturday night, the 14th inst., he by accident met a gig and waggon, passing in opposite directions, at the turnpike-gate at Merriott, when the shaft of the latter vehicle coming into contact with Mr. Cabble's horse, it entered the breast at the point of the near shoulder, and passing between the blade and chest, glanced at the ribs under the skin, and penetrated by the spinal bone behind the saddle, which forced Mr. C with violence over the horse's head. The shaft was with considerable difficulty, extricated, and the horse has since been killed. Mr. C received so much injury as to be unable to proceed further the same evening, but we hear is now doing well.' The following report also occurs in *DCC* (27 April 1826, p.4, col.5): 'A singular accident befel the Bristol Mail on Thursday night. It was passing along about four miles from hence [Southampton], when a light cart driven with great speed met the horses in front, and, singular to state, the shafts of it entered the breasts of the two unfortunate leaders in such a manner that one of them died immediately, and the other a few hours afterwards. They were very valuable horses.' The report of this accident is on the same page of *DCC* as one of a bankruptcy hearing summarized by TH as item 30a and used by him in the writing of *The Mayor of Casterbridge*. It seems unlikely that in copying the one item, TH did not notice this other item, in the adjoining column of the issue of *DCC*, in the spring of 1884.

163a–[166]

(Aug. 1830)

<u>Lulworth Smugglers</u> – Dorset Assize – ⋏ Saturday – Emmanuel

Charles, William Wiltshire & James Hewlett were indicted for that that they in

company with others were found armed with offensive weapons, in order to their

illegal landing, running & carrying away certain goods, liable to pay duties

At West Lulworth; they were also indicted for assaulting a Custom House

officer whilst in the execution of his duty. Mr Erskine said he should

not press the capital charge against the prisoners but should proceed to

the second charge. The prisoners were therefore acquitted of the first

charge, & were put upon their trial for the assault.

Andrew Jordan – I am a coastman in the Preventive Guard at West

Lulworth; I was on duty on the 28. May last; I went to Horse Wall, to

the west of Lulworth Cove; I remained on duty till between 1 & 2 o'clock

when I heard a noise from off the beach & I went to see what it was. I

was alone; I saw a party of men coming off the beach towards the

valley; there were between twenty and thirty men, several of them having

kegs upon their shoulders; the others had sticks in their hands, when

I saw they had goods I fired a pistol as a signal; the men struck

with their sticks upon the ground & told me to stand back, or I should

catch it; they used offensive language; I then fired at them; in three

[This was Hewlett, Selby's brother-in-law]
or four minutes after one man fell ʌ After this they put down some

tubs, & told me to take them and to stand off, or my life would not

be my own – Emmanuel Charles was the man who said this; it was

a bright starlight night; I was within two or three yards of him;

//

the men went on; I put fire to a blue light & followed them; I kept within

five or six yards of them; sometimes they threatened me with violence,

brandishing their sticks; sometimes they said, "Stop behind good lad

& don't come any further." I told them I could not go back, but

that I would kill two or three first if they struck me: they offered

me £1 to go back. I followed them to Dagger's Grave; ~~they put~~

~~some of the tubs into a cart~~ the second time they stopt; they said they

would leave me six tubs if I would go no further: when we got to

Dagger's Grave they put some of the tubs into a cart; they then desired me to be off or I should be murdered; I said I could not, & I would

do my endeavours to kill the first man who attempted to injure

me; they then came forward with sticks raised up & the word

was given by a man to form a half-circle, and it was formed

close to me; stones were flung at me & struck me; the three

prisoners were among them; a man struck at me, I snapt my

pistol at him, but it missed fire; they then called out "Death or

Liberty", & the stones came faster than ever; one struck me on

the nose, & knocked me down; they then rushed in upon me &

struck & kicked me. Word was given to take my arms from me.

They laid upon my face; I told them if they killed me to kill me

like a man & not to smother me in blood. They then took my

arms from me; I heard a voice say do not kill him, & then they

ceased to beat me, & left me on the ground. I got up & walked a   //

little way as well as I could. I met one of our men – he stopped with me

till Mr Roberts, the Commanding Officer, came up & they then took me

to the station at Lulworth & had my wounds dressed. I was con=

fined to my bed five days & have not been well since.

Cross-examined by Mr Earle, – John Puckett was one of the first

men I saw. I saw Hewlett & Puckett in the second ring; I con-

sidered myself within a moment of my death, & yet I can swear to the

men I saw by starlight.

Cross-examined by Mr E. Moody on behalf of the prisoner Emanuel

Charles. – I had never seen Charles before. I did not tell them I was a

Custom House Officer till long after I had fired at the man.

Rees Pritchard. – I heard a pistol fired on the night in question, & in

consequence I fired several pistols, & lighted a blue light. I fell in with

the last witness, he was so much covered with blood that I hardly

knew him.

– Roberts – Lieutenant in the Navy. – Jordan & Pritchard were

under my command. I found five tubs of spirits between 2 & 3

in the morning half-way between Dagger's Grave & Horse Walls.

I heard a pistol fired & proceeded in the direction from whence I heard

the sound, & there found Jordan covered with blood.

John Puckett – I am a labouring man & was out on the night of

The 29. May. I went out after a bundle of ~~firs~~ furze about 9 or 10 o'clock

a person came & spoke to me about 10. When he first came to me   //

I thought it was Emanuel Charles, but it was not him. In consequence

of what he said, I went on till I came to Dagger's Grave; & as I was

going on we came to 10, or 12 men who were walking along the

road; after I joined them we went on towards the coast to Horse

Walls; when we got there we took up some tubs of spirits, maybe

50. There were then about 23 or 24 of us: we took up the tubs

& went round the hill, & then we saw Jordan, he was following

us; we went on to Dagger's Grave, Jordan followed us; we then

flogged the man; we threw stones at him first: I believe he

met with a blow on the nose; he fell & we were all upon him;

some beat him with sticks, some kicked him, & others muffled

him about; James Hewlett & William Wiltshire were there.

Cross-examined – I never was out a night after tubs before:

The man I first saw I took to be Charles walked all the way with

me: I thought it was Charles all the way; but when we got before

the magistrates I found it was not him.

   This was the case for the prosecution...Objection to terms of

the indictment – His lordship (Mr Baron Bolland) s^d the prisoners had

shown great forbearance – Entered into their own recognizance for good

behaviour, & were discharged –   Old D.C.C. Aug. 5. 1830

Hand: ELH down to *This was the case for the prosecution*; TH thereafter.
Text: *(Aug. 1830)*; *[This was Hewlett, Selby's brother-in-law]*: in pencil.
Source: *DCC*, 5 August 1830, p.3, cols 1–2.
Note: *[This was Hewlett, Selby's brother-in-law]*: TH's interpolation. *Selby*: James Selby
(1798–1879) of Broadmayne, a mason who 'worked forty years for Hardy's father and had been
an ex-smuggler' (*Life and Work*, 170). In the 1912 Macmillan Wessex edition of *WT* Selby is the
'old carrier of "tubs"', the 'informant' who 'spoke ... of the horribly suffocating sensation
produced by the pair of spirit-tubs slung upon the chest and back, after stumbling with the burden
of them for several miles inland over a rough country and in darkness' (*PW*, 22–3). As an old man
Selby reaffirmed for TH the story of the execution of two York Hussars on Bincombe Down in
1801 – the event which provided the factual basis for 'The Melancholy Hussar' (see *Life and Work*,
119, also *PN*, 124–5; *Ray*, 22–4). Mr E. Moody: *DCC* gives no initial for Mr Moody. *Puckett*:
DCC has Pucket. *furze*: ELH has corrected *DCC*'s 'firs'. *I never was out a night*: *DCC* has 'out at
night'. TH already knew of this incident, and James Hewlett's part in it. In 'The Distracted Young
Preacher' (1879) the character 'Owlett' is a conflation of 'owler' (a traditional term for a smuggler)
and 'Hewlett', as Kathryn King observes (*WT*, 1991, 243). TH drew on this entry years later
(obliquely referring to 'Facts') when trying to establish details of the incident for a correspondent:
'I find on referring to the notes ['Facts'] I made for "Distracted Preacher" that the "Preventive-
men" (they were not called excisemen) each carried two pistols in his belt, which fired to give the
alarm; & then a blue-light was burnt. The smugglers carried heavy sticks' (TH to T.H. Tilley (28
October, 1911), *CL*, iv, 186); see *Ray*, 57. This item contributed to the revision of 'The Distracted
Preacher' for the 1912 edition of *WT*, where TH added the information that Owlett 'was caught
and tried with the others at the assizes; but they all got off', and inserted the name 'Dagger's Grave'
(now 'Dagger's Gate') as the site of the smugglers' rendezvous (*Ray*, 57; *WT*, 1991, 244). TH also

draws on this 'Facts' item in his review of the 'action' of 'The Distracted Preacher' in the 1912 Preface: 'I may add that the action of this story is founded on certain smuggling exploits that occurred between 1825 and 1830, and were brought to a close in the latter year by the trial of the chief actors at the Assizes before Baron Bolland for their desperate armed resistance to the Custom-house officers during the landing of a cargo of spirits. This happened only a little time after the doings recorded in the narrative, in which some incidents that came out at the trial are also embodied. In the culminating affray the character called Owlett was badly wounded, and several of the Preventive-men would have lost their lives through being overpowered by the far more numerous body of smugglers, but for the forbearance and manly conduct of the latter. This served them in good stead at their trial, in which the younger Erskine prosecuted, their defence being entrusted to Erle. Baron Bolland's summing up was strongly in their favour; they were merely ordered to enter into their own recognizances for good behaviour and discharged' (Preface to *WT* in *PW*, 23).

166a

<u>Fugitive King & Queen of France</u> & family – arrive at Lulworth

Castle – & Poole – Shooting at Lulworth – Go to Weymouth Races, &c –

ib. Sept 2, 9, et seq. //

Source: *DCC*, 2 September 1830, p.4, col.2; *DCC*, 9 September 1830, p.4, col.2.
Note: *Fugitive King … family*: Charles X (1757–1836), King of France 1824–30, exiled after the revolution of 1830. The royal family included the Duchesse de Berri, the Comte de Mesnaid, the Duke d'Angoulême. Joseph Weld of Lulworth Castle offered the castle as 'temporary asylum … the French Royal Family remained at Lulworth until October [1830]' (*Frampton*, 350–51); see also item 170b.

167a

<u>Nunnery</u> Taunton. A young lady, dau. of a resp[ble] R. Catholic

gent[n] at Axminster, takes the veil at the Franciscan nunnery –

Another the previous week did the same.   Sep. 2. ib.

Source: 'Taking the Veil', *DCC*, 26 August 1830, p.4, col.4.
Note: TH has mistaken the date of this report. *Axminster*: town in E. Devon. *the previous week*: reported in *DCC*, 19 August 1830, p.2, col.5. *DCC* commented censoriously: 'a manifest and gross perversion of the first law of nature'.

Also: –

167b

Died. Aug 5. At Albano, n^r Rome, the country residence of her husb^d,

aged 33, Sarah Emerson; wife of Lieut Col. Geo. Manley, of the Drag-

oon Guards of his Holiness the Pope, & only daughter of the late W. Stuckey

Esq. of Swaffham, Norfolk. Col. Manley is a native of Taunton.

Obituary n.   ib.

[from wh. it w^d appear that Taunton was a R.C.centre.]

Source: *DCC*, 2 September 1830, p.4, col.4.
Note: *Manley*: for Col. Manley see item 177b. *n*. notice? *[from wh. ... R.C.centre.]*: TH's addition.

167c

The widow of the late Bp. Heber is married to a Greek Count –

who is, or was, secretary to the gov^t of the Ionian Islands –   ib.

Source: *DCC*, 2 September 1830, p.2, col.4.
Note: *Heber*: Reginald Heber (1783–1826), Bishop of Calcutta and author of the hymn 'From Greenland's icy mountains'. Mrs Heber published a *Life* of Heber in 1830.

167d

Dorchester & Blandford Races, theatres, &c.   ib. Sep 2. & 9.

Source: *DCC*, 2 September 1830, p.3, col.1 and p.4, cols 1–2; *DCC*, 9 September 1830, p.4, cols 1–2.

167e

Two days post from Beaminster to Dorch^t & 10 postage.   ib.

Source: *DCC*, 2 September 1830, p.4, col.1.
Note: a complaint in *DCC* about mail being sent from Beaminster to Dorchester ('sixteen miles') via Salisbury ('nearly one hundred miles').

167f–[168]

Arson (at Kenn) One confesses… "We'll go & do it by & by." Wall s^d I have

bought the brimstone on purpose…(a large roll of brimstone was in the

cupb^d …Got up at 2 in morning to help load potatoes – "His wife

melted brimstone in a spade; dipped 3 or 4 pieces of writing paper in it

…got rags & made tinder, & went upstairs & fetched a flint, which   //

Richard Clarke took with the matches. She asked if he wanted a

steel – he s^d he sh^d strike with his knife. They (4 men) then went

out of the house – about 3 o'c. – towards the mows. Ten minutes later

he saw 3 lights, on looking out. Sentenced to Death –
                    (Mr Benj. Poole of Kenn)
(They owed the farmer ʌ a grudge, he having caused Wall to be fined

£20 for selling cider with^t a licence.). It was Wall incited the others to the act.

  Before the Judge left the City (Wells) he was pleased to reprieve

Mary Wall. (she was really the instigator & chief of the conspiracy).

                                                        ib. Sep 2. 30.

Source: 'Somerset Assizes – Wells: "Arson"', *DCC*, 2 September 1830, p.3, col.4.
Note: *Kenn*: between Nailsea and Clevedon, Somerset. *mows*: mow, a stack of hay or corn, or a
place where hay or corn is stacked (OED). *DCC* reported that 'John Rowley, Richard Clarke, John
Old and James Rowley were indicted for having set fire to a stack of corn, the property of Benjamin
Poole of Kenn; and Wm. Wall and Mary Wall were charged with having counselled, procured, aided
and abetted the other prisoners'. See also item 171a.

168a–[170]

Wreckers: bars of gold : – It is generally known that after a

continuance of gales, blowing from a certain quarter, bars of gold & silver

are occasionally picked up on the Chesil bank which unites Portland to the mainland, & as many incorrect traditions are afloat respecting the vessel at the wreck of which these valuables were lost we give the following statement which we have collected from an old pamphlet kindly lent to us by a gentleman of Dorchester. – The Hope a Dutch merchant ship Booii Cornelizs, master, sailed in the ^year^ 1747 from Amsterdam being engaged in illicit traffic with the Spanish possessions in America. On her return towards Holland she had on board no less than £50,000 sterling in specie of one kind or other besides a considerable quantity of gold dust, staple silver, & other valuable commodities. After a continuance of the most violent tempests for 14 days the vessel was driven on the beach at Portland on the night of the 16th January 1748 //

It was then excessively dark & no light could be seen from the Portland lighthouses. The crew 74 in number all got safe to land, but the ship was shattered in three parts. As soon as daylight discovered the calamitous condition of the vessel, upwards of 300 people of the parishes near the coast poured down upon the beach & plundered the wreck of all the valuables they could find & carry away, preventing the crew from saving any part of the cargo. One of these men, Augustus Elliot, was subsequently tried at Dorchester for the robbery, & the statement of the counsel for the crown, went to show that the plundering mob to the number of 300 or 400, were formed into divisions by the prisoner in order the more effectually to counteract the efforts of the crew & to secure the plunder. In addition to this number a great concourse of people were continually pouring in from all parts of the country, so that the shore was for 10

days together covered with thousands, until three of the magistrates

of the county collecting a body of men well armed, proceeded to the

beach & dispersed the mob. On the part of the prisoner it was con=

tended that it was the general opinion of the people that the crew

of the vessel were pirates & might therefore be plundered with im=

punity; but that so far from having acted under this impression

he assisted in saving some of the cargo, carrying it to his own home

to preserve for the owners on being paid the salvage. After a trial of

6 hours and a half the jury brought in a verdict of not guilty. Another

person was tried for the same offence, but the jury also brought   //

in a verdict of not guilty; & our authority then goes on to state that

"two others remained for trial on the same account, but the Court

seeing the disposition of the jury discharged them on giving bail for

their appearance at the next assizes." The affair at the time excited an

extreme degree of interest.   Old D.C.C. Sep 2. '30

Hand: ELH; *year* (l.8) in TH's hand.
Text: *year*: in pencil.
Source: *DCC*, 2 September 1830, p.3, col.1.
Note: *specie*: coinage.

170a

Dorchester – Races Ball at Kings Arms (County people – Floyers, Murrays

Pattisons, Framptons, Bankes, Damers) : "Dejeuner à la f." by officers

of Scots Greys at their Mess Room, on Saturday morning, to Sir E. Baker

&c – Dancing, continued till the company retired.   ib. Sep.9.

Source: *DCC*, 9 September 1830, p.4, col.2.
Note: *County people*: TH's words. *Dejeuner à la f.*: 'déjeuner à la fourchette'. *DCC* reported that the Ball 'was, on this occasion, graced with an unaccustomed display of united rank, beauty, and fashion, the attendance being equal both in point of extent and brilliancy, to that of any former year. Dancing commenced at ten o'clock, and was continued with the greatest spirit; indeed the amusement proved so gratifying, that the horizon was tinged with the grey of dawn long before the company separated. The refreshments were provided by Oliver with that taste which always distinguishes his house'. The families mentioned by TH are largely, in Bockhampton terms, local, the Floyers of West Stafford, the Murrays of Stinsford, the Pattisons of Wrackleford, the Framptons of Moreton, the Bankes of Kingston Lacy, the Damers of Came. Other well-known local figures attending the dinner included Mr and Mrs Bastard, Mr Wollaston, Major Garland, Mr and Mrs W.L. Henning and the Revd and Mrs Yeatman. *Baker*: Sir Edward Baker of Ranston, nr. Blandford.

170b

Ex Royal Family of France – speak English –   ib.

Source: *DCC*, 9 September 1830, p.4, cols 2–3; see also *DCC*, 16 September 1830, p.4, col.2.

170c–[171]

Dinner at Chipleigh Hall, near Wellington, given by Mr Sanford the

newly elected MP. for this county in return for the compliment of

a dinner to him at Wellington by the Freeholders...Roads towards

C. were scenes of activity and gaiety, large parties moving towards the

place of entertainment...450 assembled...Cards of admission were

intended, only for those who were at the Wellington dinner...but many

others came...advancing the valid & irresistible claim of having given

plumper. Ancient hall...gallery...family pictures. Dinner at 3.

5 tables along the hall & 1 throughout its length...On the left of M^r S.

sat Mr Carew...Gallery filled with elegantly dressed ladies, Mrs S. Lady

Langham...& other distinguished females. The tables were furnished with the following supplies : 6 rounds, 6 rumps, 12 sirloins & 14 ribs of beef:

& 12 loins veal – 12 quarters lamb – 28 tongues – 8 hams – 60 fowls

– 60 ducks – 60 turkeys – 12 savoury pies – 70 plumb puddings – & 7 haunches

& 6 ribs venison. 4 or 5 hh^s sherry & port; brandy rum & gin: several

hh^{ds} beer & cider.

   For the ladies – 6 turkeys – 12 fowls – 28 part^{ges} – 3 hams – 8 sav^y dishes –

12 dishes, jellies and creams – 10 of pastry – 6 heath poults – & dessert.

ib. Sep 16.

Source: *DCC*, 16 September 1830, p.3, col.1.
Note: *Wellington*: town in Somerset. *plumper*: a vote given solely to one candidate at an election (when one has the right to vote for two or more) (OED). *Mr S.*: Mr E.A. Sanford. The *DCC* report observed: 'When the hour of dinner arrived, upwards of four hundred and fifty persons were assembled.' TH chose only two items from the *DCC* of 16 September 1830 – this and the following item, juxtaposing a scene of conspicuous consumption with a spectacle of a very different kind.

171a–[173]

Execution of the Kenn incendiaries – (v. ante) – W.Wall 35, J. Rowley 32,

Richd Clarke 19...They were part of a gang infesting neighb^d. Wall

was in habit of taking potatoes to Bristol for sale, also proprietor of

a cider shop, where young men of idle habits resorted – the two others

were lodgers. In hope that the fate of the men might have a more

salutary effect upon such of the gang as are still at large it was

determined that the exec^n sh^d take pl. near spot where crime comm^{ted}

   Culprits taken from Ilchester Gaol at an early hour on Wedn^y &

arrived at Kenn, 42 miles (?) ½ past 10. Order of procession

Chief Constable on horseback L100 sp^l constables on foot with staves –

L High Sheriff & under Sheriff on h.b^k L Magistrates (3) & Chaplain, in

open carriage L Javelin men, with halberds, on h.b^k. L Prison Caravan

drawn by 4 horses, in wh.were the 3 culprits, guarded by Mr Hardy. gov^r

of the County gaol, the executioner, & his assistant L Party of javelin men –

L 50 constables on h.b^k L On entering village the funeral knell com^{ced}.   //

Process^n halted front of house in wh. Magistrates were assembled – &

Rowley was taken before them, full confession of guilt. He walked to

& from the van with a firm step. After necess^y arrangem^{ts} had been

concluded the cavalcade moved on to the pl. of ex^n, a field 7 acres

in extent, opposite to that in wh. mows consumed. Temporary Gallows –

on them the inscrip^n For Firing Stacks. The culprits having been

released from their fetters, ascended platform, followed by Rev^d M^r

Valentine…At his request all knelt on platform – & each holding

a prayer book, repeated Litany…"O Christ hear us!" great fervour

& emphasis. Wall was the first pinioned, & when rising from

his kneeling posture he looked tow^{ds} Magis^s & others near platform

& said in a very earnest manner, I hope, gent^n you will please

to forgive my poor dear wife & ch^n. During the time occupied in pinioning,

~~they read~~ adjusting the ropes &c, they read aloud from prayer book wh.

each continued to hold. Previously to caps being drawn over eyes

Revd V. asked if wished address multitude…Young man

Clarke s^d "Cider has been my ruin…" Wall – "If I had not opened

a cider shop…" The waggon on wh. platform was erected being

drawn from under them they were launched into eternity. – Spect^{rs}

kept at convenient distance by tenantry of late high Sheriff, $\wedge$ yeoman,
local

&c. sworn as Special constables. In the rear of these were stationed

the ~~troops~~ Bath & Bedminster troops of y. cav^y under Capt Wilkins.

Constabulary under Ch. Const. G. Emery Esq. – Cut down – coffins –   //

High Sheriff & Magis^{ts} returned thanks to the different <u>parish constables,</u>

& Chief Do., to Capt. W. & Cavalry, & others…the whole cavalcade moved

off ground, escorting caravan about a mile on its return to Ilchester –

where – bodies interred. 15,000 persons – great order – after depart^{re} of caval^{de}

Revd J. Leifchild ascended platform. & – impressive address.

  Sentence on Jas Rowley & Mary Wall – commuted to transportation. Wall

leaves 7 children, eldest 13. (Executed Sep. 8 Wed) Old D.C.C. Sept. 16. 30

Hand: ELH inserts *Prison Caravan* (l.12), otherwise TH.
Text: the query within parentheses following *42 miles*, added in pencil.
Source: *DCC*, 16 September 1830, p.3, col.4.
Note: *Chief Do.*: abbreviation not in *DCC*. *impressive address*: addressing the 'immense concourse',
the Revd Liefchild exorted 'those who had been led to improper courses to consider before it was
too late, of the dreadful consequences which inevitably follow a life devoted to intemperance,
idleness and a breach of the Sabbath day'. Entries in the journal of Mary Frampton (the sister of
James Frampton, a notoriously zealous Dorset magistrate in the period 1830–34) confirm that the
authorities were highly nervous of the threat to public order in this area of the country in the autumn
and winter of 1830–31. (*Frampton*, 360–66, 367–8.) See '*Facts*' items on incendiarism through
November and December 1830 (items 192b, 192d, 192f, [193]c). See also item 167f.

173a

<u>Hung himself,</u> – J. Davis of Abbotsbury, in the Independent Meeting

House, of which he was the proprietor.   ib. Sp. 23. 30
Cf. Rector of Stedham, Sussex – hung himself to bell rope in belfry. Ap^l 1882 DCC. Also Farmer at
Motcombe – lends £700 to build chapel – not repaid – kills his child (ante).

Text: the reports in this item are linked by a single bracket.

Source: *DCC*, 23 September 1830, p.4, col.1, *DCC* 6 April 1882, p.10, col.1.
Note: *Rector of Stedham*: The Revd H. St. George Edwards, Rector of Stedham and Heyshott, Sussex. *Farmer at Motcombe*: TH refers back to an earlier item, 147a.

173b

                        & Dance
Tenant's Horse-race ʌ – Drax – Charborough Pk. – silver cup, to be run for

by horses belonging to them (the tenants). Immense number of people – a mile course

formed, & a convenient stand erected (in the Park) – Ten horses started wh.

were handicapped by the worthy host – The leading horses came in as follows:

M^r K's b.m. Clari 1-1 M^r B's b.m. 2-2. Mr Stroud's c.g. 3-3. Race

decided in two well contested heats. At conclusion 200 of ten^y & their

friends – sumptuous dinner, given by the hosp^ble landl^d. At 5 the merry

dance commenced in the park...Mr Drax intends to make it annual.

                                                                        ib.

Source: *DCC*, 23 September 1830, p.4, col.2.
Note: *Drax*: John W.S. Sawbridge (1800–87) who assumed the surname and arms of Erle-Drax on marrying Jane Erle-Drax in 1827. *Charborough Pk.*: 5 miles W. of Wimborne Minster. As Richard H. Taylor notes, 'by TH's account', the estate is the setting of *Two on a Tower* ('Memoranda 1', *PN*, 22, fn. 56; *Life and Work*, p.475). In a note (probably of 1881) TH reports an old postilion pointing out Charborough as 'heiress land', with its owner, Miss Drax (daughter of the above), who 'lives there alone – a quiet little lady – keeps no company' (*PN*, 22). *M^r K's b.m.*: 'Mr Kitcatt's brown (or bay) mare'. *Mr B*: 'Mr Bull'. *c.g.*: chestnut gelding.

173c

The Marquis de Montmorency, who refused to take oath of allegiance to Louis

Philippe was in Poole this week [sailed across?]...Has taken Merley House,

n^r Wimborne   ib. //

Source: *DCC*, 23 September 1830, p.4, col.3.
Note: *Merley House*: Merly House, 1 mile S. of Wimborne, Dorset (built 1756–60).

174a

<u>Will</u>. Late T.Southwood Esq. (see ante) remarkable will – much attention

at the time: it now appears was guilty of the legal folly of making

his own will, & when he bequeathed his extensive property consist[g]

of manor of Taunton & T. Deane &c, to his manservant M[r] R.

Mattock he forgot to add the words "his heirs" so that M[r] M.

has only a life interest in M[r] S.'s testamentary bequest…The alleged

heir-at-law has advertised the property to be sold, subj. to M[r] M's

life interest.

ib.

Source: *DCC*, 23 September 1830, p.4, col.3.
Note: *ante*: see item 147c.

174b

Weymouth
<u>A new coach</u>, called the Tally-Ho! from Luces Hotel ⋏every M. W. & Fr morn[g]

¼ to six, through D. Bl. Sal. Stockbridge, Bas. & Egham: Old W.H.Cellar

at 9. George & Bl. Boar Holb[n] & the 3 Cups Aldersg[te] ½ past 9. Leave 3 Cups

6.a.m W.H.C. 7, Tu, Th. S. morn[g] Luce's 10 ev[g] . Adv[t]

Text: *Weymouth*: in pencil.
Source: *DCC*, 23 September 1830, p.4, col.3.
Note: *Luces Hotel*: see item 41a; *D. Bl. Sal.*: Dorchester, Blandford, Salisbury; *Bas.*: Basingstoke;
Old W.H.Cellar: Old White Horse Cellar, Piccadilly; *3 Cups*: Three Cups, Aldersgate Street, City
of London.

174c

Portland People – have been during the memory of man, almost destitute of medical assistance, the emoluments among so poor a class not being

sufficient remunerate a professional man; & the whole aid, in case

of sickness or accident, being thus obtained from Wey[th] – 5 m. distant

from nearest part of island: & communic[n] being more difficult since

Nov 1824 (gale) when arm of sea widened 4 times original head breadth...

Sum raised to retain medical man on Island.   D.C.C. Sep 30. 1830

Source: 'Royal Munificence', *DCC*, 30 September 1830, p.3, col.3.
Note: *Nov 1824 (gale)*: see item 199b. Cited by *Cullen Brown*, 164. According to *DCC*, on receipt
of a petition from the islanders, the newly acceded William IV granted £25 to be 'annually
appopriated towards the support and maintenance of a resident surgeon'.

174d–[175]

Hemp manufacture – Bridport & Beaminster – from the finest thread to the   //

enormous cable – Also sail-cloth, sacking for hammocks &c. Nets made all

along the coast – women braid them – mostly for the Newfoundl[d] & other

fisheries –   D.C.C. Oct 14. 30

Source: *DCC*, 14 October 1830, p.4, col.1.

175a

Mary Frampton's Journal.

1781. Custom to keep new married pair to dinner & not dismiss

them till evening. <   >

Source: *The Journal of Mary Frampton From the Year 1779, Until the Year 1846*, ed. Harriot
Georgiana Mundy (London: Sampson Low, Marston, Searle, & Rivington, 1885; 3rd edn, 1886),
p.7.
Note: *Mary Frampton*: (1773–1846), of Moreton, Dorset, sister of James Frampton (1769–1855)
and half-sister of the lawyer Charlton Byam Wollaston (1765–1840), of Wollaston House,

Dorchester. Frampton and Wollaston, as magistrates, were jointly responsible for the committal for trial of George Loveless and his fellow Tolpuddle workers, in 1834. The *Journal*, interspersed with letters and edited by her niece Harriot Mundy, is dated 1779–1846. *new married pair*: Phillis Wollaston (Mary Frampton's half-sister) and Mr Shirley, son of Earl Ferrers (m.1781).

Excision from f.88r&v (see Appendix One)

175b

<u>History of Lady Susan</u> O'Brien's elopement –   18–19.

"All London was wild with admiration of his (O'Brien's) person,

& his inimitable manner of acting a fine gentleman in comedy"...

"celebrated actor"..."She was reckoned the proudest of the proud"...

"Her principles & education, as well as her husband's, had been neglected.

...No two people were more liked." (vide post. 177)

Source: *Frampton*, 18–19.
Note: *Lady Susan*: Lady Susannah Fox-Strangways, later O'Brien (1743–1827), eldest dau. of Stephen Fox-Strangways, 1st Earl of Ilchester. *O'Brien*: William O'Brien (1738–1815), Irish actor, a protégé of Garrick, successful in leading roles at Drury Lane, admitted to private theatricals at Holland House, married Lady Susan, amid much scandal, in 1764. TH refers to the 'famous elopement ... so excellently described in Walpole's letters, Mary Frampton's Journal, &c.' (*Life and Work*, 264) (entry for 1892). For Frampton's full, and informative account, see item 177c; a good modern account is by Stella Tillyard, *Aristocrats* (London: Chatto & Windus, 1994), pp.183–8. TH also records Marie Liechtenstein's more censorious report of the affair (item 180f). From 1774 the O'Briens lived at Stinsford House, an Ilchester property, in the parish where TH was born. On O'Brien's death in 1815, TH's grandfather 'constructed the vault for him and his wife' and was asked by her '"to make it just large enough for our two selves only"' (*Life and Work*, 264; Pinion, 485); see 'The Noble Lady's Tale' (*TL*, *CP*, 289–95) and commentary by Hynes, *CPW*, i, 387 (citing this '*Facts*' item and 180f); see also 'Friends Beyond', (*WP*, *CP*, 60–61). 'The First Countess of Wessex' in *A Group of Noble Dames* derives from the history of the courtship and marriage of Lady Susan's parents, Elizabeth Strangways-Horner and Stephen Fox, later 1st Earl of Ilchester (*HC*, 75). MS sources for the life of Lady Susan O'Brien have been used by Susan Rands in 'Letters to Thomas Hardy from the 5th Countess of Ilchester concerning the journal of Lady Susan O'Brien', *Somerset and Dorset Notes and Queries*, 34 (September 2000): 385–92; 'Lady Susan O'Brien and her friendship with the Pitt Family', *Somerset and Dorset Notes and Queries*, 35 (March 2001): 11–21.

175c–[176]

(Frances Twysden, dau. of Bp of Raphoe, wife of 4th earl)

Countess of Jersey. ʌ The prince was under her influence...a clever, un-

principled, but beautiful & fascinating woman...By her intrigues

she persuaded the Prince to appoint her to go & meet the Princess

Caroline of Brunswick, who travelled in a mantle of green satin trimmed

with gold...& beaver hat...High spirits... 'am I not going to be m[d] to the hand-   //

somest prince in the world?' Rumours against her char[r] even then...An

officer of the King's German legion, Major Töebingen, was said to

have been admired by her...wore an ameythst pin...The King

her Uncle Geo III was much attached to his niece – the Queen never

liked the Prince to marry her, & was s[d] to be prejudiced ag[st] her –

On dit that the Prince was pleased with her at first sight, but

that Lady J. contrived to speak to him alone, & set him against

her before the ceremony.   85–6

Source: *Frampton*, 84–6.
Note: *Countess of Jersey*: sometime mistress of the Prince of Wales, later George IV. *On dit*: the text has 'the *on dit* of the time reported'. This extract from Frampton concerns the arrival of Princess Caroline from Brunswick, before her marriage to the Prince of Wales. See item 151b.

Excision from f.88r&v (see Appendix One)

176a

What an extraordinary death is that of the Duchess of St Albans

& her child! It is however considered a fortunate thing from the

rumours prevalent on the subject – (the duke died 1815 – the Duchess

Feb 19. 1816, the child Aubrey, 7th duke, a few hours after his mother. They were married 1802. The dukedom then reverted to child's uncle William).

266

Source: *Frampton*, 266.
Note: the information in parentheses is TH's summary of the editor's footnote.

176b

<u>The Pcess. Charlotte</u> was peremptorily forbidden by the Pce Regent to

remain even for a night from Weymouth. She used therefore to stay

as long as she possibly could at Melbury, Abbotsbury Castle, Moreton

&c – & return to the King's Lodge between 12 & 1 o'clock a.m.   272   //

Source: *Frampton*, 272 (fn).
Note: see item 16b. *Melbury, Abbotsbury Castle*: Dorset properties of the Earl of Ilchester.

177a

<u>Maria Louisa</u> – sitting one evening alone with Lady Burghersh –

Lady B. asked her if she had not kept up a correspondence with

Napoleon during time of his residence in Elba. She s^d yes – to

a much greater extent than was suspected. – "Then why did you not

join him during the Hundred Days?" – "I c^d not. Further pressed

ans^d for some time "it was impossible" – at last ended by stating that

her being with child by another man was the invincible reason which

prevented it. That man (Cte de Neipperg) she m^d imm^y on death of N.

having had 2 ch. by him previously, & 2 subs. to their m^{ge}. She was

much attached to him to his death – he never lost his respectful manners to

her. Was captivating, though blind of one eye. He was first introduced to her by the Emp[r] after several refusals on her part.   402

Source: *Frampton*, 399–402.
Note: *Maria Louisa*: Marie-Louise (1791–1847), second wife of the Emperor Napoleon. *Lady Burghersh*: sister of William Long-Wellesley, see item 59b and note. *the Hundred Days*: from Napoleon's escape from Elba until his defeat at Waterloo. *blind of one eye*: the text has 'blind in one eye'. *C[te] de Neipperg*: (1774–1829), General in Napoleonic wars, first on Austrian then on French side.

177b

Popery in Taunton. Convents described – occupied by Franciscan nuns

who emigrated from Brussels during Fch. Rev[n].

Chapel erected by G. Manley Esq., a native of Taunton, & now Lieut.

Col. of the reg[t] of Dragoon guards of His Holiness the Pope:

Many Catholics have come over from the continent & & taken up their

residence in the convent here – &c &c.   Old D.C.C. Oct 21. 1830

Source: 'Popery in Taunton', *DCC*, 21 October 1830, p.4, col.4.
Note: *DCC* reports: 'the state of Popery in this town begins to assume a more decided character since the Catholic Relief Bill passed last year'. The 'zeal displayed for making proselytes to the Roman Catholic Religion' is, it says, 'the foundation of the intolerant spirit of that church'. It points out the 'evil' of Protestant parents who because of 'pecuniary difficulties' allow their children 'to be brought up in the Popish religion'. The Catholic Relief Act, April 1829, substituted a new form of oath for the oaths of Supremacy and Allegiance and abolished the exclusion of Roman Catholics from public offices. *DCC* at this time reflected the strong anti-Catholic feeling in the county. See also items 167a, 167b.

177c–[179]

The union of the celebrated actor O'Brien with Lady Susan Strangw[ys].

They were thrown together by the private theatricals carried on at Holl[d]

H. & all London was wild with admiration of his person & his inimitable   //

man^r of acting a fine gentleman in comedy. He was himself of a

gentleman's family in Ireland left by some accident for education with

a R.C. priest; & considering his education, his turn for the stage, & the

society into wh. that taste must have thrown him he was certainly a

very extraordinary & amiable char^r. He lived in D^{shire} respected &

beloved by every one for many years, at Stinsford, a house belonging

to Lady Susan's b^r L^d I.

She, when young, was reckoned the proudest of the proud, & the

highest of high; her elopement, therefore, was the more wondered

at. They went to America for some years after the m^{ge}, where her

friends had procured him some trifling office – I believe as commissary.

M^r O'B followed the law, & went the western circuit for a short

time after his return from America, until they finally settled at

S. They remained always most affect^{ly} attached to each other.

Lady S. was a woman of a very strong & highly improved underst^g

extremely agreeable in soc^y, a steady warm hearted friend, & a

person in whose convers^n anything like gossip or abuse of y^r neigh^r

never held a place, but to the very latest hour of her existence

her lofty char^r was most strongly marked. Her principles & educ^n

as well as her husb^{ds} had been neglected; but whatever their

errors might be in both they were redeemed by very valuable &

amiable qualities, & no two people were more liked or their society

more courted in the middle & close of their lives. He had most amenity, she most strength of char^r...[Note –] She was eldest dau. of S.

1st E. of I. born 1743. – was one of the 10 young ladies daughters of dukes &

earls, who were bridesmaids to Q. Charlotte on her m^{ge}. The beautiful &

renowned Lady Sarah Lennox was another...Holl^d H. resid^{ce} of Hy.

Fox, 1st Ld Holland, 2^d son of Sir. S. Fox, & younger b^r of St. E. of I,

conseq^{ly} uncle of Lady Susan.   Journal of Mary Frampton
                    [vide post, 180]

Source: *Frampton*, 18–20.
Note: *Lady Sarah Lennox*: Sarah Lennox (1745–1826), dau. of Duke of Richmond, m. Col.
George Napier (d.1804), lifelong friend of Lady Susan O'Brien, to whom she was related by
marriage. *Holl^d H ... St. E. of I*: Holland House, W. London (great Whig centre of the period),
residence of Henry Fox, 1st Lord Holland, second son of Sir Stephen Fox (1627–1716), and
younger brother of Stephen Fox, 1st Earl of Ilchester (1704–76). See item 175b.

179a

Mrs Fitzherbert. – The follow^g curious anecdote was related to

me by Hon Mrs G. Dawson Damer, née Seymour, who on the death of her

parents (L^d & L^y Hugh Seymour) was adopted & educ^d by Mrs Fitz H.

   She was dining with me at Dor. & my b^r Jas. F. & Major Horatio

Shirley were also present: – "On the death of Geo IV in 30, some

jewels & trinkets were directed to be given to Miss Seymour (then

Mrs Damer); amongst others was the counterpart of a kind of brooch,

cont^g miniat^e of Geo IV set with a diamond instead of a glass. The

diamond had been cut in half, & the other part set in same way

cont^d a m^{re} of Mrs F.H. Great search made at Windsor...

   Some time aft^s D. of Wellington...s^d...that in his office as First

L^d of T. duty to remain...body of King, Quite alone who

had given him strict instruct[ns] not to leave it, & had desired to

be buried with whatever orn[ts] might be upon him time of d.

Dk. quite alone with body – lying open coffin, & his curiosity

being excited by seeing small jewel hanging round neck of King – tempt[d]

to look at it...identical port[t] of M[rs] F.H. & diamond –   ib. //

Source: *Frampton*, 12–13 (fn).
Note: *M[rs] Fitzherbert*: Maria Smythe (1756–1837), widow of Edward Weld of Lulworth Castle (1775) and also of Thomas Fitzherbert (1781), went through a form of marriage with the Prince of Wales (1785) and lived with him as his wife (in spite of his marriage to Princess Caroline (1795)) until about 1803: 'probably the only woman to whom George IV was sincerely attached' (*DNB*). *cont[d] a m[re]*: 'contained a miniature'. *D. of Wellington*: see item 68d. *First L[d] of T.*: First Lord of the Treasury. *Quite alone*: TH attempted to erase these words which were to be written three lines later, correctly. *time of d.*: 'time of death'.

180a

"<u>Holland House</u>." Pcess Liechtenstein.

<u>Mrs Fox</u>, on her husband being suddenly visited in his illness, slipped

into a closet <u>en</u> <u>déshabille</u> – Fearing the conv[n] with the visitor was

exciting her husband too much, she coughed &c...At last s[d] 'The

young man's gone I think?'   1. 131.

Source: Marie Liechtenstein, *Holland House* (London: Macmillan, 1874) ii, 130–31.
Note: *Pcess Liechtenstein*: Marie, Princess Liechtenstein (1851–78), née Marie Fox, the adopted daughter of Henry Fox, 4th Lord Holland. *Mrs Fox*: Elizabeth Armitstead (1750–1842). wife of Charles James Fox (1749–1806), great-uncle of 4th Lord Holland. *visitor*: George Jackson (1785–1861), diplomat. Liechtenstein's source for this story was Sir George Jackson, *Diaries and Letters of Sir George Jackson*, 2 vols (London: 1873), ii, 3–4; see item [204]a. See also *LN*, i, 187 (item 1454), also entered from *Holland House*, in 1886 or 1887.

180b

Henry Fox secretly m[d] Lady Caroline Lennox; eldest dau. of 2[d] D.

of Richmond. Her f. & m. w[d] not forgive her till the baby was born. 55

Source: Liechtenstein, *Holland House*, i, 55 ff, 68.
Note: *Henry Fox*: 1st Lord Holland (1704–74). *2ᵈ D. of Richmond*: Charles Lennox, 2nd Duke of Richmond (1701–50), was the grandson of Charles II.

180c

Erased item (f.90v) (see Appendix One)

180d

The Duke blames his acquaintances for furthering the secret mᵍᵉ. They

write one after another declaring they knew nothing about it –

Source: Liechtenstein, *Holland House*, i, 57–66.
Note: *The Duke*: The Duke of Richmond, see 180b. *his acquaintances*: the Earls of Lincoln and Ilchester and Henry Pelham.

180e

Fox went over Napoleon's house during the peace of 1802. Saw a bust

turned face to wall. It was his own.   ib.

Source: Liechtenstein, *Holland House*, ii, 147–8
Note: *Fox*: Charles James Fox. *Napoleon's house*: the Imperial Residence, Saint-Cloud, S.W. of Paris.

180f–[181]

                          court & assembly's
Lady Susan The talk ʌ yesterday was all of the match of Lady Susan

Strangways & O'Brien the player. It is said she went out Saturday with

a servant, whom, under the pretext of having forgotten something she sent

back, & said she wᵈ wait in the street till her return. O'Brien was waiting

in a hackney-coach, wh. she got into, & they went to Covent Garden Ch. &   //

were married. 'Tis a most surprising event, as Lady Susan was everything that was good & amiable; & how she even got acquainted with this man is not to

be accounted for: they say she sent him 200 £. a little time since. Everybody

is concerned at this rash step. She is of age.   ib. II. 46.

(Letter by Mrs Harris in "Letters by the 1st Earl of Malmesbury from 1745 to 1820".
1870).

Source: Liechtenstein, *Holland House*, ii, 46–7.
Note: this letter (5 April 1764), also appears in Earl of Malmesbury (ed.) *A Series of Letters of the
First Earl of Malmesbury His Family And Friends from 1745 to 1820*, 2 vols (London: Richard
Bentley, 1870), i, 108. See earlier item 177c. Lady Susan O'Brien was 1st cousin of Charles James
Fox.

181a

A beautiful picture of Lady Susan, by Sir J. Reynolds is at Holland House, –   ib.

Source: Liechtenstein, *Holland House*, ii, 43–4. See also Malmesbury, *Letters*, i, 108 (fn).
Note: *Sir J. Reynolds*: Sir Joshua Reynolds (1723–92), painter and first President of the Royal
Academy.

181b

Miss Read, the paintress, in Walpole's letters on this subject was Miss Cath-

erine Read, who did the pretty portrait of the <u>Gunning</u> D^chess of Hamilton –   ib.

Source: Liechtenstein, *Holland House*, ii, 47.
Note: Liechtenstein is quoting a letter from Walpole to the Earl of Hertford, (12 April 1764). *on
this subject*: the Lady Susan affair; Lady Susan and O'Brien were discovered at Miss Read's.
Catherine Read: (1723–78), fashionable portraitist in London. *Gunning*: Elizabeth Gunning,
Duchess of Hamilton and Argyll (1734–90). Read's paintings of the Duchess and of her sister
Maria Gunning, Countess of Coventry ('The Beauties'), were widely reproduced as engravings.

181c–[182]

                                  ⌠mother –
<u>Lady Sarah Lennox's</u>⌡great beauty – Her grandson, Mr Henry Napier says –

'My grandf^r 2^d D. of Richm^d was one of the L^ds of the Bedch^r to K. Geo II who then resided at Kens. Palace. He had been, as was the custom of those days

married while yet a boy to Lady Susan Cadogan, dau. of L[d] C. who as a cavalry

officer disting[d] himself in D. of Marlb'[s] wars. This marriage was made

to cancel a gambling debt, the young people's consent having been the last

thing thought of: the Earl of March [after[ds] the 2[d] D. of R] was sent for

from school & the young lady from her nursery – a clergyman was in attend[ce]

& they were told that they were immed[y] to become man & wife! The young lady is

not reported to have uttered a word; the gent[n] exclaimed: They surely are not

going to marry me to that dowdy? The ceremony however took place a post-

chaise was ready at the door, & L[d] M. was inst[ly] packed off with his   //

tutor to make the 'Grand Tour', while his young wife was returned to the care

of her mother, a Dutchwoman, daugh[t] of W[m] Munter, Counsellor of the

Courts of Holland, ~~[idle story goes on that~~ After some years spent abroad

L[d] M. returned, a well educated handsome young man, but with no agree-

able recollections of his wife. Whereupon inst[d] of at once seeking his own

home he went directly to the opera or theatre...exam[d] the comp[y]...Beautiful

woman struck his fancy...asked who she was – 'you must be a stranger in

London' replied the gent[n] 'not to know the toast of the town – the beautiful

Lady March.' Agreeably surprised L[d] M. proceeded to the box & claimed

his bride...Lived so happily that she died of a broken heart within a year

of his decease (1750). Holland House MSS   ib. II. 57.

Source: Liechtenstein, *Holland House*: ii, 51–3.
Note: *Henry Napier*: Capt. H. Napier (1789–1853), youngest of the five sons of Col. George and
Lady Sarah Napier (see item 182a).

182a–[183]

Lady Sarah Lennox, dau. of the above – Old Geo II put her in a large

China jar, & shut down the cover to prove her courage. She began singing

her French song of 'Malbruc'. Her mother died – went to live with sister

in Ireland – then with eldest sister Lady Holland. G.II – comes & jokes.

She embarassed – Future Geo III, a spectator, also embarassed. He falls

in love with her...asks Lady Susan Strangways about her – wants to

marry her – She indulges in a foolish flirtation w^h Ld Newbottle [was

she drawn into this by the King's party?] – but loved the King – makes

hay close to the road where the King passes on horseback. King's relations

& Ld Bute – A courtier advised the King to seduce her – but he w^d not –

she knew that courtier's name, < > but w^d never tell it – The King is   //

made to marry Charlotte. She was selected as one of the bridesmaids – L^d

Westmoreland kneels to her thinking her the queen. Married Sir C. Bunbury –

Divorced – married Col. George Napier, son of 4th Ld Napier – King still

thinks of her – In 1814 a sermon on diseases of the Eye. His majesty

present, blind: a lady also present, deeply affected – She also blind –

Lady Sarah, in tears for the King's suffering.   ib. II 53–70

[The story is told at length – Her character seems a guileless one]

Source: Liechtenstein, *Holland House*, ii, 53–70.
Note: *G.II - comes & jokes*: in fact this incident took place at Kensington Palace; by this time Lady Sarah Lennox was a young woman. *makes hay close to the road*: this was the road past Holland House. Liechtenstein takes this incident from Horace Walpole, *Memoirs of the Reign of George III*, 4 vols (London: Richard Bentley, 1845), i, ch.5. *A courtier advised the King to seduce her*: TH's version of 'advised the King to pursue a course injurious to herself'. *Divorced*: not mentioned in Liechtenstein. *His majesty present, blind*: an understandable misreading by TH of a report of a Charity Sermon in 1814 where the effect of a eulogy on George III 'was greatly heightened by the

recollection that His Majesty was at that time … totally and incurably blind'. Lady Sarah Napier was present, but not George III. See also item 177c.

183a

A <u>Picture</u>. With Holland House in the background. Lady Holland bought

it, but never knew whose was the portrait, or the painter.   ib.

Source: Liechtenstein, *Holland House*, ii, 172.

183b

<u>Strange Malady</u>. "I wonder in what state Ld Huntington is now

in, as last year I heard that his Bones were all crumbling to Dust

& out of the skill of the Physicians to cure his disorder – "

    (Anecdotes for 1788, from Diary of Ld Robt Seymour. <u>Murray's Mag.</u>)

Source: Sir Robert Seymour, 'Anecdotes, Reports, Truths and Falsities for the Year 1788: Passages From the Diary of Lord Robert Seymour', *Murray's Magazine*, 1 (1887): 471–90 (p.472).
Note: *Ld Robt Seymour*: Lord Robert Seymour (1748–1831), MP, 3rd son of 1st Marquess of Hertford.

183c

<u>Sir J. Rous</u>, when he went to ask for the consent of Dow^r Lady Carbery

to his marriage with her grand-daughter Miss Wilson: sh w^d not give it –

he was surprised – demanded reason – she told him it was her intention to

marry him herself. She then enjoyed the momentary pleasure of seeing

his uneasiness, & after^{ds} telling him she willingly consented.   ib.

Source: Seymour, 'Anecdotes, Reports', 472.

183d

The D. of York betted with Col.Tarleton that he w^d walk with him 6 miles in

less time for 200 guineas...declined contest – & paid forfeit of the whole stakes –   ib. //

Source: Seymour, 'Anecdotes, Reports', 473–4.
Note: *walk ... 6 miles*: between Hyde Park Corner and Kew Bridge.

184a

A Lady married in her Domino (Lady A. Campbell) to Mr Clavering,

having gone off with him from the Masquerade.   ib.

Source: Seymour 'Anecdotes, Reports', 475.
Note: *Domino*: a face mask, usually black.

184b

Duke & Duchess of Montrose – deaf & blind – (both apparently) – an "interpreter"

to enable them to communicate.   ib.

Source: Seymour, 'Anecdotes, Reports', 480.
Note: 'The Duchess of Montrose buried the 30th of June; she died at Table eating some minced
Veal. The Duke asking her thro' the means of their Interpreter (being very deaf himself, as likewise
blind) how she liked it, her Grace replied she found it *extremely* good, and sank back on her chair
lifeless' (480). The Duchess died 18 June 1788.

––––––––––

184c

Intoxication with Ideas – Men can intoxicate themselves with ideas

as effectually as with alcohol or with bang, and produce, by dint

of intense thinking, mental conditions hardly distinguishable from

monomania. Demoniac possession is mythical; but the faculty of

being possessed, more or less completely, by an idea, is probably the fundamental condition of what is called genius, whether it show it-

self in the saint, the artist, or the man of science. One calls it

faith, another calls it inspiration, a third calls it insight; but the

'intending of the mind' to borrow Newton's well-known phrase, the con-

centration of all the rays of intellectual energy on some one point,

until it glows & colours the whole cast of thought with its peculiar

light, is common to all.

Huxley, 'Science & the Bishops' – <u>19th Cent</u> Nov. 87

Source: Thomas Henry Huxley, 'Science and the Bishops', *Nineteenth Century*, no.125 (November 1887): 625–40 (p.630).
Note: *Huxley*: T.H. Huxley (1825–95), man of science and eminent Darwinist, greatly admired by TH (see *LN*, i, 377). *bang*: probably a variant on 'bhang', the Indian variety of the common hemp. Huxley was replying to a pamphlet 'The Advance of Science' which reprinted three sermons (by the Bishops of Carlisle, Bedford and Manchester), preached in Manchester Cathedral (4 September 1887) during the annual meeting of the British Association for the Advancement of Science, in Manchester.

184d

<u>Fascination</u>. Basilisk & opoblepa – kill other animals by staring at them.

Mouse running round open-mouthed snake, crying; at last as if forced, leapt in.

Same effect from eye of setter on partridge. <u>Human eyes</u> also   Old Cyclo
                                                                                                "Witchcraft".

Source: unidentified.
Note: *opoblepa*: unidentified. *Old Cyclo*: probably 'old Encyclopaedia'.

184e

Mr Arthur Symons is one of the few men writing to-day who are seriously to be reckoned with. No matter of what he writes – whether it be a piece of music or an actress, a city or a dead poet – he always gets straight to the heart of a thing; and he has the extraordinary faculty of making you see precisely what he sees and think exactly as he does. And in this book before us he is, above everything, an interpreter of his own emotions; he is so greatly interested in himself that he cannot conceive of the possibility of his readers not possessing a similar curiosity about his feelings and ideas. This attitude is typical of all men with highly developed artistic faculties and flaming imaginations. The writing is nearly always subjective: it is rarely impersonal, and never objective. In writing about ten cities of the world (Rome, Venice, Naples, Seville, Prague, Moscow, Budapest, Belgrade, Sofia and Constantinople) he has simply described in exquisitely beautiful language the varied emotions, moral, intellectual, and physical which came to him as he lived in each place. He confesses that, to him, 'cities are like people with souls and temperaments of their own'; and again, 'it seems to me that all these cities have given up to me at least something of their souls, like the people I have loved and hated in my way through the world.' It is not too much to say that no

Text: loose cutting, incomplete (10.8 x 6.8 cm).
Source: unidentified. This is a review of Arthur Symons, *Cities* (London: J.M. Dent, 1903). On reverse of cutting is material including a press announcement of Austin Dobson's edition of Burney's *Evelina* (Macmillan, 1903).
Note: Arthur Symons (1865–1945), poet, critic and editor, was on friendly terms with TH in the 1900s (see James Gibson, *Thomas Hardy: Interviews and Recollections* (Basingstoke: Macmillan, 1999), p.65). TH entered several notes and cuttings from Symons's poetry and criticism in 'Literary Notes II' for the period 1893–1904 (see *LN*, ii, items 1909, 2014, 2076, 2156, 2183, 2194, 2201, 2235, 2285, 2315, 2509, 2514).

184f

(DCC 1882)
Mr Farq^n came into the County in 1808 or 9
                      and
& bought Mr Sturts ~~or~~ Mr Wyndhams hounds

& with £40,000 a year commenced his

hunting career over the whole of Dorset
                      Solomon &
with Ben Jennings huntsman & $\wedge$ Tom Jen

nings Whips. My father was at Brasenose

when he was at Christchurch & was partly the

means of introducing him to the county. M^{rs}

F. was a superb woman with £30,000 worth

of diamonds at the Blandford Ball – & so

was his second wife Mrs Philips of Mont

acute...He hunted the hounds at his sole

expense at Eastbury & Cattistock, in

the Vale & on hills for 51 years. Billy

Butler was a constant visitor...unique

in his way...stories...gusto.

He lived at Okford Fitzpaine while in

the Vale turn & turn about, & had 3 horses –

~~favourite~~ Maximus, his best & his

two old hacks Vinosus & Spavinosus

– prided himself with his classics. His

favourite meet was at Melcombe Park.

< > hardly ever missed a day – rode a

long way to the meets – I see him

now in my minds eye on the Bulbarrow

Hills, & have often ridden home with him

– his broad brim hat, jolly handsome face

– his cut-off brown coat, brown boots &

thigh leggings to keep off the thorns, for

he often put up the fox himself &

knew exactly where the fox w^d make

for. E.B.Acton

Udalls Dorset Collection II. 50.

Text: at 90°, pencil. This, and subsequent items (184g–j) are entered onto the reverse side of a pasted-in hotel receipt.

Source: letter from E.B. Acton in J.S. Udal's 'Dorset Collection', ii, 58, a collection of cuttings assembled in the 1880s (*DCM*).

Note: *Farq*[n]: J.J. Farquharson (1784–1871), famous master of foxhounds of Langton, Blandford; see A.H. Higginson, *The Meynell of the West: John James Farquharson* (London: Collins, 1936); Hawkins, *Cranborne Chase*, pp.86–7. *Brasenose … Christchurch*: colleges of Oxford University. *Billy Butler*: The Revd William Butler, Rector of Frampton (1762–1843), the original of the sporting parson, Parson Billy Toogood, in 'Andrey Satchel and the Parson and Clerk' in 'A Few Crusted Characters' (*LLI*) (see *Brady*, 146). This item is a further source for the story. TH's 1896 Preface to *LLI* refers to a 'truly delightful personage' who had 'several imitators in his composite calling of sportsman and divine, but no rival' (*PW*, 30–31). *Udalls* [*sic*] *Dorset Collection*: John Symonds Udal (1848–1925), retired colonial magistrate and Dorset folklorist, author of, among others, *Witchcraft in Dorset* (1892), *Dorsetshire Folklore* (1922). Udal was a friend of TH (see *CL*, vi, 248). This item appears to be a letter by E.B. Acton, dated 24 November 1882, in Udal's 'Collection'; Acton was the son of the Revd Edward Acton (1786–1875), Vicar of Shillingstone, Dorset. The details of the report are reproduced in *The Victoria History of the Counties of England: Dorset* (1908; rpt Folkestone: William Dawson, 1975), ii, 301–3. This and the four items following (184g–j) are entered onto the reverse side of a hotel receipt which is pasted in. The receipt (for £1 2s. 6d.), dated 17 March 1890, covers accommodation and meals at the West Central Hotel, 97–103 Southampton Row, Russell Square, London for the period Saturday 15 March to Monday 17 March 1890. This was one of two temperance hotels favoured by TH and ELH (see Fran Chalfont, 'Hardy's Residences and Lodgings: Part Three', in *THFH*, i, 19–38 (p.22)). Assuming TH entered this information shortly after his hotel visit, the process of authentication of local information for stories either written or in the process of being written (and which were published the following year as 'Wessex Folk' in *Harper's New Monthly Magazine*, March–June 1891) is well under way.

184g

1839 – D.C.C. July 25 – John Hounsell
  for poisoning his wife.

Text: at 90°, pencil.

Source: Udal, 'Dorset Collection', ii, 201–2 ('Dorset Summer Assizes', *DCC*, 25 July 1839, p.4, cols 2–3).

Note: items 184g–i all refer to a sensational poisoning case in the then remote West Dorset village of Powerstock. Hounsell was acquitted in spite of evidence of arsenic poisoning. In her *Memories and Traditions* (see 198a), Lucia Boswell-Stone recalled the trial (p.55).

184h

(man & woman poison wife & husb[d]
respectively)   Udal II 202

Text: at 90°, pencil.
Source: Udal, 'Dorset Collection', ii, 202.

184i

"I made her a sweat of rosemary
  hyssop & beer"

Text: at 90°, pencil.
Source: Udal, 'Dorset Collection', ii, 202.
Note: *a sweat*: a medicine for inducing sweat, a sudorific.

184j

On the Dorchester Road from Sturminster

is a p.house called the King's Stag – its

sign displaying a stag with a golden collar

round its neck, & underneath it are

the following lines –

  When Julius Caesar landed here
  I was then a little deer;
  When Julius Caesar reigned as King
  Round my neck he put this ring;
  Whoever shall me overtake
  Spare my life for Caesar's sake
    (cutting from N.P. 1829).   //

Text: at 90°, pencil.
Source: Udal, 'Dorset Collection', ii, 2.
Note: *King's Stag*: the first of the 'lone inns' in TH's 'A Trampwoman's Tragedy' (*TL, CP*, 196).
(cutting ... 1829): TH's addition. See also item 203 for a variant of this rhyme found in Yorkshire.
TH also alludes to this legend in *Tess of the d'Urbervilles* (*Tess*, 1988, 18), drawing on *Hutchins*,
iii, 738. See Michael Bath, 'King's Stag and Caesar's Deer', *PDNHAS*, 95 (1973): 80–83. Bath
consulted 'Facts' for this article (n.15, p.83).

185a

<u>Revenge</u> –
Spain – 1679 – If a man receive a box on ear &c, he called

a drunkard: reflecting word passed on his wife's virtue, these

must be wiped off with blood – & by assassination. For they say

it is not just that offended party sh^d put his life in an equal

balance with the offender's. So tenacious of revenge that they will

not lay aside an injury for 20 y^{rs}. If they happen to die before they

accomplish it they will recommend the same upon their death beds

to be executed by their children. A certain person of note, dreading the

revenge of his enemy, went to West Indies, stayed 20 y^{rs}, till, hearing

that both he & his son were dead he returned to Spain, changing

his name for greater security: grandson of enemy, 12y^{rs} of age, hired

a ruffian, who assassinated soon after his return.

Cotter Morison – 'S. of Man'.

Source: James Cotter Morison, *The Service of Man: An Essay Towards The Religion of the Future* (London: Kegan Paul & Co., 1887), pp.149–50 (taken from a chapter: 'Morality in the Ages of Faith').
Note: *he called a drunkard: reflecting word passed on his wife's virtue*: 'if he be called a drunkard; or a reflecting word happens to pass on his wife's virtue'. *Cotter Morison*: Cotter Morison (1832–88) was a leading positivist, whom TH met at a Rabelais dinner in early June 1886, and whose work he evidently respected (*CL*, i, 146–7). TH also copied extracts from Morison's *Service of Man* into *LN* (*LN*, i, 1465–71).

185b

<u>Hatred for Science</u> – Mother Margaret (Hallahan) when she first

caught sight of the Britannia Bridge excl^d "Oh, how wonderful ! But

if men do such things as these they will begin to think they have no need of God." She felt a satisfaction when some of the wonderful

modern discoveries came to nought. Was glad to hear that the laying

of the first Atlantic cable had failed, & what is still worse, & is a

stain on her memory (?) she was even pleased that in spite of storm-

signals & metereological theories the wrecks on the English coast increased.

"I like these learned gentlemen to know", she w[d] say, "that God is master."

[Yet she was a warm hearted, devoted woman)   C.M.   ib. //

Source: Morison, *Service of Man*, pp.235–6 (taken from the chapter: 'What Christianity Has Done').
Note: *Margaret (Hallahan)*: although 'wholly illiterate' Mother Margaret had a 'powerful mind'. Morison claims that, as a Catholic, she showed 'the flash of anger and hatred of science so characteristic of the theologian who fears that his God is in danger' (235). *memory (?)*: there is no apparent reason for TH's query. *[Yet ... woman)*: added by TH, summarizing Morison.

186a

Religion & debauchery – D[r] Carlyle (D[r] Alex. C's father) was intimate

with L[d] Grange – used to meet for private prayer – praying alternately,

then had wine & supper. For half a year at a time there was no inter-

course between them. D[r] C's conjecture was that at those times, L[d] G.

was engaged in a course of debauchery at Eding[h]. Report, however, said

that he & his associates passed their time in alternate scenes of

relig[n] & debauch[y] – spending their days in meetings for prayer &

pious conv[n] & their nights in lewdness & revelling. "Some men are of

opinion that they c[d] not be equally sincere in both. I am apt to

think that they were."

  There are strong rumours that such contradictions between faith

& practice were not unknown in Scotland in a more recent past.

ib.

Source: Morison, *Service of Man*, pp.280–2.
Note: *Dr Alex. C*: Alexander Carlyle (1722–1805), Scots divine and pamphleteer. Morison draws on Carlyle's *Autobiography*, not published until 1860. *Ld Grange*: James Erskine, Lord Grange (1679–1754), judge.

186b–[187]

About 1850 Mr Readwin's attention was drawn to subj. of gold

mining in Wales by invitation of a gentⁿ in City, to look at some

native gold that had just come up, as he said, from a place in Wales,

somewhere near Dolgelly. He was shown an ordinary medicine bottle

marked off in the usual six doses & nearly full of water worn gold

grains & scales, a portion of wh. however, he sh^d now recognize as

angular gold separated from crushed galena or blende. Sixty or

more pounds (sterling) were required for the six doses, wh. were
          in
"taken" by "Bult ~~of~~ Cheapside." The man who had brought this bottled

gold had walked all the way from Dolgelly – some 250 miles, & had   //

done the same with a similar golden freight yearly for several years previously.

Paper read on gold in N. Wales. Times. Jan 7. 1888.

Source: 'The Gold Discoveries in North Wales', *The Times*, 7 January 1888, p.10, col.c.
Note: *Paper read*: by T.W.A. Readwin at a meeting of the Geologists' Association, University College, London.

187a

Gretna Green in 1887 – There was never any marrying blacksmith –

Being, like Coldstream & Berwick on Tweed, just over the border,

years ago it was a very convenient place for those who wished to get

married without leave...All that was needed was that the two

runaways sh^d in the presence of witnesses take one another to be husb^d

& wife, & they were properly enough married. Since 1857 residence in

Scotland 21 days by one of the parties is obligatory – but all the

rest holds good – That is, if the prospective bridegroom holidays in

Scotland for 3 weeks & his sweetheart comes down by mail at end

of time they can be m^d.   P.M.Budget. 5.1.88.

Source: *Pall Mall Budget* (5 January 1888) (no.1000), 18–19.
Note: *but all the rest holds good*: i.e. under Scottish Law. TH records an extract from an interview
by 'A Visitor' with the Registrar of Births, Deaths and Marriages for Gretna Green. For the Gretna
Green blacksmith, see item 63c.

187b

Frith's Autobiography –

Mr O. the Capt his brother in law, sleep in a double bedded room

of hotel kept by Frith's father. Capt. is awakened by his b. in law

kneeling upon his body endeavouring to strangle him...Capt flings

assailant on floor – tries to unlock door – runs downstairs – seen

by the children – O. dies in Asylum. Their father is sitting up –

dog barks at O., dazes him – pinioned by bell-rope, from behind –

thrown on sofa – O. died in asylum at York.

(con^d p.190)   //

Source: W.P. Frith, R.A., *My Autobiography*, 3 vols (London: Richard Bentley & Son, 1887–88),
i, 18–19.

Note: *Frith*: William Powell Frith (1819–1909) R.A., English painter, famous from the 1850s for his large, crowded canvasses, 'Ramsgate Sands', 'Derby Day' and 'The Railway Station'. Frith wrote appreciatively of TH's work in his *Autobiography* (1888), for which TH thanked him, recalling his view of 'Derby Day' (*CL*, i, 183). Mr O.: Owen.

188a

Hutchins: "Stinsford." [The Two Johns.]

John Syward dies 1402 – his wife & J.Jurdan being his executors –

his lands were settled in remainder (after wife's life, that is?) on John

his bastard brother

Matilda, age 26, wife to T.Brocas, & Alice (25) wife of J Shermyn

daughter of (the late?) Wm Syward (John's brother?) were his heirs ex

parte patris.

But John Heryng was his next heir on the part of Katherine his

mother.

His widow married R. Moor "holding for her life the lands formerly

John Syward's." [what became of bastard b^r? did he know that the lands sh^d come to him?]

Source: *Hutchins*, ii, 560.
Note: *(after wife's life, that is?)*; *(the late?)*; *(John's brother?)*; *[what became of bastard…come to him?]*: TH's interpolations. *daughter*: in *Hutchins*, 'daughters'. TH's own copy of *Hutchins* contains various annotations on ii, 560–61.

———————————

188b

" East Chaldon."

Philip Harang & his nephew W^m made a partition & settlement to the family

estates; also agreeing that whatever they sh^d acquire of the inheritance of

R.Harang & T. Harang their ancestors, sh. be divided between them.

Philip H. was convicted of the homicide of a certain William the Clerk,

& was outlawed; but after[ds] received pardon.

Source: *Hutchins*, i, 340.
Note: '*East Chaldon*.': or 'Chaldon Herring', near Lulworth, Dorset. *R.Harang & T. Harang*: Richard & Terricus Harang.

188c

"Bindon." There are still to be seen in the shep[ds] cottage at Little B., a

long gothic window to the east...probably once the humble church.

The Abbot...All wrecks on the coast as far as the conventual possess-

ions extended, belonged to him.   //

Source: *Hutchins*, i, 350, 352.
Note: '*Bindon*.': ruins of 12th-century Cistercian Abbey, near Wool, Dorset which figures in *Tess of the d'Urbervilles* (*Tess*, 1988, 230, 244). *Little B.*: E. of Lulworth Cove, the original site of Bindon Abbey. *conventual*: pertaining to a convent.

189a

– Melcombe Horsey"

From Sir George Clifton, the last of that family the estate came to Sir

Thomas Freke his father in law, by mortgage –

Source: *Hutchins*, iv, 367.
Note: *Melcombe Horsey*: parish W. of Milton Abbas. *Sir George Clifton*: TH's slip in referring to Sir George Horsey, whose family derived from Clifton Maybank, N. Dorset.

189b

"Ashmore."

... "He married Margaret Eliz ᵗʰ de Gury daughter of the Marquis de Gury

of the kingdom of France by whom he had no issue legitimate" – &c III. 371

Source: *Hutchins*, iii, 371.
Note: *He*: John Carver Esq. (1720–53), on the S. wall of chancel of St Nicholas church, Ashmore.

189c

"During the lives of her two last husbands & her widowhood she retained

the name of her first husband...   Cranborne. III. 377

Source: *Hutchins*, iii, 377.
Note: *Hutchins* reads: 'In 1316 the heirs of the Earl of Gloucester were certified as Lords of the vill of Cranburne. This manor, and a third part of the great inheritance of the Clares, fell to the share of Elizabeth de Burgh. By her first husband she had Elizabeth, wife of Lionel, Duke of Clarence. By Roger de Amory she had Elizabeth, wife of John, Lord Bardolf. During the lives of the two last husbands, and her widowhood, she retained the surname of her first husband [Richard de Burgh], and styled herself Elizabeth de Burgh, Lady of Clare.' Elizabeth de Burgh, lady of Clare, endowed Clare Hall (1359), later Clare College Cambridge.

189d

Adela, one of the concubines of King Hy I. Married Thoˢ Bardulff

(before or after concubinage?) Had daughter Rohesia – who mᵈ

1ˢᵗ Hy de le Pomerai, 2ᵈˡʸ John Russell, ancestor of the Dks of Bedfᵈ.

This Adela had by the King an illegᵗᵉ son, E. of Cornwall.

Hutch. II. 189

Source: *Hutchins*, ii, 189.
Note: *(before or after concubinage?)*: TH's interpolation. Hutchins traces the ancestry of the Russells of Kingston Russell back to Adela Corbet who was a mistress of Henry I. TH's own copy of Hutchins has a pencilled-in addition to the Russell pedigree which clarifies the relationship between Rohesia and Henry I's mistress, Adela, as described in Hutchins' narrative.

189e

Viscount Purbeck...m[d] "a dau of the infamous char. Sir Henry

Mildmay" – changed his name – tried to surrender his peerage –

descendants living in early part of 18th cent.   ib. I. 465.

Source: *Hutchins*, i, 465.
Note: *changed his name*: from Villiers to Danvers.

189f

"Bizzy" Sturt – very lovely woman, &c   III. 125   //

Source: *Hutchins*, iii, 125 (fn.).
Text: the full text of this item is in pencil.
Note: *'Bizzy' Sturt*: Eliza, dau. of Humphrey Sturt of Crichel, Dorset. *very lovely woman*: 'She was once the lovely Bizzy Sturt, whose external accomplishments, elegant as they were, constituted but a small part of those perfections for which she was so justly celebrated.'

190a

Frith's Autobiography, cont[d]

He sees tears chasing each other down the cheeks of a model – found

she was sitting to prevent her father going to prison for debt –

Source: Frith, *Autobiography*, i, 58–9.
Note: *cont[d]*: from item 187b. Text: *Frith's Autobiography, cont[d]*: positioned above first ruled line of page.

190b

Posts to London – as his mother's servant –

Source: Frith, *Autobiography*, i, 71–7.
Note: Frith recounts being repeatedly taken for a servant as a young boy.

190c

He & other painters accidentally choose same subject.

Source: Frith, *Autobiography*, i, 84–5.
Note: in 1840 both Frith and Daniel Maclise (1806–70) exhibited paintings of Malvolio from Shakespeare's *Twelfth Night*, at the Royal Academy.

190d

Turner – said he w^d be buried in two of his pictures: w^d not sell.

Source: Frith, *Autobiography*, i, 136.
Note: *Turner*: J.M.W. Turner (1775–1851), landscape painter. *pictures*: 'Carthage', 'Sunrising Through Mist'.

190e

Caracciolo – hanged at yard arm – next morning; King Ferdinand

shaving; saw body of C. floating, eyes open – outside cabin window.

Source: Frith, *Autobiography*, i, 145–6.
Note: *Caracciolo*: Caracciolo (1752–99), admiral of Ferdinand, King of Naples; he deserted to the French, was captured and hanged.

190f

Casts from Thurtell – his eyelashes adhere to the plaster –

Source: Frith, *Autobiography*, i, 183.
Note: *Thurtell*: convicted of a notorious murder in 1824. As a student Frith had access to casts of 'different parts' of Thurtell 'to help us in our anatomical studies'.

190g

Actress sits for personage in Derby Day – She is rubbed out – Her rage

when she sees the finished picture.

Source: Frith, *Autobiography*, i, 280–82.

190h

Picture of marriage of P. of Wales – difficulty of borrowing the dresses after[ds]

& getting the ladies to sit. With regard to Duchess of Brabant's robes he

had to pledge himself neither to smoke nor drink beer in their presence.

Source: Frith, *Autobiography*, i, 340–44.
Note: *their presence*: in the presence of the robes.

190i–[191]

Picture of Charles II – Sunday before death – "After much searching I found

a man curiously like the King. He seemed in feeble health, but without   //

any signs of fatal illness upon him; but strange to say, he sat to me for the

last time one Sunday, & 'before that day se'night all was in dust' with

him as with his royal prototype."

Source: Frith, *Autobiography*, i, 370.
Note: Frith painted 'Charles II's Last Sunday', inspired by an entry in the *Diary* of John Evelyn: 'I am never to forget the unexpressable luxury, & prophanesse, gaming, & all dissolution, and as it were total forgetfullnesse of God (it being Sunday Evening) which this day sennight, I was witnesse of; the King, sitting & toying with his Concubines ... A french boy singing love songs ... it being a sceane of uttmost vanity; and surely as they thought would never have an End: six days after was all in dust' (*The Diary of John Evelyn*, ed. E.S. de Beer, 6 vols (Oxford: Clarendon Press, 1955), iv, 413–14). Charles II died on 6 February 1685.

191a

Phillips is seized with paralysis while in Frith's studio.

Source: Frith, *Autobiography*, i, 371.
Note: *Phillips* [*sic*]: John Philip, an old painter friend of Frith's.

191b

Thackeray singing at the Club in Dean St. about 1845 – He & Dickens at

Academy banquet about this time. Also Rogers, D. of Wellington, Sir R.

Peel, Macready, Turner &c.

Source: Frith, *Autobiography*, i, 106–7; 118–21.
Note: *Academy*: Royal Academy. *Rogers*: Samuel Rogers (1763–1855), banker, poet and collector. *Macready*: William Macready (1793–1873), actor. This combines two incidents: dining at the Deanery Club and a Royal Academy banquet.

191c

Scandal about Napoleon I. – That there was an intimacy between him

& his wife's daughter Hortense, who married his b^r Louis: that Nap. was

father of her son Charles.

    Lucien advised Josephine: 'you are going to the waters: you must get

a child by another man'; or that Bonaparte must have a child by another

woman, & J. adopt it.   Bourienne.

Source: Louis A.F. de Bourrienne, *Memoirs of Napoleon Bonaparte*, ed. R.W. Phipps, 4 vols (London: Bentley and Son, 1885), ii, 98–9, 131. See *LN*, i, 400–401.
Note: *wife's daughter Hortense*: Josephine de La Pagerie (1763–1814), wife and Empress of Napoleon 1st; she had first married General Beauharnais, their dau. being Hortense (1783–1837). *Lucien*: a brother of Napoleon. *Bourienne* [*sic*]. See also item 133b.

191d

Old Coaching Days. Henry Bunbury the famous caricaturist

of road scenes. J.L. Agasse – painted a stage waggon 1820.

'Nimrod' discourses of Gigs – with its varieties, the buggy, the Stanhope,
                                     James
the Dennet, the Tilbury, – in 1837. ⁀ Pollard has preserved Stage-

Coach scenes – he was, early in the century, the painter of coaching themes.

Harpers Bazaar. 3.3.88.   //

Source: *Harper's Bazar*, XX1, no.9 (3 March 1888), p.139, cols 2–4.
Note: *Agasse*: acute accent omitted. This item is taken from 'Scenes on the road in the old London coaching days', illustrated by contemporary drawings. *Bunbury*: Henry Bunbury (1750–1811), son of a Suffolk baronet, and brother-in-law of Lady Sarah Lennox; popular amateur painter and caricaturist, and, as such, a favourite of H. Walpole. Some works engraved by Rowlandson and Gillray. *Agasse*: James Laurent Agassé (1767–1849), a Swiss settled in England. Noted for his animal paintings, espec. horses. *'Nimrod'*: pseud. of Charles Apperley (1779–1843), sporting writer, wrote on hunting in Dorset; see Higginson, *The Meynell of the West*, pp.9–21. *Pollard*: James Pollard (1792–1867), leading illustrator of coaching in its heyday; see Neville C. Selway, *The Regency Road: The Coaching Prints of James Pollard* (London: Faber & Faber, 1957).

192a

Dancing at Sun Inn, Portland Fair: floor gave way; all precipitated

into the cellar.   Old DCC. 11 Nov. 1830

Source: *DCC*, 11 November 1830, p.4, col.2.
Note: according to the report, 'nearly 200 persons … alighted on the casks of Sir John Barleycorn'; there were no injuries.

[192]b

Incendiarism – ricks – farm-buildings &c – Vigilant watch kept on most

farms – scarcely a farmer employing a machine to whom a notice has

not been sent – several farmers have removed their threshing machines

from their premises.   Nov 18.   ib.

Source: 'Outrages in the Country', *DCC*, 18 November 1830, p.2, col.5.
Note: the first entry in *'Facts'* referring to the Dorset disturbances of November 1830.

192c

<u>Stolen silver plate</u> – found concealed in a hayrick.   ib.

Source: *DCC*, 18 November 1830, p.3, col.4.
Note: the discovery took place near Melksham, Wiltshire. Thomas Marshall and Margaret Cooper were committed to Fisherton Gaol, to await trial for theft.

192d

<u>Incendiarism</u> at its climax – corn ricks & machines destroyed – special

constables sworn. At Salisbury the yeomanry were called out – Rewards of

£200 on the conviction of any incendiary – 60 rioters taken at Basingstoke. 25th

Source: *DCC*, 25 November 1830, p.4, col.2.
Note: *Incendiarism at its climax*: TH's observation. *yeomanry*: local units of volunteer armed cavalry. These summaries are from a long report detailing numerous such incidents. There is also a lengthy report in the same issue of *DCC* (25 November 1830, p.2, col.5) which observes that 'Kent, Sussex, Suffolk, Surrey, Buckinghamshire, Wilts. and Hants are now the extensive theatre of arson and disorder', also an editorial (p.4, col.1) referring to 'the torrent of insubordination'.

192e

<u>Resurrectionists</u> – People take a house at Devonport – sack seen

entering – many teeth found in house – graves empty –   ib.

Source: *DCC*, 18 November 1830, p.4, col.3. In a further report 'The Devonport Resurrectionists' (*DCC*, 25 November 1830, p.3, col.3), it emerged that 25 graves had been opened by the accused.
Note: *Resurrectionists*: see item 90a.

192f

<u>Some incendiaries killed</u> by military firing on them: sentences from

one month to transp[n] for life.

Source: 'Disturbed State of the Country', *DCC*, 2 December 1830, p.2, cols 4–5.
Note: *DCC* carried reports of disturbances closer to home, viz. Blandford, Handley, Cranborne, Mappowder, Buckland Newton, East Stour and Bere Regis. A 'corps of Yeomanry' was formed at a meeting held at the King's Arms, Dorchester, presided over by Col. Dawson Damer. Reports of

riots in the region were so numerous that, for once, *DCC* ran a 'Second Edition', with 'latest intelligence' (p.4, col.3) as it stood at 10 o'clock on Thursday morning – the day of publication. Such was the pressure on space that the newspaper's report of the 'Dorchester Annual Dinner' held at the King's Arms, (p.4, col.3) was evidently cut back to a fraction of the usually allotted portion. *DCC* reported 'threats to James Frampton Esq. of Moreton House'.

192g

Young woman returns to her g.m^{rs} cottage late: breaks key in trying

to unlock door: stays out all night –   ib.

Source: *DCC*, 2 December 1830, p.3, col.3.
Note: this is a report of an inquest on the grandmother who was found dead in the cottage. *breaks key*: cf. 'Breaking a key is a dreadful (bodement)' (*Far from the Madding Crowd*, (Oxford: Oxford University Press, 1993), p. 228).

192h–[193]

Impish tricks – servant girl to aged people at Ludgvan, n^r Penzance, plays   //

tricks of supernatural appearance – on jugs, teapots, glasses, fireirons

beer barrel – put in Bridewell. On coming out she goes as servant to

a relation – now operates on articles of food: a duck prepared for cooking

bounds to floor: pieces of pork & butter leapt about.   ib.

Source: 'Ludgvan Ghost Revived', *DCC*, 2 December 1830, p.3, col.4.

----

[193]a

Lycurgus – brother dies – Sceptre devolves upon Lycurgus' brother's widow,

then pregnant. Queen offers to marry L., promising that no son sh^d be

born to intercept L's succession –   Dic.s. e.g. Chalmers.

Source: Alexander Chalmers, *General Biographical Dictionary*, 32 vols (London: J. Nichols & Son, 1812–17), vol. 21 (1815), p.3.
Note: *Lycurgus*: traditionally the Spartan law-giver, *c.* 600 BC. *Sceptre devolves ... brother's widow*:

Chalmers has 'devolved to him by the death of his brother Polydectes', i.e. not to the widow.

---

[193]b

{ Lyserus (John)
{ Madan (Rev^d M) advocated polygamy on moral grounds. Chalmers.

Text: a bracket links *Lyserus (John)* to *Madan (Rev^d M)*.
Source: Chalmers, *General Biographical Dictionary*, vol. 21 (1815), pp.85–6.
Note: *Lyserus*: John Lyserus, d.1684, 'infatuated with the ambition of founding a sect of polygamists'. *Madan*: Martin Madan (1726–90), preacher and writer, his *Thelyphora* (1780) justifed polygamy but 'cost the author his reputation among the religious world'. Unusually, TH misplaces the centred line consistently used through the notebook to denote a switch in source material.

[193]c

The disturbances – assemblages in neighb^d of Shaftesb^y – proceeded to Stower

Provost: destroyed some machines: thence to the residence of the clergyman

from whom they demanded, with threats, a considerable reduction of tithes: 5 of

the ring leaders captured by party of armed yeoman: brought to county gaol on

following morning. One of the prisoners is a farmer named Dore, in respect^{ble} circ^s.

On Wedn^y Henstridge was in a very excited state. Messrs T.& B., Justices, at-

tended & swore in some special constables. In afternⁿ a mob collected, & openly

burnt a threshing machine...another...another...From Templecombe – Esq., &

Rev^{ds} – with 80 special constables hastened to scene – joined by strong party of

horsemen – altog^r a force of some hundreds –

Barn burnt at Bere – incendiary...[& other details] Old D.C.C. Dec. 9. 30

– Many labourers out of employ – distress great –   ib. //

Source: *DCC*, 9 December 1830, p.4, cols 1–2.
Note: *Stower Provost*: now Stour Provost, village S.W. of Shaftesbury. *Dore*: John Dore, 'the only

farmer who joined the rioters in Dorset' (Kerr, *Bound to the Soil*, p.104). *Henstridge*: another Blackmoor Vale village, S.W. of Shaftesbury. *Messrs T.&B.*: justices Thring and Bennett from the Wincanton Bench. *Templecombe*: village in S. Somerset. *from Templecombe … some hundreds*: DCC has: 'In the expectation of the mob proceeding to Temple Coombe, intelligence was dispatched to Horsington and Wincanton. From the former place, T.S.Bailwood, Esq, the Rev. Messrs. Wickham and Plucknett, and about 80 special constables, hastened to the scene of destruction.' *Bere*: Bere Regis, town E. of Dorchester, S. of Blandford. *Many labourers … distress great*: TH's interpolation. In a leading article headed in large type 'State of the Country', *DCC* now breathed a sigh of relief: 'It is with infinite pleasure that we are enabled to state that all intelligence received on this subject since our last is of the most favourable character and that the disturbed districts are generally sinking into a state of repose' (*DCC*, 9 December 1830, p.3, col.2). 'Peace has been restored to this county', noted an editorial (*DCC*, 9 December 1830, p.4, col.1). This is the last item which TH extracted from 'old DCC', entered at some time between March 1888 and September 1890.

194a

"I know a man who has been all his life subject to hallucin-

ation. This disposition is of such a nature that if he meets a friend

in the street he cannot tell at once whether it is an actual person

or a phantasm. By dint of attention he can make out a difference

between the two. Usually he connects the visual impressions by touch,

or by listening for the footfalls. This man is in the flower of his

age, of sound mind, in good health, & engaged in business. Another

member of his family has had the same affection, though in a less

degree". (Abercrombie.) Heredity by Ribot.   123

    (Other instances follow in the same book)

Source: T.H. Ribot, *Heredity: A Psychological Study of Its Phenomena, Laws Causes and Consequences* (London: Henry S. King, 1875), p.123.
Note: the passage is copied verbatim. *Abercrombie*: John Abercrombie (1780–1844), physician and author of *Inquiries Concerning the Intellectual Powers* (1830). *Ribot*: Théodule-Armand Ribot (1839–1916), French psychologist, best known for *Les Maladies de la Mémoire* (1881). There is a further interesting citation from Ribot's *Heredity* in a cutting of a 1902 article, recorded by TH in *LN*, ii (item 2197), about the nature of Mind: 'Mind has two parallel modes of activity, the one

conscious, the other unconscious' (ii, 130). TH also notes an extract from Ribot's *The Psychology of Emotions* (1897) (*LN*, ii, 63 (item 1933)).

194b

       EXTRAORDINARY CONDUCT OF A SHEPHERD. –
Considerable interest has been aroused in agricultural circles in Wiltshire by the extraordinary action of a shepherd at Ramsbury, named Hopkins, who attended the sale by auction of Lord Portsmouth's noted flock at Over Wallop, on the 18th instant, and bought sheep to the value of £1,417, without acquainting any one of his intention, and without slightest authority from his employer. We are informed that they are to be re-sold on the understanding that the deficiency, if any, will have to be made good by the shepherd, who, it is said, has £200 or £300 in the bank. D.C.C. Sep[t] 11 1890

Text: pasted-in newspaper cutting (3.0 x 7.0 cm). *D.C.C. Sep[t] 11 1890*: TH's hand on r.h. side.
Source: *DCC*, 11 September 1890, p.7, col.5.

194c

ib id [M.Chron. June 4 1811] The gibbet near Drinsey Nook, betw.

Gainsborough & Lincoln, upon wh. Thos Otter alias Temporell, was

hanged in chains murder of wife 5 years ago, presents at this time

a most extraord[y] sight. Under the jawbone of the skeleton a small

bird called the Featherpoke, has built her nest, wh. extends downwards

nearl[y] as far as to the ribs, & in that situation she has performed her incub[n]

& hatched a nest of young ones.

Text: item entered (pencil) on a pasted-in page (5.6 x 16.8 cm), ruled paper. There is no gap between this and the following item.
Source: *Morning Chronicle*, 4 June 1811, p.3, col.5.

194d

1808. July 6. Sudden death of one of the dancers at Lady Campbell's...

burst a blood vessel in going down a reel (Mr Calvert) – Terror & distress.

Lady C. fainted.   //

Source: *Morning Chronicle*, 6 July 1808, p.3, col.4.

[195]a

In the current number of *Blackwood* is an intensely interesting diary of Napoleon's voyage to St. Helena compiled by Sir George Bingham, K.C.B., with extracts from letters written from St. Helena by Sir George and Lady Bingham and Lieutenant-Colonel Mansel. There has been an abundance of Napoleonic literature of late, but we have seen nothing which gives so realistic a picture of the declining days of the great Napoleon as the diary before us. It may be interesting to note that Sir George Bingham was the son of Colonel Bingham, of Bingham's Melcombe, which had been held by the family from the time of Henry III – (a continuity only broken a few months ago, when the property passed into the hands of Mr Bosworth Smith). He had married in 1814 Emma-Septima, youngest daughter of Mr E.M. Pleydell, of Whatcombe, Dorset, who died in 1873. The papers on which the article is based were left by her to her nephew Captain A.E. Mansel, late of the 3rd Hussars, of Grove House, Dorchester, who placed them in the hands of Captain C.W. Thompson, 7th Dragoon Guards, who has edited them for *Blackwood*. Sir George was a very distinguished soldier, having gone through nearly the whole of the Peninsular War and the campaigns in the South of France, and when Napoleon was consigned to St. Helena he and his regiment, the 2nd battalion of the 53rd, were selected to accompany and guard him. He continued on the Island as second under Sir Hudson Lowe, and it was during that service that the diary and letters were written. A graphic picture is given of Napoleon when on August 7th, 1815, he went on board the Northumberland from the Bellerophon. The fallen Emperor was dressed in a plain green uniform, his hair out of powder and rather greasy, his person corpulent, his neck short, and his *tout ensemble* not at all giving an idea that he had been so great or was so extraordinary a man. Napoleon passed Sir George Bingham on his way to his cabin and asked who he was, and having been introduced put some polite questions to him. The daily life of the captive on board is fully described, and we learn with interest that Napoleon not only ate heartily but "took up both fish and meat frequently with his fingers." He discussed his battles freely and spoke without feeling as if, Sir George Bingham remarks, "he had been an actor only instead of the author of the scenes which cost so much bloodshed." Napoleon was fond of cards, and on one occasion when he lost he remarked that "good fortune of late had forsaken him." He was a bad sailor and often invisible. One day he walked the deck supporting himself on Sir George Bingham's arm, "How little did I ever think," the Dorset diarist moralises, "when I used to consider him as one of the first generals in the world that he would have ever taken my arm as support." Napoleon's ignorance was surprising, and he asked questions that any well-educated Englishman would have been ashamed to have put. At dinner the discussion turned on the invasion of England, and Napoleon amiably remarked that it was always his intention to have attempted it. He, however, expressed the opinion that he thought his life safe with the English. The only wound he ever received was from an English soldier (by a pike) at the storm of Fort Mulgrave. Of Napoleon's life on the island, Sir George Bingham gives many interesting details. One Sunday he called on him, and Bonaparte received him in his bedroom in his *robe de chambre*, "and a dirtier figure I never beheld," Sir George bluntly observes. He is equally severe on the "dirty little intrigues of Napoleon and his set," though he admits he was a favourite with the Emperor. Lady Emma Bingham once went with Sir G. Bingham and Colonel Mansel to pay a visit to the prisoner, and her ladyship found him "better looking than I expected." The diary and letters give a much more faithful account of Bonaparte and his life and manners in captivity than many of the more elaborate treatises that have been published on the subject. Dorset Chronicle 15 Oct 96

Text: pasted-in newspaper cutting (19.5 × 6.9 cm).
Source: *DCC*, 15 October 1896, p.8, col.3.
Note: *current number of Blackwood*: 'Napoleon's voyage to St. Helena', *Blackwood's Edinburgh Magazine*, 160 (October 1896): 540–49. At this date TH was particularly interested in character of Napoleon (with *The Dynasts* in view) as suggested by Bingham's comment 'as if he had been an actor only instead of the author of the scenes which cost so much bloodshed'. *Bingham*: Sir George Bingham (1777–1833), major-general. *Bingham's Melcombe*: old Dorset manor house of the Bingham family, a few miles from Whatcombe House, the home of Sir George Bingham's wife, Emma Pleydell. *Bosworth Smith*: Reginald Bosworth Smith (1839–1908), son of Canon Smith, Rector of West Stafford, near Dorchester; a friend of TH (*Life and Work*, 80, 130, 369), formerly a house-master at Harrow school, he bought Bingham's Melcombe in 1895. *Dorset Chronicle 15 Oct 96*: appended by TH.

[195]b

Lady Caroline Ponsonby married William

Lamb June 3. 1805, & became known

as Lady Caroline Lamb.

"Lady Caroline L." (Monthly Review

June '05)

Text: this and items [195]c, [195]d, below, are entered on a pasted-in page (13.2 × 9.5 cm), plain paper.
Source: Rowland E. Prothero, 'The Goddess of Wisdom And Lady Caroline Lamb', *Monthly Review*, 19 (June 1905): 12–28 (p.24).

Note: *Lady Caroline Ponsonby*: (1785–1828). *William Lamb*: William Lamb (1779–1848), succeeded as second Viscount Melbourne, 1828.

[195]c

It was in 1812 that Ld Byron & Lady

C.L. were romantically attached –

'Before Lady C. left London for

Ireland (Aug 15. 1812) she had already

one dangerous rival in Miss Milbanke

(aft^ds Lady B) & another in Lady Oxford

in whose neighb^d B. spent Sept. & part

of autumn of 1812.   ib.

Source: Prothero, *Monthly Review* (June 1905): 26.
Note: *Lady B*: Lady Byron.

[195]d

Their intimate friendship lasted from

the spring of 1812 till the following August.   //
                                                                                       ib.

Source: Prothero, *Monthly Review* (June 1905): 28.
Note: Prothero writes that 'when Lady Caroline returned from Ireland in the winter of 1812 she burned Byron in effigy at Brocket Hall.'

196a

THE DOMESTIC BRUTALITIES
OF MEN.

D. Chron. Aug 26.99

THE EDITOR OF THE DAILY CHRONICLE

SIR, – Reckless and foolhardy as it may be to expose myself to the torrent of feminine vituperation which seems certain to follow upon your reviewer's denunciation of the author of that courageous little book "The Domestic Blunders of Women," common fairness obliges me to hasten to his support. Because his is the first voice to catch the public ear, let none imagine he is the only man disappointed in his home, in the ideal of home; I venture to say there are thousands, perhaps hundreds of thousands, who have married with the same hopes that he had – that I had – who, but for that craven desire for "a quiet life" (the thing we aim at on seeing that "a happy life" is unobtainable) would place on record the story of their deplorable disillusioning. This becomes inevitably a personal matter, so I will beg you to excuse the personal pronoun. I, Sir, married upon a small income, a girl from a home where there had never been plenty. Because my wife sometimes appeared in garments which she had made herself, and hats which she had trimmed, I believed, and was encouraged to believe, that she was likely to be a thrifty housewife, capable of making money go far and home comfortable. Let me describe my circumstances previous to my marriage. I occupied one bed-room in a house twelve minutes from the City, and about as far by omnibus from the Strand. There I had breakfast and dinner, with midday dinner upon a Sunday. Always careful of my appearance, my income as clerk in a business house enabled me, as my position obliged me, to dress well. I could afford a weekly visit to a theatre or music-hall, and, being fond of such entertainments, managed to see all that was going. I had my bicycle, and on Saturdays and Sundays could take a long spin with friends into the country, if it were not the football season, when I made a practice of seeing as many important matches as possible. A fairly abstemious man, I was still able to have as much liquor as was good for me, and to stand a friend. A smoker, my pipe was well supplied. I will not say that I never betted, but I was lucky and never "hurt myself" much that way. This was my life when I "fell in love." We courted for a couple of years, during which I cut down my expenses to save money for furnishing, and six years ago I opened the gate of my little Eden – one of the villas your reviewer alludes to, I fancy, with a covert sneer. Now for my life since. I will be brief. Marriage has meant the sacrifice of most of my personal tastes. That is the sheer truth. My income has increased slightly, and I can only wonder what would have happened to us if it had not. I have had to give up most of my friends, for, though my wife did not dislike them, I found that there is considerable difference to the exchequer between standing a man a glass of bitter and asking him to sit down to the Sunday supper table, and do what he likes with the cold beef. As to theatres, I can seldom visit them. My wife would think it selfish if I went alone, and if she accompanies me it has to be "upper boxes," or at least the pit, and she likes to have something smart to wear. Her sewing she "puts out" now, as she has not "time" to do much herself. Saturday afternoons she likes me to take her out, and as she hates football matches because they "lead to gambling," I may say that I seldom, if ever, see one. Now, what is this home-life that we all hear so much about, and think that we shall like so much before we get it? A few hours in the evening, over a meal more or less satisfactory, conversation concerning the enormities of the "girl" (and as it is a fresh "girl" every few months, this is always on top). Breakfast in a rush, when your poached egg, not very fresh, is accompanied by an equally stale request for money. A flight to the train, during which I ask myself what I have got in place of the things I gave up when I married?

My wife is not bad-tempered, nor (I hope) am I; but she constantly complains of not having this and not being able to do that. She is not very fond of housekeeping; thinks her servant should do everything, and is angry when mistakes occur. I do not think she is clever with children – we have two – but she is an affectionate mother, and does her best. No doubt she, too, is disappointed, though she has a house of her own and pretty things in it. What is the prospect before me? Nothing but continual effort to pay for things, to make money go further, to make more money. Pleasures, if they may be spoken of at all, will decrease as years go on. We have a garden, but it grows nothing but cats, and I do not care for gardening. I like my children, but they are too little for me to understand, and I only see them on Sundays and Saturday afternoons; so far, I do not know them, except by their clothes, from anyone else's children. How should I? The conclusion is forced upon me that this ideal of "home" is too much "cracked up"; a young fellow likes a bit of love-making and taking out a smart girl – but that is no reason why he should enjoy the real realities of married life. I don't see that young men are much to blame; they have often never seen a home-life before they see it in the home they have scraped and saved to furnish. A girl likes presents and someone to dress for, and to take her out – but *she* doesn't like the real realities of married life a bit better when she gets them. At home she has left most unpleasant things to her mother, and beyond a little drawing-room decoration and rating the servant, she knows nothing of what is before her. I don't blame her, or call her "a depreciating property," as does the mere man. My own wife is better-looking now than she was when I married her; but I do think there is something wrong somewhere. Homes may be necessities, to bring up children in, but I don't see that they should be called "pleasures" or a source of "happiness." Who is it that gets up all this talk about homes? That person is responsible for a lot of disappointment. I should think these furnishing warehouses must put about the notion; it's to their interest, anyhow.

I have found mine a continuous opportunity for self-sacrifice, and I beg boldly to subscribe myself, yours faithfully,

Aug. 24.   A MARTYRED DUPE.

What does the man want?   //

Text: pasted-in newspaper cutting (20.7 x 12.9 cm). *D. Chron*: in pencil on lh side of heading. *Aug 26.99*: pencil on rh side of heading. *What does the man want?*: pencil, below end of cutting.
Source: 'The Domestic Brutalities of Men' ('Letter to the Editor'), *Daily Chronicle*, 26 August 1899, p.3, col.3.
Note: *D.Chron*; *Aug 26.99*; *What does the man want?*: additions in TH's hand.

[197]a

"Sept. 9. 1806. This day was married at Slinsford [Stinsford]

Ch. Dorset, Visc^t Marsham, son of Earl Romney, to Miss Pitt,

only daughter & heiress of Wm Morton Pitt Esq. with a fortune of

60,000 £. & an estate of 12,000 £ per ann. – independent of the estates

of her father. The ceremony took place in the presence of Ld Rivers,

M^r & Miss Lascelles, Ld Barham, M^r and Mrs M. Pitt, M^{rs} Ir<^{e}>monger

&c. M^r & Mrs M.P. gave the lady away, while Col. Noel & Miss

Beckford officiated on the occasion. In the early part of the morning

the whole of the unmarried female branches of the neighbouring tenantry

& villages attended at Kingston House, the seat of W.M.P. Esq., each

female attired in an elegant white muslin dress provided for them

as a present on the occasion by Miss P. After refreshments about

40 couple proceeded, 2 & 2, before the procession to the church,

strewing the way (before the happy couple) in the ancient style with

flowers of ev^y descrip^n. After the ceremony they returned in the same

order, attended by nearly 300 spectators where a dinner consist-

ing of Eng. hospit^y was provided on the occas^n in booths on

the lawn; & the festive eve concluded with a ball on the green,

in wh. the nobility present shared in the mirth. At an early

hour in the even^g the hap^y couple & suite set off in p.chaises

to pass the honeymoon at the lady's own seat Enchcome [Encombe]

House, Dorset."   <u>Annual Register</u> – 1806 .   //

Source: *Annual Register* (Chronicle), 1806: 443.
Note: an abbreviated verbatim transcription, with two corrections by TH. *[Stinsford] Ch.*: St Michael, Stinsford, parish church of the Pitts of Kingston Maurward and of the Hardy family. *Miss Pitt*: Sophia Pitt (1784–1812), dau. of Morton Pitt. *Wᵐ Morton Pitt*: William Morton Pitt (1754–1836), of Encombe and Kingston Maurward, Dorset, MP, notable philanthropist and reformer, cousin of William Pitt, Prime Minister. He sold Encombe to John Scott, later Earl of Eldon, in 1807. Landlord of the Hardys at Higher Bockhampton, although himself a long-standing mortgagor. TH included an anecdote about him in *Life and Work*, 428; see also *Public Voice*, 398–400. The 2nd edn of Hutchins's *Dorset* (1803) was dedicated to Morton Pitt. See *Hutchins*, index; *Gentleman's Magazine* (June 1836), 663–4; *Boswell-Stone*, 60; Tresham Lever, *The House of Pitt* (London: John Murray, 1947), p.362; Rands, 'Lady Susan O'Brien', 11–21. *Rivers*; *Beckford*: relatives of the Pitt family. *Lascelles*; *Barham*; *Iremonger, Noel* : relatives of Mrs Pitt. *Encombe*: Encombe House, S.W. of Corfe Castle, Dorset.

198a–[199]

Memories & Traditions Recorded by L.C.Boswell-Stone –

Printed by Richᵈ Clay & Sons Lᵈ London & Bungay.

1895

It was Xmas Eve 1814, & the custom every year on that day for

the clerk & Sexton to decorate the Ch. in the primitive manner of those

times, after cleaning the brass furniture – among wh. I certainly

remember < handsome > candlesticks on the altar; they could not then have

been considered Popish. Branches of evergreens, holly & mistletoe

were stuck in every available place; the largest branch of the last-

named, being the rarest, was put in front of the Mayor...Clerk

Hardy, & Ambrose Hunt the Sexton, after carefully locking themselves

in, had been the best part of a winter's day engaged in their work,

& sat down at last on a settle near the vestry, where a view down

the ch. of St. Peter, esp. of the N. aisle, was obtained. Then a sudden

temptⁿ seized these 2 men. It was very cold, a glass of wine wᵈ do them good; the wine was in the vestry, easily come at. So, having

taken some appropriated for the Holy Comm^n they seated thems^s, but had

hardly tasted the wine when they became aware of a well-known
                    [Revd Nathan^l Templeman – died 1813 –]
figure seated between them – their late rector ⌃ They did not see him

come: he seemed to rise up suddenly. He looked from one to the

other with a very angry countenance, shaking his head at them just

as he did in life when displeased, but with a more solemn aspect.

Then rising & facing them he slowly floated up the n. aisle &   //

sank down gradually out of their sight. The clerk swooned, the sexton

tried to say the Lord's Prayer, &, when the apparition vanished he

after some trouble unlocked the ch. door & got help for H. They

were both so frightened that concealment was impossible. The story

spread through the town, soon reaching the ears of the rector M^r

Richman who determined to search into the truth, & submit the men

to a rigid examin^n. Mrs R. & her sis. Mrs Williams were ill & nervous

at the time, hence Mr R. asked my aunts to let him see the men

at their house…They came, looking very dismal, but…never varied

from their first account. Rector forgave them…after exhortation.

p.20.

Source: *Boswell-Stone*, 19–20. The volume is compiled by W.G. Boswell-Stone and has a dedication
'To Miss Pettigrew From the Children of Her Old Friend'.
Note: *L.C.Boswell-Stone*: Lucia Catherine Boswell-Stone (1806–91) of Dorchester, only daughter
of Edward Boswell, Deputy to William O'Brien in his office as Receiver-General for Dorset and
author of *The Civil Division of the County of Dorset*, m. in 1831 Joseph Stone, Town Clerk of
Dorchester; see *CL*, v, 194. *St Peter*: St Peter's, Dorchester. *[Revd Nathan Templeman – died 1813]*:
TH's addition from information in *Boswell-Stone*, 17; see item 202a. *Mr Richman*: The Revd Henry
John Richman of Holy Trinity with St Peter's Dorchester; see items [199]b, 218a.

[199]a

Houses burnt down where the "Kings Arms" now stands – 1775.

Town in ruins from this fire – Mayor & Corp[n] sat on fallen trees

in "Burnt Gardens" (now New St) smoking pipes & drinking Dorchester

beer, debating how to restore the houses –

New Town Hall built – 1793. [Replaced by present one about 1840]

After the B. of Waterloo the Barracks were for many years untenanted

A sketch of Lady Abingdon's House in S. Street (corner of Durngate St)

is given in the Gent[ns] Mag. for 1840 – by Mr Barnes the poet.

Text: [Replaced by present one about 1840], in pencil.
Source: Boswell-Stone, 38–9.
Note: [Replaced by present one about 1840]; (corner of Durngate St): TH's additions. Barnes: The
Reverend William Barnes (1801–86), Dorset dialect poet and philologist; TH knew Barnes from
about 1856.

[199]b–201

The Great Storm of 1824 wh. caused so much destruction in West

of Eng[d] …Lived in the old house…a young girl. Being a

corner house we were much exposed. As far as I remember the   //

wild weather began about 9 or 10 on even[g] of 23 Nov. when

we went to bed, 10, or 11, wind blowing fiercely from S.W. I was

awakened by a tremendous roar of wind & a breaking of glass in the

direction of the staircase window toward the East. (I suppose the

wind had shifted to the S.E: this caused the greatest damage.) Much

startled I ran into my father's and mother's room, next door to mine.

They were both awake: my father immediately got up & I took

his place. Before doing so, however, wrapped in my dressing gown

I went into his dressing room & looked down the street. The oil

lamps were nearly all blown out; just a faint glimmer c^d be

seen here & there. I c^d barely see the tiles & slates flying about in

all directions; the day had not yet dawned. My father soon came

& took my place at the w^w & I went into my mother's room. A

trem^s blast of wind took the curtains of the bedstead up entirely

(it was a 4 poster) & made the rings run along the iron rod. The

only door open was the door between b. r^m & dress^g r^m where my

f. was sitting. A short time after that gust he s^d "There is a crowd

of people at the Richmans' door" (it was now getting lighter).

"Why," he added, "there is Richman standing among them without

a hat!" Soon after came a knock at the b. r^m door: the cook

entered very agitated: M^r & Mrs R. were both killed. A stack

of chimneys had fallen upon them. We got up: my <u>mother</u> went

to see Miss R. their niece...staying with them. I watched my m^r //

down the st. with great anxiety: there seemed to be a storm of slates &

tiles rushing against each other. Miss R. gave a descript^n. She

slept next to her u. & aunt – When the storm was increasing M^{rs}

R. knocked at the wall, & Miss R. went in to her aunt's room.

Mrs R. seemed alarmed, & asked her to light another rushlight,

fearing the one they had might go out. Her uncle seemed to be

quietly sleeping, for (nervous man as he was) he always said he

c^d sleep best in a high wind. Miss R. had hardly got back

to her own bed before...a tremend^s crash...next room. Tried to open door...c[d] only manage just a chink – cold air blew

through. Rushed into st. gave alarm...first to D[r] Cooper, who

lived opposite. It was long before the mass of brickwork c[d] be

removed...bodies found without any mutilation – Miss R's eyes

open – husb[ds] closed, as in deep sleep. Her gold repeater

was ticking by her side uninjured – It was a childless union –

they were much attached to each other, & wished that they might

die together.

Large tree...roots lifted up the earth across the road...horse

removed from stable owing to dangerous state of tree...

At Wey[th] the 2 seas met over "The Narrows" – most of Esp. washed

away – stone chair carried away...found[ns] of house laid bare, esp.

Johnstone Row: sea flooded the basement, esp. Gloucester Row:

people went down the st. in a boat: two houses burning.   ib.

Text: there is no gap between this and following item, [201]a.
Source: Boswell-Stone, 26–8.
Note: *The Great Storm of 1824*: in *The Woodlanders* old apple trees retain 'the crippled slant to north-east given them by the great November gale of 1824, which carried a brig bodily over the Chesil Bank' (*Woodlanders*, 1985, 141) and in *The Well-Beloved* Jocelyn making for Chesil Bank passes 'the ruins of the village destroyed by the November gale of 1824' (*The Well-Beloved* (Oxford: Oxford University Press, 1986), p.20). The devastating effects of this storm on the region were widely reported in *DCC* and in the *Sherborne and Yeovil Mercury*; see Gordon Le Pard, 'The Great Storm of 1824', *PDNHAS*, 121 (1999): 23–36. *stone chair*: this was 'at the end of the Esplanade'. *Richman*: see item [198]a. *At Wey[th] the 2 seas met over 'The Narrows'*: that is, where the isthmus of the Chesil Bank joins Weymouth and Portland; see 'The Night of Trafalgar (Boatman's Song)': 'the Back-sea met the Front-sea' (*The Dynasts*, Part First, V, 7). In *The Dynasts* (1919) TH inserted a note to this song: 'In those days the hind-part of the harbour ... was so named, and at high tides the waves washed across the isthmus at a point called "The Narrows"' (*CPW*, iii, 335; iv, 416).

201a

Farringdon Ch. destroyed by the owners of the estate –   ib. //

Source: *Boswell-Stone*, 14.
Note: *Farringdon Ch.*: the remains of the church of Winterborne Farringdon (nr. Winterborne Came, S. of Dorchester), a village 'entirely depopulated' (*Hutchins*, ii, 519). Boswell-Stone recalls childhood fears that the ruin was haunted (p.14). In *The Trumpet-Major* John Loveday standing by 'Faringdon Ruin', tells Anne Garland, 'my grandfather could call to mind when there were houses here. But the squire pulled 'em down, because poor folk were an eyesore to him' (*Trumpet-Major*, 1991, 326.)

202a

Revd N. Templeman (died in 1813) a little old man pottering

along the st., with a gold headed cane, wh. he tapped on the pavem^t

at every step: full curled wig, on the very top of wh. reposed a

shovel hat; a dress of square old fash^d clerical cut, ruffles, cravat,

& bright buckles in his shoes.   ib.

Source: *Boswell-Stone*, 17.
Note: *Templeman*: The Revd Nathaniel Templeman (1728–1813), Rector of Holy Trinity with St Peter's, Dorchester.

---

[202]b

(married 1808, when he was Visc^t Primrose)
Earl v. Countess of Rosebery ʌ – a proceeding for divorce (her maiden

name Harriett Bouverie, dau. of the Hon Mr Bouverie) Annual Register 1815

Lady Rosebery's sister was wife of Sir Henry St John Mildmay – Bart –

& another sister married Mr Mildmay, Sir H's brother.
(then a happy couple)
Sir H's wife dies. He stays with the Roseberys ʌ for consolation at first

Attachment between Sir H.M. & Lady R. w^d meet in Kensington gardens...Ld R. suspecting, took his wife away to Scotland –

Sir H. disguising himself, & suffering his beard & whiskers to grow, takes

up his abode at an inn near. (Oct 1814) under the name of Col. de Grey.
                                        (Mr Primrose)
L^d R's family – i.e. his mother, wife, b^r ʌ & himself, dined at 6. Ladies

retired at 7 – gent^n joined them at 9: Lady R. w^d disappear

from drawing room. Dow^r Countess watched – There was a bedroom on

ground floor of the wing...Mr Primrose, instructed by Dow^r from what she

had seen, & with some servants, broke open the door of bedroom, wh. was locked,

& caught the couple, who went away together...Divorce obtained.

(Sir H. was dressed in large blue jacket & trousers, & red waistcoat covered with
                                    & armed with brace of pistols
a profusion of pearl buttons ʌ when the room was burst into, & "the handk^f wh.

Lady R. had worn round her neck at dinner was off & her gown unpinned.")   //

Source: Earl v Countess of Rosebery, *Annual Register* (Appendix to Chronicle), 1815: 283–6.
Note: *Earl*: Archibald Primrose (1783–1868), 4th Earl of Rosebery: *Annual Register* has
'Roseberry'. *(then a happy couple)*: TH's summary of 'in the most uninterrupted state of domestic
happiness'. *away to Scotland*: to Dalmeny, the Rosebery's Scottish seat. *caught the couple*: *Annual
Register* has 'Sir Henry was discovered by the side of the bed, dressed etc.' In a subsequent
crim.con. trial, Rosebery obtained £16,000 damages from Mildmay, who had to spend the rest of
his life abroad, with the Countess; see Lawrence Stone, *The Road to Divorce. England 1530–1987*
(Oxford: Oxford University Press, 1990), pp.239–40.

[203]a

Times – 1808. Aug 2. Salisbury races ended on Thursday last. Very little

sport. The ball, however, was attended by all the fashion of the county.

Match of singlestick, &c.

Source: *The Times*, 2 August 1808, p.3, col.2.
Note: *Match of singlestick*: a chaotic match was played which 'did not at all answer public
expectation ... for want of previous proper arrangement by persons skilled in the game'; the
'Wiltshire men uniformly play with the arm naked' while the 'Somersetshire men generally play

with the arm padded'. See Ruth A. Firor, *Folkways in Thomas Hardy* (1931; New York: A.S. Barnes & Co, 1962), p.175, who cites a reference to singlestick in *The Dynasts* (Part First, II, 4.) (*CPW*, iv, 73).

[203]b–[204]

The Saturday Review.   [January 14, 1882.

THE FOLK-LORE RECORD. – VOL. III. PART II.*

This volume, like the volumes which have preceded it, contains some papers of considerable interest, and exhibits also some of the faults which we have been obliged to point out in previous notices of the records of the Folk-lore Society. In books which must necessarily be a miscellaneous gathering of contributions from many hands this is perhaps hardly to be avoided; but it would be well if the limits of the subjects legitimately falling under the head of folk-lore were more clearly defined and more carefully kept. All superstitions probably fall within these limits, and it is certainly matter of some importance to ascertain how far old superstitions still have a practical hold on the people of this country. A few remarks contained in this volume may well startle those who are not aware of the facts. From the evidence here given it would seem that the state of things in Dorsetshire and Devonshire is by no means what it should be. At the Shaftesbury Union a few months ago a middle-aged man applied for relief, as being unable to work. The surgeon could assign no cause for his inability, nor could he assert its existence; and the only reason given by the man was that he had been "over-looked" by his sister-in-law. His wife had been to a wise woman at Stalbridge, whose prescriptions or advice had relieved him for a few days; but the spell had again become too potent for him to resist, and he was helpless. Hence he refused absolutely to work. His application for relief was not granted; but it must probably be allowed that there remains still in some parts of the country a mass of absurd fancies which modern education has not yet been able to root out. It is not a little disgusting to learn that an annual gathering is, or was until lately, held in the same neighbourhood, called the Toad Fair, because a cunning man "of great fame there sold to crowds of admirers legs torn from the bodies of living toads. These, placed in a bag, and worn round the neck, were declared to be a sovereign remedy for scrofula, for the 'over-looked,'" and for sufferers generally. This is, of course, superstition of the most grovelling and mischievous kind, as there is no conceivable connexion between the supposed cause and the supposed effect. But it may perhaps be doubted whether the following story of wart cure should be taken as an instance of the superstitions attached to this subject. Earlier volumes of the *Folklore Record* have given some nauseous specimens of these delusions, in all of which the result is as entirely unconnected with the cause as in the talisman of the toad's legs. A Liverpool lad, we are told, had his hands covered with warts, and a lady seeing them, gave a recipe which she declared to be trustworthy. "Get one or two cowrie shells," she said, "and put them into an eggcup or other small vessel, and then get a lemon, and squeeze the juice from it on the shells. In a few hours the shells will be dissolved into a white paste; put the paste on the warts with a piece of stick two or three times a day, and before many days are over the warts will vanish." The writer asserts that the application in this case was entirely successful; and certainly one does not see that there is more of superstition in the outward form of the prescription than there would be in the assertion that warts may be burnt out with nitric acid. *The Folk-lore Record. Vol. III. Part II. London: Folk-lore Society. 1881.

A paper on rural weddings in Lorraine shows perhaps as strong an instance of survival as may be found in any land. The old custom of obtaining a bride by force is here indicated by no mere faded sign or symbol, but by a veritable trial of strength, which taxes the muscles of the combatants to the uttermost, although care is taken that no serious mischief shall be done. The contest is redeemed from brutality, not merely by these cautions, but by the fact that it becomes almost as much a trial of wit as of bodily powers. Readiness of speech is, indeed, a weapon as necessary for success as stoutness of arm and readiness of nerve. The first battle being over, and a truce granted, the admission of the assailants into the house is made to depend on their singing a verse or a song unknown to any of the defenders, and which, therefore, none can go on with in reply. In a large number of instances the assailants are pulled up at the first line; but sometimes they are allowed to go through twenty or thirty verses of a long story without interruption, and then the defenders chime in with the first line of the last strophe, and tell their opponents that they need not weary themselves by going through so long a song. This tournament of ballad-singing is followed by another struggle to place the goose upon the hearth, which is worth notice only as showing how completely the notion of fighting for a wife has taken possession of the people. Even when this is accomplished, there remains the further ordeal in which the bride and three of her companions, of precisely the same height with herself, are placed on a bench, with a white cloth thrown over them, while the bridegroom has to touch with a stick the form which he supposes to be that of his bride. If he succeeds in so doing, he dances with her without changing partners during the rest of the evening. If he fails, he must content himself with dancing with her companions. The sports, on the whole, may be somewhat boisterous; but there is no evidence that they are marked by anything to which serious objection could be taken.

From the Danish of Professor Grundtvig Miss Mully translates three tales which are of great interest, not only for purposes of comparison, but for their own merits. Neither of the three contains many incidents which are not found in the traditions of other countries; but all are told with singular purity and tenderness of feeling. The story of Prince Wolf adds another to the vast family of legends the framework of which is furnished by the love and sorrows of Eros and Psyche. Prince Wolf is, in fact, the Beast who has Beauty for his bride; but, even in his bestial form, he appears in no terrific guise. He wins his wife by answering a question which baffles all others; but the severance comes only after the wife has thrice proved faithless to the letter of his commands. The tinder-box and taper take the place of the torch or the lamp of oil; and Wolf, in his human shape, is awakened, not by the dropping of the spark or the burning liquid, but by the kiss of his wife, who throws her arms round his neck, forgetting to extinguish the taper. Then follows the parting, and the awful ordeals which must be passed through before they may meet again. She must find her way to the castle far off to which the wolf has been taken; and she is guided on her journey by the wolf's track all stained with blood. This is the veritable Lykabas, the path of the wolf, the path of light, the journey of the sun through all the stages of the changing year. She has the same impossible tasks to perform, the same implacable monsters to appease; and she surmounts all her troubles by the force of gentleness and love. The doors of the palace of Hebbenfeld refuse // to crush her at the bidding of the demon queen, because she has oiled their hinges. The dogs will not tear and bite her, for though they had been yelping and barking for ages, no one had ever fed them till she came. It is the same with all the other servants of the witch. The wicket-gate is the last of all; and the gate will not squeeze her, because she had given it a bolt for which it had been longing for many hundred years. But she encounters a greater danger when, as she sinks in utter despair on the loss of the jewels which she had got from the witch of Hebbenfeld, a youth in the full vigour of manly beauty accosts her kindly, and asks the reason for her grief. Not once only or twice he aids her effectually, although each time to the condition that she must take him for her sweetheart she replies, "Nay, I had a sweetheart once, but I shall never see him more." At last she regains the lost jewels and brings them to the witch, who is the Aphrodite of the ancient story. Prince Wolf is now in his human form, but he is to marry the witch's daughter, and his wife is to hold the torches in her hands at the wedding feast. There was a spell upon her, and she could not move though the torches burned on until her fingers were almost on fire. "My hands are burning," she moaned. "Burn then, candle and candlestick too," said the witch; but the bridegroom heard the curse, and, starting forward, recognized his lost love. Seizing the torches, he hands one to the witch and the other to her daughter. On these the spell at once works. The torches burnt on until they and the whole castle were turned to ashes. But Wolf and his bride were far away, as far as the dawn leaves behind it the murky abodes of darkness.

It may be a pardonable fancy if in the adaptation of these stories we ascribe to the Teutonic and Scandinavian races a power scarcely equalled by another peoples of the great Aryan family. How far the harvest of these traditions has been gathered in and safely stored in printed volumes it would be rash to say; that materials of the highest value still remain to reward future search there can be no doubt. An interesting paper by Mr. Coote on the source of some of Galland's "Arabian Nights" tales seems to prove that the last four stories of his collection were obtained directly from oral informants at Constantinople or Smyrna, and that he could not have obtained them from any written documents, inasmuch as no Arabic, Persian, or Indian MS. of any of these four tales has ever been found, and no hope exists in the minds of Orientalists that any ever will be found. It is strange, as Mr. Coote remarks, that Galland should thus have learnt by word of mouth four stories which are undoubtedly "the most brilliant fictions of that unequalled *corpus fabularum*."

Mr Lach-Szyrma's paper on folk-lore traditions of historical events is perhaps less attractive than some others in the volume; but it is the only one which touches questions of importance not only for the comparative mythologist, but for the historian. Mr Lach-Szyrma seems, like Professor Blackie, to be impressed with the idea that the general talk of the people will preserve a remembrance of great events in such a way as to give the record a practical value. He speaks of Cornish traditions as dwelling much on Judge Jeffreys and Oliver Cromwell, and says that they further commemorate "the terror of the Armada, the burning of the Mousehole, and the Buccaneer wars." But of these and other traditions Mr Lach-Szyrma unluckily gives no details; and it is by the details only that they can be judged. According to Professsor Blackie, oral tradition may, after centuries, and even millenniums, "be more true to the real character of the fact than the written testimony of this or that particular witness." As a special instance of this he adduces the tradition which points out the summit of a hill near Scarborough as the spot where Cromwell encamped during the siege of the castle in the Great Rebellion. The tradition, he admits, is so far inexact that Cromwell was at the time in quite another part of the country; but the inaccuracy, he maintains, touches only the point of Cromwell's absence. This, in his eyes, is a very small matter; and there remains, as he holds, the triple fact "that there was a great civil war in England between the Crown and the Commons at the time specified; that in this war the castle of Scarborough was an object of contention between the parties; and that in the same war a man called Oliver Cromwell was one of the principal generals of the popular party." To be sure, if this was all that we knew of the reign of Charles I., it would not be very much; and Mr. Blackie admits that the tradition would tell us no more. But it is exceedingly doubtful if it tells us nearly so much. Professor Blackie has probably read into it from his own knowledge the controversy between the Crown and the Commons; and in all likelihood local memory troubles itself as little about the cause of the blockade as about the explanation of the siege of castles in the days of King Stephen. The overthrow of Harold Hardrada and Tostig, coming as it did only a few days before a fight still more memorable, would, we might suppose, leave an impression on local tradition never to be effaced; yet the memory of the battle in which the English Harold defeated and slew his Norwegian namesake seems to have died out utterly in the neighbourhood of Stamford Bridge, unless the selling of cakes fashioned in the form of a horseman carrying a spear can be taken as an historical reminiscence of it. The cakes are sold in a November fair; and from this it would follow that the people remember neither the cause of the quarrel nor the day on which it was decided. It would be probably nearer the truth to say that popular traditions never can be trusted, and that, even when they correspond with the historical record, they are of little or no use, inasmuch as in such cases we gain our knowledge not from the local tradition, but from the written chronicle. But in the vast majority of cases they run counter to the historical evidence. It is so, as Mr Lach-Szyrma admits, with the traditions of Cornwall. These "represent the Spaniards as the fiercest and the most deadly foes of England; history represents Spain as a nation that scarcely ever achieved a great victory over the English." Nor is it otherwise with matters strictly local. "Tradition describes John Tregeagle and Job Militon as incarnate demons; locals history describes them as quiet country gentlemen." In spite of this we are told, oddly enough, that "the memory of Caesar's conquest is preserved in Yorkshire legends," a stag having been found near Leeds, with a ring of brass around its neck, bearing this inscription:–

> When Julius Caesar here was King,
> About my neck he put this ring.
> Whosoever doth me take,
> Let me go for Caesar's sake.

But Caesar was never north of the Humber, nor even of the Thames, and, in Lingard's words, he was never master of a foot of British ground. What is the value of a tradition, if it be a tradition, which preserves a memory of imaginary conquests and fictitious kings?

Text: pasted-in periodical cutting f.102r, (18.7 x 17.3 cm), f.102v, col.1, (21.4 x 8.7 cm), col.2, (13.4 x 8.7 cm).

Source: *Saturday Review*, 53 (no 1368), 14 January 1882, pp.56–7. (Review of 'The Folklore Record', vol. III, Part II (Folklore Society, 1881).)

Note: *Shaftesbury Union ... unable to work*: see J.S. Udal, *Dorsetshire Folk-lore* (1922), pp.205–6. *Bag ... worn round the neck*: see reference to 'Toad-bag' in *The Mayor of Casterbridge* (*Mayor*, 1987, 187). *When Julius Caesar ... for Caesar's sake*: see also item 184j for a variant of this rhyme found in Dorset. This issue of the *Saturday Review* also carried a review of TH's *A Laodicean* (pp.53–4). See also item 110a.

204a

Lady Jackson on Louis XV

Aided by the fertile fancy of the celebrated *coiffeur*, Leonard, the Duchess had invented, exclusively for herself, a head-dress, which she christened *"le pouf sentimental."* The scaffolding was two inches higher than that of the head-dress worn by the queen, and which was also invented for the occasion, and named *"coiffure à loge d'opéra."* It was composed of numberless plumes, waving at the top of a tower. Leonard had used fourteen yards of gauze or lace for the duchess's "pouf" and folds and plaits surrounding it. The ornaments employed were two waxen figures, representing the little Duke de Beaujolais (afterwards King Louis Philippe) in his nurse's arms. Beside them was placed a parrot pecking at a plate of cherries; and reclining at the nurse's feet was the waxen figure of a black boy. On different parts of the edifice were the initials of the Dukes de Chartres, de Penthièvre, and D'Orleans, formed with the hair of those princes – the husband, father, and father-in-law of the fair wearer of the sentimental *coiffure*.

Forgetting the height of her *"pouf"*, the duchess in the course of the evening leaned forward to speak to the Duke de Penthièvre, when her head-dress became entangled in the ornaments of a girandole on the opposite side of her box. On resuming her upright position the girandole remained firm, but drew out a long piece of the gauze and displaced the parrot and the cherries. Luckily they fell on the duke, who caught them, and, with great presence of mind, prevented a further fall into the *parterre*. Thus, saving his daughter from becoming the object of mirth to the audience, and perhaps saving also Gluck's opera; but the incident occasioned much merriment among the royal party.

Text: pasted-in periodical cutting f.102v, col.2 (6.5 x 8.6 cm). *Lady Jackson on Louis XV*: in pencil.

Source: 'Lady Jackson on the French Court', *Saturday Review*, 53 (no.1368) (14 January 1882): 55–6.

Note: *Lady Jackson*: Catherine, Lady Jackson d.1891, wrote on French court life. Wife of Sir George Jackson, she edited his *Diaries and Letters* (1873), see item 180a.

[205]a:i

'The Toldoth Jeshu is the most ancient Jewish writing that has descended to us

against our religion. It appears to be of the first century, & even to have been written

before the Gospels.'

————————

Text: this and subsequent three items ([205]a: ii–iv) are pasted-in extracts from a notebook, (17.8
x 10.0 cm) (unruled paper); pages 1–9 recto only, 10, recto and verso (1–9 numbered on top lh
corner; 10 recto and verso, unnumbered). The line is regularized.
Hand: Florence Emily Dugdale (FED).
Source: Voltaire, *Lettres sur les Juifs*, cited by G.W. Foote and J.M. Wheeler in their Preface to *The
Sepher Toldoth Jeshu: The Jewish Life of Christ* (London: Progressive Company, 1885), vi.
Note: *Jeshu*: TH also used the spelling 'Jeschu'. This is one of several sources for TH's 'Panthera'
(*TL*, *CP*, 280–86). The others include Basnage's *History of the Jews*, Crawley's *Tree of Life*,
Origen's *Contra Celsum* (see items [205]a:ii–[205]d) and the 1898 edition of George Eliot's
translation of Strauss's *Das Leben Jesu* (1837) (which TH owned). Hynes records a 'footnote in
Strauss concerning the name Panthera; Strauss's note cites Origen, Schöttgen (a name that appears
in Hardy's holograph) and *Toledoth Jeschu* (the spelling that Hardy used, and then altered, in the
holograph)' (*CPW*, i, 386). Florence compiled (in the British Museum) the copies necessary for the
background of the poem some time before August 1909, when she and TH were guests of Edward
Clodd at Aldeburgh (*Millgate, 1982*, 461–7). TH added to these notes from Florence his own
transcriptions from *Origen Contra Celsum* ([205]a–[205]c). It appears that TH was able to read a
draft of the poem to Clodd, and possibly fellow guests, during that August visit, presumably having
used Florence's transcripts. In September TH was sending MSS of poems for what was to be *Time's
Laughingstocks*, to Macmillan, and immediately asking for the MS of 'Panthera' back (*CL*, iv,
44–5, 47–8; *Millgate, 1982*, 466). On 6 October TH thanked Clodd for sending 'notes on
Panthera' (*CL*, iv, 47–9). See also the annotation of 'Panthera' by Hynes (*CPW*, i, 337, 386).

[205]a:ii

From Basnage's "<u>History</u> of the Jews" Taylor's translation

—

'Celsus is excusable in having upbraided Christians with the virgin being forced by a

soldier called Pandera, but how can St Epiphanius (A.D.367) be excused, who assures

us that Jesus was the son of Jacob surnamed Panthera? // And indeed the name given here to the soldier, Panther, is a Greek one; how then can it be introduced into the genealogy of J. Christ as the surname of a family. There is good reason to believe that it was invented only to make the birth of the Messiah more odious. The manuscript of a Rabbi is also quoted, wherein it is said that as the leopard is produced by the mixture of a species, so J.Christ sprung from a Greek soldier and a Jewish woman. Those who reckon Panthera among Christ's ancestors, fall into the snare which the most inveterate // enemies of the Christian religion have laid for them. Emanuel de Tesauro is one of these, for he blesses the fate of Marham and Panther because Jesus Christ came from them " (B. iv., ch.27.)

Hand: FED.
Source: Jacques Basnage, *History of the Jews* (trans. Thomas Taylor) (London: J. Beaver & B. Lintot, 1708), Book 4, ch.27, pp.376–7; translation of *Histoire des Juifs* (1706).
Note: *Basnage*: (1653–1723), French Protestant historian. *St Epiphanius*: St Epiphanius, d.403, early Christian scholar, opponent of Origen.

[205]a:iii

The Jewish Life of Christ.

Chapter I.

In the year 671, of the fourth millenary [of the world], in the days of Janneus, the king, a great misfortune happened to the enemies of Israel. 2. There was a certain idle and worthless debauchee named Joseph Pandera, of the fallen tribe of Judah. // <3> He was a man of fine figure and rare beauty, but spent his time in robbery & licentiousness. He lived at Bethlehem of Judea. 4. Near by there lived a widow who had a daughter named Miriam, of whom mention is several times made in the Talmud as a dresser of women's hair. 5. This daughter was betrothed by her mother to a very chaste, gentle & pious youth named Jochanan. 6. Now it happened that Joseph

occasionally passed by Miriam's door & saw her. Then he began to have an //

unholy affection for her. 7. So he went to & fro about the place, and at length the

mother said to him, What maketh thee so thin? He replied, 'I am madly in love with

Miriam.' 8. Then, said the mother, I would not deny thee the favor; see if she is

willing <to> do with her as thou pleasest. 9. Obeying her counsel, Joseph Pandera went

frequently by the house, but did not find a suitable time until one Sabbath evening,

when he // happened to find her sitting before the door. 10. Then he went into the

house with her, & both sat down in a dormitory near the door, for she thought he was

her betrothed, Jochanan. 11. Tum ea homine ait: Ne me attingio; in menstruis <s>um.

Sed is morem illi non gerebat, cumque circa <e>am voluntati suae obsequatus fuisset,

in domum suam abit. 12. Circa medium noctis <i>terum in eo exardescere desiderium

malum. Ergo // somno levatus ad domum Miriamis viam affectans, <a>d cellam se

confert, factumque repetit. 13. Valde autem exhorruit puella, et quid hoc, ait, tibi

vult, Domine, quod eadem nocte his me convestisti? idque non passa sum ab eo inde

tempore quo sponsam me tibi elegisti? 16. After three months, Jochanan was told that

his betrothed was with child. 17. In great agitation, he went to his preceptor, Simon

// Ben Shetach, and, telling him about the matter, asked him what he ought to

do. 18. The preceptor inquired, Dost thou suspect anyone? Jochanan said,

Nobody, except Joseph Pandera, who is a great debauchee, and liveth

near her house. 19. The Preceptor said, My son, take my advice, and keep silent; for if

he hath been there he will surely go there again. Therefore be wise, and get a witness,

so that thou mayest bring him before the great Sanhedrim. // 20. The young man went home and was sorely troubled during the night. He thought to himself, 'When

this thing becometh known the people will say it was my doing. 21: Therefore, to

avoid the shame and disgrace, he ran away to Babylon and there took up his abode.

22. In due time Miriam brought forth a son and named him Jehoshua, after her

mother's brother.

Hand: FED.
Text: *sum*; *eam*; *iterum*; *ad*: words obscured by paste-in.
Source: Foote and Wheeler (eds.) *The Jewish Life of Christ*, 13–16.
Note: *Tum ea homine … me tibi eligisti*: these sections (11–13) are translated as: 'Then she said to him: "Don't touch me; I am having my period." But he did not comply with her wishes, and after gratifying his desire for her he went home. In the middle of the night he was again inflamed with a terrible longing, and so getting up from his sleep he made his way to Miriam's house, went to her room and repeated the deed. The girl was completely terrified and said to him: "My lord, what is the meaning of this? You have visited me twice in the same night, something which I have not had to suffer since you chose me as your fiancee."' Of these sections, the editors explain 'we are obliged to keep these passages veiled in Latin. There are worse things in the Bible, but we do not feel at liberty to emulate the indecency of the inspired writers. A reference to *Leviticus*, xx.18, will give a fair idea of the meaning of Miriam's exclamation in the first sentence' (p.15 (note 5)). The two verses (14 & 15) which Florence Dugdale had omitted from the transcription passed onto TH, are as follows: 'Verum in silens repetit, nec verbum ullum proloquitur. Ergo Miriam queri: Quousque tu peccato scelus addis? annon pridem tibi dixi esse me menstruatam? Verum ille non attendebat ad ejus verba, sed desiderio satisfaciebat, ac tum postea iter pergebat suum.' (But he remained silent and said nothing. So Miriam complained: 'How far are you prepared to compound your crime? Did I not tell you just recently that I was having my period?' He took no notice of her words, however, and after satisfying his desire he went on his way.) *convestisti*: a mistranscription of 'convenisti'.

[205]a: iv

Pandera

The Jewish tradition, from which Celsus drew, was later incorporated

in the Talmud, & later still amplified & altered in the medieval 'Sepher Toldoth

Jeschu.' The following are the chief details of the Talmudic account. Jeschu, as the

name is written, the omission of the 'ain' changing the meaning to 'his name &

remembrance shall be be blotted out,' is described as Ben Stada, the son of Stada, or Ben Pandera, the son of Pandera. By Stada, Miriam (Mary) is implied; She is

described as a dresser of women's hair and a sinner. Pandera, a Roman soldier,

was her paramour & the father of her child. Her husband, Paphos // ben Jehuda,

divorced her.   //

"The Tree of Life'. Pp. 158–9. by Ernest Crawley

Hand: FED; *by Ernest Crawley* in TH's hand.
Source: Ernest Crawley, *The Tree of Life: A Study of Religion* (London: Hutchinson, 1905),
pp.158–9.
Note: *is described as Ben Stada*: Crawley's text has 'described either as'.

[205]b

Origen against Celsus. (Origen contra Celsum)

(Trans by Bellamy.)

"The Jew, whom Celsus personates…says that the Virgin Mary being

big with child was divorced by her husband the carpenter, for committing

Adultery with one Panthera, a soldier, & being got with child by that

scandalous wretch."   (Chap. XXIX. Bk 1.)

Source: Origen, *Origen contra Celsum* (trans. as *Origen against Celsus* by James Bellamy)
(London: B. Mills, 1660), Book 1, ch.29, p.119.
Note: *Origen*: Origen (186–253), an Alexandrian, one of the greatest early Christian philosophers.
He recovered and largely reproduced the anti-Christian work of Celsus, written *c*. 180, in order to
refute it.

[205]c

"Then he [Celsus] reproaches him [Christ] with being born at an obscure

village, & having a woman to his mother that got her livelihood by going

out to service, who, he says, being convicted of Adultery, was divorced

from her husband, who was a Carpenter by trade.

"Then he says, That after this indignity wand'ring from place to

place, she was privately brought to bed of our Saviour, & that he being

forced, by reason of want, to work in Egypt, & having learn'd there

some of those arts for which the inhabitants of that country are so

famous, return'd into his native country, & swelling with a vain

conceit of the miracles he sh^d do, gave out that he was God –"

Chap. XXVI. Bk.1

Source: *Origen against Celsus*, Book 1, ch.26, p.108.

[205]d

"He goes on in the same bantering strain...she...[the mother of

Jesus]...led so obscure a life that she was scarce known by those

who were her nearest neighbours." Chap XXXIV. Bk.1

[Vide also Haeckel, Strauss. etc.] //

Source: *Origen against Celsus*, Book 1, ch.34, p.136.
Note: *[Vide also Haeckel, Strauss. etc.]*: TH had read *The Riddle of the Universe at the Close of the Nineteenth Century*, a translation of Ernst Haeckel's *Die Welträtsel* (1899), and David Friedrich Strauss's *Das Leben Jesu* in George Eliot's translation (1898); see *CPW*, i, 386 and *LN*, i, 1297n., *LN*, ii, 2069, 2069n., 2341.

f.103v is blank

[207]a–[209]

Grove's Dic. of Music. "Barthélémon, François

Hippolite, born at Bo^urdeaux July 27. 1741, was the son of a Fch

gov^t officer & an Irish lady. He commenced life as an officer in

the Irish brigade, but being induced by the Earl of Kelly, a well-known amateur composer, to change his profession for that of music,

he became one of the most disting^d violinists of the time. In 1765

he came to England & was engaged as leader of the opera band. In 1766

he produced at the King's Theatre a serious opera called 'Pelo-

pida', & in the same year married Miss Mary Young, a niece

of Mrs Arne & Mrs Lampe, & a favourite singer. In 1768

Garrick engaged him to compose the music for the burletta of

'Orpheus' introduced in his farce 'A peep behind the curtain',

the great success of wh. led to his composing the music for other pieces

brought out at the same theatre. In 1768 he went to Paris, & produced

there a pastoral opera called 'Le Fleuve Scamandre'. In 1770

B. became leader at Vauxhall gardens. In 1776 he left

England with his wife for a professional tour through Germany,

Italy, & France. At Florence, B. at the request of the Grand

Duke of Tuscany, set to music the Abate Semplici's oratorio

'Jefte in Masfa'. He ret^d to Eng. late in 1777. An acquaint^ce

with the Revd Jacob Duché, chaplain to the Female Orphan Asy^m

led to his composing, about 1780, the well-known tune for the Morn^g

Hymn 'Awake my Soul'. In 1784 B. & his wife made a profess^l

visit to Dublin. In 1791–9 he contracted an intimacy with Haydn   //

then in London – On Sept. 20. 1799 Mrs B. died. Besides the

comp^ns above named B. wrote the music for the following dramatic

pieces: – 'The Enchanted Girdle" 'The Judg^t of Paris' 1768; 'The Election'

1774; 'The Maid of the Oaks' 1774; 'Belphegor' 1778; & sev^l quartets for stringed inst^ts concertos & duos for the violin, lessons for the p.forte,

& preludes for the organ. As a player he was disting^d by the firmness

of his hand, the purity of his tone, & his adm^ble manner of

executing an adagio. died July 20. 1808 [W.H.Husk].

Source: George Grove (ed.) *A Dictionary of Music and Musicians (A.D. 1450–1880) By Eminent Writers, English and Foreign*, 2 vols (London, Macmillan, 1879), i, 145.
Note: *the time*: Grove has 'his time'. *Vauxhall gardens*: see also 'Trumpet-Major Notebook' (*PN*, 163). '*Awake My Soul*': the title of the hymn is "Morning Hymn", with words by Bishop Ken. According to TH (for whom it was a personal favourite), it was 'the most popular morning hymn ever written.' (see Peter Coxon, 'Hardy's Favourite Hymns', *THJ*, 13 (2) (May 1997): 42–55 (42–3)). TH's assessment prefaces his 'Barthélemon at Vauxhall' (*LLE*, *CP*, 567–8), first published in *The Times* (23 July 1921) to mark the anniversary of the composer's death in 1808 (see *Life and Work*, 447). *W.H.Husk*: William H. Husk (1814–87), Librarian to the Sacred Harmonic Society; Grove has 'W.H.H.'. TH wrote that he 'had often imagined the weary musician, returning from his nightly occupation of making music for a riotous throng, lingering on Westminster Bridge to see the rising sun and being thence inspired to the composition of music to be heard hereafter in places very different from Vauxhall' (*Life and Work*, 447). TH wrote 'three drafts of a story' from these materials (*Pinion*, 236–7); see Evelyn Hardy, 'Thomas Hardy: plots for five unpublished short stories', *London Magazine*, 5 (1958): 33–45. A contemporary reference to Barthélemon as violinist occurs in Fanny Burney's *Evelina* (1778), Letter lii: 'a player of exquisite fancy, feeling, and variety'.

[211]a

Last Journals of Horace Walpole. Edited by A.F.Steuart. 2 vols.

A Drama (1772) Caroline, sister of Geo III. Kept in close

retirement by her mother Pcess. Dowager of Wales – suddenly married

at 16 to the K. of Denmark. At 21 she was seized at a mas-

querade, with Struensee the physician & prime minister, her

lover. Sent prisoner with her youngest child (whom the K

of Denmark disowned) to the Castle of Cronenburg. Three or four

noblemen arrested at same time & accused of having par-

taken of her favours of wh. she was said to be very liberal.

Struensee's father: fit of apoplexy on hearing of son's im-

prisonment – when he had been made Prime minister his

father had said he w^d sooner have heard of his death.

King of D. dosed with laudanum –

Pcess. Dowager of Wales, mother of Caroline, wasted her

money on Ld Bute her favourite &c

1.3.et seq. 73, 109, &c.

Source: Horace Walpole, *Last Journals of Horace Walpole During the Reign of George III From 1771–1783*, ed. A.F. Steuart, 2 vols (London: John Lane, The Bodley Head, 1910), i, 3–6, 73, 112, 19.
Note: *Struensee*: Johann Friedrich Struensee (1737–72), physician at the Danish court, raised to the rank of Count and Chief Minister, charged with plotting against the King and executed. *King of D. dosed with laudanum*: the English Ambassador to the Danish Court reported to Walpole that 'the junto certainly had meant by drugs to hurt the King's understanding' (p.112). *Pcess. Dowager of Wales*: Augusta, Princess Dowager of Wales (d.1772). *Ld Bute*: John Stuart, 3rd Earl of Bute (1713–92). TH's page references are partially incorrect.

[211]b–212

Romance. Edward Walpole, one of Sir Robert's sons: fell in

love with a miliner at his lodging. When he left she came

to him, said she was turned out: he told her to sit down at

the foot of his table...she had 4 children by him & died.

He reared & educated them as if they were legitimate.

Maria, the second, married 1st Earl Waldegrave. She   //

after his death fascinated the d. of Gloucester, b^r of Geo III, whom

she married, marriage kept secret for many years – I. x.&c

Source: Walpole, *Last Journals*, i, vii–xviii (editor's Introduction).
Note: *Edward Walpole*: second son of Sir Robert Walpole. *miliner*: [sic], Mary Clement. *Maria, the second*: Walpole and Mary Clement had three daughters, Laura, Maria and Charlotte. Maria

(1736–1807) became Countess Waldegrave and later Duchess of Gloucester. It was Maria's marriage to the Duke of Gloucester which led to the Royal Marriage Act (1772) prohibiting marriage by members of the Royal Family with commoners. TH summarizes not Walpole here, but the editor's introduction.

212a

Afterwards the marriage was publicly declared...The duchess

maintained a degree of State, &c. Parl^t made provision for the

children. It was on these that the later interests of the Dss.

centred for her husband in his latter years fell under the

influence of the Dss's beautiful & intriguing Lady in waiting, Lady

Almeria Carpenter...She reigned at Gloucester House, the Duchess

remaining its nominal mistress indeed, but Lady A. constituting

its ornament & its pride – a galling position enough for the sup-

planted ex-beauty   I. xxii.

Source: Walpole, *Last Journals*, i, xxi–xxii (editor's Introduction).

212b–[213]

"My Recollections" – By the Countess of Cardigan.

   Lady Anne Brudenell, dau. of the 2^d E. of Cardigan,

was one of the most lovely of the beauties associated with

the Court of Charles II. She married the Earl of Shrewsbury,

& the story is well known of how she, dressed as a page,

held the Duke of Buckingham's horse whilst he fought with

& slew her husband.

Allan Fea describes how "some time before the poor little

plain Duchess (of Buckingham) suspected that she had a

formidable rival in the beautiful Countess, she was returning

from a visit to Deene to her house at Stamford, where her   //

reckless husband found it convenient to hide himself, as a warrant

for high treason was < > out against him, when she noticed a

suspicious little cavalcade travelling in the same direction.

Ordering the horses to be whipped up she arrived in time to give

the alarm. The Duke had just then set out for Burleigh House

with some ladies in his company...& he escaped.

The wicked Countess & her lover lived at Cliveden – "the

bower of wanton Shrewsbury & of love" – & her spirit is suppos[d]

to haunt the beautiful riverside retreat.   125

Source: Countess of Cardigan and Lancastre, *My Recollections* (London: Everleigh Nash, 1909),
124–5.
Note: *story is well known*: the story is fiction; Lady Shrewsbury was in France when the duel was
fought. *Allan Fea*: author of *Nooks and Corners of Old England* (London, Everleigh Nash, 1907).
Deene: Deene Park, Wansford, Northamptonshire. *'the bower ... of love'*: a quotation from
Alexander Pope, *Epistle to Bathurst*, l.308 in *Epistles to Several Persons (Moral Essays)*, ed. F.W.
Bateson (London: Methuen, 1961). This item is the source for TH's 'The Duel' (*MV, CP,*
449–50).

[213]a

Lady Amelia Blackwood was with her husband until

he died [from a fall from his horse: unconscious 3 days]

but another lady whom he had dearly loved would not be

denied admittance to the death-chamber. Lady Amelia did

not object, so the dying man's mistress & his wife waited

for the end together – truly a strange situation.   137

Source: Cardigan, *My Recollections*, 135.
Note: *husband*: Henry Blackwood, on his way to Newmarket races.

[213]b–[215]

A Grim story. Constance de Burgh...one of my great
                [1851]   [afterwards 1ˢᵗ Earl of Dudley – born 1817]
friends...married ʌ Lord Ward ʌ...Not in love with husband...

but made accept him...Ward...extraordinary ideas –

...worshipped the beautiful – had a barbaric passion

for precious stones...made her put them on her unclothed

figure...wᵈ admire her for hours, contrasting the sheen of

the ropes of pearls with the delicate skin as she sat on a   //

black satin covered couch. She timid & tactless – terrified

– then disgusted. Appealed to her father & mother – they

decided her h.'s peculiarities came within the meaning of

the marriage vows...told she must submit – Fate threw
                [b. 1827 – aftᵈˢ E.of Kinnoull. Life guards – capt. 1851]
Lᵈ Dupplin ʌ across her path...I knew Blanche [his wife]
[m. 1848 – son b 1849 – dau. Constance Blanche Louisa 1851 &c]
very well ʌ She wᵈ· tell me sorrowfully of her husbᵈˢ infatuation.

    Matters came to a crisis at a fancy dress ball given by

Lady Londonderry at Holderness House...Constance looked

delicate...was <u>enceinte</u>...had to go home. Husbᵈ remained

till 3...As he approached his house he noticed a man

leaving it – Lᵈ Dup. who turned & disappeared.

L[d] W. went up to his wife's bedroom. Accused her –

made her get up…tears & entreaties useless…led her past

the scandalized servants & turned her out of doors –

The poor frightened girl managed to reach her parents

house in Grosvenor Crescent – implored shelter – heartless as

her husband – would not take her in. More dead than alive

turned to Conduit St. where her singing master lived…took

her in till next day, when she went to Ostend.

Ostend to Ems – where a child was prematurely born,
                [1851 – Husb[d] remarried 1865]
& unhappy young mother died ∧ Husb. brought body to

England. & once again she lay in her darkened room

On the evening of the day before the burial Lord Colville

came to see L[d] W…"Colville, you admired my wife?"   //

"Yes – I did" – "Well then, come & look your last on her", &

lighting a candle he led the way upstairs…"Still admiring

my wife? Well – she was a pretty woman – but – you'd never

credit she had such bad teeth." Put down candle…raised

wife's head – wrenched the jaws apart…"Look here"…

But L[d] C. had hurriedly left the room.   50.

Source: Cardigan, *My Recollections*, 44–50.
Note: the words in square brackets, inserted by TH, derived from a peerage, presumably Debrett.
worshipped the beautiful: the text at this point also includes: 'he had selected his wife partly on
account of her beauty and he treated her like some lovely slave he had bought' (p.45). *she timid &
tactless*: the text reads: 'not tactful, and not accommodating' (p.45). *L[d] Dup. who turned &
disappeared*: the text has at this point: 'ran for his life down the street'. *scandalized servants*: whom
Lord Ward had asked to 'assemble in the hall' (p.47). In her memoirs, *Under Five Reigns* (London:
Methuen, 1910), Lady Dorothy Nevill asserted that it is 'impossible to place any credence in the

ghastly story which Lady Cardigan retails with such gusto' (p.165).

[215]a

King of Spain admires married lady. Sends husb^d away

like Uriah to the war. But he bears a charmed life.

Somebody in camp tells him of the intrigue. He rushes

back secretly. King & his attendant officer are just going

to the lady's house. Husband enters. Officer kills husband.

Body removed & interred secretly. Given out that he died

at the seat of war.   170.

Source: Cardigan, *My Recollections*, 167–9.
Note: *King of Spain*: Alphonse XII (1857–85).

---

[215]b-[216]

Life of Bp. Walsham How.
"Exceeded the limits of decency…On one occasion one of his sons

had tried to read a more than usually nasty book of this description…

…Finding it impossible to go on with it he took it down to the library

& told his father that, though not over-particular, he was quite unable to

wade through the unclean matter contained in the book in question. The

Bishop's sole reply was to take an envelope out of his paper stand &

address it to W.F.D.Smith Esq. M.P. The result was the quiet

withdrawal of the book from the library, & an assurance that any

other books by the same author w^d be carefully examined before they   //

were allowed to be circulated.

On June 8 1896, the Yorkshire Post had a leading article strongly condemning this class of literature, & on that day Bishop Walsham How wrote to the editor as follows:

Bishopgarth, Wakefield.

"Sir: Will you allow me to publicly thank you for your out-spoken leader in your to-day's issue denouncing the intolerable grossness & hateful sneering at all that one most reveres in such writers as Thomas Hardy.

"On the authority of one of those reviews which you justly condemn for this reticence, I bought a copy of one of Mr Hardy's novels, but was so disgusted with its insolence & indecency that I threw it into the fire. It is a disgrace to our great public libraries to admit such garbage, clever though it may be, to their shelves.

I am, sir,   Yours &c

Wm Walsham Wakefield.

Source: Frederick Douglas How, *Bishop Walsham How: A Memoir* (London: Isbister & Co., 1898), 343–4.

Note: *Bp. Walsham How*: Walsham How (1823–97), Bishop of Wakefield from 1888. The 'Life' was the *Memoir* written by his son the Revd Frederick Douglas How (b.1852/3–?), rector of Frome St Quintin, Dorset (1879–84). *Exceeded the limits of decency*: the *Memoir* has: 'his indignation knew no bounds when a book which exceeded the limits of decency came into his hands' (p.343). *description ... Finding*: in transcribing from How's *Memoir*, TH omitted the following clause: 'which had been sent up from Smith's library to fill up the number of volumes required'. *W.F.D. Smith*: (1868–1928), son of W.H. Smith II, head of the firm W.H. Smith & Son, newsagents, booksellers and owners of a circulating library, from 1891. *Yorkshire Post*: published in Leeds; an influential provincial daily newspaper. *one of Mr Hardy's novels*: although the Bishop did not name the novel which he had burnt, TH supposed, three weeks later, that it had been *Two on a Tower* (letter to Richard Le Gallienne, 29 June 1896, *CL*, ii, 125). By 1899 he had become convinced that the book was *Jude* (letter to Florence Henniker, 13 April 1899, *CL*, ii, 218–19). It is likely that TH inserted this extract from How's *Memoir* into 'Facts' at about the time that he was revising his novels for the Wessex edition of his work, begun in 1911. His 'Postscript' to *Jude the Obscure* in that edition included his first public reference to his belief that the book which the Bishop 'threw into the fire' was indeed *Jude*: 'After these verdicts from the press its next misfortune was to be burned by a bishop – probably in his despair at not being able to burn me.' TH returned to the subject in *Life and Work*, 294–5, where he also assumed that the book which had been burnt was also the book which the Bishop complained of to the owner of Smith's subscription library. The words in How's memoir which TH had omitted in his transcription make it clear that the book complained of, although not named, was a book which the Bishop had on loan from the library. It therefore seems impossible that the Bishop would have burnt a library book. So there were two books that had roused the Bishop's 'indignation', but in the course of time TH conflated the two complaints into one and remained convinced that there was one book, *Jude*, the subject of 'a precious conspiracy'.

216a

On this subject he also had some correspondence with the late M^rs

Oliphant...

   "My Lord, I am very glad to have your approval of my little

paper, all the more as I hesitated whether it was right for me, my-

self a novelist, to say so much concerning others of my trade, in

my own person...I suspect it is much more easy to make an ex-

ample of the comparatively unknown than of a man like Hardy, who

commands a great sale.

M.O.W.Oliphant. "

[From "Bp. Walsham How, A Memoir. By Frederick Douglas How. 1901."]   //

Source: How, *Bishop Walsham How*, 345.
Note: *M.O.W.Oliphant*: Margaret Oliphant, novelist (1828–97) castigated *Jude the Obscure* in 'The Anti-Marriage League', *Blackwoods*, 159 (1896): 135–49, having earlier heaped praise on *Tess* in 'The Old Saloon', *Blackwoods*, 151 (1892): 455–74. TH had been in correspondence with Oliphant, back in 1882, over her suggestion that he writes a 'series of sketches' about the 'labouring poor' for *Longmans Magazine*: the result was 'The Dorsetshire Labourer' essay, published in June 1883. *1901*: the date of publication of How's memoir was 1898.

[217]a

DORCHESTER AND EDMUND KEAN

In reply to "Durnovarian's" enquiry, I hear that Kean's son died at Glyde Path-hill, Dorchester, and was buried in the churchyard of the Holy Trinity in November, 1813. The poor boy's ashes, therefore, peacefully lie at rest within a few paces of the *Dorset County Chronicle* Office door. "Durnovarian" says that he died at an inn. If so, the one in question must have been "The Little Jockey," kept by a man named Thomas Ellis, who was horse dealer, blacksmith, and innkeeper, rolled into one, but withal did not prosper and finally emigrated to the States with his big family of sons. On Ellis leaving, the inn was closed, but the forge was taken over by a man named Moody, who lived there many years, being succeeded by a noted old shoeing smith named James Spencer, who had been a farrier to the Oxford Blues in his day, and now the house is held by Mr H. Martin. Its front has been rebuilt, and it is totally different to the old structure, and nothing but the site appeals to sentiment in respect to Kean. The Mason's Arms is the only inn in Glyde Path-hill at the present time, but it did not exist in 1813, not being built until about 1830, when it was opened as an inn by a man named Thomas Spencer. It stands on the site of a mason's yard, hence its name

PEREGRINE

Text: this and the following item [217]b are on a pasted-in newspaper cutting f.109r, col.1 (21.6 x 6.9 cm); col.2 (21.6 x 6.9 cm), f.109v, col.1 (3.2 x 6.9 cm).
Source: *DCC*, 15 May 1902, p.11, col.3.
Note: *Kean*: Edmund Kean (1787–1833), actor (see *CL*, iii, 19, 28; vi, 248; *Life and Work*, 339–40. For a reference to TH's three contributions to this correspondence to *DCC*, see note to 82c. See also [217]b, 218a, 218b, [219]a, below. *PEREGRINE*: unidentified.

[217]b–218

Your readers will be glad to hear that within twenty-four hours of my query of the above-mentioned subject in your columns the Rev Canon Hill found the sought-for entry in the registers of Trinity Church. It was as follows: – "1813, No 10, name, Edmund G.W. Howard, son of Edward and Mary Kean. Residing at Glyde Path Hill in this Parish, Nov. 29, age 4. Henry John Richman." It is interesting as showing the precocious boy, "dead before his prime," bore other names than that of Howard and that Kean himself (although within six months of that time he had indisputably become the most brilliant star in the British dramatic firmament) was then so little known, that a mistake was made in recording his own Christian name. The entry moreover, indicates pretty clearly the precise locality in which the "player-folk" were living, and it is not impossible that the very house in which the great tragedian lodged, may be identified, as well as the theatre in which he acted. Within a few weeks of his quitting Dorchester Kean (like Byron a short time before), woke up to find himself famous. The part played by the humble provincial theatre of Dorchester in the life of Edmund Kean is so important, and the incident itself so extraordinary, that I may be pardoned if I ask your permission to place the story of Kean and his Dorchester adventures as briefly as may be before your readers. I write of no romance, but of historical facts, resulting from a perusal of Kean's correspondence and now confirmed by the brief entry in the registers of Trinity Church.

In the early days of 1813 Kean and his family arrived at Brixham from Guernsey in "a little dirty vessel," laden with skins. Leaving his trunk in pledge, the player and his little party pushed on to Exeter, where on the 1ˢᵗ March, he played "Shylock" and stoutly refused to appear at Weymouth as "second" to Master Betty. He obtained a brief engagement at Teignmouth, where his performance was witnessed and admired by Dr. Drury, the celebrated Head Master of Harrow, some of whose descendants still reside at Torquay. During his temporary absence Mrs Kean accepted an engagement for him with Mr Elliston (George III's favourite actor at Weymouth) at a weekly salary of three pounds. Meanwhile Dr. Drury had promised to bring his name before Mr. Pascoe Grenfell and the Committee of Drury Lane. Kean therefore received his wife's news with reproaches, and serious domestic disputes ensued. At this juncture a hopeful letter came from Dr. Drury, requesting Kean's presence in London. Funds however, were wholly wanting, and after Kean and his son Howard, had taken part in some semi-private performance at the hotel hear the cathedral church-yard (doubtless the Royal Clarence) he started for Barnstaple and Dorchester where he had accepted engagements at two pounds a week. His elder boy fell ill and Kean (who loved him dearly) insisted on Mrs. Kean and the children rejoining him at Barnstaple. Mr. Barry Proctor gives the following graphic account of this memorable journey in the late autumn of 1813: – "They set off indeed in a postchaise and accomplished the first stage of their journey, but an accurate survey of their exchequer being then made, it was found necessary that Mrs. Kean and the eldest child, Howard, whose illness (whooping-cough) was increasing, should proceed in the coach, and that Kean himself, with his youngest son on his back, should trudge forward on foot. One or two of the actors relieved Kean of his child-burden occasionally, particularly a goodnatured comedian of the name of Clifford, who several years afterwards was introduced by the celebrated actor Kean, as the gentleman who had carried him in his infancy." Doubtless many of your readers will remember in the "fifties" and "sixties" of the last century having enjoyed the acting of Charles Kean, who, in November, 1813, arrived in Dorchester, on his father's shoulders, with his child's hat and coat torn to pieces, and "the dust of Barnstaple still sticking to clothes." The theatre at Dorchester was, by a degree, worse than that at Barnstaple, and to crown the general distress and anxiety of the time, Howard's condition became hopeless. The violence of the cough brought on water-in-the brain, and one night, well-nigh distracted by grief, Kean went to the theatre to act "Octavian" in "The Mountaineers." Mrs. Kean remained at home nursing the dying child in the only little room they had. About midnight Kean returned to their humble lodgings at Glyde Path Hill. He was in a state of extreme agitation and for a long time could not speak. At last he made an effort and cried out "my fortune is made! My fortune is made!" adding in a softer voice "Let but Howard live and we shall all be happy yet." He then related to Mrs. Kean, how the house when the curtain rose was three parts empty, with only a few spectators in the pit and gallery and three persons in the boxes, but that the presence of a gentleman in the stage-box "who evidently understood acting" arrested his attention. At the end of the piece it turned out that the appreciative stranger was no lesser a personage that Mr S J Arnold (son of the great musician) and manager of Drury Lane Theatre, come down expressly to see with his own eyes, the actor of whose merits Dr. Drury had spoken so warmly to the omnipotent committee. Next morning, Kean (dressed "as respectably as he could") repaired for breakfast to Mr. Arnold's hotel (was it the King's Arms or the Antelope?), and before the meal was over Edmund Kean had a contract from Drury Lane for a term of three years, at a salary of eight, nine and ten pounds per week, for each successive year. On the 21ˢᵗ November Kean wrote a long letter of gratitude to Dr. Drury; on the 23ʳᵈ Howard Kean died, and on the following day was buried in Trinity church yard. The scene at the funeral must have been a most melancholy one, but no record of it has survived, nor can the spot where the clever child, whose powers of mimicry had so charmed the good folks at Exeter, rests be any longer traced. Kean wrote, on the 24ᵗʰ to Dr. Drury, "Howard, sir, died, on Monday morning last. You may conceive my feelings and pardon the brevity of my letter." In the interval Kean had endeavoured to drown care in drink, but the brandy he took had maddened instead of stupified him. "He returned to his house" writes Mr. Proctor, "in an outrageous state, his grief still uppermost, wept and lamented the child, and swore that he would wake it from the dead. At last exhausted by his anguish and affected of course by the liquor which he had drunk, he fell into a hot and uneasy sleep. In the morning he was more composed." The morning was that of the funeral, the expenses of which (as well as the doctor's bill) he earned by a few more nights work at the Dorchester Theatre and a benefit. He was entirely without funds for his London journey, but Mr. Lee, the still remembered Dorchester manager, advanced him five pounds, with a portion of which – (for Mrs. Kean and her son Charles remained sometime longer at Glyde Path Hill) – he set forward "with a beating heart to try his fortunes on the metropolitan stage."

Such in brief is the story of Edmund Kean's season at Dorchester, which proved to him as sure a road to safety, as Lee Lane did to Charles II. A Dorchester play bill of that period, and especially that of the night of "The Mountaineers" or the final benefit, would doubtless be of some considerable value, and any information leading to the identification of Kean's Dorchester home, the theatre managed by Mr. Lee, or the grave of Howard Kean would be welcomed by the student of dramatic history. The annals of the stage as far as Weymouth and Dorchester are concerned (and much could be said of both places) have yet to be written. Although barely ninety years have passed by since Edmund Kean arrived // T.O. in Dorchester, travel-stained, bedraggled, and foot-sore, one of his autograph letters is now worth several pounds and collectors search in vain for a Dorchester bill of the play. The writer has in his possession a letter of Charles Kean (the infant who rode from Barnstaple on his father's shoulders in 1813,) in which he thanks a Brighton book seller for accepting £5 for 65 letters and 50 documents of his father's, "which he had carefully burned." They would now be worth at least £500. Such is the cruel irony of the whirligig of fate, and in the fate of Edmund Kean Dorchester certainly played an all-important part.

Bradpole, May 5ᵗʰ, 1902.   A. M. BROADLEY.   //
       D.C.C.   _____   May 15. 02

Text: *T.O.*: in ink, after *arrived*. *D.C.C., May 15. 02*: in ink, at end of item.
Source: 'Dorchester and Edmund Kean', *DCC*, 15 May 1902, p.11, cols 3–4. (Letter from A.M. Broadley.)
Note: *BROADLEY*: Alexander Meyrick Broadley (1847–1916), barrister, and author of works on freemasonry and Napoleonic subjects; he lived at Bradpole, Bridport, Dorset. *T.O.*; *D.C.C.*; *May 15. 02*: TH's insertions.

218a

EDMUND KEAN AND HIS DORCHESTER ASSOCIATIONS

May I be permitted to turn the hose of real facts upon the speculative sentimentality which is being excited over the connection of Edmund Kean with Dorchester? Ten years after he visited Dorchester under circumstances which were undoubtedly painful, when his dire poverty and family troubles made him an object of commiseration, an episode occurred which showed that prosperity had made him, if richer, certainly not better. Like Jeshurun of old, Kean "waxed fat and kicked." On January 17th, 1825, Kean, was the defendant in a case of *crim.con.* tried in the Court of King's Bench, in which the plaintiff was an Alderman Cox, a Dorchester magnate, whose wife, well known in Dorchester and Somerset, had been infamously seduced by the great tragedian. There is no need to go "scavenging over human dust heaps," as Mr. Brodrick would say, to learn the ugly facts of this dark scene in Kean's palmy days, for it is fully set out in the file of the *Dorset County Chronicle*, which not only devotes space to the trial, but in an editorial denounces it as "one of the most flagrant cases of the violation of the marriage vow that ever came to our cognisance as journalists." Since the day when Kean tramped into Dorchester a miserable player, with a dying child and all but penniless, his circumstances had vastly changed. In one of his letters to Alderman Cox's faithless wife Kean says "I am living in first style, travel magnificently, and transmit £1,000 a month." Kean was a seducer and a false scoundrel. *De mortuis nil nisi verum!* In the thick of his amour with Mrs. Cox he wrote to the worthy and rather short-sighted Alderman thus – "I must be the worst of villains if I could take a man by the hand while meditating towards him an act of injustice." On the very same day he penned a billet to Mrs. Cox informing her that he had deluded her confiding husband and urging her to join in the deceit. These letters were produced in court, and Kean was called upon to salve the Alderman's wounded honour with the sum of £800. If your readers care to plumb the depths of the great tragedian's infamy let them turn to the *Chronicle* of January 20th, 1825.   DORSET.

Text: this and the subsequent item 218b are on a pasted-in newspaper cutting f.109v, col.1 (17.5 x 6.9 cm), col.2 (5.0 x 7.2 cm).
Source: 'Edmund Kean and His Dorchester Associations', *DCC*, 22 May 1902, p.11, cols 4–5.
Note: *DORSET*: unidentified.

218b

I have done my best to localise the theatre in which Kean played "Octavian," and have doubtless succeeded. I had the good luck to hunt up Mr. Henry Davis, an old and much respected tradesman of Dorchester, living now with his son, Mr. Charles Davis, in Durngate-street, who was born in High West-street in 1824. He told me that in the rear of the house was a large building which had long before his birth been used as a theatre, but Messrs Curme and Mondey had used it for a lengthy period prior to his birth as a builder's workshop, after which it became his father's shop for cabinet-making and is now used by Mr. Godwin as an earthenware store. When moved from this building the players used a room which stood on the site now occupied by the Masonic Hall, and it was there that Kean played in 1813. From thence, about 1831 or 1832, the theatre migrated to a large brick building standing at the highest point of Friary-lane, and then it was shifted to a large room in Prince's street exactly opposite the Plume of Feathers Hotel, where it gave up the ghost, and the building was afterwards turned into a wine cellar by Colonel Stickland's son, Robert, and a long time after (in 1853) it became the store-room and armoury of the Dorset Militia, ultimately being taken over by the Volunteers, who still hold possession. From this it may confidently be assumed in connection with Kean's visit in 1813 that he played in a building standing where the Masonic Hall is now located, and that his poor boy yielded up his last breath in one of the rooms of the dingy "Little Jockey" in Glyde Path-hill. I may add that there is small hopes of recovering a playbill of the day. A Mr. Zillwood was a jobbing printer, living next to the County House, as also was Mr. Clark in the Cornhill. These were the only two printers in the town, but now the rubbish heaps have long ago vanished, and with them I fear any hope of the recovery of a stray playbill of the day.

PEREGRINE.

P.S. – As a bit of gossip in connection with old parson Richman, the "Henry John Richman" who buried Kean's boy, he with his wife was killed in bed by a huge chimney stack falling on them in the awful November gale of 1824, exactly 11 years after he had buried Kean's little one. The house where this happened is still standing, and is at present occupied by Mr. Pinnick, who keeps the branch post-office there.

D.C.C. May 22.02 //

Text: *D.C.C. May 22. 02* (in ink).

Source: 'Edmund Kean and His Dorchester Associations', *DCC*, 22 May 1902, p.11, col.5.

Note: *he with his wife ... November gale of 1824*: see item 199b for Boswell-Stone's account of this fatality. *PEREGRINE*: unidentified. *D.C.C. May 22. 02*: TH's insertion.

[219]a

DORCHESTER AND ITS THEATRES

A Satisfactory Solution

With the kind assistance of Captain J.E.Acland and by the aid of certain facts gleaned from the amusing but very discursive memoirs of Herbert Lee, the well-known impresario, who, between 1792 and 1830 (when this book was published), had to do with Dorset playhouses at Poole, Weymouth, Lyme Regis, and Bridport, as well as at Dorchester, I am able to offer your readers what we believe to be a satisfactory identification of all the Dorchester theatres.

1.– The "New Theatre," inaugurated in 1786 with a prologue in verse composed by the Rev. Thomas Russell (1762-1788), whose sonnets are strongly commended in the Dictionary of National Biography, was more or less a temporary structure – "Wood was its walls, and furze its roof."

2.– Writing in 1830 Henry Lee speaks (Vol. II, p.141) of "the theatre near the Antelope Inn Yard." This was doubtless the first theatre built in 1792 for Lee by Mr Curme, sen., on the Trinity-street site, now occupied by Mr. Godwin's china shop. This, in all human probability, was the theatre in which Edmund Kean played before his engagement at Drury Lane. The exterior of the existing structure bears a strong resemblance to that of the old Theatre in Orchard-street, Bath, and other 18th Century houses.

3.– The third theatre erected for Lee, by Mr. Henning, "on his own land," and which only lasted two years, as "the owner needed the site for his own purposes," was that erected in North-square and afterwards occupied by the Salvation Army.

4.– Then comes the theatre built for Lee by Mr Curme, jun., in 1828, and opened on Monday, February 25th, of that year by Mr. Lee. The prologue, for which Mr Lee was responsible, and of which I possess a copy, is full of smart and telling allusions to Dorset topography, the proximity of the Roman Wall, &c. An advertisement in the *Dorset County Chronicle* of February 21st, 1828, shows that this was the "Loyalty Theatre" in High West-street, and in 1832 Savage writes of "a small but neat theatre in High West-street, erected in 1828." The existing Masonic Hall stands on the ground once occupied by the Loyalty Theatre.

Mr. Lee speaks of having "acted in the County Hall." The building he refers to occupied the site of the present structure, and programmes in the County Museum show that it was occasionally used in the early part of the 19th Century for public entertainments. The County "House" is shown in its present position in very early maps of the town.

A reference to early 19th Century rate books would give absolute certainty to our contention as to the second of Lee's Theatres being in North-square. Mr. Lee's labours as a builder of theatres in Dorchester, however, did not cease with the Loyalty Theatre in High West-street. In the *Dorset County Chronicle* of 1834 there is an advertisement "of the opening of the Roscius Theatre, so named," says Mr. Herbert Lee, "from the well-known circumstance that the theatre now in preparation is the very last in which the Modern Roscius (Kean) appeared before going to Drury Lane." We take this to mean that the building in Trinity-street, spoken of by Henry Lee as "close to the Antelope Yard," was once more turned to its original use in 1834.

Here again a reference to rate-books would be invaluable. Henry and Herbert Lee both ran the Barnstaple Theatre, and it was from Barnstaple that Kean trudged to Dorchester in the autumn of 1813 with the son, who now lies in Trinity Church graveyard, on his back. In the Barnstaple programmes of 1820-21 figure the names of Henry Lee, Mrs. Lee, Herbert Lee, Miss Lee, and Miss E Lee. Many of your readers will doubtless remember the Misses Lee, who taught "dancing and deportment" at Bridport and elsewhere in the "fifties" and "sixties" of the last century. I believe they were the daughters of Herbert Lee. Henry Lee married his wife, the mother of Herbert Lee, at Blandford about 1790. Dyer, one of Lee's actors, published his theatrical reminiscences about 1834. He gives a ground plan which the elder Lee sent him for the erection of the theatre at Bridport in the passage immediately to the west of the Bull Hotel, described as "the principal inn of the place." Dyer speaks of Lee as a man of much wit, but enormously stout and unwieldy. He ridicules his pretentions to have written "Caleb Quotem" (a play usually ascribed to one of the Colmans), but he wrote three or four other little books besides his memoirs. A reference to the Blandford registers would fix the identity of Mrs. Lee, whose acting at Weymouth, was so greatly admired by George III., who showed so much kindly solicitude about her health.

I should be glad to have further information as to the full names of the Misses Lee, the granddaughters of Dorchester's energetic impressario. It is difficult to understand why Henry Lee omits all mention of Kean in 1813. Had the great actor slighted or forgotten the humble country manager who had given him the chance which led to fame and fortune? In 1830 the sun of Edmund Kean had already begun to set.

A.M. BROADLEY,   //

The Knapp, March 1, 1912.

Text: pasted-in newspaper cutting f.110r, col. 1. (21.2 × 6.2 cm); col. 2 (8.0 × 6.2 cm).
Source: 'Dorchester and its Theatres', *DCC*, 7 March 1912, p.14, cols 1–2. (Letter from A.M. Broadley.)
Note: *Herbert Lee*: this should be Henry Lee; see item 82c. *The third theatre*: a mistake (by Broadley) for 'second' theatre.

220a

PAGANINI

Paganini was born at Genoa on the 18th February, 1784. After exhausting his father's instruction, he was taken in hand by Signor Servetto, of the Genoese theatre; then Giacomo Costa, chapel master, taught him, and the child was often seen playing in the Genoese churches on a violin almost as large as himself; but, like Mozart before him, and

Mendelssohn after him, Nicolo was the despair of his masters, who were in turn angry with his innovations, and astonished at his precocious facility. In his ninth year he appeared at a concert, and electrified every one with variations on the French air, *La Carmagnole*. This triumph impelled his avaricious father to discover some one who could further teach him; the young talent was to be pressed and squeezed to its utmost limit, in order to produce the golden harvest.

At Parma lived the celebrated musician Rolla. To Rolla the boy was taken, but Rolla was ill. Whilst waiting in the ante-room little Nicolo took up a violin, and played off at sight some difficult music which he found lying on the table. The invalid composer raised himself on his bed to listen, and eagerly inquired who the great master was who had arrived, and was playing in his ante-room? "A mere lad! – impossible!" but on Paganini's making his appearance as an humble pupil, Rolla at once told him that he could teach him nothing. Thence to Paer, who was glad to make his difficult charge over to Ghiretti, and this master gave him three lessons a week in harmony and counterpoint. It is not clear that this extraordinary genius owed much more to any one but himself – his indomitable perseverance and his incessant study. His method is to be noted. For ten or twelve hours he would try passages over and over again in different ways with such absorption and intensity, that at nightfall he would sink into utter prostration through excessive exhaustion and fatigue. Though delicate, like Mendelssohn, he ate at times ravenously, and slept soundly. When about ten he wrote twenty-four fugues, and soon afterwards composed some violin music, of such difficulty, that he was unable at first to play it, until incessant practice gave him the mastery.

In 1797, Paganini, being then thirteen years old, made his first professional tour, but not as a free agent. His father took him through the chief towns of Lombardy, and not unnaturally prescribed the task and pocketed the proceeds. But the young neck was already beginning to chafe against the yoke. In 1798 he escaped, with his father's tardy consent, to Lucca, where a musical festival in honour of St. Martin was going on. He there gave frequent concerts, and was everywhere met with applause, and, what was more to the purpose, with money. Surrounded by men of inferior talents, a mere inexperienced youth, without education, without knowledge of the world, with nothing but ambition and his supreme musical genius, he now broke wildly away from all wise restraints, and avenged himself upon his father's severity by many youthful excesses. He gambled – he lost – he was duped by his companions; but he made money so fast, that he soon owned about £1,000. It is pleasant to think that he at once thought of giving some of this to his father and mother; it is unpleasant to record that his father claimed, and eventually got, almost the whole sum from him. But it did not much matter now, for everything seemed literally to turn into gold beneath those marvellous fingers, and bad luck proved nearly as profitable to him as good.

By the time he had reached seventeen, Paganini was a confirmed gambler. He had little left but his Stradiuarius violin, and this he was on the point of selling to a certain prince, who had offered him £80, a large sum at the beginning of the century even for a Stradiuarius. Times have changed, and in these latter days we think nothing of giving £300 for a genuine instrument of the first class. But the reckless youth determined to make a last stand for his violin. "Jewels, watch, rings, brooches," to use his own words, "I had disposed of all – my thirty francs were reduced to three. With this small remains of my capital I played, and won 160 francs! This amount saved my violin and restored my affairs." "From that time," he adds, "I abjured gaming, to which I had sacrificed a part of my youth, convinced that a gamester is an object of contempt to all well-regulated minds." The violin he narrowly missed losing was given by Pasini, the painter, who on one occasion brought him a concerto of extraordinary difficulty to read at sight, and placing a fine Stradiuarius in his hands, said "This instrument shall be yours if you can play that concerto at first sight in a masterly manner." "If that is the case," replied Paganini, "you may bid adieu to it;" and playing it off at once, he retained the violin. Easy come – easy go. Some years later, at Leghorn, being again in great straits, he was obliged to part, for a time at least, with this same Stradiuarius; but this disaster was only the means of procuring him the favourite Guarnerius, upon which he ever afterwards played. In his need, Monsieur Livron, a distinguished amateur, lent him this splendid instrument, and was so enraptured by his playing, that he exclaimed, "Never will I profane the strings that your fingers have touched. It is to you that my violin belongs." The violin is still shown at Genoa under a glass case.

At the age of twenty-one (1805) he made a second professional tour, passing through Lucca and Piombino, and in one convent church where he played a concerto, the excitement was so great that the monks had to leave their stalls to silence the uproar in the congregation. It was at the end of this tour that Napoleon's sister, the Princess Eliza, offered the new violinist the direction of the court music, and gave him the grade of captain in the royal guard, with the privilege of wearing that officer's brilliant uniform on state occasions.

Being in love with a lady of the court, who reciprocated his attachment, he gave out that he would depict upon his violin a *Scène Amoureuse*; the treble string, we presume, was the lady, and the fourth string the gentleman. The emotional dialogue was carried on between the two in a manner which fairly overcame the audience with delight, and led to the Grand Duchess requesting him to try one string alone next time. How he succeeded in that exploit is known to all the world, for he ever afterwards retained an extreme partiality for the fourth string.

In 1808 he obtained from the Grand Duchess leave to travel. His fame had preceded him. Leghorn, where seven years before he had forfeited his famous Stradiuarius and won a Guarnerius, received him with open arms, although his appearance was marked by an amusing *contretemps*. He came on to the stage limping, having run a nail into his heel. At all times odd-looking, he, no doubt, looked all the more peculiar under these circumstances, and there was some tittering among the audience. Just as he began, the candles fell out of his desk – more laughter. He went on playing the first string broke – more laughter. He played the rest of the concerto through on three strings, but the laughter now changed to vociferous applause at this feat. The beggarly elements seemed of little consequence to this magician. One or more strings, it was all the same to him; indeed, it is recorded, that he seldom paused to mend his strings when they broke, which they not unfrequently did. Whether from abstraction or carelessness he would allow them at times to grow quite ragged on the finger board, and his constant practice of plucking them, guitar-like with the left hand, as well as harp-like with the fore-finger of the right hand, helped, no doubt, to wear them out rapidly.

At Ferrara both he and his violin met with a different reception. A singer had failed him, and he had induced a *danseuse* who had a pretty voice to come to the rescue. Some graceless fellow in the audience hissed her singing, which caused Paganini to take a revenge little suited to the occasion. In his last solo he imitated the cries of various animals, and suddenly advancing to the foot-lights, caused his violin to bray like an ass, with the exclamation, "This is for him who hissed!" Instead of laughter, the pit rose in fury, and would have soon made short work of him and his violin, had he not escaped by a back door. It appears that the country folk round Ferrara called the town's people, whom they hated, "asses," and were in the habit of singing out "hee-haw!" whenever they had to allude to them, hence the angry reception of Paganini's musical repartee.

No one ever saw the principal parts of his solos, as he played by heart, for fear of the music being copied. The rehearsal over, he carried even the orchestral parts away with him. He would then go strait home, take a light meal, throw himself on his bed, and sleep profoundly until his carriage arrived to take him to the concert. His toilet was very simple, and took hardly any time; his coat was buttoned tightly over his chest, and marked the more conspicuously the impossible angles of his figure: his trousers hung loose for trousers of the period; his cravat was tight about his neck. He sweated so profusely over his solos, that he always carried a clean shirt in his violin trunk and changed his linen once at least during the concert. At concert time he usually seemed in excellent spirits. His first question on arriving was always, "Is there a large audience?" If the room was full he would say, "Excellent people! good! good!" If by any chance the boxes were empty he would say, "Some of the effect will be lost." He kept his audience waiting a long time, and he would sometimes say, "I have played better," or "I have played worse," and occasionally his first solo would be more effective than his last. After once or twice trying the music of Kreutzer and Rode in public, he decided never to play any but his own, and said to his secretary, Mr. Harris, "I have my own peculiar style; in accordance with this I regulate my compositions. I had much rather write a piece in which I can trust myself entirely to my own musical impressions." "His art," observes M. Fetis, "was an art born with him, the secret of which he has carried to the grave." – *Good Words.*   //

Text: pasted-in periodical cutting f.110v, col.1 (21.4 x 7.0 cm); col.2 (21.5 x 7.0 cm); col. 3 (2.6 x 7.0 cm); col.4 (2.3 x 7.0 cm), pasted-in at 90°.
Source: unidentified; the article in *Good Words* was reprinted in an unidentified newspaper (TH's source).

[221]

152   The Periodical   [Vol. IV, No. LXXI
        April 1913.

'When we came into the city [Gaza], in the place that is called the Four Ways, there was a statue of marble which they said was a statue of Aphrodite; and it was upon a base of stone, and the form of the statue was of a woman, naked, and having all her shame uncovered. And all they of the city did honour to the statue, especially the women, kindling lamps and burning incense. For they reported concerning it that it giveth answer in dreams unto those who wish to make trial of marriage, but they deceived each other, speaking falsely. And oftentimes, being bidden by the demon to make a contract of marriage, they were so unfortunate that they came even to divorce, or lived together in evil wise. ...When we came unto the place where was the aforesaid idol of Aphrodite (but the Christians were carrying the precious wood of Christ, that is to say the figure of the Cross), the demon that dwelt in the statue beholding and being unable to suffer the sight of the sign which was being carried, came forth out of the marble with great confusion and cast down the statue itself and brake it into many pieces. And it fell out that two men of the idolaters were standing beside the base on which the statue stood, and when it fell, it clave the head of the one in twain, and of the other it brake the shoulder and the wrist. For they were both standing and mocking at the holy multitude.'...

[From *The Life of Porphyry, Bishop of Gaza, by Mark the Deacon*. Translated, with introduction and notes, by G.F. Hill (Oxford Translations.) *Published by Henry Frowde*. Price 3*s*.6*d*. net ($1.00).]   //

Text: pasted-in periodical cutting f.111r (11.0 x 12.2 cm). *April 1913*: at head of article (pencil).
Source: *The Periodical*, 4 (no.71) (April 1913), 152. The journal reproduces material taken from *The Life of Porphyry Bishop of Gaza by Mark the Deacon* (Oxford: Clarendon Press, 1913), 69–71.
Note: *April 1913*: insertion by TH.

Appendix One: Erasures and Excisions

Erasures

1. *12r item 23c*

Text: 1.5 lines. Scraped out. Only identified words are 'the' and, possibly, 'succession'.
Source: almost certainly from *Walpole, Letters* vol.1, since the preceding and following items are taken from this source.

2. *15v item 30b*

Text: one line. Scraped out. Almost completely erased. Only identifiable letters are 'Ex'.
Note: the next-but-one item (30d) is 'Exchequer bills stolen', *DCC*, 13 April 1826, p.1, col.5. But another report, *DCC*, 13 April 1826, p.2, col.4, deals with the same incident from another perspective: 'a gentleman was robbed of a valuable watch and pocket-book, containing £800 in Exchequer bills' etc. It is possible that TH wrote a summary of this report; he then noticed the item on p.1, col.5 (on the same case) which he preferred to the first, and which he then erased.

3. *24r item 47e*

Text: two lines. Scraped out. Almost completely erased. Only identifiable word is 'of'.
Source: note: traced by Millgate to *DCC*, 17 August 1826, p.4, col. 5. Report of trial of Phoebe Hooper. *Millgate 1971*, 240–41, 396.
Note: it is possible that the erased matter may have come from a report on Phoebe Hooper, 'an apparently respectable woman' accused of marrying her former husband still living. She is acquitted on poor evidence. *DCC* notes: 'The prisoner, from her appearance and manner, as well as from her deportment through the trial, excited the sympathy of every person in the court. Nothing was alleged against her character in any respect' (*DCC*, 17 August 1826, p.4, col.5). Millgate suggests this passage offers 'the basis not only of important plot elements in *The Mayor of Casterbridge* but of much of the actual characterisation of Susan Henchard' (*Millgate, 1971*, 240–41, 396).

4. *26v item 52c*

<u>Soldier</u>. M. Quin, 65th, private; a party ordered out at 4.a.m. to fire

at a target in a field near the town (Kilkenny, where reg[t]. quartered) <

> On

the ground Q. found opp[y] to load his musket – muzzle to right breast &

naked toe to trigger. "I can endure this no longer:" died of the shot.   ib.

Text: the last word of the second line and the entirety of the subsequent five lines have been heavily scrawled through by overwriting with a different pen: the last three are partially recoverable: 'ghosts but somebody said there were no ghosts there and then on the // matter being by [?] said [?] that though the ends of the city // with prayer book in his hand and nothing else but and smiled to the sea'.

Source: traced by Millgate to *DCC*, 14 September 1826. p.3, col.3 (*Millgate, 1971*, 239–40).

Note: what follows is the relevant part of the report from which TH made the subsequently erased summary: 'A party had been ordered out at four in the morning of that day to fire at a target, in a field near the town. From some cause, yet unexplained, Quin was not in attendance at the time appointed. A few minutes after, the drill-sergeant, whose name is John Kitchen, came to his bed-side, and compelled him to get up instantly; he then hurried him out of the room, without allowing him to put on shirt, stockings or shoes; at the same time giving orders to a corporal to march him to the ground, through the town of Kilkenny, in that state, and to keep him moving in double quick time, at the point of his bayonet' (see *Millgate, 1971*, 239–40). It is likely that this erasure was made to disguise the close re-working of this incident for the humiliation of Abel Whittle by Henchard in *The Mayor of Casterbridge*, ch. 15 (*Mayor, 1987*, 99–100).

5. 30v item 60a

Text: 2.5 lines. This is heavily scrawled through and overwritten in a different pen; the overwriting is not decipherable.

Source: Millgate suggests (personal communication) that a possible source is the story of a suicide in *DCC*, 9 November 1826, p.3, col.4 ('Man in the parish of Mearns'). Both the previous and the following items (59f, 60b) are taken from *DCC*, 9 November 1826.

Note: identifiable words may be: 'Old', 'woman', 'floated', 'they', 'dribbled', 'this, prey', 'upon'.

6. 56r&v item 111d

Text: this is a near-illegible item of five lines, the last four of which are heavily scrawled through. Identifiable from the first, scored-through, line is the figure '7', possibly part of a phrase 'for 7 years'. Other identifiable words are: 'strong', 'kept', 'oath', 'expired'.

Source: Millgate correctly traces this to a *DCC* report, 'Sobriety and Its Beneficial Consequences', *DCC*, 9 July 1829, p.2, col.2 (*Millgate, 1971*, 239–40, 396).

Note: this item is a direct source for *Mayor of Casterbridge*, ch.2. For Millgate 'the relevance to the story of Henchard seems plain … it is perhaps of some significance that an attempt has been made, presumably by Hardy himself, to render the notebook entry illegible' (240). The *DCC* report runs as follows: 'A man, who is now a respectable tradesman in Chelsea, was for many years one of the most profligate of the out-pensioners of Chelsea Hospital, and was known only as a common nuisance in the neighbourhood by his constant inebriation, suddenly took it into his head to swear that for *seven years* he would not taste of any liquid stronger than tea. This oath he kept most inviolably, and by his regularity obtained a friend who put him into business. In November last the term of his oath expired, and he anxiously looked forward to the day, that he might enjoy himself without infringing upon his conscience. In fact he did get as much intoxicated as he ever had been, but on the next day renewed his oath for *twelve years*, since which he has gone on in the steady money-getting way in which he had passed the last seven years.' Henchard's 'oath before God' is to 'avoid all strong liquors for the space of twenty-one years to come' (*Mayor, 1987*, 19).

7.   *59r item 117f*

Waggoner asleep in his waggon – night Bridport R^d – meets coach – shaft

of waggon enters breast of leader

Source: 'Shameful Negligence', *DCC*, 8 October 1829, p.4, col.1. This source has been traced by Simon Gatrell, 'The Early Stages of Hardy's Fiction', in Norman Page (ed.), *Thomas Hardy Annual*, no.2 (London: Macmillan, 1984), 3–29 (p.21), although he dates the entry from *DCC* as 15 October.
Note: the whole of this item is scrawled through, but has been convincingly recovered by Gatrell. The *DCC* report reads: 'It is too often observed that men who are in charge of carts and waggons, are frequently found sleeping in them whilst on a journey, leaving the horses to proceed at will, and endangering the safety of every vehicle which may meet them. An instance of this kind occurred on Friday, from which the most serious consequences were likely to have resulted. As the Age, a daily coach between London and Plymouth, was coming from Bridport to this town [Dorchester], on reaching Askerswell's Hill a cart was met, and owing to the darkness of the night, before the coachman could pull his horses to the other side of the road, one of the shafts of the cart entered the breast of the near leader and killed him on the spot. The driver of the cart was at the time fast asleep, and consequently unable to se the coach lamp. No blame whatever can be attributed to the coachman who was on the right side of the road. It is to be regretted that such instances of neglect are not more frequently punished.' This item is a source for the disastrous accident in *Tess of the d'Urbervilles*, Bk.1 ch.4, in which 'the pointed shaft of the cart had entered the breast of the unhappy Prince like a sword' (*Tess, 1988*, 37).

8.   *90v item 180c*

Text: this is heavily scrawled-through item of 1.25 lines which is not recoverable.
Source: to judge from the items which both precede and follow this one the erased passage is almost certainly taken from Liechtenstein, *Holland House*, vol.1.

Excisions

1.   *28r&v*

Note: the possible sources of this excised item are:

i. A notice by bankruptcy Commissioners of an announcement of Examinations of an innkeeper, declared a Bankrupt, to take place at Henstridge, Somerset (*DCC*, 19 October 1826, p.1 col.1).

ii. An examination by bankruptcy Commissioners of a London broker whose integrity a lawyer said 'he … did not for moment intend to question' (*DCC*, 19 October 1826, p.3, col.5). Millgate suggests (personal communication) that this item is a possible source for Henchard's examination for bankruptcy in *The Mayor of Casterbridge* (ch.31) (*Mayor, 1987*, 219–20).

iii. Millgate also suggests (personal communication) that the excised material could contain a *DCC* report of an old woman who died of starvation after being denied admittance to a workhouse (*DCC*, 26 October, 1826, p.3).

2. 34r&v

Note: in the edition of *DCC* from which the previous item (67d) is drawn (2 August 1826) is the following item: 'Last week, the wife of a seaman at Sunderland chastised a stepson rather severely, and the neighbours were in consequence about to burn her in effigy. As the figure was approaching her house, a person informed her of the circumstance; which so affected the woman, that she fell down in a fit of apoplexy, and expired. She was advanced in pregnancy, and the child was expected, but it lived only a short time' (*DCC*, 2 August 1826, p.3, col.3). The closeness of the parallel between this episode and the miscarriage and death of Lucetta Farfrae in *The Mayor of Casterbridge* (chs 39–40) makes it almost certain that amongst the excised material was a summary of this report. In *The Mayor* Lucetta suffers 'the paroxysms of an epileptic seizure', provoked by the traumatic effect of the skimmington-ride (*Mayor, 1987*, 279).

3. 88r&v

Note: in *The Journal of Mary Frampton* there is a letter from Lady Elizabeth Talbot to Lady Harriot Fox Strangways (3 March 1797) which contains the following passage: 'One of the Directory was seen a few days ago in the Strand, and recognized by a French lady whose father, mother, and brother he had murdered. She fainted away in the street, and before she recovered enough to speak he had escaped in the crowd' (p.94). Kristin Brady noted that 'there is an excision in the "Facts" notebook at a point between passages that come before and after this source for the story in *The Journal of Mary Frampton* ... It is likely ... that Hardy did copy down this letter and later cut it out either to cover his tracks or simply to make use of the note' (*Brady*, 216). Simon Gatrell makes a similar observation, adding that an 'erased line in the notebook just below the excision appears to read "& before she recovered, he had disappeared"' (see Gatrell, 'The Early Stages of Hardy's Fiction', 4–5). Gatrell writes that TH 'used this incident as the opening crisis of his story "A Committee-Man of 'The Terror'"', transposing the scene from the Strand to Budmouth/Weymouth. The connection is made quite certain when Hardy has his French lady say to the committee-man (who does not vanish, but stays to help her after she has fainted), 'You guillotined my father, my brother, my uncle – all my family, nearly, and broke my mother's heart' (CS, 676; Gatrell, 5) This source was first identified by Richard Little Purdy, 'A source for Hardy's "A Committee Man of 'The Terror'"', *Modern Language Notes*, 58 (1943): 554–5.

Appendix Two: 'Accidents of Locality'

From his youth Hardy could not fail to have been aware of the unusually marked location of families of national importance and influence in this area of Dorset. The Fox and the Pitt presences at Stinsford House and at Kingston Maurward House are familiar enough from the early pages of the *Life and Work*. In the vaults of Stinsford Church 'lie many members of the Grey and Pitt families ... there also lies the actor and dramatist William O'Brien with his wife Lady Susan' (*Life and Work*, 13). Lora Grey brought the Kingston Maurward estate into the Pitt family on her marriage to George Pitt (d.1734), whose bust in the church, together with the Grey monument with its skull, and the memorial to the O'Briens, were so familiar to the young Hardy, whilst the story of O'Brien and Lady Susan, a first cousin of Charles James Fox, was recorded by Hardy in 'Facts', from Frampton's *Journal* and Liechtenstein's *Holland House* (175b, 177c, 180f, 191a, 181b). George Pitt's grandson, William Morton Pitt (1754–1836), of Kingston Maurward and Encombe, landlord of the Hardys at Bockhampton, also has a place in 'Facts', with its report of the marriage of his daughter at Stinsford in 1806 ([197]a). The wealth of this interesting but unlucky philanthropist was heavily mortgaged, a fact to which Hardy subtly alludes in *Under the Greenwood Tree* (Part 11, ch.vii), where Dick looks out at 'a vast expanse of mortgaged estate' (*Under the Greenwood Tree*, ed. Simon Gatrell (Oxford: Oxford University Press, 1985), p. 108). The affairs and the fortunes of the two neighbouring houses of Stinsford and Kingston – Fox and Pitt – must have been ever-present in the talk of generations of Hardys. In his will of 1815, O'Brien of Stinsford acknowledged the friendship of Morton Pitt of Kingston, 'during nearly forty years'.

Within walking distance, across the heath, lay two other houses associated with families of great note. Hardy's own extended family in Puddletown could not have escaped knowledge of the comings and goings at Ilsington House (also known as Piddletown Manor) in the heart of the little town. Ilsington had become a Walpole property through the marriage of Robert Walpole (Horace's elder brother, and 2nd Earl of Orford) to the heiress Margaret Rolle in 1724. It remained so until 1862; but from the 1790s until 1829 it was let to General Thomas Garth, Principal Equerry to George III, and was much used, and liked, by royal princesses on their visits to Dorset. Ilsington was the childhood home of Lady Dorothy Nevill (a Walpole) with whom Hardy was later well acquainted. Hardy's insertion of 'Tom Garth' in a 'Facts' report from *DCC* of 1826 (45b) suggests a long-standing familiarity with the recent history of the house and its tenants.

In the next parish lay Athelhampton, also known as Admiston or Adminston (82a). This ancient mansion which Hardy knew in his youth, and which his father helped to restore in the 1850s, had been the property of the Long family of Draycot, Wiltshire, since the seventeenth century, but through a Wellesley marriage with a Long heiress, in 1812, it became for 40 years a Wellesley property, owned by William Long-Wellesley (1788–1857), nephew of the Duke of Wellington. The sad story arising from this wholly mercenary connection with Athelhampton was closely followed by Hardy, particularly in the longest entry in the notebook (120e). By 1848 George James Wood (1807–67) a well-to-do farmer, had acquired Athelhampton from the Wellesley estate. His nephew George Wood Homer, and his family, were well known to Hardy and to his cousin Tryphena Sparks.

Bibliography

Annual Register (Chronicle), 1806: 443.

Annual Register (Appendix to Chronicle), 1815: 283–6.

Anon., *Gentleman's Magazine* (June 1836): 663–4 (obituary of William Morton Pitt).

Anon., Review of *The Life of Porphyry Bishop of Gaza by Mark the Deacon*, *The Periodical*, 4 (no.71) (April 1913): 152.

Anon., Review of Sir George Bingham's account of Napoleon at St Helena (*Blackwoods Edinburgh Magazine*, 160 (October 1896): 540–49), *Dorset County Chronicle*, 15 October 1896.

Anon., 'Paganini', *Good Words*.

Anon., 'The Crown Treasures of France', *Graphic*, 27 March 1886.

Anon., Review of J.E. Thorold Rogers, *History of Agriculture and Prices in England 1259–1793*, vols 3&4, *Spectator*, 21 July 1883 (no. 2873): 938–9.

Archer, William, 'Conversations with Mr Thomas Hardy' in Norman Page (ed.), *Thomas Hardy: Family History*, 5 vols (London: Routledge/Thoemmes Press, 1998), iii, 27–50.

Bailey, J.O., *The Poetry of Thomas Hardy: A Handbook and Commentary* (Chapel Hill, NC: University of North Carolina Press, 1970).

Basnage, Jacques, *History of the Jews* (trans. Thomas Taylor) (London: J. Beaver & B. Lintot, 1708).

Bath, Michael, 'King's Stag and Caesar's Deer', *Proceedings of the Dorset Natural History and Archaeological Society*, 95 (1973): 80–83.

Berrow's Worcester Journal.

Bettey, J.H., *Man and Land: 150 Years of Farming in Dorset 1846–1996* (Dorchester: Dorset Natural History and Archaeological Society, 1996).

Boswell-Stone, L.C., *Memories and Traditions Recorded by L.C. Boswell-Stone* (London: Richard Clay, 1895).

Bourrienne, Louis A.F. de, *Mémoirs de Monsieur de Bourrienne...sur Napoléon* (Paris, 1829–31).

Bourrienne, Louis A.F. de, *Memoires of Napoleon Bonaparte*, ed. R.W. Phipps, 4 vols (London: Bentley and Son, 1885).

Brady, Kristin, *The Short Stories of Thomas Hardy: Tales of Past and Present* (Basingstoke: Macmillan, 1982).

Briggs, S., 'An instrument from the equestrian figure of Osmington Hill', *Proceedings of the Dorset Natural History and Archaeological Society*, 98 (1976): 63–4.

Broadley, A.M., 'Dorchester and Edmund Kean', *Dorset County Chronicle*, 15 May 1902, p.11.

Broadley, A.M., 'Dorchester and its theatres: a satisfactory solution', *Dorset County Chronicle*, 7 March 1912, p.14.

Brown, Joanna Cullen, *Hardy's People* (London: Allison & Busby, 1991).

Cameron, David Kerr, *The English Fair* (Stroud: Sutton Publishing, 1998).

Cardigan and Lancastre, Countess of, *My Recollections* (London: Everleigh Nash, 1909).

Carter, John, 'A further note on A.E. Housman', *Times Literary Supplement* (14 March 1968), p.278.

Chalfont, Fran, 'Hardy's Residences and Lodgings: Part Three', in Norman Page (ed.), *Thomas Hardy: Family History*, 5 vols (London: Routledge/Thoemmes Press, 1998), i, 19–38.

Chalmers, Alexander, *General Biographical Dictionary*, 32 vols (London: J. Nichols & Son, 1812–17).

Cornhill Magazine.

Couzens, Tim, *Hand of Fate: The History of the Longs, Wellesleys and the Draycot Estate in Wiltshire* (Bradford-on-Avon: ELSP, 2001).

Cox, G. Stevens, '"A Trampwoman's Tragedy", Blue Jimmy and Ilchester Jail', *Thomas Hardy Year Book*, 1 (1970): 82–5.

Coxon, Peter , 'Hardy's favourite hymns', *Thomas Hardy Journal*, 13 (2) (May 1997): 42–55.

Crawley, Ernest, *The Tree of Life: A Story of Religion* (London: Hutchinson, 1905).

Cunningham, Hugh, 'The Metropolitan Fairs; A Case Study in the Social Control of Leisure', in A.P. Donajgrodzki (ed.), *Social Control in Nineteenth Century Britain* (London: Croom Helm, 1977), pp.163–84.

Daily Chronicle (London).

Daily News (London).

Davies, E.W.L., *Memoir of the Rev. John Russell and his Out-of-door-Life* (1878; new edn, London: Richard Bentley & Son, 1883).

Davis, Glanville J., 'John Fitzgerald Pennie – "Sylvaticus"', *Proceedings of the Dorset Natural History and Archaeological Society*, 118 (1996): 7–12.

Debrett's Peerage, Baronetage, Knightage And Titles of Courtesy (1878).

Doheny, J.R., 'Thomas Hardy's Relatives and Their Times', in Norman Page (ed.), *Thomas Hardy: Family History*, 5 vols (London: Routledge/Thoemmes Press, 1998), i, 47–81.

Donajgrodzki, A.P. (ed.), *Social Control in Nineteenth Century Britain* (London: Croom Helm, 1977).

'Dorset' (pseud.), 'Edmund Kean and his Dorchester associations', *Dorset County Chronicle*, 22 May 1902, p.11.

Dorset County Chronicle, Somersetshire Gazette, And General Advertiser For the South and South-West of England.

Dorset Evening Echo.

Dorset Militia Ballot Lists 1757–1799 (Index), 2 vols (Somerset and Dorset Family History Society, 1999).

Edwards, P.D., *Dickens's 'Young Men': George Augustus Sala, Edmund Yates and the World of Victorian Journalism* (Aldershot: Ashgate, 1997).

Evans, Eric, *The Forging of the Modern State: Early Industrial Britain 1783–1870* (1983; 2nd edn, London: Longman, 1996).

Evelyn, John, *The Diary of John Evelyn*, ed. E.S. De Beer, 6 vols (Oxford: Clarendon Press, 1955).

Fea, Allan, *Nooks and Corners of Old England* (London: Everleigh Nash, 1907).

Fern, Khinlyn, 'Visitor's book for the Loyalty Theatre, Dorchester', *Proceedings of the Dorset Natural History and Archaeological Society*, 121 (1999): 145–50.

The Field.

Firor, Ruth A., *Folkways in Thomas Hardy* (1931; New York: A.S. Barnes & Co., 1962).

Fletcher, James, M.J., '"The Man in the Wall" at Wimborne Minster', *Proceeedings of the Dorset Natural History and Archaeological Society*, 37 (1916): 26–39.

Foote, G.W. and J.M. Wheeler (eds), *The Sepher Toldoth Jeshu: The Jewish Life of Christ* (London: Progressive Company, 1885).

Frampton, Mary, *The Journal of Mary Frampton From the Year 1779 Until the Year 1846*, ed. Harriot Georgiana Mundy (London: Sampson Low, Marston, Searle, and Rivington, 1885).

Frith, W.P., *My Autobiography*, 3 vols (London: Richard Bentley & Son, 1887–88).

Fuller, H.T. and V. Hammersley (eds), *Thackeray's Daughter: Some Recollections of Anne Thackeray Ritchie* (Dublin: Euthorion Books, 1951).

Gatrell, Simon, 'The Early Stages of Hardy's Fiction' in Norman Page (ed.), *Thomas Hardy Annual*, no.2 (London: Macmillan, 1984): 3–29.

Gatrell, Simon, 'Wessex' in Dale Kramer (ed.), *The Cambridge Companion to Thomas Hardy* (Cambridge: Cambridge University Press, 1999), pp.19–37.

Gibson, James (ed.), *Thomas Hardy: Interviews and Recollections* (Basingstoke: Macmillan, 1999).

Giordano, Frank, *'I'd Have My Life Unbe': Thomas Hardy's Self-Destructive Characters* (Montgomery, AL: University of Alabama Press, 1984).

Gissing, George, *The Nether World*, ed. John Goode (1889; Brighton: Harvester Press, 1974).

Graphic (London).

Greenslade, William, *Degeneration, Culture and the Novel 1880–1940* (Cambridge: Cambridge University Press, 1994).

Greenslade, William, 'Rediscovering Thomas Hardy's "Facts" Notebook' in Phillip Mallett (ed.), *The Achievement of Thomas Hardy* (Basingstoke: Macmillan, 2000).

Gronow, R.H., *Reminiscences and Recollections* (London; Smith, Elder & Co., 1862).

Gronow, R.H., *Reminiscences...being Anecdotes of the Camp, The Court, and the Clubs, at the close of the last War with France* (London: Smith, Elder & Co., 1862).

Gronow R.H., *Recollections and Anecdotes, being a second series of Reminiscences by Capt. R.H. Gronow* (London: Smith Elder & Co., 1863).

Grove, George (ed.), *A Dictionary of Music and Musicians (A.D. 1450–1880) By Eminent Writers, English and Foreign*, 2 vols (London: Macmillan, 1879).

Hardy, Evelyn, 'Thomas Hardy: plots for five unpublished short stories', *London Magazine*, 5 (1958): 33–45.

Hardy, F.E., *The Early Life of Thomas Hardy 1840–1891* (London: Macmillan, 1928).

Hardy, F.E., *The Later Years of Thomas Hardy 1892–1928* (London: Macmillan, 1930).

Hardy, Thomas, *Time's Laughingstocks and Other Verses* (London: Macmillan, 1909).

Hardy, Thomas, 'Which is the Finest View in Dorset?', *The Society of Dorset Men in London Year-book, 1915–16*, pp.31–2.

Hardy, Thomas, *The Architectural Notebook of Thomas Hardy*, ed. C.J.P. Beatty (Dorchester: Dorset Natural History and Archaeological Society, 1966).

Hardy, Thomas, *Thomas Hardy's Personal Writings*, ed. Harold Orel (London: Macmillan, 1967).

Hardy, Thomas, *Thomas Hardy: The Complete Poems*, ed. James Gibson (London: Macmillan, 1976).

Hardy, Thomas, *The Collected Letters of Thomas Hardy*, eds Richard Little Purdy and Michael Millgate, 7 vols (Oxford: Clarendon Press, 1978–88).

Hardy, Thomas, *The Personal Notebooks of Thomas Hardy*, ed. Richard H. Taylor (London: Macmillan, 1979).

Hardy, Thomas, *The Complete Poetical Works of Thomas Hardy*, ed. Samuel Hynes, 5 vols (Oxford: Clarendon Press, 1982–95).

Hardy, Thomas, *The Life and Work of Thomas Hardy*, ed. Michael Millgate (Basingstoke: Macmillan, 1984).

Hardy, Thomas, *Jude the Obscure*, ed. Patricia Ingham (Oxford: Oxford University Press, 1985).

Hardy, Thomas, *A Pair of Blue Eyes*, ed. Alan Manford (Oxford: Oxford University Press, 1985).

Hardy, Thomas, *The Woodlanders*, ed. Dale Kramer (Oxford: Oxford University Press, 1985).

Hardy, Thomas, *The Literary Notebooks of Thomas Hardy*, ed. Lennart A. Björk, 2 vols (Basingstoke: Macmillan, 1985).

Hardy, Thomas, *The Well-Beloved*, ed. Tom Hetherington (Oxford: Oxford University Press, 1986).

Hardy, Thomas, *The Mayor of Casterbridge*, ed. Dale Kramer (Oxford: Oxford University Press, 1987).

Hardy, Thomas, *Tess of the d'Urbervilles*, ed. Tim Dolin (London: Penguin, 1988).

Hardy, Thomas, *Tess of the d'Urbervilles*, eds Juliet Grindle and Simon Gatrell (Oxford: Oxford University Press, 1988).

Hardy, Thomas, *A Laodicean*, ed. Jane Gatewood (Oxford: Oxford University Press, 1991).

Hardy, Thomas, *The Trumpet-Major*, ed. Richard Nemesvari (Oxford: Oxford University Press, 1991).

Hardy, Thomas, *Wessex Tales*, ed. Kathryn R. King (Oxford: Oxford University Press, 1991).

Hardy, Thomas, *Thomas Hardy: The Excluded and Collaborative Stories*, ed. Pamela Dalziel (Oxford: Clarendon Press, 1992).

Hardy, Thomas, *Far from the Madding Crowd*, ed. B. Suzanne Falck-Yi (Oxford: Oxford University Pess, 1993).

Hardy, Thomas, *Thomas Hardy's 'Studies, Specimens &c Notebook'*, eds Pamela Dalziel and Michael Millgate (Oxford: Clarendon Press, 1994).

Hardy, Thomas, *Under the Greenwood Tree*, ed. Simon Gatrell (Oxford: Oxford University Press, 1995).

Hardy, Thomas, *Life's Little Ironies*, ed. Alan Manford (Oxford: Oxford University Press, 1996).

Hardy, Thomas, *Thomas Hardy: The Complete Stories*, ed. Norman Page (London: J.M. Dent, 1996).

Hardy, Thomas, *Thomas Hardy: Selected Poetry and Non-Fictional Prose*, ed. Peter Widdowson (Basingstoke: Macmillan, 1997).

Hardy, Thomas, *A Pair of Blue Eyes*, ed. Pamela Dalziel (1873; Harmondsworth: Penguin, 1998).

Hardy, Thomas, *Thomas Hardy: The Withered Arm and Other Stories 1874–1888*, ed. Kristin Brady (Harmondsworth: Penguin, 1999).

Hardy, Thomas, *The Mayor of Casterbridge*, ed. Phillip Mallett (New York: Norton, 2001).

Hardy, Thomas, *Thomas Hardy's Public Voice: The Essays, Speeches, and Miscellaneous Prose*, ed. Michael Millgate (Oxford: Clarendon Press, 2001).

Harper's Bazar (New York).

Harrod's Postal and Commercial Directory of Dorsetshire and Wiltshire (1865).

Harrop, A.J., *The Amazing Career of Edward Gibbon Wakefield* (London: George Allen & Unwin, 1928).

Hawkins Desmond, *Cranborne Chase* (London: Victor Gollancz, 1980).

Higginson, A.H., *The Meynell of the West: John James Farquharson* (London: Collins, 1936).

Hobsbawm, E.J. and George Rudé, *Captain Swing* (London: Lawrence and Wishart, 1969).

Hone, William, *The Every-day Book: And Table Book; or Everlasting Calendar of Popular Amusements, Sports, Pastimes, Ceremonies, Manners, Customs and Events etc.*, 3 vols (London: William Tegg, 1826–27).

How, Frederick Douglas, *Bishop Walsham How: A Memoir* (London: Isbister & Co., 1898).

Howkins, Alun, 'The Taming of Whitsun: the Changing Face of the Rural Holiday', in E. Yeo and S. Yeo (eds), *Popular Culture and Class Conflict 1590–1914* (Brighton: Harvester Press, 1981), pp.187–208.

Hutchins, John, *The History and Antiquities of the County of Dorset* (1774), eds W. Shipp & J.W. Hodson, 4 vols (3rd edn, Westminster: J.B. Nichols & Sons, 1861–73; rpt East Ardsley, Wakefield: E.P. Publishing, 1973).

Huxley, T.H., 'Science and the Bishops', *Nineteenth Century*, no.125 (November 1887): 625–40.

Jackson, Sir George, *Diaries and Letters of Sir George Jackson*, 2 vols (London: 1873).

Jackson-Houlston, C.M., *Ballads, Songs and Snatches* (Aldershot: Ashgate, 1999).

Jones, David, 'Rural Crime and Protest', in G.E. Mingay (ed.), *The Victorian Countryside*, 2 vols (London: Routledge, 1981), ii, 566–79.

Kelly's Directory of Dorsetshire (1880).

Kerr, Barbara, *Bound to the Soil: A Social History of Dorset* (1968; East Ardsley, Wakefield: E.P. Publishing, 1975).

Kramer, Dale, 'A Query Concerning the Handwriting in Hardy's Manuscripts', *Papers of the Bibliographical Society of America* (Third Quarter, 1963): 357–60.

Lang, Andrew, 'Literary Forgeries', *Contemporary Review*, 44 (December 1883): 837–49.

Le Pard, Gordon, 'The Great Storm of 1824', *Proceedings of the Dorset Natural History and Archaeological Society*, 121 (1999): 23–36.

Lee, Henry, *Memoirs of a Manager; Or Life's Stage with New Scenes*, 2 vols (Taunton: W. Bragg, 1830).

Lever, Tresham, *The House of Pitt* (London: John Murray, 1947).

Liechtenstein, Marie, *Holland House*, 2 vols (London: Macmillan, 1874).

Lindgren, Charlotte, 'Thomas Hardy: grim facts and local lore', *Thomas Hardy Journal*, 1 (3) (October 1985): 18–27.

Lockie, John, *Topography of London* (2nd edn, London: 1816).

Longford, Elizabeth, *Wellington: Pillar of State* (London: Weidenfeld & Nicholson, 1972).

Mallett, Phillip (ed.), *The Achievement of Thomas Hardy* (Basingstoke: Macmillan, 2000).

Malmesbury, Earl of (ed.), *A Series of Letters of the First Earl of Malmesbury His Family And Friends from 1745 to 1820*, 2 vols (London: Richard Bentley, 1870).

Manford, Alan, 'Emma Hardy's Helping Hand', in Dale Kramer (ed.), *Critical Essays on Thomas Hardy: The Novels* (Boston, MA: G.K. Hall, 1990), pp.100–121.

Mayo, C.H., *Bibliotheca Dorsetiensis* (London: C. Whittington and Co., 1885).

Millgate, Michael, *Thomas Hardy: His Career as A Novelist* (1971; London: Macmillan, 1994).

Millgate, Michael, *Thomas Hardy: A Biography* (1982; Oxford: Oxford University Press, 1985).

Millgate, Michael, *Testamentary Acts* (1992; Oxford: Clarendon Press, 1995).

Molloy, Joseph Fitzgerald, *Court Life Below Stairs – Or, London Under the Last Georges 1760–1830*, 4 vols (London: Hurst & Blackett, 1882–83).

Molloy, Joseph Fitzgerald, *The Life and Adventures of Peg Woffington With Pictures of the Period In Which She Lived* (London: Hurst & Blackett, 1884).

Morison, James Cotter, *The Service of Man: An Essay Towards the Religion of the Future* (London: Kegan Paul & Co., 1887).

Morning Chronicle (London).

Musson, Jeremy, 'Ilsington House, Dorset', *Country Life* (12 June 1997): 158–63.

Nevill, Lady Dorothy, *Under Five Reigns* (London: Methuen, 1910).

Newth, John, 'Ilsington', *Dorset County Magazine* (May 1992): 12–14.

Oliphant, Margaret, 'The Old Saloon', *Blackwood's*, 151 (1892): 455–74.

Oliphant, Margaret, 'The Anti-Marriage League', *Blackwood's*, 159 (1896): 135–49.

Origen, *Origen Against Celsus*, trans. James Bellamy (London: B. Mills, 1660).

Page, Norman, *Thomas Hardy* (London: Routledge, 1977).

Page, Norman (ed.), *Thomas Hardy Annual*, nos 1–5 (Basingstoke: Macmillan, 1982–87).

Page, Norman (ed.), *Thomas Hardy: Family History*, 5 vols (London: Routledge /Thoemmes Press, 1998).

Pall Mall Budget (London).

Pall Mall Gazette (London).

Pennie, J.F. (pseud. Sylvaticus), *The Tale of a Modern Genius; or, the Miseries of Parnassus*, 3 vols (London, 1827).

Pevsner, Nikolaus, *Cornwall (The Buildings of England)* (Harmondsworth: Penguin, 1951).

Phipps, R.W. (ed.), *Memoirs of Napoleon Bonaparte*, 4 vols (London: Bentley & Son, 1885).

Pinion, F.B., *A Hardy Companion* (1968; London: Macmillan, 1976).

Plomer, William (ed.), *Kilvert's Diary 1870–1879* (London: Jonathan Cape, 1944).

Pope, Alexander, *Alexander Pope, Epistles to Several Persons (Moral Essays)*, ed. F.W. Bateson (London: Methuen, 1961).

Powell, Anthony, *John Aubrey and his Friends* (1948; rev. edn, London: Hogarth Press, 1988).

Proceedings of the Dorset Natural History and Archaeological Society.

Prothero, Rowland, 'The Goddess of Wisdom and Lady Caroline Lamb', *Monthly Review*, 19 (June 1905): 12–28.

Purdy, Richard Little, 'A source for Hardy's "A Committee Man of 'The Terror'"', *Modern Language Notes*, 58 (1943): 554–5.

Purdy, Richard Little, *Thomas Hardy: A Bibliographical Study* (Oxford: Oxford University Press, 1954).

Rands, Susan, 'Letters to Thomas Hardy from the 5th Countess of Ilchester concerning the journal of Lady Susan O'Brien', *Somerset and Dorset Notes and Queries*, 34 (September 2000): 385–92.

Rands, Susan, 'Lady Susan O'Brien and her friendship with the Pitt family', *Somerset and Dorset Notes and Queries*, 35 (March 2001): 11–21.

Ray, Martin, *Thomas Hardy: A Textual Study of the Short Stories* (Aldershot: Ashgate, 1997).

Reid, Fred, 'Art and Ideology in *Far from the Madding Crowd*', in Norman Page (ed.), *Thomas Hardy Annual*, no. 4 (Basingstoke: Macmillan, 1986).

Renan, Ernest, *Recollections of My Youth*, trans. C.B. Pitman, revised by Madame Renan (London: Chapman & Hall, 1883).

Reynolds, Frederick, *The Life and Times of Frederick Reynolds, Written By Himself*, 2 vols (London: Henry Colburne, 1826).

Ribot, T.H., *Heredity: A Psychological Study of Its Phenomena, Laws, Causes and Consequences* (London: Henry S. King, 1875).

Rosenbaum, Barbara, *Index of English Literary Manuscripts Vol. IV (1800–1900), Part Two (Hardy–Lamb)* (London and New York: Mansell, 1990).

Rudge, James, 'Description of the Field of Waterloo by James Rudge', *Dorset County Chronicle*, 6 November 1828.

Sadlier, Michael, *Blessington-D'Orsay. A Masquerade* (London: Constable, 1933).

Saturday Review.

Savage, James, *Dorchester and Its Environs* (Dorchester, 1832).

Scott, Sir Walter, *Woodstock; or, The Cavalier* (1826; London: Oxford University Press, 1912).

Selway, Neville C., *The Regency Road: The Coaching Prints of James Pollard* (London: Faber & Faber, 1957).

Seymour, Sir Robert, 'Anecdotes, Reports, Truths and Falsities for the Year 1788: Passages From the Diary of Lord Robert Seymour', *Murray's Magazine*, 1 (1887): 471–90.

Shepton Mallett Journal.

Sheridan, Ann, 'Circuit theatres in Dorchester and Bridport', *Theatre Notebook*, 53 (1) (1999): 19–40.

Silver, Brenda R., *Virginia Woolf's Reading Notebooks* (Princeton, NJ: Princeton University Press, 1983).

Simcox, Edith, 'Eight Years of Cooperative Shirtmaking', *Nineteenth Century*, 15 (June 1884): 1037–54.

Singer, S.W. (ed.), *The Dramatic Works of Shakespeare*, 10 vols (1826; London: Bell & Daldy, 1856).

Spectator.

Stephens, F.G. and George, M. Dorothy (eds), *Catalogue of Political and Personal Satires...in the British Museum*, 11 vols, 1870–1954 (London: The Trustees, 1949), ix.

Stone, Lawrence, *The Road to Divorce: England 1530–1987* (Oxford: Oxford University Press, 1990).

Stuart, Dorothy Margaret, *The Daughters of George III* (London: Macmillan, 1939).

Symons, Arthur, *Cities* (London: J.M. Dent, 1903).

Taunton Courier and Western Advertiser.

Thompson, E.P., *The Making of the English Working Class* (1963; Harmondsworth: Penguin Books, 1968).

Tillyard, Stella, *Aristocrats* (London: Chatto & Windus, 1994).

The Times (London).

Tomalin, Claire, *Mrs Jordan's Profession* (1994; London: Penguin, 1995).

Treves, Sir Frederick, *Highways and Byways in Dorset* (London: Macmillan, 1906).

Udal, J.S., 'Dorset Collection' (n.d.) (Dorset County Museum, Dorchester).

Udal, J.S., *Dorsetshire Folklore* (1922; Guernsey: Toucan Press, 1970).

Verey, D. (ed.), *The Diary of a Cotswold Parson* (Gloucester: Alan Sutton, 1978).

The Victoria History of the Counties of England: Dorset (1908; rpt Folkestone: William Dawson, 1975).

Wagner, A.R., *English Genealogy* (Oxford: Clarendon Press, 1972).

Walpole, Horace, *Memoirs of the Reign of King George III*, 4 vols (London: Richard Bentley, 1845).

Walpole, Horace, *The Letters of H. Walpole, Earl of Orford*, ed. Peter Cunningham, 9 vols (London: Richard Bentley, 1857–59).

Walpole, Horace, *Last Journals of Horace Walpole During the Reign of George III From 1771–1783*, ed. A.F. Steuart, 2 vols (London: John Lane, The Bodley Head, 1910).

Walpole, Horace, *Horace Walpole's Correspondence with Sir Horace Mann*, eds W.S. Lewis, W. Henry-Smith and G.L. Lam (London: Oxford University Press; New Haven, CT: Yale University Press, 1960).

Western Gazette.

Weymouth, Portland and Dorchester Telegram.

'Which is the Finest View in Dorset?', *The Society of Dorset Men in London* (Year-book, 1915–16) (London, 1915): 31–2.

Williams, Raymond, *The Country and the City* (1973; London: Hogarth Press, 1985).

Winfield, Christine, 'Factual Sources of Two Episodes in *The Mayor of Casterbridge*', *Nineteenth-Century Fiction*, 25 (2) (September 1970): 224–31.

Woolf, Virginia, *The Diary of Virginia Woolf*, ed. A.O. Bell, 4 vols (London: Hogarth Press, 1980).

Yates, Edmund, *Edmund Yates: his Recollections and Experiences*, 2 vols (London: Richard Bentley & Son, 1884).

General Index

Indexing of the *'Facts' Notebook* is by *item numbers*, derived from Hardy's own pagination. Thus on his page 2, he made four entries, here now numbered (and indexed as) 2a, 2b, 2c, 2d. Although towards the end of the Notebook Hardy abandoned pagination, it has been maintained editorially, e.g. [203]a.

Indexing of introductory matter is by *page numbers*.

* An asterisk denotes a source from which Hardy made an entry or entries into the Notebook.

Subject Index